Foreword

In 1992, the CIPFA's Financial Management Panel produced guidance on the form, content and development of business plans within public services. Following the publication of this guidance – *Business Plans – A move in the right direction* – many requests have been received for copies of 'live examples'. The Financial Management Panel has responded to these requests by compiling this compendium, which reproduces a selection of existing business plans from across the public services. It also contains the key sections of the Institute's published advice which should be considered alongside the examples shown. The compendium illustrates that public services have adopted a wide variety of approaches to the business planning process and provides an excellent opportunity for sectors to learn from each other's experiences.

Nigel Palk
Chairman, Financial Management Panel

Caveat

The examples included in this compendium have been amended only to exclude personal and financial details. In all other respects they are reproduced as provided by the organisation to illustrate the variety of approaches adopted. CIPFA does not express a view on individual business plans but merely reproduces them to assist organisations in their own developmental work. This document is not, therefore, a 'best practice guide' but a compendium of actual business plans which are already in use. CIPFA is extremely grateful to all those organisations which supplied copies of their business plans. Due to the scale of the response, only a selection of those received are included. This selection has been made on an entirely random basis and does not imply that those business plans that are reproduced have more merit than those which have not been used.

Contents

Local Authorities

CIPFA

BUSINESS PLANS

A Compendium

INTRODUCTION

Institute Guidance on Business Plans

The following material is taken from 'Business Plans – A move in the right direction', published by CIPFA in 1992.

1 – Business plans: what they are

"I will go anywhere, provided it be forward."

– David Livingstone

1.01 Business plans are statements of the objectives of any business and the actions which it intends to take for these objectives to be achieved.

1.02 They were first used in the private sector, mainly to **support applications** for credit; grants; investments; and other sorts of financial support. Few if any providers of such support now give it without first seeing and approving business plans. They give an indication of the quality of management as well as a measure of the business risk.

1.03 They were, therefore, designed primarily to secure such approval. To do this they had to convince outsiders that managers had thought out where their businesses are going. Managers in the public sector have to be equally clear where their businesses are going, and business plans **give them a sound framework** within which to commit their planning to writing.

1.04 They are now the subject of an extensive literature. Some excellent guides are available but these are, for the most part, directed towards the needs of new private sector businesses. The Post Office has however produced a very readable and informative guide for its own managers. This guide on the other hand is intended to illustrate the scope for business plans in the public sector as a whole, and to set out their essential features.

1.05 It does so under the following heads

- the purposes of public sector business plans (*Chapter 2*)

- putting them together (*Chapter 3*)

- their contents (*Chapter 4*)

- their form (*Chapter 5*)

- the contribution which accountants can make (*Chapter 6*)

- the appraisal and interpretation of business plans (*Chapter 7*).

1.06 A simple checklist for the drafters of business plans is included on page 20.

1.07 Innumerable technical terms are used by the officers of different types of public bodies for the different types of organisations into which their structures are subdivided, for the different financial bases on which these organisations work, and for their various users. Often different people use the same terms for different things, and different terms for the same things. This guide therefore tries to define each such term when it is first used, and all these definitions are repeated in a glossary on page 19.

2 – Their purposes in the public sector

"It is and it must be in the long run be better for man to see things as they are than to be ignorant of them."

— Alfred Edward Houseman

2.01   Different organisations within the public sector have differing roles, and are funded and constituted in differing ways, so need business plans for different purposes. The three main types of organisation are

- **support services** whose work comes to them through internal markets

- **trading organisations**, including those which sell services to the public and other external customers, support services which compete for their work with external suppliers and (in local government) direct service organisations (DSOs). If local authorities want to carry out work in a number of specified categories in-house they may lawfully do so only if their DSOs win the work in open competition

- all other departments of public bodies, and subdivisions of departments which deliver **services to the public**, and support services whose work is decided corporately, rather than by an internal or external market. For convenience this guide refers to all such organisations as 'service units'.

For support services which operate in an internal market

2.02   Support services normally seek work, not finance. Like all businesses, to do this they must **show their clients and trading partners** that they are businesslike and that clients' requirements have been understood. Most clients have their own business problems to think about and will need to rigorously review the cost; efficiency; and quality of all the services which they obtain.

2.03   Consequently the managers of support services need to plan for the development of these services, so as to **maintain their usefulness to clients** in a period of rapid changes in the statutory basis of services and in what the public expects from them, and to match other suppliers. They need in addition to carry out SWOT analyses – of **Strengths, Weaknesses, Opportunities and Threats**.

2.04   Business plans for support services serve a third purpose, in providing a vehicle for **conveying information about the organisation** to recruits, potential users, and new council and board members. They may also provide a much needed way of bringing not-so-recent recruits and members up to date about the position of the business.

For trading organisations

2.05   Few trading organisations are required to submit business plans in support of their tenders. Prospective clients usually make their own independent enquiries to test the soundness and competence of all their tenderers. Nevertheless, it is increasingly common for direct service organisations to offer business plans in support of tender documents. For the other (non-DSO) trading organisations of some public bodies, this is now standard practice.

2.06 In addition some trading organisations, including local authority waste disposal companies and NHS trusts, prepare business plans as part of their preparations for independent status.

2.07 All such organisations need business plans for their second and third purposes – to focus the minds of their managers and their staff on **the real needs of their users**, and to **keep third parties informed**. In these respects their business plans are the same as those of support services.

2.08 Above all, trading organisations have to keep their competitive position uppermost in mind if they are to survive and prosper. Managers need to be clear how they propose to stay competitive – whether by specialising or diversifying, and whether by increasing market penetration or by sticking to the safest lines. This gives them the choice of aiming to be

- market dominators, **doing as much work as possible** for as many clients as possible

- in-house competitors, who **quote for all the main types of work offered**. They do whatever work this generates for them, and thereby provide their clients with a yardstick by which to check the prices and quality of services from all sources. The size of in-house competitors therefore tends to fluctuate inversely to market pressures

- niche-market suppliers, who concentrate on **whatever types of work they do best**; this is often work which other providers cannot readily do, such as work in uneconomically small parcels, or of special types.

For service units

2.09 Even if they do not have to compete for work (or not overtly) all service providers in the public sector need to plan for the development of their services, to show their staff what they have to do, and to keep their own support services informed about their likely future requirements. Their business plans are sometimes called 'service plans', although most of the points made in this guide apply equally to both.

 2.10 One further factor applies to most service plans. They are normally parts of, and responses to, the **service strategies** of their departments and, often, of overall **corporate strategies**.

2.11 Many service units have to compete in more subtle but increasingly demanding ways and all have to become more consumer-orientated. Schools, for example, need to attract parents and pupils; hospitals have to attract doctors and patients; housing departments need to convince tenants that alternative landlords could not provide a better service; and planners and other regulators need to satisfy potential appellants that decisions have been made fairly and promptly.

2.12 Most service units, therefore, need to plan for a continuous rise in service standards by the progressive adoption of improvements already adopted by front runners elsewhere, or generated locally. This is not necessarily to enable them to move up market, but to keep abreast of rising public expectations (as reflected by both the Citizen's Charter and Quality Street) and to keep their value-for-money ahead of any possible competitors.

2.13 Different service units differ in how much freedom of action they are given by top management to pursue such improvements. Some authorities leave them free to do so at their own initiative. Others expect them to follow as closely as possible departmental and corporate strategies.

2.14 Other service units may have to work hard just to maintain the present quantity and quality of services where, for example, they know that their budgets will decline in real terms.

3 – Putting business plans together

"Adventure is the result of poor planning."

— Colonel Blatchford Snell

Who should participate?

3.01   Managers have to have the last word in drafting business plans, as they carry the responsibility, but they need to involve their workpeople as much as possible in their preparation. This is because staff are more knowledgeable than anybody else about many aspects of their work, and because staff need to identify with plans and give their commitment .

3.02   One way of involving staff is to arrange 'workshops' for the various teams. Several meetings, preferably of between five and ten participants, spread over about two months, have been found to stimulate the greatest degree of participation. Meetings may be turned into 'brainstorming' sessions.

3.03   All except the smallest organisations may find that a number of parallel workshops provide the best way of involving all their staff. In this way, workshops can then be devoted to subdivisions of the organisation. However, in this case, further workshops for key workers will be needed, to cover the organisation as a whole.

3.04   Workshops are best held away from the usual workplace. This enhances the feeling that they are special events, and makes it less likely that their participants will be interrupted.

3.05   All participants should be briefed about what is expected of them, and should be given the latest available information about customer satisfaction, and performance indicators.

3.06   Participants must also keep the needs of their clients uppermost in their minds. A good way of doing this is to invite client officers to join in for part of the sessions. They should be encouraged to say what service improvements they would most appreciate, and why. Client officers who are known to be friendly but candid are likely to contribute most to the exchange. Improvements can rarely be offered there and their clients, and which are of only marginal value. Any improvements sought will of course have to be costed at the first opportunity.

Outside help

3.07   Managers may find it constructive to stand off from some of the proceedings, by bringing in facilitators to **hold the ring** and to **challenge the time-honoured methods** of operation and organisation with which managers may be identified. Facilitators may be professionals, or officers with the necessary abilities who may be borrowed for the purpose from other departments.

3.08   Consultants and other specialists are sometimes called in not only to facilitate but also to advise on the planning itself and to take the initiative by recommending new objectives and methods.

3.09   They may do this work better and more quickly than managers and they may know more about the outside world and new opportunities, methods and dangers. But they are seldom seen as offering permanent commitment whereas even the most sceptical of staff can be sure that managers will identify with, and be responsible for, business plans which they have taken a lead in drafting.

Feedback

3.10 The more enterprising the staff who participate and the more forthrightly they can be encouraged to talk about performance then the more fruitful their involvement. Managers too may be prompted to raise their own sights – team members may, for example, know more about new methods and equipment.

3.11 On the other hand, the more unexpected the difficulties which are raised in workshops (such as restrictive practices among staff not present) the greater the need for business plans to spell out how such difficulties should be overcome. In either case, the involvement of workpeople can feed back decisively into planning.

On-the-job discussions

3.12 Not all managers rely on workshops when drafting business plans. Some prefer to visit all their workpeople in their normal places of work and preferably on the job as often as they can. Managers have been known to elicit all the necessary participation and feedback by these means.

Coordination

3.13 Service units are not free agents. Nor are trading organisations, however successful they may be in competition. All are integral parts of the departmental structures of public bodies, and their planning needs to be accommodated to their authorities' corporate strategy and thinking. Corporate strategy may, for example, cover the roles of in- house service suppliers, pricing, cross-subsidisation and the conditions of service of staff.

3.14 Managers who are in any doubt about whether higher management will be comfortable with either the means or ends which they propose to adopt, may submit draft business or service plans for approval. Their proposals can then be seen in perspective.

3.15 This is usually the best way in which to invite elected and board members to view proposals, and the most likely to secure their approval to any change in the ground rules within which organisations are required to operate. Members may in any case have modified their views about conditions of service from those previously understood by managers.

3.16 Many public bodies now make their own strategic plans for some years ahead, and commit them to writing in some detail. Business plans then need to be reconciled with any such strategic plans.

3.17 Unless planning is restricted to the organisation under consideration, the business plan needs to reconcile with other organisations' plans. To secure this result, drafters at all levels need to check that their respective plans are in line with one another. Even when agreement about this has been secured, any subsequent changes have to be checked, to make sure that plans still reconcile with those above and below.

3.18 Referring to business plans is then the quickest way in which managers can demonstrate that their planning is in line with corporate planning.

3.19 One local authority uses a matrix to demonstrate the relationship between planning at different levels.

Timing

3.20   It is usual for business plans to follow a rolling programme. Each business plan should cover a period of about three years, and be updated every year. The best time of year, for any trading organisation which depends on a single contractor for the majority of its work, is usually just after such a contract has been awarded. A suitable time for many other organisations is usually just after budgets have been set.

3.21   There is no need for a workshop every year, because meetings might then be seen by staff as routine, and by managers as being too time- consuming. The best occasions for workshops are probably before the initial business plan is made and whenever major threats or radical changes have to be planned for thereafter.

3.22   However fundamental the changes adopted in the course of the planning, business plans need to be drafted and circulated – at least in outline – immediately following workshops. Delay for any reason damages any sense of ownership on the part of team members who feel they have contributed. Drafters have to be ready to start work and to be clear about the separate needs of substance (the **contents** of business plans) and **form** (how they should cover it).

4 – The contents of business plans

"Let our advance worrying become advance thinking and planning"
— Sir Winston Churchill

4.01 Four distinct sets of points need to be covered. They are

- the **context in which the organisation works**, as dictated by its relationship with its users and other agencies

- its **current position**

- the **action** which it plans to take

- other **information** which help to put business plans in perspective for their various readers.

Context

4.02 Every business plan needs to start with a statement covering

- the place of the organisation in the **departmental structure**, and who its manager reports to

- its **history** – why it was set up, and what major tasks it has since been given

- the purpose or '**mission**' of the organisation in a few pithy lines, such as '*clients depend on us to pay all their staff precisely what they are entitled to, on time, to record all their deductions, and to answer all foreseeable queries immediately*'. Such statements carry all the more weight if staff can be seen to 'own' them, and if they are backed up (as provided for here) by evidence of commitment to the practical action necessary to delivering such a service. Their purpose is to provide a clear statement of the goal of the organisation for all staff involved

- the **range of services to be offered** to clients and customers. This is of course in addition to, and not instead of, the other documents which constitute bills of fare for trading organisations. Support services should also make clear that they are always open to suggestions as to new types of work; new methods of working; and different bases for charges

- **the main clients of support services and DSOs, such as district health authorities, governing bodies, and other support services and DSOs** (all of which should be listed if not too numerous) and the many consumers of services, such as students; patients; passengers; and planning applicants

- the principal strengths of the organisation and (for clients who are free to choose) **why they have chosen to use it so far**, such as coverage of all the trades and specialisms needed; or willingness to do the awkward jobs.

Current position

4.03 Other factors may then need to be explained in order to provide an up to date analysis of the current position of any organisation. The following factors are normally common to all business plans

- for trading organisations, the **current trading position**, even if it is unfavourable. If business plans are to be seen as realistic, the current trading position has to be spelled out. There is no point in trying to conceal the truth

- for non-trading organisations, the **budgets** allocated to them, with an analysis of differences between the current and the previous budget

- for in-house suppliers which compete for their work with external suppliers, the **budget allocations of their clients** for which they will be competing

- **any threats which clients may shortly face**, such as constitutional change; compulsory competition; expected legislation and EC Directives; budget reductions; clients' plans for change to deal with these threats, as stated in their own service plans; and how such clients are to be helped

- threats which will **directly affect the organisation itself**, particularly competition and budget reductions

- the **main opportunities for new business for in-house suppliers**, such as work currently done by contractors or consultants; and any new business targeted

- **notable successes or failures** in the period just past, and the reasons for them

- any **long-standing problems** for which no solutions have yet been found, for example

  - inefficient buildings

  - corporate decisions (for example about gradings) which managers believe are damaging their organisation's competitiveness

  - centrally negotiated but uncompetitive pay rates, and other problems in industrial relations, such as insistence on payment in cash, or resistance to shift working.

The action planned

4.04 Objectives and readily measurable performance criteria, for the organisation and all its workpeople, are central to any business plan, because

- promised improvements in abstract terms are unlikely to impress anybody. The **words in business plans need to reconcile to the facts and figures**

- setting out quantified objectives **quickly identifies conflicting objectives** held by others in the organisation.

4.05 For both local authorities and the National Health Service, indicators are now available for most types of work. They are well summarised in the Audit Commission's guide 'Performance Indicators in Local Government' and in the Department of Health's 'Health Service Indicators'.

4.06 The planned action is likely to cover the following heads

- **improvements in standards of service** which are

  - required by contracts or service level agreements called for now by external agencies, such as British Standards; statutes and regulations; and codes of practice

  - or shown to be necessary by consumer surveys

- **proposals for further improvements** and why they are being made. The most successful businesses are constantly searching for further improvements in their performance or standards over and above those required or sought by clients. This is a fundamental principle of the 'total quality' movement. Managers can safely assume that their most serious competitors are already doing the same

- **performance indicators** which have been adopted as measures of progress by service units. This enables specific targets to be set, such as the dates by when contact-hours per lecturer; costs per 100 articles laundered in hospital laundries; average chargeable hours per week; or library books borrowed per student; are raised to specified levels; or by when unit costs or numbers of defects are reduced below specified levels. Dates may also be specified for the completion of specified jobs, such as drawing up and agreeing strategic plans and service level agreements

- **what has to be done, and by whom**, to achieve improvements of both sorts, and also the milestones by which their progress will be regularly measured (such as the dates by when specified jobs will be done) . All staff need to know where they are going, how they will get there, and the criteria by which their efforts will be judged

- the **planned trading position**, identifying separately the effects of volume changes, new work, higher standards and new methods

- **approved or proposed changes in numbers; skills; training or types of staff**, for example

  - any **reductions which may have to be made in staff numbers, or in tiers of management**, the reasons why; and what is being done to ameliorate their impact

  - how any **scarce expertise** is to be secured. If for example greater use is to be made of married women (wishing to resume their careers) former permanent staff on contract, or work-sharing

  - the **minimum qualifications** which will now be looked for in appointees to specified jobs, and the training plan which will be followed to give existing staff these qualifications

- agreed improvements in

  - **premises, transport, plant or equipment**, and the use to be made of them

  - **computers, IT and management information**. Computer software and hardware are getting cheaper; more user-friendly; and more reliable. Consequently managers should be planning to take advantage of the gains offered

  - any other capital expenditure, including any increase in **working capital** where plans provide for taking on additional work

- any other proposals for **reducing unit costs**

- the **contingency plans** which have been made for all eventualities, including the worst possible scenario. For example, what would be the consequences and necessary action should expansion plans fail; existing demand unexpectedly decline; or should clients be lost as a result of competition or constitutional change? Could performance or services still be maintained at the quoted rates for the lower level of output? Have sensitivity analyses been carried out? Is there a danger of a small reduction in demand requiring a disproportionately large reduction in jobs?

4.07   The list is long and could no doubt be made longer still because there are so many factors in good management which may usefully be planned for. As this guide is about business plans and planning, not about management, it lists only the features commonly seen in the best business plans in the public sector, and not all the entries which may be made in them.

Other information

4.08   Other points which are often added for the information of third parties include

- the **internal structure** of the organisation, showing the main divisions and subdivisions and how many staff there are in each. This will give clients a clearer understanding of an organisation than other sources such as telephone directories, which are otherwise all that they often see

- the **names, qualifications, experience and biographical details** of its manager, team leaders, and leading staff, together with an analysis of the staff, analysed by skill, location or grade

- the names and telephone numbers of staff who act as **contact points** for clients.

6 – The contribution of accountants

"The winds and the waves are always on the side of the ablest navigators."
– Edward Gibbon

6.01 Business plans need to carry conviction with many different types of readers, and at many different levels. Often the hardest readers to satisfy are those who want to see that figures have been put on everything which can be counted or measured, and that all such figures cross-check, internally, with one another and, externally, with any comparable figures available from other sources.

6.02 Banks and other providers of finance in the private sector often use accountants to carry out the necessary scrutiny of business plans and, not surprisingly, their drafters often employ accountants to make sure that their own plans stand up to such scrutiny.

6.03 Public sector managers are entitled to the same service from their accountants. The many jobs which accountants are usually best placed to do are to

- set out the current trading or budgeting position (*para 4.03*)

- show how the current position of the organisation, as thus set out, is intended to change. This is usually best done by analysing all variations in income and expenditure between volume changes, new work, new methods, higher standards and inflation. This is often the hardest factor to price, especially where organisations are cash-limited or where long-term contracts require income to be indexed. Accountants must then spell out the risks to organisations if inflation thereafter exceeds the rates provided for (*para 5.10*)

- set out the current budgeting position of the clients whose work is being competed for (*para 4.03*)

- reconcile planned trading and budget positions with those of parent and subordinate organisations, and with long-term plans (*para 3.17*)

- reconcile planned expenditure with inputs, for example by relating planned expenditure on salaries and wages with planned staff numbers and grades (*para 4.06*)

- make sure that planned capital expenditure is included in corporate capital programmes (*para 4.06*)

- make spot estimates of the likely cost of possible variations in services (*para 3.06*).

6.04 These jobs are clearly over and above the friendly advice which accountants, like all advisers and associates, should try to give to all their clients. Accountants do by definition see all the business of the organisation, albeit from a different angle from many other observers, so that managers are rightly disappointed if accountants fail to identify with their own clients, or to keep their eyes open for ways of helping them.

6.05 For organisations which provide accounting services, the duties of accountants are different again. Their duties then include those of operational managers. It is then their turn to look for help and advice from their clients.

7 – Appraisal

"If you understand everything, you must be misinformed."

– Japanese proverb

7.01   Practitioners often need to make their own appraisals of the business plans drawn up by others. The three key features to look for in a plan are

- user orientation

- realism

- checkability.

User-orientation

7.02   Every plan has to demonstrate a clear vision of what users want and will pay for, and how they can best be helped.

7.03   This can be tested by looking for

- a precise statement of **who the clients and customers are**

- descriptions of the steps which have been taken to ascertain **what service they want**, what improvements they would most appreciate, and what expensive features of the service they would most readily dispense with

- a summary of the threats faced by clients (such as competition, budget reductions and constitutional change) and **how clients can be helped** to meet them

- a list of **the changes specified** by contracts and service level agreements

- the results of any **consumer or customer satisfaction surveys**.

Realism

7.04   Are business plans 'pie in the sky'? Do they look as if their authors are just going through the motions, or have they been well thought out? Do they reflect cautious but soundly-based optimism? These are the hardest questions for anybody not directly involved in the planning to answer. Readers should, however, begin by asking themselves if the plans spell out

- all the likely **threats** to the organisation (particularly greater exposure to competition, and increasing interest among competitors)

- the organisation's **weaknesses** (as perceived by users) and its strengths

- its **current budget, compared** with

- the overall budget

- clients' budgets

- its own budget for last year, or probable actuals

● its **projected trading position, compared** with

- the estimated trading position for the period preceding the first period covered by the plan

- the clients' budget provision which the organisation will be competing to share

● for both budgets and trading positions, **why projected figures differ** from those immediately past. Are changes analysed to show separately the effects of volume changes; new work; new methods and different standards? Do the figures in the plans agree with the words?

● whether there is any **doubt about the lawfulness** of working for the clients or customers intended

● any additional accommodation; vehicles; plant and equipment; computer hardware and software; or **working capital** which may be needed. If needed, how will they be funded? Have any projected calls on capital programmes been agreed by higher management?

● the **training needs** of staff at all levels

● coordination with

- **corporate aims** and policies

- any corporate **ground-rules** as to pricing, cross-subsidy, surpluses and deficits

- **centrally determined pay rates** or conditions of service

- the plans, where known, of both **parent and component organisations**. The plans of the whole need in both cases to equal the sum of the plans of the parts

● the various **contingencies** which may arise, and the action planned if they do. Has a sensitivity analysis been carried out to forecast the effect on jobs and unit cost levels of marginal reductions in business?

● are any **fundamental problems unresolved**, such as poor accommodation, and inefficient working practices.

7.05 There are two other key questions about which plans commonly make claims but confirmation usually needs to be sought. The first question is **how far staff have been involved** in the plan, to tap their knowledge, seek their consent to the relevance and constructiveness of any changes proposed, and thereby to secure their commitment.

7.06 The second question is whether the plan is **part of a rolling programme**, or a one-off, with no provision for updating. If it is part of a rolling programme, is this year's plan reconcilable with year two of last year's ?

7.07 Are assumptions about the volume of business consistent with information about the volume available, and with the share of such business expected to be won? Are these assumptions consistent with the resources (including manpower) assumed to be available? Are assumptions about manpower realistic, given the pay rates assumed?

Checkability

7.08 It is normally obvious straight away if plans are rigorous, and seriously thought through. On the other hand, the use of words when figures should be available, and of abstract terms instead of concrete, is ominous and suggests that plans are cosmetic.

7.09 Readers should also look out for quantified performance indicators, both to measure the improvement in the performance of the organisation itself, and to give staff targets at which they can aim.

7.10 Budgets and trading figures provide further sources of check, especially if they are reconciled with the other data referred to in para 7.04.

Glossary of terms

public bodies – local authorities, health authorities, NHS trusts, the boards of nationalised industries, and other autonomous bodies in the public sector

organisations – departments and divisions of public bodies, and all sub- divisions thereof

support services – organisations which provide services, not to the public, but to other organisations which do so, or to other support services

direct service organisations (DSOs) – support services in local government which are required by statute to compete for their work with external service- suppliers

in-house suppliers – DSOs and support services

trading organisations – DSOs, other support services which compete for their work with external suppliers, and organisations which sell goods and services to external customers

service units – organisations which provide public services, and support services the volume of whose work is decided corporately

clients – in-house users

customers – external paying users

consumers – external non-paying users.

Checklist for drawing-up business plans

Ascertain client base

1   List current clients

2   Meet them to discuss

  ● what service they really want and what, if any, improvements they would particularly value

  ● what these might cost and whether clients would pay

  ● what features of present service they would dispense with, for agreed credits

  ● what threats they face to their own organisation, and how they may be helped in meeting them

  ● what changes they might prefer in the bases for charges

  ● their estimated budget provision

    – so far as committed to the organisation, or

    – so far as open to competition by it

3   Summarise service improvements required by contracts and service level agreements

4   Gather and tabulate all possible data about customer or consumer satisfaction

5   List potential additional clients or customers

6   Ascertain for them as far as possible the same data as in 2

7   Confirm lawfulness of working for them

8   Summarise service improvements required by external agencies

9   Update range of services

10   Update mission statement

Draw up SWOT analysis

11   Strengths **(S)** – consider why the services of the organisation have been used to date

12   List weaknesses **(W)** – including

  ● those specified by clients

  ● long-standing problems, such as inadequate buildings and equipment, centrally negotiated but burdensome conditions of service, and inefficient working practices which have not yet been successfully renegotiated

● inadequate training or out-of-date qualifications

13 Opportunities **(O)** (as noted in review of client base)

14 List threats **(T)** – including the extension of competition and increasing contractor interest

Summarise trading position

15 Set out estimated totals and main headings, for period now ending

16 Set out corresponding figures for period covered by plan

17 Analyse differences, apportioned between revised charges; volume changes; new work; new methods; and different standards

Summarise budget position

18 Set out probable actual totals and main headings for period now ending

19 Set out corresponding budget totals for first year of plan

20 Analyse differences (as in 17)

21 Reconcile budget of organisation with budget of parent department

22 Make sure same price-base used throughout

Staff participation

23 Circulate all staff – stress receptiveness of management to constructive proposals for radical changes in methods and working practices

24 Decide whether or not to hold workshops

25 For workshops

● decide which staff should attend which workshop

● select facilitator (if manager is not going to lead)

● select other participants (such as client officers)

● arrange suitable venue (away from workplace)

26 For visits to workplaces, arrange for both manager and staff to be free for long enough for useful dialogue (as 23)

Coordination with higher management

27   Ascertain corporate policies as to use of in-house suppliers' conditions of service and complements

28   Ascertain ground-rules as to cross-subsidisation, pricing, surpluses and deficits

29   Submit draft of plan for approval of principles, and reconciliation with departmental plans

Coordination with lower management

30   Collect and summarise subordinate plans

31   Reconcile their totals with organisation's plan

Summarise resources

32   Estimate manpower needed

33   Reconcile with budget

34   For any required increases in categories of staff who have proved difficult to recruit, decide how recruitment should be effected now

35   Ensure any additional incentives allowed for in budget reconciliation

36   Discuss with staff

   ● any changes in promotion, training and recruitment procedures

   ● any reductions in manpower

37   List any improvements needed in premises; vehicles; plant and equipment; computer hardware or software; or working capital

38   Decide method of funding

39   If to be charged to capital, secure agreement to inclusion in corporate capital budget

Agreeing facts with figures

40   List all readily measurable performance indicators available, to enable

   ● performance of organisation (in securing promised improvements) to be monitored

   ● staff to know what they have to do, and whether they are succeeding

CIPFA

BUSINESS PLANS

A Compendium

EDUCATION

The University of Edinburgh

Corporate Plan 1993-1998

THE UNIVERSITY *of* EDINBURGH

CORPORATE PLAN
1993 - 1998

June 1993

THE UNIVERSITY *of* EDINBURGH

CORPORATE PLAN 1993-1998

MISSION STATEMENT

The University's fundamental mission is the advancement and dissemination of knowledge and its understanding. As a leading European centre of academic excellence, the University's core strategic objectives are: to sustain and develop its identity as a research and teaching institution of the highest international quality; to provide an outstanding educational environment, supporting study across a broad range of academic disciplines and serving the major professions; to produce graduates equipped for high personal and professional achievement; and to enhance the scientific and cultural vision of society as well as its economic well-being. As a great civic University, Edinburgh especially values its intellectual and economic relationship with the Scottish community that forms its base and provides the foundation from which it will continue to look to the widest international horizons, enriching both itself and Scotland.

THE UNIVERSITY *of* EDINBURGH

STRATEGIC OVERVIEW

I. Research

1.0 The University of Edinburgh has recently been confirmed as the leading research University in Scotland, and amongst the top ten in the United Kingdom. More than 97% of all eligible staff were submitted for assessment in the 1992 Research Assessment Exercise, and two-thirds of all departments at Edinburgh were assessed to be in the top two grades. The University intends to maintain, and where possible, to strengthen this position.

1.1 The University's pre-eminence in research is based upon a complex range of factors. Foremost amongst these are: the high quality of the University's staff; the opportunities available to pursue interdisciplinary research in an academic environment characterised by breadth and excellence; the close proximity and interdependence of research and teaching; the provision of access to a major research Library within the University, and to an exceptional computing and communications infrastructure.

1.2 To sustain and build upon these advantages, the University intends to ensure that resources continue to be allocated selectively through a planning and budgeting process that seeks to integrate academic, financial and physical planning, and which takes account not only of quantitative information and performance indicators, but also, and importantly, of academic plans and priorities. In addition, it intends: to review, and if necessary to improve the systems and structures that facilitate interdisciplinary activity; to enhance postgraduate research by increasing further the number of such students and by improving the facilities available to them; to organise teaching in ways that permit academic staff adequate time for research; and to improve the University's research support services.

1.3 The University also intends to increase further its income from research grants and contracts over the planning period, whilst continuing to attract at least two-thirds of this income from peer-reviewed sources including the UK Research Councils, UK charities and the EC; to strengthen its links with, and to increase its income from, industry and commerce; and to continue to improve the rate at which indirect costs are recovered from industrial sponsors.

1.4 These and related developments are in future to be overseen by a Vice-Principal (Research) who will advise the Principal, chair a newly-reconstituted Research Committee, and be a member of major decision-making bodies within the University, including the Central Management Group.

THE UNIVERSITY *of* EDINBURGH

1.5 Nevertheless, research management is and will remain strongly devolved at the University of Edinburgh, with resource decisions being taken as close as possible to the point at which research itself is pursued, subject to the need for appropriate forms of accountability. This reflects the University's belief that the role of central management should be to facilitate local research strategies rather than to impose corporate ones.

2. Teaching

2.0 The University of Edinburgh is, and intends to remain, one of the most broadly-based Universities in Scotland and the UK, offering students an academic education of the highest quality across a wide range of disciplines, including the major professions. This teaching, which will be of a level and quality appropriate to our student intake, will continue to take place in the distinctive context of a strong research environment where every student can expect to be taught by academic staff who are active in research.

2.1 The University is also firmly committed to the provision of student choice and to the maintenance of a flexible degree structure, both of which reflect the best traditions of higher education in Scotland. These objectives are underpinned by the breadth of provision available at Edinburgh. This facilitates flexibility in the curriculum as well as interdisciplinarity in research.

2.2 There is strong demand for places at the University, and the quality of the intake reflects this very high level of competition for entry. The University's graduates are also very much in demand, especially in Scotland. Both of these factors suggest that the quality of teaching in Edinburgh is in general high, but more specific indicators of teaching quality will also start to become available over the next few years as a result of the quality assessment programme. In the course of the current planning period, and in the context of these assessments, Edinburgh will therefore be seeking to maintain, and wherever possible will continue to improve, the quality of its teaching.

2.3 The number of undergraduate students has grown rapidly over the past few years. However, the rate of growth is now slowing down, as previously planned, and consistent with the Funding Council's declared policy of consolidation. Subject to the need for annual review in the light of future changes to the funding environment, the total number of full-time home/EC undergraduate students is expected to level out at around 11750 by 1996/97. The total student population is expected to reach approximately 16500, including about 2000 postgraduate students, 1500 part-time students, and 1000 overseas students. There are not expected to be any radical changes in the composition of the undergraduate population during this period, although the University is considering ways in which it might attract more students from Scotland. In addition, the University will continue to develop Continuing Education as an integral component of the University's teaching activities.

CORPORATE PLAN

THE UNIVERSITY of EDINBURGH

2.4 The recent period of growth has posed new challenges and there have been many positive responses throughout the University. A comprehensive review of teaching is underway with the aims of: identifying examples of good practice and promoting them across the University; increasing efficiency whilst maintaining the quality of teaching; and ensuring that academic staff have adequate time to pursue their research. The recommendations of this review are likely to include greater encouragement of active-learning and further changes in teaching methods, especially in the first two years of the undergraduate curriculum. The University is extending formal research training, and promoting computer-literacy, language skills, and environmental awareness within the student body as a whole. Additionally, the University will review the efficiency with which it uses its teaching accommodation, and the adequacy of its academic support structures, including the provision of library facilities, student services, and residential accommodation.

2.5 The majority of these and related developments will be overseen by a Vice-Principal (Teaching) who will advise the Principal, chair the University's Teaching Committee, and be a member of major decision-making bodies within the University, including the Central Management Group.

3. Management and Finance

3.0 Over the past two years, the University has substantially revised its management structure, strengthened its financial control procedures, increased the extent to which responsibilities are devolved within the context of these reforms, and introduced new systems of planning and budgeting. This process of reform will continue over the next few years as the new systems and structures develop and mature. Change will consequently be continuous, but not dramatic. Priorities over the planning period will be: to consolidate the revised management structure; to further devolve responsibility within that structure; to continue to improve the flow of management accounting and other information to budget-holders, making use of all the relevant MAC systems as they become available; to refine further the University's planning and budgeting process; and to provide staff with adequate support and training in pursuit of these changes.

3.1 The new management structures and systems have been designed to restore and secure the University's financial position, which is recognised to be a necessary precondition of continued academic excellence. There is already evidence of success, upon which the University intends to build. Having incurred losses for a number of years, the University achieved a surplus on ordinary activities of more than £2m in 1991/92. It plans to continue to make operating surpluses for the rest of the planning period in order to rebuild reserves, and to provide resources for capital expenditure. The University remains committed to its plan to eradicate the accumulated deficit by no later than July 1994.

CORPORATE PLAN

3.2　The University also intends to ensure that it maintains an adequate level of financial flexibility throughout this period. Since staff costs are the single largest category of University expenditure, this will involve: raising the proportion of fixed-term appointments; increasing the use of hourly-paid teaching staff; and introducing teaching studentships. These initiatives are also consistent with the academic plans and priorities described above.

3.3　In addition, the University will continue to pursue unrestricted funds from sources other than the Funding Council, in particular by the sale of services, through the work of its company UnivEd Technologies Ltd in negotiating research contracts, mounting short courses for industry, and arranging consultancies, and through the fund-raising activities of the University's Development Office.

3.4　One area that will receive special attention over the next few years will be estate management. In addition to the preparation of a strategic estate plan, the University will be improving the efficiency with which existing building stock is utilised, and seeking to integrate the management of space within the new planning and budgeting process. Central timetabling will be extended further next year, and work is already in progress which will enable attributable premises costs to be taken into account when future budgets are considered.

3.5　All of these developments will be overseen by the Central Management Group, reporting to the Finance and General Purposes Committee and the Court. However, the Vice-Principals with responsibility for strategy and for planning and budgeting will continue to play a particularly important role in ensuring that the above changes are successfully implemented, and the relevant targets met.

4. Benefits to the community

4.0　In keeping with its history and traditions, the University will also strive to benefit the community, both directly via the provision of expertise, facilities and services, and indirectly by the contribution that it makes to the reputation, identity and cultural life of the city, and to the stimulation of economic activity in the region.

4.1　These objectives will be pursued in a variety of ways, for example: by attracting students, clients and customers to Scotland from throughout the world; by training undergraduates, many of whom contribute to the life and work of Edinburgh and Scotland after graduation; by widening access to undergraduate degree courses with special references to students who attend schools in the Lothian region, and to mature applicants from the East of Scotland; by providing continuing education and PEVE courses that are of interest to the local community, and others; by developing further cooperative links at postgraduate level with associated institutions in and around Edinburgh; by contributing to the organisation of prestigious civic events; and by working with local government, including the city and its agencies, to make the region increasingly attractive to potential investors, for example by developing the Technopole at the Bush Estate.

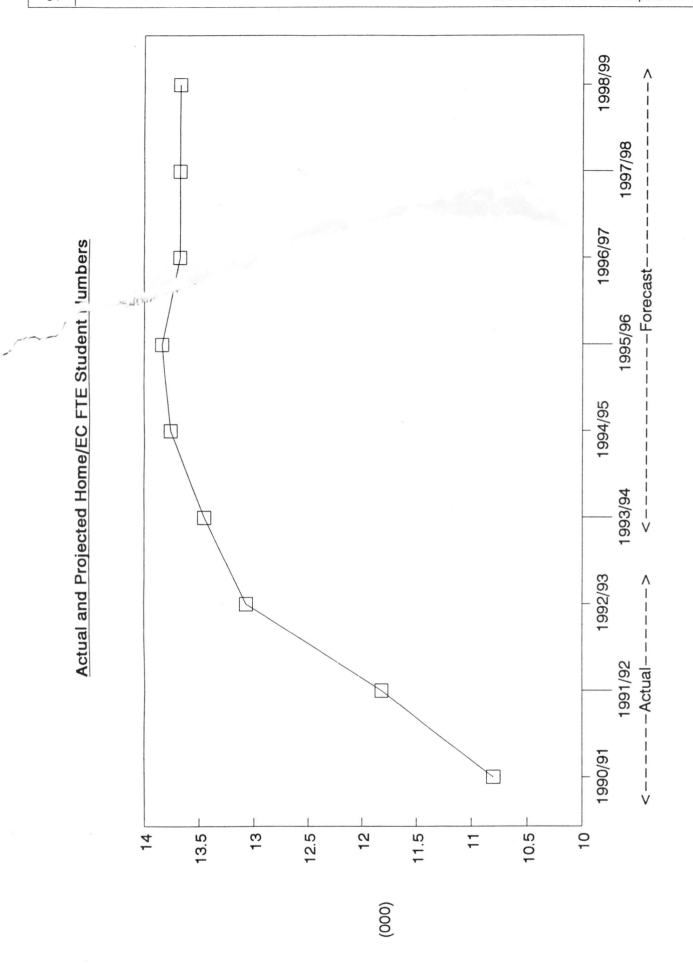

Actual and Projected Home/EC FTE Student Numbers

Income from Research Grants and Contracts

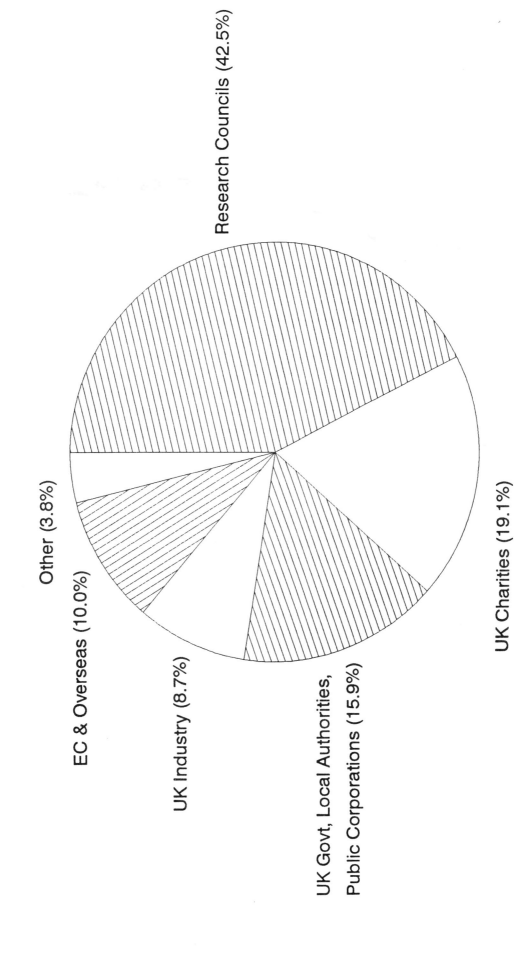

Research Councils (42.5%)

UK Charities (19.1%)

UK Govt, Local Authorities, Public Corporations (15.9%)

UK Industry (8.7%)

EC & Overseas (10.0%)

Other (3.8%)

Source : Form 3 1991/92

Income and Expenditure : Year to 31 July 1992

(Excluding Depreciation, Research Grants & Contracts, Residences & Catering, Equipment and Other Services Rendered)

Income

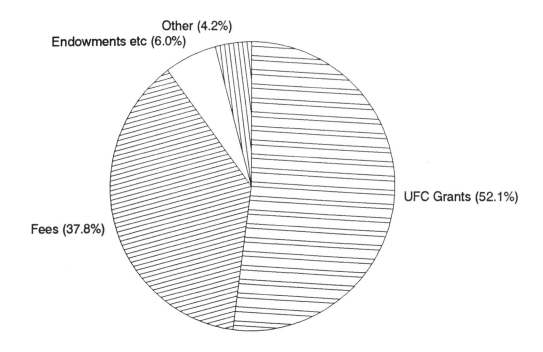

Expenditure

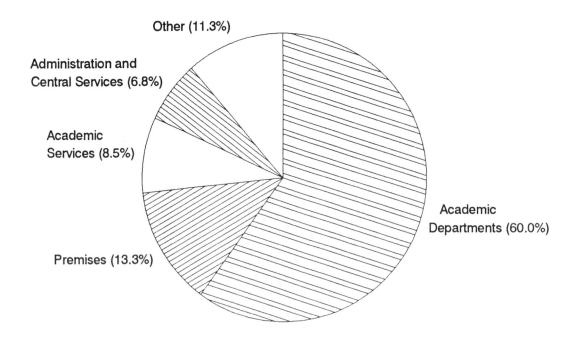

Source : University Accounts 1991/92

CIPFA

BUSINESS PLANS

A Compendium

EDUCATION

Weymouth College

Summary Plan, February 1993

Weymouth College

Summary Plan, February 1993

Weymouth College produces three planning documents:

◆ Strategic plan

◆ Operational plan

◆ Summary plan.

The Plan reproduced here summarises the College's five year strategic plan. In addition, Weymouth College has produced a detailed operational plan for the period April 1993 to August 1994, the first funding cycle with incorporated status. This operational plan is split into six key sections:

◆ Introduction – what the plan is, its relationship to the Strategic plan, review processes.

◆ Background information – operational issues; strategic objectives

◆ Academic operational plan*

◆ Human resources operational plan*

◆ Resources operational plan*

◆ Physical resources strategy*.

* Each of these 'plans' identifies in tabular form operational objectives, targets, management responsibilities, resource implications and evaluation.

Both the operational and strategic plans will be reviewed on an annual basis.

Weymouth College

SUMMARY

Published February 1993

Weymouth College

INVESTOR IN PEOPLE

Weymouth College aims to meet the needs of the community by providing a quality service which achieves positive outcomes by:

- ensuring proper guidance and induction to new students to the College;

- providing excellent on-course support in a safe and attractive learning environment;

- working closely with schools, parents, employers and local interests to serve their needs and maintain the broad waterfront of provision ;

- encouraging and facilitating staff to operate with maximum professional and personal effectiveness in meeting College aims;

- making continuous improvements in efficiency and effectiveness in its use of resources;

- demonstrating a commitment to quality through all aspects of its operations.

1.0 Background

Weymouth Tertiary College is the foremost provider of post sixteen education and training in South Dorset. The College operates on two sites across the town. The College has grown rapidly since its inception in 1985, having nearly doubled its full-time enrolments over the last four years. The College works closely with the local community and has a good reputation for excellent examination results, high staying-on rates, development and innovation.

2.0 Needs Analysis

2.1 The College aims to meet the diverse training and education needs of South Dorset. This varied provision includes bespoke special needs provision, most technical and vocational skills and the full range of academic subjects.

The Strategic and the derivative Operational plans have been based on a preliminary analysis of the local markets and the factors affecting demand for the College's services.

2.2 The key factors we have identified in our needs analysis are:

- the statistical data on school roll numbers for the local area show a steady increase for the 1994/95 period.

- enrolment data from schools for statemented special needs students indicate that demand for the College's dedicated provision will continue.

- there is likely to be an increase in demand for the special needs supported employment programmes.

- in the medium term the recession will continue to depress work placements and day release and also to increase full-time enrolments of adults.

- 96% of Dorset private sector firms employ less than 25 people, and 15% of employers have fewer than six, therefore training and marketing has to be tailored to their needs.

2.3 Other factors likely to affect future enrolment include:

- the decline of the local defence industry;

- the average age of the population in Dorset increasing due to the numbers of retired people and the national downturn in the birthrate;

- the increase of women returning to the workplace;

- the increased competition between Colleges, sixth forms and other providers with the introduction of training credits;

- the changes in the employment base away from manufacturing towards service industries;

- optimistic forecasts for local industries in the vocational areas serviced by the College, such as Business and Management, Hospitality, Electronics and Leisure.

2.4   In addition to examining these needs we have also identified the College's opportunities and constraints in responding to them. Particular constraints include a lack of appropriate accommodation, a past history of under funding and lack of a coherent capital replacement programme. In responding to market needs the College will draw upon its high reputation in the local areas and the commitment and quality of staff, recognised through achievement of the Investor in People Award.

2.5   The Strategic Objectives in the following sections show how the College will be responding to the market needs identified in this analysis.

3.0   Academic Strategy

3.1   Background

Weymouth College aims to continue to meet the needs of its traditional clients and be responsive to new demands. The College has achieved several years of considerable growth whilst maintaining quality standards. Our strategy is to continue this growth but at a level which relates to lcoal market needs and enables us to maintain quality and access.

3.2   The strategic objectives which will determine the nature of our provision over the planning period are:

- **to continue to offer a high quality service as a Tertiary College through provision of student support services, an entitlement curriculum and high examination pass rates;**

- **to recognise the unique needs of a rural environment and provide a range of programmes for education, training, updating, recreation, leisure and culture;**

- **to provide a wide range of teaching and learning styles which cater for differentiation of achievement and need, enable the maximum number of students to achieve their full potential, and emphasise equality of opportunity for all.**

3.3   The strategic objectives related to growth and development are:

- **to expand its student population by 20% over the five year planning period to contribute to the achievement of national and local targets;**

- **to continue to develop strong links with other providers, to include local schools, adult education and higher education, to ensure continuity and progression for clients;**

- **to minimise barriers to access and maximise resources through the modularisation of courses, provision of flexible learning and the introduction of a non-traditional academic year.**

4.0 Human Resources

4.1 Introduction

It is recognised that staff are the College's most valuable resource and the quality of the service we offer depends on employing staff who are appropriately skilled, qualified and motivated. The Staff also need support and appropriate development to ensure optimum performance. The College's commitment to these principles was confirmed through the achievement of the Investor in People Award in December 1992. Clearly, the challenges posed by Incorporation and other developments will require review of the structure of the organisation, as well as changes to the specification of skills required from individuals.

4.2 The strategic objective related to this is:

- **to be staffed by qualified and trained staff and will provide a comprehensive staff development programme which supports the academic strategy and meets the needs of individual staff.**

5.0 Financial Resources

5.1 Introduction

In order to successfully achieve its aims, the College will have to manage all its resources efficiently and effectively. The development of a Management Information System has been the initial step in gaining management control and information on utilisation of resources. Further work in this area will continue to enhance sophistication.

5.2 The budget in 1992/93 was approximately £8 million, with the main income of £6.5 million being derived from the LEA. Other sources of income were:

- Government Training Programmes;

- European Social funding;

- Work Related Non-Advanced further education;

- Commercial activities.

5.3 Strategic objectives in this area are:

- **to increase its income by accessing new sources of funding and producing surplus income equivalent to 5% of the College gross budget.**

- **to maintain financial efficiency through an effective system for financial management.**

5.4 A variety of measures, including increasing the capacity and flexibility of the accommodation should enable us to increase our SSR at the end of the planning period to 1:15.

6.0 Physical Resources

6.1 Introduction

Weymouth College is a two site operation. Unfortunately, the longer term strategy of the local authority was to have a one site operation, which has meant that investment in the Newstead Road site was severely limited for a number of years. This lack of funding is reflected in both fabric and equipment. Overall there has been spasmodic capital investment which has resulted in the acquisition of temporary accommodation on both sites - 17 temporary buildings in all. Although annual surveys of replacement and depreciation needs of equipment have been undertaken, a coherent investment and replacement programme has not been implemented.

6.2 In order to meet the need for increased student numbers, alterations and additions to existing accommodation are essential. Additional work needs to be undertaken, alongside the annual maintenance programme to ensure our strategic objective of:

-   **providing a safe, healthy, attractive and well equipped working and learning environment for all its clients.**

7.0 Quality

7.1 A consistent theme running through all the planning statements has been the College's commitment to maintain the quality of its provision to all its clients. Specific measures we will be taking during the planning period to ensure this are:

-   introducing a system of internal programme verification, including employer perceptions, by September 1994;

-   monitoring examination results against national average;

-   monitoring and responding to non-completion data;

-   producing accurate value-added data.

7.2 The strategic objective related to quality is:

-   **to demonstrate its commitment to quality through the achievement and maintenance of the Investor in People award, the achievement of BS 5750 by two sectors and the enhancement of its quality assurance mechanisms.**

8.0 Sensitivity Analysis

The key planning assumptions are set out in the section 3.5.11 of the main document. Because of our record of historical growth and our links with the local community, we have considered the likely impact of foreseeable variations on our assumptions and, although these would alter the details of our plan, we believe the fundamental strategy remains achievable.

CIPFA

BUSINESS PLANS

A Compendium

EDUCATION

A Large University

Institutional Plan, 1992/93 - 1995/96

Note:

Annexes B to F not included.

UNIVERSITY OF

INSTITUTIONAL PLAN

1992/93-1995/96

DECEMBER 1992

Institutional Plan 1992/93 – 1995/96

Contents

1   NATURE OF THE UNIVERSITY, AIMS AND OBJECTIVES

1.2   The University's three main Aims are:

a)   Research and Scholarship

To advance research, scholarship and learning and to disseminate knowledge as a University of international repute, ensuring that 'academic staff have freedom within the law to question and test received wisdom, and to put forward new ideas and controversial or unpopular opinions, without placing themselves in jeopardy of losing their jobs or privileges'*.

b)   Teaching and Learning

To provide education for students, intended to give them competence in their chosen discipline, to encourage them to develop their intellectual capabilities and personal aspirations and to enable them to be responsible and questioning members of society.

c)   Service Outside the University

To act as a major resource for the   of England, forming effective links with regional communities and organisations and offering a range of services based on the academic activities of the University and including some specifically targetted to meet needs identified in the region.

1.3 As part of the planning process the University has established specific objectives, to be achieved during the planning period. Progress towards these objectives is reviewed annually and the objectives restated where necessary. They are reflected in the sections below and are summarised in Annex A.

1.4 Key Elements of the Plan

(a) Financial Strategy

The University will plan for an annual breakeven position on its income and expenditure account and will restore the University's uncommitted general reserve to £2.7M by 1995/96 through the application of funds derived from the suspension of ERBS contributions.

(b) Student Population

* 1988 Education Act.

Page 1

The University will grow to a fte student population of 8,200 by 1995/96.

(c) Teaching Quality

The University is committed to the provision for teaching quality, through the operation of established assurance and enhancement mechanisms and through resourcing policies.

(d) Research

The University is committed to the enhancement of research performance across its range of disciplines. Its strategy, which incorporates an element of selectivity to reflect the outcomes of Funding Council assessment exercises, co-ordinates resourcing, staffing and equipment policies.

(e) Continuing Education

The University plans to increase continuing education activity to 1115 fte by 1995/96.

(f) Use of Resources

Within the context of devolved resource management arrangements, and so far as is compatible with the planned expansion of student numbers, the University intends that any additional planned resources should be used mainly for the support (departmentally and centrally) of existing academic staff, rather than the appointment of new academic staff.

(g) Capital Programme

The University will implement a capital programme to enhance academic, residential and social provision by 1995/96.

(h) Maintenance Programme

The University will maintain a rolling five-year programme of long-term maintenance.

2   ACADEMIC DEVELOPMENTS

2.1   TEACHING

2.1.1 Following agreement by the Secretary of State for Education and Science,
                        is planning to merge with the University on 1 August 1993. This will be a major addition to the profile of the University. However, the merger has not been taken into account in the student number plans, financial or other statements including in this document. The next iteration of the University's Institutional Plan in 1993 will take into account the full effect of the merger.

2.1.2 The University is planning to increase its student population from 6,837 fte in 1991/92 to 8,200 by 1995/96. This entails a 20% expansion over the period. The detailed student number plan for 1995/96 is given in Annex B. This will be subject to annual review.

2.1.3 The University will aim to increase the proportion of mature home/EC undergraduates and those entering without standard A/AS level qualifications towards a target of 14% by the end of the planning period.

2.1.4 The University expects to increase numbers of overseas students on regular courses to 452 within the planning period from a base of 309 in 1991/92.

2.1.5 The University intends to increase the proportion of postgraduates within total student numbers from 21.5% of the total population in 1991/92 to 23.9% by the end of the planning period (including students on self-financing courses).

2.1.6 The current academic mix will be largely continued over the planning period although there will be an increase in the proportion within the Social Science subject category arising from the proposed developments in the Department of Law (see para 2.1.7).

Subject Categories	1991/92	1995/96
Science	13.7%	13.7%
Engineering	5.7%	5.4%
Mathematics	7.0%	6.8%
Social Science	27.1%	30.6%
Humanities	26.0%	25.3%
Education	20.5%	18.2%
	-----	-----
	100.0%	100.0%

2.1.7 Fundamental changes are taking place in legal education nationally. The Department of Law through its Centre for Legal Practice is one of the selected locations for the provision of a conversion course for non-law graduates recognised by the Law Society as covering the academic stage of their professional training to become solicitors. Its first intake was taken in 1992/93. Following further discussion with the Law Society, major growth is anticipated in self-financing postgraduate taught numbers by the end of the planning period. This is likely to involve a Legal Practice Course starting in 1994/95 with an annual intake rising to 200 fte students.

2.1.8 During the period 1988-1991 the University undertook a major physical expansion of its School of Education. This was achieved through a £5m grant from the UGC in order to extend the School's teaching facilities and by major residential developments funded by the University. This physical expansion underpinned the growth in student numbers within the Faculty of Education from 1,030 in 1988/89 to a planned total of 1,497 by 1995/96. A major concern over the planning period will be the proposals announced by the Secretary of State for Education and Science for changes in Initial Teacher Training. The University will respond positively to the challenge when the implications become clearer.

2.1.9 Links will be maintained with the local Health Authority to continue the jointly-funded Postgraduate Medical School. The University will further develop as a focus for the health care professions in this country and elsewhere, with an endowed Chair being established in the Centre for Complementary Health Studies, through its own Institute of Population Studies, and through links with School of Occupational Therapy and College of Health.

2.1.10 As part of its programme of regional collaboration, the University acts as a validating body.

2.1.11 The   became an affiliated institution with effect from 1991/92. The association, central to which is degree validation, is expected to extend to research collaboration, joint teaching of certain advanced courses, cooperation in overseas recruitment and the development of distance learning and part-time degrees based on certificate courses.

2.1.12 As detailed in paragraph 2.1.1 discussions are advancing with   directed towards a merger from 1 August 1993 of the two institutions, with the School becoming an academic department within the Faculty of Engineering. Developments which would follow from a merger include work with the University's Earth Resources Centre and the School's cooperation in course provision and research with associated departments in the University. Following the merger,   will offer HND courses under the auspices of the BTEC. Although the School is located   from the University it is only a short distance from the University's   The University already has a landline to the Institute and the development of other IT facilities will be a priority. The prospect of merger has provided the catalyst for the University's current reappraisal of its presence in   (see Section 9.8 EXTERNAL RELATIONS AND COMMUNICATIONS).

2.1.13 The University has introduced a first stage of unitisation of its courses, a standardised degree structure and a pilot modular degree option to students after their first year. These changes will permit further developments as thought appropriate in the direction of greater flexibility in course provision.

2.1.14 Student exchange arrangements at undergraduate and postgraduate level are expected to increase. There will be further expansion to link departments with partner institutions in Europe through ERASMUS schemes. In 1992/93 will be involved in 32 student mobility programmes involving 250 students in exchange arrangements.

2.1.15 With the expansion of ERASMUS and other overseas programmes and the increased flexibility of the University's degree courses, the importance of language-teaching provision across the subject range will grow (see Section 6.4 LANGUAGE PROVISION).

2.1.16 The University will continue to optimise its use of both the teaching day and academic space.

2.1.17   has a good record for graduate employment reflecting its reputation for quality of output. With the evolving needs of the employment market in mind, the University will seek to produce graduates with enhanced transferable skills. This will be achieved through curriculum developments (informed by teaching quality assurance), the University's IT strategy and the work of the Staff Development Unit. In 1991/92 the University established a teaching development fund of £50,000 pa to promote innovation in teaching and reinforce its commitment to quality.

2.1.18 The University will seek to increase the proportion not only of students from under-represented educational, social and cultural backgrounds but of disabled students, and will monitor progress in this aim.

2.2   CONTINUING EDUCATION

2.2.1 The following objectives have been established for the period to 1995/96:

- To maintain and extend the University's programme of continuing, professional and adult education by making all appropriate aspects of the University's research, scholarship, teaching and expertise more widely accessible to the adult population and particularly the local community.
- To promote a growing range of CE which reflects the character of university higher education in general and the University of   in particular, and combines vocational and more general non-vocational objectives.
- To provide professional updating, and continuing education and training (CET) for industry, business and commerce, and the professions.
- To maintain the high quality of this provision by carrying out research into aspects of adult education and CE, and appropriate staff development.

2.2.2 A crucial aspect of the University's strategy is to ensure that provision is of high quality and of university standard. This is a major responsibility of the academic staff of the University's Department of Continuing and Adult Education (DCAE), which also undertakes delivery of part of the Continuing Education programme and facilitates the involvement of all subject departments in this work. This integration of CE with the main stream of University teaching has made considerable progress during the past few years and will continue to be a major objective for the planning period. There is also major involvement of the School of Education which is responsible for INSET work, currently around one quarter of the University's CE provision.

2.2.3 The objectives set out in 2.2.1 will be met by offering an extensive programme of liberal education (some of which may be accredited for the purposes of credit accumulation and transfer), certificate courses, ACCESS to HE, CET and INSET. The programme will grow to a projected 1115 fte's in 1995/96. One half will be a combination of liberal education and CET (promoted by DCAE) and professional updating carried out by the Management Studies Centre and Postgraduate Medical School. Approximately one quarter of the programme will consist of one/two term courses, short exchanges, English for Academic Purposes, part-time EFL etc and another quarter will be INSET. The detailed student number plan for Continuing Education is given in Annex C.

2.2.4 The University regards Continuing Education work as a major part of its service to the   region and will continue to maintain a significant presence in   alongside an extensive provision in   The University will explore areas of CE provision in   with other appropriate HE institutions.

2.2.5 With a change of Funding Council from 1993/94, the method of funding continuing education may vary in the future. The University will respond positively to any such changes when the implications become clearer.

2.3 **RESEARCH**

2.3.1 The University plans and reviews research activity on a systematic basis, in order to pursue policies of selective support. In the light of submissions, the University Research Committee identifies selected departments/subjects for priority support to maintain or improve their existing research ratings. In addition, the resource allocation system incorporates an element of differential research support reflecting UFC/HEFCE research ratings.

2.3.2 The University aims to attract postgraduate students in increased numbers, post-doctoral staff and academic visitors of a quality to enhance its academic reputation. The University will continue to develop partnerships with industry and commerce, with professional and government bodies and with other educational institutions both national and worldwide. In support of collaborative research activities the University will seek to build on its success in gaining funding under various European Commission research programmes to raise the University's research profile in Europe. There will also be further emphasis on nationwide industrially-linked activity such as LINK DTI/SERC grants obtained by the Department of Chemistry and School of Engineering

2.3.3 The University plans to increase research income further, and has set a target of 13% of total recurrent income (excluding catering and residences, and the effects of the shift in dual support funding) by the end of the planning period. External research income will continue to be regularly monitored and assessed by Research Committee against national comparators.

2.3.4 As part of the systematic implementation of the University's research policy, departmental study leave programmes will be monitored and developed in furtherance of agreed research plans.

2.3.5 Research performance will be monitored through the system of departmental profiles, updated annually, and through departmental and research centre reviews. Both mechanisms will inform the work of the Research Committee in making subject-specific decisions in the allocation of the following funds allowing for the optimisation of research outcomes within the resources available :

a) the Research Selectivity Fund: allocated to competing departments on the basis of departmental proposals;

b) the Research Fund: allocated to individuals in support of research;

c) Postgraduate studentships.

In addition part of the equipment grant is deployed on a discretionary basis in support of research.

2.3.6 The transfer of funds from the UFC to the Research Councils has resulted in a differential impact across the University. In response to this the University has adopted a mechanism to address in the short-term, the financial and staffing implications for individual departments. In the longer term the University proposes to move to an arrangement which channels an increasing element of indirect funding from Research Councils to the relevant departments.

3 STAFFING POLICIES

3.1 The University will continue to aim to attract and retain high calibre staff who will enhance its national and international reputation for research, scholarship, and teaching. The University will provide conditions that encourage motivation and job satisfaction for all employees and assist the effective use of resources. Provision under the following heads will be regularly reviewed in the light of expansion of student numbers:

> (a) non-staffing expenditure intended to enhance the performance of existing staff
>
> (b) additional support staff (eg technical, clerical/secretarial and other ancillary grades)
>
> (c) a limited number of permanent appointments of extra academic staff, who subject to the 1988 Education Act, should have career prospects and terms and conditions of service equivalent to those of existing staff.

The University will guard against pressure of financial circumstances leading to a disproportionate increase in short-term posts at the expense of permanent longer-term appointments and thus to a decline in research performance.

3.2 Under the resource management arrangements operative since 1991/92 departments have increased freedom over the use of their departmental resources to facilitate changes in their staffing structure.

3.3 Staff training and development procedures within the University were the subject of a major review in 1989/90 and a co-ordinated approach covering all categories of staff is now being implemented with the objective of increasing levels of skill, job satisfaction, motivation and personal development.

3.4 Expenditure directly attributable to staff development and training has increased some 25% in real terms since 1989/90 primarily through the expansion of the University's Staff Development Unit (See Section 6.3 STAFF DEVELOPMENT UNIT).

3.5 Staff development and appraisal schemes are now fully operational for both academic and academic-related staff. These arrangements will be reviewed during the planning period to ensure that full advantage is taken of opportunities for institutional and personal development. It is the intention of the University to extend this initiative to include all categories of staff and steps have already been taken to this end. This will be developed as appropriate over the planning period.

3.6 The University will continue to maintain a rolling fund of £250,000 to permit selective early retirement particularly to assist enhancement of research performance and changes of direction within departments.

3.7 The increasing academic management role of heads of department has been recognised and additional emoluments made available to reward them. In addition new training programmes for this management role will be provided by the Staff Development Unit.

3.8 The University is committed to a policy of Equal Opportunities employment and to implementing, consolidating and extending Equal Opportunities policy measures for all employees of the University.

4. PHYSICAL RESOURCES

4.1 Capital expenditure remains one of the major constraints upon the University in formulating its strategy for the planning period. It is determined not to undertake commitments which it cannot match in terms of necessary capital expenditure.

4.2 The University is aware of the pressures that increases in student numbers put on student residential accommodation. By October 1992 the University will have completed construction of 600 new self-catering places at the cost of some £14m (loan financed) to accommodate an increase in population of 800 fte. To cater for further planned growth by 1995/96, various options are being considered, including increased head-leasing accommodation and substantial use of third party off-campus developments. The University intends to reach decisions in 1993 which will ensure provision of extra residential accommodation to meet the needs of the expected student population by 1995/96.

4.3 A £500,000 refurbishment programme to existing academic buildings has just been completed and by October 1994 the University will have constructed a teaching/conference complex at a cost of £1.3m, part supported by £506,000 by the UFC. These developments will form a solid base for planned student expansion.

4.4 The University has committed £2.25m of non-UFC funds up to 1994/95 for capital programmes associated with the various student support services and social facilities, reflecting the growth of student numbers in the planning period. The capital projects planned are detailed in Annex F and include increases in social space, dining and shopping facilities and the extension of the Student Health Centre at

4.5 The University sees the equipment grant as a major concern over the planning period and will look to supplement it, for example from research contract overheads and other non-UFC income streams. New arrangements for managing equipment funds have been introduced as from 1991/92 and these will involve the production of indicative five-year equipment plans for departments under the supervision of Academic Policy Committee.

4.6 Based on condition surveys by external consultants, the University has established a new 5 year rolling programme to address the identified problems and increased its basic annual provision for long term maintenance from £100,000 pa in 1989 to £600,000 pa from 1992/93 onwards. It will maintain this programme throughout the planning period. By 1993 it will have completed a £3.5m project to repipe and rewire the Physics/Chemistry complex of which £2.4m will have been financed from non-UFC funds.

5 FINANCIAL STRATEGY

5.1 The University had a small deficit on the income and expenditure account for 1991/92, after the application of funds resulting from the discontinuation of the superannuation contribution in respect of the non-academic pension scheme (ERBS). This discontinuation will last until April 1997 and will result in £3M becoming available over a 5 year period. The University has identified the following objectives for the period to 1996:

- To break even on the income and expenditure account each year to 1995/96;

- To eliminate the accumulated deficit, which at 31 July 1991 amounted to some £1.1m (excluding Residence and Catering balances),by the application of funds accumulated from the suspension of the ERBS superannuation contributions;
- To restore the University's uncommitted general reserves to some £2.7m by 1995/96;
- Within increasing total income, to reduce the proportion deriving from UFC/HEFCE grant and fees of funded students;
- To make a financial provision of £600,000 pa for a programme of essential building maintenance.

5.2   In order to increase total funding the University will be looking to:

- increase the number of overseas students on non-self-financing courses to 452;
- develop self-financing courses to increase ftes to 650;
- increase externally funded research income to 13% of recurrent income (excluding Residence and Catering and the effects of the switch in dual support funding);
- increase the recovery of indirect costs on research contracts etc;
- raise increasing resources (£0.5m per annum by 1994/95) through a development Campaign from external sources including Alumni, to be used mainly for capital purposes, library purchasing and selective academic posts;
- increase contributions from conferences etc, to finance new student residential accommodation and the new teaching/conference complex, and to make a contribution to funds for the selective support of research;
- increase income from other activities such as validation of courses for other HE institutions;
- increase income from consultancy and professional services, including

5.3 The University generates considerable income from conference and other vacation lettings. This income finances some academic activities, for example a contribution of 10% of surpluses to the Research Fund, but much the greater part goes to residential accounts, facilitating the building of further residential developments on a self-financing basis. With the new residences recently completed and the planned provision of further places, the University has set a target of a tripling of conference income attributable to self-catering units by the end of the planning period through the increase in places and the proposed teaching/conference complex.

5.4 Using procedures based on the Hanham recommendations the University will continue to seek increased indirect cost recovery on research and similar projects to a minimum of 50% of staffing costs.

5.5 The University will give priority to better support of academic staff to meet identified needs in their departments. In selected areas this policy will mean increased academic staffing, but most increased support will be given to existing academic staff, through greater expenditure under other staffing and non-staffing heads.

5.6 The resource management arrangements effective from 1991/92 give more discretion to academic departments to determine the disposition of resources within a given envelope. Thus implementation of the policy set out in paragraph 5.5 will fall to academic departments under the supervision of the Academic Policy Committee.

5.7 Established mechanisms will continue to ensure that self-financing courses contribute to the central costs and income of the University.

5.8 The planned resources for the academic, non-academic and student services sectors will be the subject of annual review each Autumn, with annual budget decisions and detailed resource allocation decisions being made each Spring. Following reviews in the Michaelmas Term 1992 the planned resources for the academic sector for 1995/96 are detailed in Annex D.

5.9 The allocation of validation income will shift from University general funds to those departments involved in validation, less a topslice to support the central Validation Office. The total annual income is expected to exceed £150,000.

5.10 In the event of significantly adverse financial developments, the University would expect to reassess its plan in a coherent way, using reserve funds to finance variations temporarily. The rate at which some objectives could be achieved would inevitably be effected.

5.11 The Development Office Strategic Plan falls into two distinct parts, the first of which is the development of the alumni relations programme, which should result in some financial support for the University in the medium to long term. In respect of fund raising, the Development Office closed the University Development Appeal in 1992 with its target of £1.50 million comfortably exceeded. A longer term Development Campaign, with a target of £0.5m per annum by 1994/95, will begin in 1993. The aim of the Campaign will be to secure annual giving in support of a range of core activities (such as Library provision, scholarships, equipment, student facilities) and one-off support for a changing portfolio of special projects. The Development Office's Strategic Plan will be submitted annually to P&RC for approval and rolling forward.

5.12 Over the planning period and beyond, the Development Office is expected to improve progressively the ratio of funds raised to the cost of operations.

6.   **ACADEMIC SERVICES**

6.1   **COMPUTER SERVICES**

6.1.1 The University has undertaken a substantial review of its IT strategy as an integral part of its planning process. A review of the Computer Unit, the replacement of equipment funded by the Information Services Committee of the UFC in 1991/92, the installation of a new computer for the Library and participation in the UFC's MAC Initiative have enabled the University to plan a comprehensive and integrated set of services.

6.1.2 The University will extend IT to all aspects of its academic and administrative work. It will continue to support a strong computing infrastructure on a high speed data communications network covering the whole site, enabling users to access the set of centrally managed local services from any workstation. Provision has been made to extend and enhance the network over the planning period.

6.1.3 High priority will be given to providing network access points in all offices and lecture rooms through a wiring installation programme spread over a number of years. Provision of network access points in Halls of Residence remains desirable but has had to be given a lower priority for the planning period. Alternative funding arrangements will be sought.

6.1.4 The University will encourage faculties, departments and centres to provide all staff and students with access to computing facilities at or near to their normal place of work through the provision of equipment connected to the network. They will also be encouraged, through guidelines for good practice, to make appropriate use of IT facilities in the teaching process (see section 2.1.17 TEACHING).

6.1.5 The local network is connected to the national JANET network and users will be encouraged to make use of appropriate facilities and services at other sites, including Regional or National Centres.

6.1.6 The University's Computer Unit will continue to provide computing services for the departments and faculties. An internal review has concluded that it should reduce its programming services, develop as a repository of technical expertise and advice and continue to provide a computing network and infrastructure together with certain specialist services. Though the Unit will continue to develop its responsibilities for standardisation, coordination and purchasing, the extension of the network will permit a greater devolution of computing resources throughout the University during the planning period.

6.1.7 All service machines including those operated by the Computer Unit, the Library and the Registrar's Department will be required to offer systems that can be connected as servers to the network so that they can be accessed from any terminal or workstation.

6.1.8 The University welcomes national, collective initiatives such as the JANET network and the CTISS teaching projects. It is a member of the LIBERTAS/SSLSCAP group of universities for Library computing and of the Powerhouse Group for administrative computing. The University will support the Computer Unit in maintaining its expertise in networking so that it can contribute to the development of national and international standards and manage the data communications infrastructure which is crucial to the success of the IT Strategy.

6.2 LIBRARY

6.2.1 The University recognises the central importance of the Library for both research and teaching and the need to enhance its resources and facilities for the increased demands in the planning period. The system of resource allocation gives departments more scope and flexibility for their own purchasing programmes and will allow the Library, its collections and services to benefit from planned growth in student numbers. The University Development Campaign will have the Library collections as a major objective.

6.2.2 The Library will continue to develop as a major information resource for the   of England as well as supporting the academic work of the University in the most effective way. The Library will complete in the planning period:

- complete conversion of the old card catalogue into electronic form
- integration of the Library system with the campus computing network
- harmonisation of Library strategies with the University's declared strategy
  for Information Technology.

The University is aware of the increasing pressure upon Library space, both for the storage of the collections and for readers' places, and will examine strategies to meet these problems.

6.3 STAFF DEVELOPMENT UNIT

6.3.1 The University's Staff Development Unit combines both staff development and appraisal work with support for the maintenance of teaching quality. A significant investment has been made in developing these mechanisms which are seen to be of great importance over the planning period.

6.4 LANGUAGE PROVISION

6.4.1 In recognition of the importance of language teaching provision across the subject range, the University's Language Centre has been reorganised with enhanced language provision being provided from 1992/93 by a now separate Foreign Language Centre.

6.4.2 English as a Foreign Language is taught by the English Language Centre in its dual capacity as a central service to the academic department and as a self-financing unit. Its activities are expected to expand with the growth of the University's overseas links and recruitment.

6.5 UNIVERSITY PRESS

The University Press, which provides a major resource for the publication of research and scholarship, will expand further over the planning period largely on a self-financing basis. The University will provide a financial contribution in recognition of the service to the University which the Press performs in delivery of its objectives.

7 STUDENT SERVICES

7.1 The University intends that the resourcing of the Guild of Students, the Athletic Union and the various student support services should reflect the growth of student numbers in the planning period. New formula-based arrangements for the allocation of resources to the Guild and Athletic Union were agreed and implemented from 1991/92. Similar arrangements will be considered for the Family Centre and the Student Counselling Service.

7.2 As part of its sports development policy for the planning period, the University continues to seek non-UFC finance and collaborative developments with local bodies for the enhancement of its sports facilities.

7.3 The University is aware of the pressures that increases in student numbers place on student residential accommodation (see Section 4.2 PHYSICAL RESOURCES). To cater for further planned growth, various options are being considered, including increased head-leasing of accommodation and substantial use of third party off-campus developments. The University will maintain its commitment to provide places for all first-year students in University accommodation and, given the pressures on local accommodation in   , for a significant proportion of senior years, most in self-catering units. The University remains aware of the difficulties of building extra residences and recognises the burden that loan financing places on student rents and is determined to minimise its impact. The income generated from conference and other vacation lettings will continue to provide a significant subsidy contribution to the student residence accounts

7.4 The University has made a major commitment for capital programmes associated with the various student support services and social facilities, reflecting the growth of student numbers in the planning period (see Section 4.4 PHYSICAL RESOURCES).

8 NON-ACADEMIC SERVICES

8.1 The University has taken the view that the increase in expenditure from general funds for the non-academic sector should be proportionately less than that planned for the academic sector, reflecting a judgement that improvements in performance can be obtained by increased efficiency and by the provision of improved computing infrastructure.

8.2 Within the constraints noted in paragraph 8.1 the University will ensure expenditure is appropriate to:

- support the projected increase in student numbers;
- support the demands of academic development;
- meet the demands placed on the University by external agencies;
- provide a quality service.

8.3 The University continues to develop central administrative services to provide effective support for agreed activities and policies. Information systems have been reviewed in conjunction with the MAC Initiative, and will be enhanced during 1993 to provide the integrated and easily-accessed data essential to the managerial developments for the planning period. A major objective will be to ensure adequate financial management and student information is provided to underpin the resource management arrangements for the academic sector.

8.4 In support of the major investment in MAC software and replacement hardware, additional terminals and PCs are planned which will improve access to management information and support changes in operational systems and procedures.

8.5 Planned expansion of the University will by 1993/94 exceed the capacity of the present PABX telephone exchange. Additional exchange and extension lines are proposed phased over a three year period.

8.6 A major review of archiving and retrieval systems is planned to improve access to student records and committee papers currently retained in paper format.

8.7 A Non-Academic Sector Plan to 1995/96 has been approved. A summary of its financial implications is given in Annex E.

9 EXTERNAL RELATIONS AND COMMUNICATIONS

9.1 The University's External Relations strategy has several strands

- Public relations and publicity
- Industrial liaison and technology transfer
- Promotion and marketing of courses
- Development (fund-raising)
- Research promotion
- International affairs and links
- Relations with the region

The External Relations Division will continue to provide direction in many of these areas, particularly public relations and publicity, the promotion and marketing of courses and relations with the Region. Other matters will be handled by   the Development Office, the Research and External Support Office, the International Office and the Erasmus Office in conjunction with academic departments.

9.2 As an outward-looking university,   has long-standing links with many institutions in other parts of the world and continues to forge new ones. Some of the relationships are consolidated by formal agreements relating to the exchange of staff and students. Within Europe the availability of funds through various European Commission programmes (ERASMUS, COMETT, TEMPUS, LINGUA, ESPRIT, BRITE/EURAM and Environment) has encouraged new links and the University will continue to develop these.

9.3 The University will promote, through the activities of a Regional Advisory Group, its accessibility as a major source of high-level expertise for the

                                                           A pump priming fund for regional activities is administered by the Group.

9.4 The University will continue to market its consultancy and other professional services. This will be supported in part by the University's consultancy company,   The company also administers the   on behalf of the European Commission. A branch office has been opened in   to promote both the Centre and company throughout the Region. A wholly owned subsidiary company,   has been formed to promote consultancy and commercial opportunities related to the biotechnology field.

9.5 The University is exploring a range of relationships with institutions in the region (see Section 2.1.10 TEACHING), and looks forward to collaboration where appropriate with the new University of

9.6 Through its long-established patronage of the visual and performing arts, the University provides a cultural centre which draws attendances from all parts of the County of   and beyond. Its Great Hall, with an annual series of concerts by the Bournemouth Symphony Orchestra, is a major performance venue, and the University itself promotes annual programmes of concerts, public lectures and exhibitions. Council approved a revised policy for the Arts in July 1992 and over the planning period these detailed recommendations will be implemented.

9.7 The   Theatre, on the University campus, maintains a permanent professional repertory company with the support of the Arts Council of Great Britain, local authorities in   and the University. Continued support for the Theatre, for music and visual arts, will be kept under review.

9.8 The University's strong links with   will be further reinforced in 1993 by the merger with   (see Section 2.1.12 TEACHING). The incorporation of so significant an institution will provide the University with a major base, and the opportunity to consolidate all its activities in   of which the most notable are the
          jointly funded since its inception in 1971 by the University and
                              and the Department of Continuing and Adult Education
at   The University will also explore areas of CE provision in
and   with other appropriate HE institutions.

10 QUALITY : MEASUREMENT, EVALUATION AND MANAGEMENT

10.1 The University is under strong external pressure to grow but is committed to providing a high quality experience, both academic and non-academic, for its students and has thus decided on an expansion programme over the planning period which will allow this to be achieved.

10.2 The University has introduced a range of teaching quality assurance policies resulting from a comprehensive review began in 1989, the key elements of which are:

- revised procedures for considering and approving proposals for new taught courses;
- the introduction of a system of departmental reviews operating on a 5 year cycle, forming one of the principal instruments for departmental planning and for securing accountability from its academic units;
- the introduction of teaching quality audits, concentrating on the department's teaching quality assurance policy. The results of these audits feed into and inform departmental reviews;
- the adoption of the main points concerning postgraduate research students and supervisors contained in the CVCP's code of practice.

10.3 In November 1991 the CVCP Academic Audit Unit undertook an audit of the University, examining existing systems and procedures for academic quality control and assurance. The University was commended for its many good practices. Some areas were identified as requiring further attention and the University aims to address these through its established mechanisms.

10.4 The University's quality assurance work is strongly supported by the Staff Development Unit which will combine both staff development and appraisal work with maintenance of teaching quality.

10.5 The University is committed to emphasising quality in all aspects of its work and has put in place a wide range of managerial reforms. Central to these was the introduction in 1991/92 of a revised committee structure and of managerial arrangements based on increased devolution of authority and accountability.

10.6 Fundamental to the new committee structure has been the development of the Planning and Resources Committee. The Committee is the focus for a wide-ranging and integrated planning process in the production, review and restatement of the University's Institutional Plan. The Committee will monitor progress against the Plan on a systematic basis, supported by appropriate management information, reviewing and updating the Plan annually. The work of the Committee will be informed routinely by the arrangements for departmental reviews and departmental profiles.

10.7 New resource management arrangements effective from 1991/92 have given more discretion to academic departments to determine the disposition of resources within a given envelope, under the supervision of the Academic Policy Committee. This Committee works interactively with Planning & Resources Committee in the development of academic aspects of the University's Institutional Plan.

10.8 Following the development of a programme of reviews of academic departments, a 5 year cycle of systematic reviews of all service areas (Academic, Administrative and Student) will begin in 1992/93. As with academic departments, this will form one of the principal instruments for service area planning and for securing accountability.

10.9 The University has adopted a new code of practice for internal audit and has strengthened the terms of reference of its Finance Committee so as to enable it to act as an Audit Committee.

10.10 The University has established a Purchasing Coordination Group reporting direct to Finance Committee so as to provide a continuous review of arrangements for the purchase of supplies and services. Further attention will be given over the period to improving policies and practices for purchasing.

DAW/JKC
A:\PLAN4A
11 November 1992

UNIVERSITY OF   ANNEX A

INSTITUTIONAL PLAN 1995/96

Summary of Objectives in relation to the Institutional Plan
To be achieved by 1995/96 unless indicated.

Academic Developments

1   To increase the student population from 6,837 fte in 1991/92 to 8,200 by
        1995/96 [para 2.1.2].

2   To increase the proportion of mature home/EC undergraduate entrants and
        those entering without standard A/AS level qualifications to 14% by
        1995/96 [para 2.1.3].

3   To increase the numbers of overseas students on regular courses to 452
        by 1995/96 from a base of 309 in 1991/92 [para 2.1.4, 5.2].

4   To increase the proportion of postgraduates within total student numbers
        from 21.5% of the total population in 1991/92 to 23.9% by 1995/96
        [including students on self-financing courses] [para 2.1.5, 2.3.2].

5   To increase the number of students on self-financing courses to 650 by
        1995/96 [para 5.2].

6   To largely maintain the current academic mix (as measured by proportion
        of the student population) over the planning period [para 2.1.6].

7   To maintain links with the local Health Authority, to continue the
        jointly funded Postgraduate Medical School and to further develop as a
        focus for the health care professions [para 2.1.9].

8   To extend the association with the
                [para 2.1.11].

9   To reappraise the University's presence in   [para 2.1.12, 9.8].

10   To develop further modular, other inter-disciplinary degrees and credit
        transfer schemes [para 2.1.13].

11   To expand departmental links with partner institutions in Europe through
        ERASMUS schemes, expanding from a base of 32 student mobility programmes
        in 1992/93 [para 2.1.14].

12   To continue to optimise use made of both the teaching day and academic
        space [para 2.1.16].

13   To produce graduates with enhanced transferable skills [para 2.1.17].

14   To increase the proportion of students from under-represented
        educational, social and cultural backgrounds and from disabled students
        [para 2.1.18].

15   To maintain and extend the University's programme of continuing,
        professional and adult education [para 2.2.1].

16   To increase the volume of CE activity from 960 fte in 1990/91 to 1115
        fte by 1995/96.

2

17   To provide priority support to selected departments/subjects to improve
        or maintain their research ratings [para 2.3.1, 2.3.5].

18   To monitor and enhance research performance through the work of the
        Research Committee [para 2.3.5].

19   To develop a mechanism which channels an increasing element of indirect
        funding from research councils to the relevant departments [para 2.3.6].

20   To continue to develop partnerships with industry and commerce,
        professional and government bodies and with other educational
        institutions [para 2.3.2].

21   To increase funding from EC research programmes and to raise the
        University's research profile in Europe [para 2.3.2].

22   To increase research income to 13% of total recurrent income by 1995/96
        [para 2.3.3].

Staffing Policies

23   To work to recruit and retain high calibre staff who will enhance the
        University's standing in research, scholarship and teaching [para 3.1].

24   To increase levels of skill, job satisfaction, motivation and personal
        development for all categories of staff [para 3.3, 3.5].

25   To optimise the operation of the staff development and appraisal schemes
        for academic and academic-related staff and where appropriate to
        introduce analogous schemes for other categories of staff [para 3.5].

26   To continue a rolling fund of £250,000 to permit selective early
        retirement [para 3.6].

27   To maintain and extend Equal Opportunity policy measures [para 3.8].

Physical Resources

28   To ensure adequate provision of residential accommodation to meet the
        needs of the expected student population by 1995/96 [para 4.2].

29   To provide appropriate teaching and social provision to reflect the
        growth in student numbers [para 4.3, 4.4].

30   To maintain a £600,000, 5 year rolling long term maintenance programme
        [para 4.6].

Financial Strategy

31   To break even on the income and expenditure account each year to 1995/96
        [para 5.1].

32   To eliminate the accumulated deficit by the application of funds
        accumulated from the suspension of the ERBS superannuation contributions
        [para 5.1].

33 To restore the University's uncommitted general reserves to some £2.7M by 1995/96 [para 5.1].

34 To reduce the proportion of total income deriving from UFC/HEFCE grant and fees of funded students [para 5.1].

35 To raise £0.5M pa by 1994/95 through a Development Campaign [para 5.2, 5.11]

36 To increase the contribution from conference and other vacation lettings generally, and by tripling conference income attributable to self-catering units by 1995/96 from a base of £102,000 in 1989/90 [para 5.3].

37 To increase the recovery on indirect costs on research and similar projects to a minimum of 50% of staffing costs [para 5.4].

38 To increase validation income to £150,000 pa [para 5.9].

39 To improve the ratio of funds raised to the cost of operations within the Development Office [para 5.12].

Academic Services

40 To implement progressively the agreed strategy for the development of IT for teaching, research and administrative purposes [para 6.1.1 - 6.1.8].

41 In respect of the library, to complete during the planning period:

a) conversion of the old card catalogue into electronic form
b) integration of the Library system with the campus computing network
c) harmonisation of Library strategies with the University's declared strategy for Information technology [para 6.2.2].

42 To examine strategies to meet the increasing pressure on Library space [para 6.2.2].

43 To expand the University Press over the planning period, largely on a self-financing basis [para 6.5].

Student Services

44 To ensure that the resourcing of the Guild of Students, the Athletic Union and the various student support services reflect the growth in student numbers over the planning period [para 7.1].

45 To continue to seek non-UFC finance and collaborative developments for the enhancement of the University's sports facilities [para 7.2].

46 To maintain the University's commitment to provide residential places for all first-year students [para 7.3].

Non-Academic Services

47 To continue to develop central administrative services to provide effective support for agreed activities and policies [para 8.3].

4

48   To provide additional IT equipment to improve access to management information and support changes in operational systems and procedures [para 8.4].

49   To expand the PABX telephone exchange to meet the growing needs of the University [para 8.5].

50   To undertake a major review of archiving and retrieval systems [para 8.6].

External Relations and Communications

51   To develop further the University's international links in both teaching and research [para 9.2].

52   To promote, through the activities of a Regional Advisory Group, the University's accessibility as a major source of high-level expertise for the   [para 9.3].

53   To continue to market consultancy and other professional services [para 9.4].

54   To implement progressively over the planning period the Arts Policy recommendations as agreed by Council [para 9.6].

Quality: Measurement, Evaluation and Management

55   To implement agreed teaching quality assurance policies [para 10.2].

56   To monitor, through the work of P&RC, progress against the Institutional Plan on a systematic basis, reviewing and updating the Plan annually [para 10.6].

57   To implement a programme of reviews of service areas [para 10.8].

58   To improve policies and practices for purchasing [para 10.10].

CIPFA

BUSINESS PLANS

A Compendium

HEALTH

Rochdale Healthcare NHS Trust

Business Plan, 1993/94

BUSINESS PLAN
1993/94

MISSION STATEMENT

"Our mission is to provide high quality services to all of our patients respecting their dignity and putting their interests first. Services will be efficient and effective and it is our aim to ensure integration with all other agencies. We are committed to sound medical, nursing and other professional standards and wish to support our staff with excellent training and development opportunities."

OCTOBER 1992

Rochdale Healthcare NHS Trust

ROCHDALE HEALTHCARE NHS TRUST

BUSINESS PLAN 1993/94

I N D E X

ROCHDALE HEALTHCARE NHS TRUST

BUSINESS PLAN 1993/94

1. THE MISSION

1.1   Rochdale Healthcare NHS Trust has recently produced its first "Strategic Direction" covering the five years to 1997/98. This document identified the Trust's strategic objectives, setting out a broad plan for their achievement and established the direction in which the Trust wishes to move forward. The Business Plan 1993/94 identifies the short-term objectives which will move forward the implementation of the Trust's strategy and reviews the objectives currently being pursued from the 1992/93 Plan in the light of the Strategic Direction and progress to date. Central to the Trust's development is the Mission Statement:-

> *"Our mission is to provide high quality services to all of our patients respecting their dignity and putting their interests first. Services will be efficient and effective and it is our aim to ensure integration with all other agencies. We are committed to sound medical, nursing and other professional standards and wish to support our staff with excellent training and development opportunities."*

1.2   A number of key objectives have been developed to underpin the mission statement and these are grouped under five headings. All are critical to the mission and they provide a focus for the Business Plan, setting out the areas within which the key management tasks for 1993/94 and the subsequent two years will be focused:-

*   Services

*   Quality

*   Efficiency and Effectiveness

*   Integration

*   Manpower, Training and Development

1.3   The Department of Health has identified three top priorities for 1993/94 which are reflected in this Business Plan:-

    (i)   implementation of "Health of the Nation";

    (ii)   ensuring high quality health and social care in the community, in partnership with local authorities;

    (iii)   developing the "Patients' Charter" at national and local levels.

1.4   Rochdale Health Authority and FHSA's document "Purchasing for Health", a joint Purchaser Plan for 1993 onwards, has recently been issued and sets out the Purchasers' wish to:-

    (i)   develop community based services;

    (ii)   see benefits for their patients as a consequence of change in medical practice and technological developments;

    (iii)   purchase services which are efficient and effective, demonstrating increased value for money;

The Business Plan takes account of the views and plans set out by the Trust's main Purchaser, particularly the issues it has highlighted for possible inclusion in 1993/94 contracts.

1.5   The Business Plan incorporates the following key issues:-

    (i)   targets for quality improvements against which performance can be measured;

    (ii)   targets for improving efficiency in the use of resources;

    (iii)   justification for planned capital expenditure;

    (iv)   broad activity and financial plans against which performance can be measured;

    (v)   plans to improve the management of the Trust's business.

2. SERVICES

2.1 Strategic Objectives

The Trust's strategic objectives in terms of Services are centred on the following:-

* to be the main supplier of quality services to the population served by Rochdale Health Authority;

* to manage areas of increased demand resulting from demographic changes, achieving significant increases in workload levels within existing resources;

* to continue to improve existing services and, in some cases, to extend the range of care provided in response to the demands of patients and Purchasers;

* to target ophthalmology services for development to a wider population;

* to implement the Community Care Plan in the best interest of Rochdale people;

* to provide integrated hospital and community services in Rochdale;

* to incorporate the views of Purchasers, General Practitioners, service users, the F.H.S.A., the C.H.C. and voluntary bodies in the Trust's planning mechanisms;

* to help achieve the "Health of the Nation" targets in Rochdale.

2.2 Existing Service Provision

The Trust provides a comprehensive range of hospital in-patient, out-patient and day care services for a catchment population of 165,000 and community services for Rochdale Health Authority's resident population of 217,000. For geographical reasons, the bulk of the populations of Middleton and Heywood, which form part of the Rochdale Metropolitan Borough, have traditionally looked to hospitals in North Manchester, Oldham and Bury for their acute services, while at the same time, Rochdale Hospitals have historically provided services to areas outside the borough boundaries, in particular Whitworth, Todmorden and parts of Oldham.

Birch Hill Hospital provides most acute in-patient services for the existing catchment area and includes a Younger Disabled Unit and Haemodialysis facility which provide services for a number of surrounding Districts. Ophthalmology in-patient services are provided for the residents of Bury Health Authority as well as Rochdale, while Rochdale residents receive ENT in-patient treatment in Fairfield Hospital, Bury. Rochdale Infirmary provides out-patient and accident and emergency services, together with in-patient facilities for orthopaedics, oral surgery and an E.S.M.I. Unit.

The full range of community services for the whole population of Rochdale are provided in co-operation with General Practitioners, the local authority and voluntary sector and carers and users; this includes community nursing services, paramedical services and specialist learning disabilities and mental health services. Other services include dental, G.U. medicine, diabetic services and an extremely well developed, high quality audiology service.

2.3 Integration

A key objective for the Trust concerns the integration of services and a number of issues will continue to be addressed during 1993/94 to ensure that the excellent progress to date is continued.

(i)   further integration of hospital and community services by continuous updating and improvement of the existing admission and discharge protocols and providing total care packages;

(ii)   building on the excellent links that exist in Rochdale with the Health Authority, Local Authority and Family Health Services Authority, to facilitate implementation of the Community Care Plan and to ensure excellent community based services for the people of Rochdale;

(iii)   building effective links with all Purchasers that will facilitate the planning and development of services and ensure maximum effectiveness and value for money in service provision;

(iv)   further improving communication and collaboration with General Practitioners in planning and running services in the interest of patients;

2.4 Service Objectives 1993/94

The 1992/93 Business Plan set out a number of objectives which are still relevant to the Trust's strategy. In addition to continuing with their implementation the Trust has identified further objectives in support of the Strategic Direction, largely in conjunction with Purchasers. The following paragraphs set out the 1993/94 Service objectives:-

2.4.1   Contracted Activity Levels

The Strategic Direction assumes a continuing need to achieve increases in activity levels within existing resources and identifies an annual growth rate across all Specialties, with differential increases. The Table opposite shows the anticipated contracted activity levels for 1993/94 and the achievement of these levels in each service group will be a key objective.

2.4.2   Day Case Proportions

The proportion of day case provision in Rochdale is already high, as evidenced by the recent Audit Commission Report which identified Rochdale amongst the top performers in a sample of fifty-four authorities. Nevertheless targets have been set to achieve improved performance in this area which is at the top of the Purchasing agenda and details are set out in the Table on the opposite page. The overall day case proportion is planned to move from   in 1992/93 to   in 1993/94 and   by 1995/96, with larger increases in general surgery, orthopaedics and ophthalmology. The achievement of these targets will be critical to the success of the Trust in 1993/94 and beyond.

2.4.3   Implementation of Community Care

Rochdale Healthcare NHS Trust is totally committed to the implementation of community care in Rochdale and is determined to make the new arrangements work in co-operation with the other agencies. The production of Rochdale's Community Care Plan has involved total co-operation between the Health Authority, Rochdale M.B.C., Rochdale F.H.S.A. and the Trust. A "Working Together" initiative was established to prepare the Plan and will continue through the implementation and review processes of the government's "Caring for People" programme which will be implemented from 1 April 1993.

Specific objectives to be addressed by the Trust in 1993/94 will include the following:-

(i)   full and appropriate participation in the assessment and care management process, ensuring that the needs of patients and carers are covered;

(ii)   Defining discharge arrangements for all patient groups and ensuring that individual discharge plans give full consideration to nursing and social care needs and carer requirements;

(iii)   preparation and implementation of joint training programmes relevant to community care;

5

TABLE

ROCHDALE HEALTHCARE NHS TRUST

BUSINESS PLAN 1993/94

Contracted activity levels for 1992/93, 1993/94 and 1995/96 projections

SPECIALITY	CONTRACTED 1992/93			PROJECTED 1993/94			PROJECTED 1995/96			Projected Annual Growth Rate
	% In-Patients	% Day Cases	Total Cases	% In-Patients	% Day Cases	Total Cases	% In-Patients	Day Cases	Total Cases	
General Medicine										
Elderly										
General Surgery										
Orthopaedics										
Ophthamology										
Gynaecology										
Dental										
Anaesthetics										
Paediatrics										
Maternity										
Mental Health & ESMI										
TOTAL										

6

(iv)   development of information systems which enable the accessing and sharing of data;

2.4.4   Community Care Plan

Specific objectives which are set out in the Community Care Plan and which the Trust plans to implement in 1993/94, with the support of Rochdale Health Authority are:-

(i)   the appointment of a Consultant Community Paediatrician to provide high level input in the community, to achieve better integration between primary and secondary care and to facilitate the revision of the existing Child Health Services to take account of current practice and local need;

(ii)   the development of the Floyd Unit (younger disabled) to become a resource centre for advice and information on all aspects of physical disability and to work closely on training with Community staff and Social Services;

(iii)   the continuing implementation of the extremely successful strategy to resettle people with learning disabilities from the large hospitals outside Rochdale to community-based accommodation in the town, ensuring that everyone is able to live and work alongside the rest of the population and to use the same facilities;

(iv)   moving residential services out of Scott House into ordinary houses in the community;

(v)   opening the new Mental Illness Unit at Birch Hill Hospital with 48 beds and 80 days places, to replace old and inadequate facilities;

(vi)   opening of the Mental Health Resource Unit at Sudden and further development of Community Mental Health Teams to work from Centres across the Borough in providing local assessment, therapy and treatment;

(vii)   appointment of a psychiatrist to work with people who have learning disabilities and who are also experiencing mental health problems.

In addition, it is proposed to examine further the development of peripheral clinics in Middleton as this would improve services for the local population. Rochdale Health Authority is known to support community developments of this nature. Furthermore, following discussions with the Purchaser, it is proposed to review access to the psychology service.

Other developments which are being considered with Purchasers include a strengthening of the Challenging Behaviours Team and the provision of respite care for older children with difficult health and behavioural problems.

2.4.5 "The Health of the Nation"

The Trust is committed to the improvement of health in Rochdale and will seek to achieve the broad aims and targets set out in "The Health of the Nation". It is acknowledged that the prime responsibility to achieve the targets rests with Rochdale Health Authority as Purchaser, but the Trust will give its full support in working with the Health Authority and Primary Healthcare Teams to achieve the objectives in the timescales laid down. It is anticipated that local action programmes will be developed during 1993/94 and the Trust will co-operate in this process and in their implementation.

2.4.6 Medical Services

A number of significant developments have been achieved in the medical specialties in the past twelve months, including the extension of the Endoscopy Department and the appointment of an additional Consultant Gastroenterologist; the further extension of the Renal Unit's capacity; an additional full-time consultant post in paediatrics; an expanded service in Genito-Urinary Medicine and significant improvements to the Coronary Care Unit and Intensive Therapy Unit. These changes have signalled a tremendous move forward in the quality of medical services offered by the Trust and further developments planned with Purchaser support for 1993/94 include the following:-

(i)   the further development of the cardiology specialty to enable procedures such as pacemaker implants to be carried out in Rochdale, thereby reducing patient waiting, anxiety and travel, and improving the quality of the local service;

(ii)   the introduction of composite Downs Syndrome screening;

(iii)   the undertaking of all cervical cytology work for local hospitals, clinics and GP's by the Trust's pathology department, removing the need for some tests to be carried out elsewhere.

In addition, it is proposed to review the provision of facilities for the victims of stroke which would enable the rehabilitation of patients back into the community. In carrying out this review, the Purchaser's view will be sought as it is known that the improvement of rehabilitation services is high on their agenda.

2.4.7 Surgical Services

Recent developments in surgical services have been centred on the appointment of a fourth Consultant Ophthalmologist and a newly funded consultant post in urology, the first specialist urologist appointment to Rochdale. In addition, substantial investment in equipment has been made in orthopaedics, ophthalmology and urology. The Trust, therefore, offers much improved surgical services and is looking to achieve significant business development once the constraints of block contracts are lifted. However, for 1993/94 the Trust's objectives are limited to the following tasks:-

(i)   the formation of a joint ophthalmology service with Oldham NHS Trust, whereby a population of around six hundred thousand would be served, with all major ophthalmic surgery being undertaken in Rochdale;

(ii)   discussions with Rochdale Health Authority, GP Fundholders and other Purchasers on the major developments in orthopaedic surgery that were outlined in the Trust's Strategic Direction, with a view to completing contractual arrangements for 1994/95 and beyond;

(iii)   further consideration to the provision of a combined oncology service for Rochdale, a development which is supported in principle by managers of the main Purchaser;

(iv)   examination of future requirements for scanning facilities in Rochdale;

(v)   development of proposals for private patient facilities in Rochdale.

2.4.8 1992/93 Objectives

The 1992/93 Business Plan set out a target to reduce DNA's in out-patients to a maximum of   in all specialties. Monitoring to date indicates that while the proportion of DNA's is reducing, the target is unlikely to be achieved in all specialties by 31 March 1993. Consequently, the objective is being restated in the 1993/94 Business Plan and further action will be taken to ensure its achievement.

9

3. QUALITY OF SERVICES

3.1 Strategic Objectives

Rochdale Healthcare NHS Trust sees the development of quality issues as paramount to its success and gives quality the utmost priority in its forward planning. The Trust's strategic objectives are as follows:-

* **to achieve and maintain a high level of quality in the delivery of patient services;**

* **to implement and improve upon the Patients' Charter Standards and local standards.**

3.2 Implementation of Quality Management

All doctors, nurses, professional, technical and managerial staff in Rochdale are committed to achieving and maintaining a high level of quality in the services which they provide. A Quality Strategy has been adopted by the Trust Board which will guide the organisation to full implementation of Total Quality Management (T.Q.M.). An extensive, continuous programme of training and development is being implemented so that all managers and staff are actively involved and committed. Quality measurement and monitoring systems are being developed using the "Lake View" standard setting and audit system and a Quality Monitoring Team has been established with representatives from Rochdale Health Authority and the Community Health Council. The key functions of the Monitoring Team are:-

(i)   developing and monitoring the implementation of the Trust's Quality Strategy, providing regular reports to the Trust Board;

(ii)   ensuring that Patient's Charter Standards are implemented and maintained;

(iii)   co-ordinating patient satisfaction survey work;

(iv)   implementing a co-ordinated standard setting and audit process across the Trust services;

(v)   co-ordinating clinical and services audit.

The "Quality of Service" initiative (QOS) has been established to help encourage quality initiatives from the staff themselves at work place level, giving them power to take action on their own ideas. There are now seventeen QOS teams, each working in a particular area or department of the Trust, identifying and taking action on quality improvement issues/targets. Many excellent quality improvements have already been achieved at minimal cost and it is intended that all clinical and non-clinical departments will have a QOS team by late 1993 involving around thirty teams.

10

3.3   Quality Objectives

The 1992/93 Business Plan set out a number of key objectives which are being addressed. These will be continued into 1993/94 and some new targets set. The following paragraphs set out current progress and future objectives:-

3.3.1   National Charter Standards

The nine National Charter Standards have all been addressed; specific objectives are as follows:-

(i)   Charter Standard No. 2

Access for the disabled is being improved by:-

*   All capital schemes being arranged with access for the disabled;

*   All clinics being altered to improve disabled access;

*   Provision for disabled parking being planned on the Birch Hill Site;

*   Further initiatives to improve access for the disabled being planned.

(ii)   Charter Standard No. 5

The Accident and Emergency Department at Rochdale Infirmary is currently being upgraded and restructured and supports the "Triage" arrangements. The local standard for waiting time after the need for treatment has been assessed is currently two hours, but it is planned to improve this to one hour by the end of 1993/94.

(iii)   Charter Standard No. 6

Important objectives are being pursued in 1992/93 concerning the planning and operational procedures in the Main Out-Patients Department, including the National Charter Standard that patients will be given a specific appointment time and be seen within thirty minutes of that time. Other issues include:-

(a)   communicating to GP's details of their patients' visit within ten days of their appointment;

(b)   providing customer relations training for staff;

11

(c)   providing communications skills training for staff dealing with patients, relatives and other staff members;

(d)   upgrading reception and waiting areas;

(e)   introducing smart, attractive uniforms for receptionists.

These issues are being addressed through a RMI sub-project team and good progress has been achieved with (b)-(e). Consultants have been asked to review their appointment arrangements and needs, and it is expected that in order to ensure achievement of the required Standard in every clinic, work will need to continue into 1993/94.

(iv)   Charter Standard No. 9

Reference has been made at paragraph 2.4.3 (ii) to action taken in relation to the discharge of patients from hospital.

(v)   Other National Charter Standards

The National Charter Standards not referred to above, ie. respect of privacy, dignity and religious and cultural beliefs; information to relatives and friends; cancellation of operations; and a named qualified nurse, midwife or health visitor responsible for each patient, will be achieved in 1992/93.

3.3.2   Local Charter Standards

Specific local standards have been set in relation to waiting times in Accident and Emergency [paragraph 3.3.1 (ii)] and waiting times for first out-patient appointments. The latter are specialty specific, the majority being twelve weeks. However, the 1992/93 Business Plan set out a target to reduce the maximum wait for non-urgent appointments to ten weeks. As progress with this objective is extremely varied both across the specialties and within specialties, it will be necessary to carry it forward to 1993/94 when new initiatives will be planned. Purchasers have expressed particular dissatisfaction over waiting times in orthodontics, dermatology, neurology, rheumatology and orthopaedics and these specialties will be closely examined.

Steps are being taken in 1992/93 to ensure that staff wear name badges and to improve signposting arrangements, so that visitors can find their way around Rochdale's hospitals more easily.

It is intended that in 1993/94 the Trust, in co-operation with Rochdale Health Authority and F.H.S.A., will seek to develop local quality standards in primary care; these will complement the national standards that are expected to be published by the Department of Health in 1993.

3.3.3   Waiting Lists

The 1992/93 Business Plan set two key objectives:-

*   seek to have no patients waiting over 18 months in any specialty by 31 March 1993;

*   reduce waiters over twelve months by   in all specialties by 31 March 1993.

It is anticipated that these targets will be achieved and revised targets established in discussion with Purchasers for 1993/94. As a minimum, a further   reduction in waiters over twelve months across all specialties will be targeted.

3.3.4   Other Quality Objectives

The 1992/93 Business Plan set out a further three objectives in relation to quality:-

*   Improve admission policies in all specialties;

*   Review all ward booklets and other patient information;

*   Plan and implement a patient satisfaction programme in conjunction with Purchasers and the C.H.C.

Significant progress has been achieved with each of these objectives and admission policies and patient booklets and information will be completed by 31 March 1993. However, work will continue into 1993/94 with the development of a rolling programme of patient satisfaction programmes which are critical to the Trust's quality assurance programme.

13

4. FINANCE

4.1 Strategic Objectives

The Trust's strategic objectives are as follows:-

* **to achieve the Trust's financial targets which are set by Statute and the Department of Health;**

* **to ensure that resources are managed in the most efficient and effective way for the benefit of patients, GP's, Purchasers and staff.**

* **to achieve cash savings which enable the Trust to achieve its financial targets and at the same time fund desirable service changes and take advantage of medical innovation.**

4.2 Resource Expectations

The past two years have seen higher than expected resources made available to Health Authorities, but plans for 1993/94 are being made against an expectation of a bleak public spending round.

The North Western Regional Health Authority has recently adopted a formula for determining the weighted per capita allocations for Purchasers based on the full weighted under 75 Standard Mortality Rate and Family Health services Authority spend. On this basis, Rochdale Health Authority, the Trust's major purchaser, is   below target; consequently it may receive a small amount of differential growth money over and above the minimum apportioned to all Districts. However, this will probably be less than   and depending on the outcome of the Public Expenditure settlement there could be no differential growth for Rochdale. Furthermore, the Regional Health Authority is currently giving consideration to the pace at which the equalisation of resources should be achieved and if the NHSME imposes short timescales for this task, it is conceivable that the "minimum growth" could be negligible or non-existent. A further complicating factor that could affect Rochdale's position concerns the inclusion of capital charges in the equalisation process, if it is decided by NHSME that they should be made "live" from 1 April 1993.

Consequently, this Plan assumes that no growth monies (other than the RCCS for the new Mental Illness Unit and funding for Learning Disabilities Resettlements which are earmarked by the NWRHA for these specific purposes), will be available to the Trust's Purchasers.

Based on experience over many years, it is unlikely that the provision for pay and price increases funded by the Department each year will be adequate to cover the actual costs; consequently, it is assumed that the Trust will have to achieve savings in 1993/94 in order to fund short-falls. Furthermore, the reduced level of additional resources which are expected to be available means that Purchasers will have limited scope to finance increases in costs arising from non-inflationary pressures.

4.3 Strategy to Achieve Cash Savings

4.3.1 The Trust has, therefore, identified a requirement to achieve cash savings for the following purposes:-

(i)   to facilitate investment in service improvements and developments;

(ii)   to maintain prices at a competitive level;

(iii)   to meet non-inflationary pressures;

(iv)   to fund shortfalls on inflation which are expected to be imposed by Purchasers.

It is anticipated that a minimum   per annum will be required in 1993/94. Savings will be achieved by reviewing all baseline budgets and embarking on a programme to review value for money throughout the organisation. A thorough examination of the Trust's services in the light of its business objectives will be made as set out in the Strategic Direction, in order that the achievement of the financial objectives can be assured for 1993/94 and beyond. The Trust Board is committed to this approach.

4.3.2 As part of the strategy to release cash and improve value for money, the ownership and management of budgets will be subject to continuous review during 1993/94. As clinical directors become more experienced, their accountability will be strengthened.

4.3.3 The 1992/93 Business Plan incorporated a number of objectives which were planned to achieve greater efficiency in the use of resources:-

*   Investigate the costs/benefits of pre-admission liaison and screening in ophthalmology, general surgery and gynaecology;

*   Review theatre utilisation and operating list planning;

*   Produce service agreements to formalise the interface between clinical directorates and paramedical services;

*   Review and report on the effectiveness of community locality management;

*   Review the arrangements for supplies contracts and ordering;

*   Identify skill mix targets and prepare an activity/mix analysis for all staff;

15

* Analyse the role and usage of Care Assistants and Health Care Support Workers with a view to increasing their deployment;

* Reduce the cost of maintenance per square metre of estate by in real terms.

Substantial progress has been made with each of these objectives and it is expected that resources will be released towards the 1993/94 cash savings programme as a consequence of work that has been done and is continuing in these areas.

4.4 Summary

The financial prospects for the National Health Service in 1993/94 look bleak at the present time. This Business Plan is being prepared in advance of the Public Expenditure settlement, but all the signs point to a high level of control on public sector expenditure and little new resource. Therefore, the Trust is preparing its plans for 1993/94 on the basis that any improvements in its services will have to be funded from cash savings. Rochdale Health Authority's "Purchasing for Health" identifies a possible differential growth sum of around   and the Trust expects that if this materialises, and if any resource is made available to the Trust, the Purchaser will rightly seek improvements in both activity levels and quality of care as a return on its investment.

5. CONTRACTS

5.1 Strategic Objectives

The Trust's strategic objectives are as follows:-

*   **to introduce more responsive forms of contracting after 1993/94;**

*   **to develop systems that link finance with patient data so that pricing can reflect the cost of treating specific conditions.**

Block contracts were established from the start of the contracting process within the North Western Region in order to minimise risk and disruption within the internal market. They have enabled Purchasers to buy access in accordance with their historic referral patterns and Providers have been assured of their income levels. However, while the system has enabled Purchasers to know their commitments from the start of the financial year, most of the risk is carried by Providers who have to fund any workload increases in excess of planned levels and cannot seek to extend service beyond their traditional points of referral since contract prices are effectively fixed. Consequently, the Trust is keen to see new forms of contract coming in from 1994/95 and will work during 1993/94 to facilitate the introduction of the contracting methods that are to be established within the North Western Region from 1 April 1994.

5.2 Costing of Contracts

Substantial progress has been made during the past two years in the area of episode costing, mainly in response to the requirement to manage the GP Fundholding and Extra Contractual Referral schemes. It is now essential to obtain a better understanding of the link between costs and patient data, so that prices for services can more accurately reflect the cost of treating specific conditions. With this objective in mind, work is being done with the obstetric specialty to identify fixed, variable and semi-variable costs. The outcome of this will assist with budget monitoring by relating income to expenditure, in addition to providing a better understanding of the specialty's costs, in particular how they react to changes in throughput, both in volume and mix terms.

In order to move towards a form of "cost and volume" contract from 1 April 1994, the Trust is committed to a substantial amount of development work in 1993/94 in the light of the NHSME guidance on costing and in support of the piloting work that is being carried out in the North Western Region. This work will help the Trust to understand the effect on its costs of marginal increases in output, and it will be necessary to develop pricing systems which are responsive to these factors.

5.3   1993/94 Contract Income

The absence of financial resource assumptions means that it is not yet possible to assess the Trust's planned income for 1993/94, although the continuation of block contracts and the expectation of minimal growth money for the major Purchaser would suggest little change from 1992/93 where   of patient services income is covered by contract, with   being totally secure as it is subject to the block contract arrangements. The only significant change concerns the GP Fundholder arrangements, as it is expected that a major practice will become a third-wave fundholder from 1 April 1993 and all fundholders will have budgets for community services from the same date. Consequently, the Trust's block contracts with Rochdale Health Authority will be reduced and the value of fundholder contracts will increase provided the business can be retained. The form of contract with the new fundholder is still to be agreed, but it is assumed that all community service contracts with GP Fundholders will be on a "block" basis.

6. MANPOWER, TRAINING AND DEVELOPMENT

6.1 Strategic Objectives

The Trust's strategic objectives with regard to manpower, training and development are as follows:-

* **to continue to develop a high level of commitment to training and personal development within the organisation;**

* **to promote a human resource strategy which facilitates achievement of the Trust's business objectives;**

* **to ensure the further development of clinical directorates.**

The Trust continues in its determination to provide high quality management of its most valuable resource, its staff. This will be reflected in its plans for manpower planning and information systems, in its commitment to providing appropriate and effective personal and professional development, in its policies for the recruitment and deployment of staff and other Human Resource issues.

6.2 Manpower Planning

Manpower planning is becoming an integral part of the corporate strategy and objectives for 1993/94 include:-

(i) the production of an annual manpower plan to coincide with the corporate business plan;

(ii) the development of high quality information systems relating to staff numbers and their deployment, building on progress that has been made during 1992/93;

(iii) the introduction of a new system of performance appraisal which has been piloted over the past few months, initially for those currently subject to the existing IPR system but eventually to all appropriate groups of staff;

(iv) the monitoring of performance management and labour costing systems.

6.3   Staff Training and Development

The Trust plans to build on its already excellent reputation for the training and development of staff and objectives for 1993/94 include:-

(i)   undertaking an annual training needs analysis for all staff, building on work that has already been done with clinical directors, care managers and business managers;

(ii)   producing from this an annual training programme with priority being given to those staff who are seen as key to the current development of the organisation, including the continuation of the management development programme and the development of medical staff in management;

(iii)   continuing a development programme for senior nurses; in particular Sisters and Charge Nurses;

(iv)   linking the introduction of a new performance appraisal system to the training programme to ensure that the training provided will lead to the achievement of personal and organisational goals;

(v)   striving towards the official accreditation of our existing and future training programmes to allow the Trust to be able to offer its own in-house Diploma in Management equivalent to DMS;

(vi)   continuing to provide opportunities for Enrolled Nurses to convert to General Registration or other professional development;

(vii)   becoming an accredited provider of First Aid training;

6.4   Other Human Resource Issues

It is recognised that the development of Human Resource strategies resulting in change in a well established culture is not achieved overnight. Amongst the objectives designed to further the change process in 1993/94 are:-

(i)   the continuous review of pay and conditions, introducing such changes as are appropriate and feasible after suitable consultation with staff, including analytical evaluation of jobs;

(ii)   continuing the process of improving communications with staff and ensuring the success of initiatives already introduced, including Team Briefing;

(iii)   further strengthening of the relationships between managers and their staff and encouraging matters involving staff representation to be dealt with at the lowest appropriate management level with local employee representatives;

(iv)   building upon the work already undertaken to create an equal opportunity environment for all staff and potential staff taking into account the requirements of the Opportunity 2000 project;

(v)   developing existing good practices with regard to recruitment and deployment of staff and ensuring that managers are sufficiently trained to deal with these matters;

(vi)   encouraging the further building of good relationships between the Trust, its managers and its staff that reduces the need for external influences in the way the Trust is managed.

6.5   Junior Doctors' Hours Initiative

The Department of Health requirement to reduce the hours of duty undertaken by junior doctors requires significant change to the number of doctors employed, to their working patterns and to the support that can be given to them by non-medical staff.   The first stage of the process has already been implemented, but by 1994 the final stage in the reduction has to be completed. The Trust will work during 1993/94 to achieve the targets that have been set.

6.6   Project 2000

The Trust is committed to the introduction of Project 2000 in Rochdale and will manage the radical effect on staffing levels within training areas. The effect of implementation will be a gradual reduction in the learner population over a three year period as the existing training curriculum terminates. It is not clear when implementation will commence in Rochdale, but further planning and preparation will be carried out during 1993/94.

6.7   Post Registration Education and Practice Project

The Trust is committed to continuing education which will involve personnel from both service and education departments working with practitioners to identify continuing education needs, set priorities and formulate strategies for continuing professional development. Targets for action in 1993/94 include:-

(i)   opportunities for Enrolled Nurse conversion to recognise and enhance their contribution to care;

(ii)   development of periodic and continuing education within the area of post-registration education and practice;

(iii)   the development of a comprehensive framework which allows the accumulation of credits towards graduate status.

21

7. INFORMATION, I.T. AND RESOURCE MANAGEMENT

7.1 Strategic Objectives

The strategic objective is to develop information, I.T. and resource management plans which respond to the Trust's corporate objectives. Consequently, the Trust's information strategy considers the total implications for information and IT, including organisational issues, an assessment of information priorities and current initiatives which impact on the strategy.

7.2 Implementation of Information Strategy

Detailed action plans have been prepared to implement the strategy which incorporates the following key features:-

(i)   Relating information to the business needs and objectives of the organisation.

(ii)   Full integrated information systems which meet the requirements of users.

(iii)   Participation in system specification and design by managers.

(iv)   Full ownership by users of the information and commitment to data quality.

(v)   Accessible, accurate and timely information for effective decision-making.

The short-term plan to be addressed in the latter part of 1992/93 and 1993/94 is concerned with the implementation of departmental feeder systems and associated networks, as follows:-

*   Pathology and Radiology systems
*   Theatre and Pharmacy systems
*   Accident and Emergency system
*   Maternity and Child Health systems
*   Out-patient systems

At the same time, decisions will be made on key resource management issues such as a case mix management system, nurse management and order communication systems.

The Resource Management Project is firmly linked with the Trust's organisational, cultural and managerial development, and the Trust Board is committed to its objectives. However, there is considerable concern about the capital and revenue costs of implementing the IT systems. Ensuring value for money from the investment is, therefore, an issue that is being vigorously pursued, and it is intended to carry out a full cost benefit exercise.

8. ESTATES

8.1 Strategic Objectives

The Trust's strategic objectives in terms of the estate are centred upon the need to remove the "millstones" of backlog maintenance (   ) and the cost of bringing the whole of the estate up to Condition B (   ). At the same time there is an urgent need to provide a fully integrated acute service on one site in a single phase development, thereby removing the present problems of split site working and its accompanying inefficiencies.

8.2 The Estates

The Trust comprises of two major Hospital Sites at Birch Hill Hospital, Littleborough and the Rochdale Infirmary, together with four Health Centres and ten clinics throughout Rochdale. The value of the Trust's capital assets at 31 March 1992 was as follows:-

	£000
Land	
Buildings, Installations and Fittings	
Assets Under Construction	
Plant and Equipment	_____
	_____

8.3 Development of the Estate

As previously stated, the Trust has a substantial problem in terms of the condition of its estate and has identified a major acute development on the Infirmary site as the preferred way forward. In April 1992 the North Western Regional Health Authority announced that a first phase of the major development of Rochdale Infirmary had been included in its 1994/95 Capital Programme at a total estimated cost of   million. The Regional Health Authority noted that the Rochdale submission "allowed for a phased approach which would demonstrate a commitment to the whole development, but would spread the spend over a slightly longer period".

In approving a first phase of redevelopment, the Regional Health Authority gave an indication as to which elements of the total scheme the   million might fund. However, rather than commit the funds in this way, the Trust considers that a more prudent and economical solution would be to obtain approval to the balance of funds to a total of   million, thereby enabling the full development to be designed, constructed and commissioned from the start. The Business Case will be submitted shortly and an Approved in Principle document is being prepared for submission once the Business Case has been accepted by the NHSME. Work on the planning and development of this major capital scheme will continue during 1993/4.

23

8.4 Capital Programme

The Trust's External Financing Limit (E.F.L.) for 1992/93 includes a sum of for resource management, including the case mix and nursing systems. The bulk of this will not be spent until 1993/94, therefore, expenditure on a number of current schemes has been brought forward to 1992/93, with substantial service benefits. However, this means that there is expected to be little cash available for new schemes in 1993/94.

The estimated outturn 1992/93 and provisional capital programme for 1993/4 - 1994/95 are set out on the opposite page. The funding assumed to be available for 1993/94 capital expenditure is based on the 1992/93 programme adjusted for commitments which have been taken over from NWRHA in respect of major capital and delegated schemes. The capital availability is uncertain at this stage. It is emphasised that it is a provisional capital programme which seeks to give a broad indication of the Trust's priorities for the next two years.

The provisional programme for 1993/94 is designed to achieve a reasonable balance between the many competing priorities that need to be addressed with both the hospital and community services. Improving the quality of services is a key objective of the Trust, so a substantial amount of the capital programme is concerned with the upgrading of patient facilities, in particular those "public" areas such as out-patients and accident and emergency which are critical to development of a good patient perception for Rochdale's services.

The objectives of the capital programme are also to enable the Trust to replace medical and other equipment as it becomes life-expired and to satisfy the likely demands of the information strategy in terms of computer hardware. However, it is acknowledged that the amount of capital available makes it extremely difficult to achieve the Trust's aspirations, but at least substantial progress is being achieved with regard to the identification of planned replacement programmes.

It is important to state that the majority of the 1993/94 building and engineering schemes are existing commitments carried over from 1992/93. The following paragraphs detail the major schemes on which expenditure will be incurred in 1993/94.

(i) Mental Illness Unit

The scheme at Birch Hill Hospital is a two-storey scheme providing two 24-bedded units on the First Floor with day rooms, Dining Rooms, Sitting Areas and Day Care on the Ground Floor. This scheme which is a key priority of the Purchaser will be opened early in 1993, the patients being transferred to the Unit from existing pre 1900 Ward Blocks.

24

CAPITAL PROGRAMME

ESTIMATED OUTTURN 1992/3 AND PROVISIONAL PLANS 1993/94 – 1994/95

	1992/93 Est. Outturn £000	1993/4 Plan £000	1994/5 Plan £000	1995/6 Onwards £000
BUILDING & ENGINEERING SCHEMES				
Acute Services Redevelopment (fees)	-			Continuing Project
Mental Illness Unit			-	-
Doctor's Residence Upgrade		-	-	-
Incinerator Upgrade		-	-	-
Moorland Upgrade				-
Eye & ENT Department Upgrade		-	-	-
Maternity Block Upgrade				-
Upgrade Radio Paging System				-
Endoscopy Department Upgrade		-	-	
Main Theatre Upgrade	-			-
Accident & Emergency Department Upgrade			-	-
Out-Patient Department Upgrade				Continuing Programme
Room 2 Out-Patients, X-Ray, Rochdale Infirmary - B&E		-	-	-
Room 2 X-Ray, Birch Hill - B&E		-	-	-
Female Examination Room		-		-
Pathology Department Upgrade				-
Medical Records Upgrade	-			-
Lower Kitchen Sandwich Room	-		-	-
Provide Laundry Shower	-		-	-
Day Surgery Upgrade		-	-	-
Office Accommodation		-	-	-
Hunter Ward Upgrade	-	-		
Calorifier Plant Replacement	-	-		-
Sudden Resource Centre			-	-
Clinic Roof Repairs	-	-		
Fire Precautions, Health & Safety, Security				Continuing Programme
Disabled Access				Continuing Programme
Estates Service Executive				-
Quality of Service Initiatives	—	—	—	Continuing Programme
Total Building & Engineering				
	———	———	———	
MEDICAL EQUIPMENT				
Urology Equipment		-	-	-
Video Information System (Endoscopy)		-	-	-
Bulk Work Analyser (Pathology)		-	-	-
Room 2 Out-Patients, X-Ray, Rochdale Infirmary - Equipment		-	-	-
Room 2 X-Ray, Birch Hill - Equipment		-	-	-
Faxitron Specimen Radiography System	-		-	-
Microbiology Bacteria Detection System		-	-	-
Cardiac Ultrasound System		-	-	-
X-Ray Room No. 1 (RI) Upgrade and Table	-	-		-
Ultrasound	-	-		-
Mobile X-Ray Machine	-	-		-
Daylight System	-	-		
Medical Equipment	—	—	—	Continuing Programme
Total Medical Equipment				
	———	———	———	
OTHER CAPITAL				
Ward Equipment				Continuing Programme
Computers (information strategy)				Continuing Programme
Vehicles				Continuing Programme
Minor Capital (under)				Continuing Programme
Schemes carried over from 1991/92		-	-	-
Resource Management			-	-
Word Processing for Ward Secretaries, etc.	-	—	—	-
Total Other Capital				
	———	———	———	
GRAND TOTAL				
	═══	═══	═══	

(ii)   <u>Accident and Emergency Unit - Upgrade</u>

The scheme at Rochdale Infirmary involves a completely new layout to provide the facilities necessary for modern and efficient treatment of patients speedily and effectively. This scheme is also supported by the Purchaser and was funded initially from the Regional Capital Programme.

(iii)   <u>Resource Centre - Sudden</u>

The conversion of an existing Health Centre into a Resource Centre to provide facilities for Mental Health Day Care on a multi purpose use basis. It is anticipated the building will be ready for occupation by the spring of 1993, the scheme having been funded initially from the Region's capital programme.

(iv)   <u>Maternity Block Upgrade</u>

A phased programme to provide modern facilities and a much improved environment within the Birch Hill maternity unit, upgrading the existing poor quality buildings.

(v)   <u>Out-Patients Department Upgrade</u>

A phased programme to improve all patient areas within the Trust's major Out-Patients Department at Rochdale Infirmary. The initial phase covers waiting and other public areas and subsequent phases will systematically improve the treatment and consultation suites.

(vi)   <u>Pathology Department Upgrade</u>

A programme of work at Birch Hill Hospital which has been identified following a report from the Health and Safety Inspectorate.

CIPFA

BUSINESS PLANS

A Compendium

HEALTH

**Southport and Formby
Community Health Services
NHS Trust**

The Business Plan for 1993/94

COMMUNITY
HEALTH SERVICES
NHS TRUST

THE

BUSINESS

PLAN

1993-1994

SOUTHPORT AND FORMBY COMMUNITY HEALTH SERVICES NHS TRUST

Chairman – Miss Linda Brown LL.B. (Hons), A.C.I.Arb., Barrister Chief Executive: Finlay Robertson MSc., Dip.N(Lond), RMN, RGN

Hesketh Centre 51-55 Albert Road Southport PR9 0LT Telephone 0704 547471 Fax 0704 530714

CONTENTS

EXECUTIVE SUMMARY

The Business Plan for 1993/94 sets out the priorities for action in what promises to be a challenging and exciting year for our newly established NHS Trust.

It is intended to be a working document for Managers and Staff in the Trust and relates to local priorities for healthcare identified in conjunction with the commissioners of service and is aligned with National priorities such as "CARING FOR PEOPLE", "THE HEALTH OF THE NATION" and "THE PATIENTS CHARTER".

The aim of the Trust is to provide the best possible healthcare to the people of Southport and Formby and we recognise that this can only be achieved if we have a clear vision of the future and specific plans for the forthcoming year.

The Business Plan will therefore lay the foundations for the strategic direction of the Trust and plans for future years.

The Trust Board is determined that its plans are appropriate and achievable and that we make every effort possible to involve the users of service in shaping the future.

We have a capable and dedicated workforce who are committed to the challenges ahead and in whom we have every confidence in their ability to deliver the plans described in this document.

PREFACE

This Business Plan identifies the objectives and key management tasks for Southport and Formby Community Service NHS Trust for the year 1993/94, in accordance with the Management Executive Letter - "Priorities and Planning Guidance in 1993/4". The Trust will operate in accordance with the intent laid out in the Trust Application, April 1992 .

During 1992/93 the Unit worked with enthusiasm for the challenges and opportunities that the Trust Status will bring by building on its major strengths:

> Ability to perform consistently well against budget and achieve substantial efficiency savings, whilst maintaining services.

> Involvement of clinicians and professionals in management at all levels in the Unit.

> An emphasis on standards, quality and innovation in patient services.

> A commitment to staff development, professional education and learning.

The Unit's performance will be presented in the Annual Report 1992/93.

Looking ahead to 1993/94, service strategies will consistently identify a community focus, and the Trust board believes that, over the year, health care services will be improved by developing services more responsive to the needs of local people.

The Trust's Business Plan for 1993/94 has been developed after involvement and consultation with Managers and key personnel. Discussions with Purchasers, and a response to the Sefton Purchasing Plan for 1993/94, have been a major consideration, emphasising the opportunities for changes in delivery of health services.

1. STATEMENT OF INTENT

SOUTHPORT & FORMBY COMMUNITY HEALTH SERVICES (NHS) TRUST

MISSION STATEMENT

OUR PURPOSE IS TO PROVIDE AND PROMOTE IN PARTNERSHIP WITH OTHERS, QUALITY HEALTH CARE TO PEOPLE IN SOUTHPORT AND FORMBY DELIVERED BY SKILLED AND RESPONSIVE STAFF.

The development of this mission statement was achieved by a representative group of managers and staff working together.

The Trust Board believes this Statement of Intent accurately reflects the current NHS priorities which are:

Improving Health

Better Services

Efficiency & Value for Money

Effective Organisation

2. KEY VALUES

The Trust is commited to the following Key Values and will strive to ensure that:

Everyone has an equal right to quality health care and services

Emphasis is on ease of access for those in need, with no discrimination on any grounds. The Trust must be sensitive to the needs of the individual, putting people first and aiming for high standards.

People working together is the key to providing these services

Effective teamwork is a vital component in the successful delivery of the Trust's objectives with an inter-agency approach strongly encouraged.

The contributions and achievements of all staff are recognised and rewarded

To build on our strengths and minimise our weaknesses by recognising the staff of the Trust as our key resource. We will actively promote and encourage reward systems which will value people's contributions as individuals.

We communicate effectively with honesty and clarity

The Trust recognises that effective communication must be a priority, contributing to full participation and commitment of its staff. Two - way communication provides opportunity for facing the changing environment and the identification and development of appropriate skills and behaviour.

3. CORPORATE OBJECTIVES

The Trust has identified and approved seven key objectives for the period 1993/94. These are clearly defined and detailed plans are described in the Business Plan.

Care in the Community

To promote and develop Community Care with a commitment to the relocating Mental Health and Learning Disabilities Services being fully integrated into planned collaborative programmes.

Retraction of Greaves Hall Site

To improve Mental Health In-Patient facilities by reproviding services in a higher quality environment closer to the local community with benefits of greater accessibility and integration with related services.
To continue as a consequence the completion of the retraction plan for the closure in March 1994.

Primary Health Care Focus

To provide a comprehensive range of Community Health Services on a locality and practice basis, in agreement with General Practitioners, that meet the needs of both the population and the GP's.

Trust Opportunities for staff

To develop plans which demonstrate the value of staff in the delivery of service improvements and which recognise and reward good performance.
To ensure strategies fully subscribe to the Healthy Employer and Workplace priorities.

Quality Service Provision

To establish Quality Assurance as a key element in all activities of the Trust, incorporating the Patients Charter and Health of the Nation strategies.

Effective Information and Financial Strategies

To deliver services within resources and maximise use of these resources.
To deliver effective contracting procedures for Community Health Services and to establish systems for monitoring and ensuring performance targets and quality standards are met.

Trust status benefits and local community

To participate fully in planning service improvements by working closely with other agencies and providing care and support.

4. CURRENT POSITION - BACKGROUND TO THE PLAN

STRENGTHS

The main strength of the Trust lies in its ability to provide a wide range of community services. It has an excellent record of monitoring and evaluating the level and quality of services and being able to respond quickly to the changing needs of the local population. Many of the services are already GP focused and delivered on a locality basis. A sound relationship has been established with Sefton Family Health Services Authority and Sefton Social Services Department, in addressing collaborative Primary Care and Care in the Community issues.

One of the Trust's main objectives is to relocate and improve Mental Health and Learning Disability Services. There is a firm commitment from The Mersey Regional Health Authority for the financial support necessary for the closure of Greaves Hall Hospital in March 1994. There are plans in Receiving Districts to achieve the majority of resettlements of people with learning disabilities within this timescale.

CHALLENGES

A major change agenda faces the Trust over the next year, with staffing and training implications being a high priority. Financial projections of capital costs and revenue consequences of the move to a community- based service must be carefully managed. As residents are resettled into the community outside the Southport and Formby District, that element of the contract income will reduce. Future income will depend upon provision within existing resources of a cost effective, quality service to people, in order to attract referrals and contracts from Purchasers.

OPPORTUNITIES

The Trust's commitment to the development and improvement of community-based services gives opportunities to influence the future shape and provision of effective domiciliary community care. Population projections indicate an increasing proportion of very dependent elderly people (85 + years age group), and high levels of ischaemic heart disease, particularly in women. By working with Purchasers, it will be possible to tailor service provision to match local people's needs and expectations.

5

4. CURRENT POSITION - BACKGROUND TO THE PLAN (continued)

KEY ASSUMPTIONS

Financial Assumptions

It is anticipated that the majority of income to be received in 1993/4 will remain on a block contract basis with the local Purchaser.

The West Lancashire Health Authority contract of   covers both long-stay and Acute Admissions. As work is continuing with the West Lancashire Resettlement Team to eventually resettle all their 14 patients, this element of the contract is under discussion. Initial indications are that the Acute element of the contract will continue for at least five years.

The Southport and Formby Health Authority contract includes long-stay people with learning disabilities who are being transferred within the Region, which results in a reduction in income after resettlement.

GP Fundholding contracts covering four GP Practices, total   and indications are that this will continue in 1993/94. Two additional Practises within Southport and Formby will become GP Fundholders, and we are calculating prices for services offered to all GP Fundholders for 1993/4. Draft contracts are currently under discussion.

Staffing Assumptions

Due to the retraction of Greaves Hall Hospital no significant recruitment problems are envisaged.

The risks of potential over-staffing have been greatly reduced by the temporary filling of vacancies and redeployment of staff within the service and with other agencies. Schemes have Regional support.

Service Managers, working with the Human Resources Department, have produced a detailed profile of the future employment options of staff working in the retracting services.

Activity Assumptions

Retraction in Learning Disabilities will result in a decline in activity as residents are resettled into other Districts.

Arrangements for Care in the Community for the increasing number of dependent people living at home are likely to lead to the current general increase in activity continuing and perhaps accelerating.

Using the contracting process and in particular the G.P. Fundholders, activity will be closely monitored through referral rates, clinic attendances and staff/patient contact times.

5. PLANS FOR 1993/94 IMPROVING HEALTH AND BETTER SERVICES

MAIN SERVICE CHANGES - FOCUS FOR THE YEAR 1993/94

5.1 LEARNING DISABILITIES

Will continue to move away from institutional-based care serving a Region wide resident population at Greaves Hall Hospital, to a Community based model of care to the local population, served by Southport and Formby Health Authority. The objectives are consistent with hospital retraction and eventual closure, together with developments that ensure a comprehensive service is available, reflecting philosophies and service principles detailed in Care in the Community, Health of the Nation and Patients Charter.

In-Patient Facilities

From April, as few as 26 residents will remain on site at Greaves Hall, housed in 2-3 wards. Confirmation of individual plans is progressing rapidly, and options are being carefully considered for the most effective means of maintaining services on site as the number of residents reduces during the year, this being dependent upon individual clinical needs.

Community Support Team

This will be established for people with a learning disability, who challenge services. The team is to be managed by a Clinical Psychologist. Initial funding of   per annum confirmed by the purchaser.
Confirmation of a model of service has to be agreed with Southport and Formby Health Authority following results of a comprehensive review of assessment and admission facilities provided within Birchwood.

5.2 MENTAL HEALTH SERVICES

Will be provided more locally giving better access, choice, assessment, treatment, care and support, either at home or close to peoples homes. Only where Specialist care is needed should this be in a hospital environment. The public consultation process has been successfully completed.

In-Patient facilities

Current service provided in the main at Greaves Hall will be relocated to the Southport General Infirmary and the Hesketh Centre to provide a in-patient service in support of extended community services.

7

5. PLANS FOR 1993/94 IMPROVING HEALTH AND BETTER SERVICES (continued)

Elderly Mentally Ill

Relocation into two wards at Southport General Infirmary providing 42 assessment beds. This accommodation will provide a higher quality environment, be more accessible and linked with other elderly services on site.

Day Hospital facilities will be relocated to the ground floor of the Hesketh Centre, operating in conjunction with existing adult services. Benefits include maximum utilisation of space, a community site with easier accessability and the opportunty to provide a fully integrated Mental Health Day Centre strategy.

Ward 14 - Alternative arrangements are being pursued for the remaining 11 residents who require long stay care, this is to be provided within Southport and Formby. This facility together with the re-provision of beds at the Southport General Infirmary will provide a respite care facility.

Resources released from a reduction in beds, and the closure of ward 14, will be reinvested in the appointment of Community Mental Health Support Workers.

Some EMI out-patient clinics to be relocated to a community setting , this will improve access and increase domiciliary support to benefit patients and carers.

Adult Mental Health Services

Acute facilities will be relocated to the first floor of the Hesketh Centre, providing 20 beds to accommodate people who cannot be supported by community intervention alone. Access to the Acute Day Hospital on site will provide supporting assessment and rehabilitation services. Beds will be significantly reduced by the provision of extended community based services for people with alcohol and drug abuse problems, crisis and respite facilities and an acute psychiatric Day Hospital. These will be funded from existing resources.

Paterson Unit at The Hesketh Centre

Services will be reprovided in :

An 8 bed community unit, which will provide short and medium term support to people in crisis and needing respite facilities.

Revenue implications have been examined and indications are that they will be contained within existing resources.

5. PLANS FOR 1993/94 IMPROVING HEALTH AND BETTER SERVICES (continued)

A 13 place community facility provided in collaboration with the National Schizophrenia Fellowship to provide long term care and rehabilitation.

Funding - Calculated on Paterson Unit current costs of   , funding obtained through Section 64 Grant   - to support the N.S.F. scheme and is dependent upon secondment of Trust nursing staff.

Benefits of these Mental Health Services developments will be to alleviate pressure on Acute beds by offering alternatives to hospital admission.

Purchasers support the scheme and are in agreement with the need to provide some respite and residential facilities as part of the overall package of health care.

Establish a Community Mental Health Team

To develop and improve domiciliary support. Will provide a central referral point, promote clear access to services, quick response and early assessment. The Team will be organised to deal with rapid response to referral .

An initial analysis has shown that funding can be met from within existing resources following reprofiling. By a reduction in beds, resources can be used to extend manpower in the community.

5.3   COMMUNITY SERVICES

Children's Centre

Completion this year of the planned refurbishment of 52 Houghton Street will provide comprehensive services to children with Special Needs.

estimated costs, funded via Capital and Revenue monies already allocated.

Establishment of a Co-Ordinator Post -   Funding from within internal resources.

9

5. PLANS FOR 1993/94 IMPROVING HEALTH AND BETTER SERVICES (continued)

This represents a major service development which will result in better access for families, improved assessment facilities and a comprehensive range of specialist services. Services included are Physiotherapy, Occupational Therapy and Speech Therapy. There is a commitment to joint working from other agencies working with children. The opening of this Centre will further develop this collaborative work.

Child & Family Therapy Services will be incorporated within the Children's Centre, provided by a specialist team led by a Consultant Psychiatrist. Appointment of a Clinical Psychologist will complete this team (funding agreed in 1992).

Primary Health Care Team (Developments)

Named District Nurse, Nursing Team, Health Visitor and MacMillan Nurse. These will be attached to GP practices.

Provision of extended domiciliary services - Home sitter and Crossroads Care Scheme. Funding for scheme agreed with Purchasing Authorities and Social Services and managed by a voluntary organisation..

Improvement of discharge liaison by provision of ansaphones for key staff. Funding through internal resources.

Extension of Hospice Home Care Team - - Central Funding issue in discussion with Purchaser.

Third MacMillan Nurse - - Cancer Relief funding. Pick up after 3 years - Health Authority.

Additional open referral clinic for Churchtown Community Clinic - planned to open May 1993. Funding from internal resources.

Educational Resource Teaching Pack for diabetic patients used by Health Visitors and Practice Nurses. Funding by Health Promotion service - agreed.

Stoma Care open self referral clinic planned for Churchtown Community Clinic. Funding within internal resources.

5. PLANS FOR 1993/94 IMPROVING HEALTH AND BETTER SERVICES (continued)

5.4 HEALTH OF THE NATION

The Health Promotion service is targeting the five key areas of the "Health Of the Nation" document:

Coronary Heart Disease/Stroke
Cancers
Accidents
Mental Illness
HIV/AIDS

In addressing these issues, **"healthy alliances"** have been established with service providers and other organisations such as Sefton Family Health Services Authority, LEA and local employers.

As part of this strategy, a **"Health at Work" project** will be launched. The aim of this project is to promote a healthy working environment and healthy workforce.

Targeting of Health Promotion activities will continue to take place with the funded appointment of two specialist posts:

The Asthma Educationalist will work in conjunction with existing community staff. Weekly drop-in clinics, a register of all asthma patients and telephone support network are the initial priorities.

The Nutritionist will offer specific dietary analysis and diet plans to a range of projects including Well Woman/Well Man Clinics, GP's and "Look After Yourself " classes.

A mobile resources service will be developed in January 1993 to facilitate Health Promotion activities with other individuals and agencies.

5. PLANS FOR 1993/94 IMPROVING HEALTH AND BETTER SERVICES (continued)

> **Health of the Nation Targets**

The Trust will respond to the future objectives listed in the Purchasing Plan and has developed a programme of planned supporting initiatives for 1993/94.

Details in Appendix F.

5.5   PATIENTS CHARTER

A service matrix has been developed to allow the monitoring of all service and quality targets on a monthly basis.

The Trust will publicise detailed information on:

Services available
Referral
Complaints
Waiting Times

A public Newsletter will be produced and links with the local press will be extended to publicise appropriate initiatives.

Primary Care Charter

Plans are well under way to agree practice-based targets, monitored jointly with F.H.S.A. and South Sefton D.H.A. Returns will be produced quarterly.

Waiting Times

The Trust performs well in this respect, with waiting lists for only two services. In 1993/94 priority will be given to reducing these.

Psychology : Number on waiting list   51
             Average length of wait   16 weeks
             Target 1993/94   12 weeks

12

5. PLANS FOR 1993/94 IMPROVING HEALTH AND BETTER SERVICES (continued)

The main initiative will be to review and carry out an initial assessment of the total waiting list.

Chiropody : Number on waiting list 50
Average length of wait
at Church Street Clinic 12 weeks
Target 1993/94 8 weeks

This has reduced considerably since the introduction of an Open Access System. The impact of refurbishment at Church Street Clinic and consequent re-organisation of clerical support, will result in some reduction of this waiting list, effects to be monitored and additional initiatives will be planned.

There is no waiting list for either domiciliary or GP practice based services.

Response to referral at all other clinics is good - 3 days.

Consumer opinion

The Trust recognises that close links must be maintained with those who represent consumer views, and will actively seek opinions and initiate involvement for improvement of service.

Developments:

User groups in Community Clinics and Day Units.

Support Group for the bereaved.

Public Forum for Learning Disabilities.

Planned programme incorporating Q-Map initiatives to survey targeted services within the Trust.

5.6   CARE IN THE COMMUNITY

Whilst not identified as the lead agency in this process the Trust recognises the high priority being given to "Caring For People" and its effective implication and operation. Managers will participate in the setting of targets and monitoring of progress.

5. PLANS FOR 1993/94 IMPROVING HEALTH AND BETTER SERVICES (continued)

Collaboration with Sefton Social Services has focussed on reviewing and agreeing:

Admission and Discharge protocols

Assessment   determining the Health Role
                     screening process for Care Planning

Referral   access to teams/named professionals

Review of Community Health Services.

Recommendations published in a Report by the Audit Commission in October 1992 highlighted areas for improvement.

Summary of Action Plan for Key Tasks for 1993/94.

Many of the initiatives operating within the Community Services have been highlighted as "good practice", with the recommendation to extend the principles to other groups across the Trust.

Initiatives to develop needs assessment data.

Active involvement in joint planning with Sefton Social Services and Southport and Formby Health Authority.

Training programme for staff in residential homes in caring for people with behavioural problems.

Activity analysis to be extended to skill mix issues in Mental Health and Learning Disabilities Services.

Implement a formal caseload review system for monitoring Team Leaders/Managers.

Staff monitoring system to investigate lost time in Nursing.

Audit out-of-hours services and Hospice care for the dying, to test out the extent of service flexibility.

5. PLANS FOR 1993/94 IMPROVING HEALTH AND BETTER SERVICES (continued)

5.7 GP FUNDHOLDING

From April 1993 there will be six fundholding practices in Southport and Formby, four having joined the scheme in the previous year with agreed block contracts for Community Services.

Extensions of the scheme to include a range of additional services has involved staff in a detailed exercise to provide a comprehensive contracting process across the Trust. As part of this, a Contracting Team has been established to develop a co-ordinated approach for negotiations with GP Fundholders.

In preparation for 1993/94 Contracts, excellent groundwork, on an informal discussion basis with the G.P.'s, has been accomplished by service managers. Draft contracts have been sent to G.P. Fundholders and the negotiating process is well under way with the majority of Community Nursing Contracts agreed and signed.

The demands of the extended GP Fundholding scheme will require the Trust to collect additional activity information. Arrangements to collect the appropriate information will be in place from 1 April 1993.

The Trust is aware that the role of the GP is critical to future developments in community health care, and the ability to secure contracts with GP Fundholders will be a major priority during the year.

Good relationships have been established and the intention is to build on these and ensure effective monitoring and exchange of information.

The Trust recognises that provision of an equitable level of service to both GP Fundholders and non-fundholders is crucial and will ensure that service developments reflect this.

5.8 PURCHASING AND CONTRACTS

Future income is dependent upon the continued provision of a cost effective and quality service to people in order to attract referrals and contracts from Purchasers.

The Trust recognises the value of maintaining good relationships with its Purchasers. It will continue to pursue increased efficiency and to generate income through the provision of services to additional Purchasers.

15

5. PLANS FOR 1993/94
IMPROVING HEALTH AND BETTER
SERVICES   (continued)

Risk-analysis Community Services.

It is evident from the changes occurring in Acute Services Clinical Practice that demands on the community services as a whole will increase. The Trust's approach to service development and planning for Community Services recognises there are certain services which in all probability will:

- be provided by other agencies primarily as part of a managed process e.g. increased GP's role in Cervical Cytology, Family Planning, Vaccination and Immunisation, Child Assessment Screening and Health Promotion.

- be subject to competition as the purchasing role develops. Other providers may also recognise the opportunity to provide competitive service briefs to the Purchasers.

At present the implications in the short term are expected to be minimal as nearly all the services provided by the community service will be part of a contract already agreed in principle with the Purchasing Consortium.

Locality Purchasing

The Trust will develop localities of general management which will provide an opportunity for contracting Community Care Services using a locality and practice based approach as indicated in the Sefton Health Authority's Purchasing Plan 1993/94.

Marketing

A Marketing Strategy will be developed by March 1993. This will be based on work currently being carried out in analysing current and future contracts and will focus on clear, achievable targets relating to the securing of future business for the Trust.

16

6. SUPPORTING PROGRAMMES - EFFECTIVE AND EFFICIENT ORGANISATIONS

6.1 HUMAN RESOURCES

Focus for the year

The key issues relate to the relocation of Mental Health Services into Southport and the resettlement of people with learning disabilities into their own areas of origin. The staffing implications of this latter issue are considerable. In addition, the extension of GP Fundholding will lead to a requirement to manage staff in a more flexible way to respond to the obligations of contracts. Thirdly, coherent Human Resources Plans will be completed to take advantage of the greater freedoms available with Trust status. Training strategy will focus on the management of service change issues, equipping staff and Managers to respond to new opportunities.

Key objectives as an NHS Trust

The key features of this will be:

Developing a system of performance management to link the objectives of individuals and groups to the Business Strategy of the Trust, with the extension of individual and team rewards for effective performance.

Developing a Pay & Rewards Policy to progressively extend the flexibility and local determination of pay and non-pay benefits, thereby seeking to maximise the number of staff transferring to Trust Contracts and enabling the Trust to take local control of pay.

Upon receipt of the Government's Public Sector Pay Restraint circular, the Trust intends to slowly consolidate work on this policy during the year in order to maximise any opportunity for implementation next year.

Trust contracts based on job evaluation, monthly pay, flexible leave, grading on a single pay spine and Performance Management Schemes.

Progressively implementing the "Benefits to Staff" commitments in the Trust Application and consolidating work already undertaken in this area.

Key objectives for Mental Health Services

Implementing workforce profiles and establishments appropriate for the relocated services, with improved skill mix within available resources.

Managing any staffing reductions resulting from these changes through the "Managing Staff Changes" Policy as far as possible without recourse to compulsory redundancy.

6. SUPPORTING PROGRAMMES - EFFECTIVE AND EFFICIENT ORGANISATIONS (continued)

Training and developing the staff for the new service through Management Development and Staff Development Programmes so that the service is reorientated to a Community Care model.

Key objectives for Learning Disabilities

Concluding the workforce profiles for the local services and completing the review of the structure of the workforce.

Minimising redundancies resulting from the resettlement through the "Managing Staff Changes" Policy.

Continuing the programme of individual interviews and counselling on the future employment opportunities of all affected staff.

Securing job opportunities for staff with other employers such as Social Services and other Health Districts where this is appropriate and to minimise potential redundancies.

Continuing control of local vacancies to maximise the opportunities for redeployment throughout the Trust during the resettlement period.

Maintaining regular information to all staff on the closure process.

Implementing the Manpower Plan agreed with the Regional Health Authority to fund redundancies resulting from the resettlement.

Key objectives for Community Services

Responding to the changes resulting from the extension of GP Fundholding by restructuring the workforce to secure contracts.

Develop a locality based model of care, with staff decentralised to GP practices and clinics wherever possible.

Undertaking a skill mix review in support of locality development to ensure that maximum staff time is deployed into patient contact and managerial and other overheads are consequently reduced to support this.

6. SUPPORTING PROGRAMMES - EFFECTIVE AND EFFICIENT ORGANISATIONS (continued)

Junior Doctors hours

The Trust will implement a Plan to reduce the contracted hours for Junior Doctors to 72 hours or less. This is a reduction in 8 from current contractual commitments for the small number of doctors involved.

The transfer of EMI Wards to the Southport General Infirmary will provide an opportunity to establish links with the Geriatric Rota operating in the Acute Hospitals Trust. Consideration will be given to any legal implications in such a cross Trust arrangement.

Opportunity 2000

Continued implementation of plan and monitoring systems to maintain compliance with the NHS ME's goals.

Review and re-negotiation of Equal Opportunity Policy in conjunction with staff representatives.

Development of a Career Break Scheme and selective child care vouchers.

National Vocational Qualification Accreditation

Building upon City & Guilds accreditation to deliver vocational assessment and training. The numbers and scope of Health Care Support Workers will continue to be expanded. Candidates have been identified and registered from 38 areas within the Trust.

Training Plans

The main focus will be for Managers to ensure that staff throughout the Trust participate in specific training programmes to develop and utilise skills needed for the provision of Community Services and the national requirements of Health of the Nation, Patients Charter and the Community Care Act.

19

6. SUPPORTING PROGRAMMES - EFFECTIVE AND EFFICIENT ORGANISATIONS   (continued)

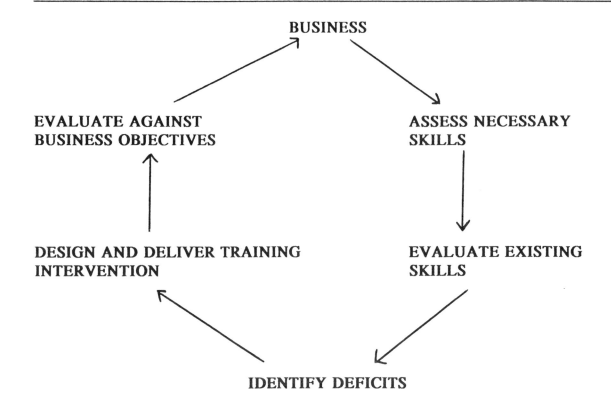

This process will be frequently monitored and reviewed throughout the year as the Community Care Model continues to change and develop.

Additional Planned Training Initiatives 1993/94

Trust Induction Programme

Care in the Community - Residential and Day Care Settings

Mental Health Act - Update workshops

Mental Health problems with people with learning disabilities

Customer Relations Programme - "You make the difference"

Health Pick- up pilot scheme - series of Open Learning modules
e.g. team working in the community/moving from hospital to community settings

In-house multi-disciplinary programme - costing, contracting, audit, business planning and Marketing workshops

"Updating of Clinical Skills in the Community" programme.

20

6. SUPPORTING PROGRAMMES - EFFECTIVE AND EFFICIENT ORGANISATIONS (continued)

Mental Health problems in the Elderly

MESOL Programme - Open University "Managing Health Services" course

Pre-Retirement courses

Management Development Programme - for Managers at all levels

Risk Analysis & Contingency Plan

The Trust will continue to work with the Regional Health Authority in minimising the necessity for compulsory redundancies resulting from the resettlement of learning disabilities. A programme of funding to support these staff changes is being discussed and staff numbers are expected to reduce in line with service changes.

In Mental Health there are fewer risks expected with the numbers of staff involved but the success of the Workforce Reprofiling Exercise will be crucial in ensuring that the service is reorientated into its new locations and decentralised form.

In Community Services, current dialogue with General Practitioners includes minimising the loss of income to the Trust through the placement of contracts with other agencies, thereby also minimising any ensuing staffing implications.

6.2 INFORMATION

There is a clear recognition within the Trust that there is a need for accurate, relevant, timely and accessible information. Good systems are essential in order to provide data for the contract monitoring process and supporting future planning.

Planned developments include:

Centralise information systems following a comprehensive review of all supporting technical, medical and clinical activity services.

The implementation of new asset accounting system - purchases 1992/93.

Links between Ross Ledger and Powertec Manpower System.

21

6. SUPPORTING PROGRAMMES - EFFECTIVE AND EFFICIENT ORGANISATIONS (continued)

Refining of costing and pricing systems using the Bradford system - purchased 1992/93.

Clinical Activity Collaboration and Analysis

Develop a system to integrate individual and localised population need with the monitoring of clinical activity to meet that need.

Provision of a Standard Information Pack to all GP practices. Reports will include comprehensive patient and activity data by teams, types of care, details of clinic sessions and identification of the specific Public Health work.

Pilot Project of the Workload Unit System

A workload unit system is a simple and effective way of measuring and monitoring the volume and cost of a service, either on an individual patient basis or for the delivery of a complete service by one member of staff, a staff team or whole department. The Trust is piloting this system for use in some therapy services and later for use in District Nursing.

This system will be of benefit in the contracting process with Purchasers or GP Fundholders for a specific level of service provision. We will develop the system in tandem with a model for identifying and planning skill mix in District Nursing. This will enable us to deliver a high quality yet cost effective service.

Resource Centre

To give wide access to up-to-date hardware and software for staff across the Trust. Training will continue with the aim of achieving widespread computer literacy.

Korner Returns

To include additional staff groups in the refined Comcare System using the ASQ for collection of data information, specifically Occupational Therapists and Physiotherapists.

6.3   FINANCE

Financial Plans for 1993-96

Details of the Income and Expenditure Accounts, Balance Sheets and External Financing Limit Statement are shown in the full set of Financial Pro-Formas and outline the Trusts revenue assumptions, asset base and capital developments.

6. SUPPORTING PROGRAMMES - EFFECTIVE AND EFFICIENT ORGANISATIONS (continued)

Expenditure

During 1993-94 the Trust will receive bridging from the Regional Health Authority for resources which are transferring to other Districts. It is important however, that during this period the Trust take every opportunity to make inroads into the fixed overhead costs of Greaves Hall.

Efficiency Savings

The Trust will achieve a programme of efficiency savings of   in accordance with the NHS ME requirement of 2%. A combination of factors will influence the final plan identifying the source of savings to be found.

- financial adjustments as a result of the ongoing retraction process

- through increased activity targets

- reviewing existing services to identify savings

- possible use of pay and price monies

We recognise the importance of ensuring robust figures and calculating the consequent impact on the contracting process

Income Generation

The Trust will achieve a target of   in 1993/94 by further extending the existing commercial business e.g. cook, freeze and laundry.

Retraction of Greaves Hall Site

Financial Implications of the closure of Greaves Hall Hospital are profound and need to be considered very carefully. There are three major stages to the task.

agree the retraction model with the R.H.A.

live within available resources during the closure period

cost of the new service within remaining resources

The first task has been completed, dowries are agreed and the R.H.A. has confirmed its commitment to bridging funds.

23

6. SUPPORTING PROGRAMMES - EFFECTIVE AND EFFICIENT ORGANISATIONS (continued)

The second is largely a question of good housekeeping of managing the service as flexibly as possible, minimising redundancies but maintaining services until the eventual closure of Greaves Hall Hospital. Work is well underway on the Manpower Plan, the estimates of bridging funds required and the detailed examination of costs.

The third task will be undertaken within the next few months as the Mental Health Strategy is firmed up. Service Managers are determining staffing levels required and infrastructure costs can be determined when the physical location of services has been finalised.

Capital Plans

Capital Plans need to be finalised but the intention is that Acute Mental Health Services will re-locate to Trust premises at the Hesketh Centre and Elderly Mental Health Services will mostly re-locate to leased accommodation on the Southport General Infirmary site. The latter is planned to take place by April 1993 subject to Regional agreement on the capital costs of moving the displaced services from the S.G.I. site into alternative accommodation. has been earmarked within the Regional Capital Programme for 1992/93 for this element of relocation and initial costings indicate that this will be sufficient.

The remainder of the relocation is more complex and an initial estimate of   within the Regional Capital Programme for 1993/94 has been used for planning purposes. This will cover the alterations required for the Hesketh Centre move, day care for the elderly and the provision of accommodation for any service displaced from the Hesketh Centre and the reprovision of some support services currently located on the Greaves Hall Site.

The relocation of services from Greaves Hall will vacate the whole site with the exception of the Laundry and Catering blocks and will enable the site to be closed in 1994. These two blocks will remain and are within the site development plan.

Greaves Hall will not be vested in the Trust but will be leased from the Regional Health Authority until March 1994. The lease cost has been assumed to be equivalent to the capital charges payable on the site.

Costings for Retraction

Work has been completed on separating the direct care and central costs to enable the release of resources that will facilitate the resettlement of residents to their own District.

6. SUPPORTING PROGRAMMES - EFFECTIVE AND EFFICIENT ORGANISATIONS (continued)

6.4 ESTATES

The development of Estate Strategies are closely aligned with the Trust's delivery of health care in the community. This is a major change and at the end of the strategy review the estate for the Trust should be concentrated on a central core facility at the Hesketh Centre with beds for the elderly and Day Hospital supporting facilities located at the Southport General Infirmary.

A strategy review and rationalisation of the estate for the community facilities will be carried out using similar methodology. This will enable both the hospital and community facilities to have clearly identified operational plans and performance targets for bringing the estate up to as new a condition as possible. This will be achieved utilising the estate quality model. Results of a review of space utilisation exercise will give optimum use of the estate.

The outcome of the surveys will be incorporated in the Business Plan as part of an overall Capital Programme identifying individual schemes, the associated cash flows, priorities and timescales for achieving their completion within the finances available.

Management of the Estate

Management of the estate will be carried out in two main areas of responsibility:

Estate business planning, development and standards which will oversee the general policy for the estate and set the standards for implementation either through an in-house team or external Consultants. Current managerial arrangements will be subject to a review by December 1993.

An operational arm which will carry out the day to day function of maintaining the estate and the environment to the standards laid down in the environmental charter. The operational service will utilise a mixture of in-house and outside contractors for delivering this service.

Assumptions

Laundry and kitchen will remain open if justified following a strategic review as a Trust asset, but are an integral part of site development.

Wards 6, 8, 14, 15, 16, and 20 will be closed during this period.

Energy Use

Current high efficiency practices will be maintained. Savings achieved over last year were

6. SUPPORTING PROGRAMMES - EFFECTIVE AND EFFICIENT ORGANISATIONS   (continued)

Maintenance

The remaining estate will be maintained in the period, along with the removal of both domestic and clinical waste and the insurance inspections of all necessary plant.

Staffing Levels

The present level of staff is 19. This will reduce as the site contracts.

Legislation

The requirements of all the recent legislation have been addressed and no additional costs are expected. These are as follows:

Environmental Protection Act 1990
Electricity at Work Regulations
C.O.S.H.H.
Pressure Systems Regulations

Southport General Infirmary

This space will be occupied on a basis of a lease with the rent being paid for the accommodation reflecting the responsibility of the Trust to maintain the building fabric service inside and out to Estate-code Condition B standard.

Assets Transferred

By 1 April 1993 transfer of a wide range of assets including contracts for Services, consumable stock to debtors and creditors and other financial issues will have been completed in accordance with NHS Management Executive Guidance EL (90) 153 and FOL (91) 12.

Estate planning for the accommodation to be agreed on an annual basis, including response times for the carrying out of Category 'C' breakdown maintenance.

Reassess budget levels for estate maintenance and upgrading in accordance with the estate quality model and the need for Capital Asset Management Programme to ensure that assets are replaced before they become uneconomical to operate and maintain.

Capital Planning Policy

Formulate a Capital Planning Policy which will enable a bottom-up approach to be taken to identifying future schemes, incorporating those identified in the estate quality model and future service provisions planned by the Directors of the Trust to meet the requirements of the Purchasing Authority.

26

6. SUPPORTING PROGRAMMES - EFFECTIVE AND EFFICIENT ORGANISATIONS (continued)

6.5 QUALITY

The Trust will continue to build on the commitment to provide high quality services, incorporating The Patients Charter issue as a priority.

Planned Quality Initiatives	Objectives	Agreed Funding
Service standards	Introduce formal system for monitoring	No funding implications
Audit child protection	Examine child health care service on an inter-disciplinary basis. Produce an action plan for future improvements.	funding in place from Regional bid for Audit monies.
Child Health Services	Hospital and community clinical activity to be examined. Aim to indicate current needs, plan future delivery of a service.	funding in place from Regional bid for Audit monies.
Monitor for District Nursing, Health Visitors, Psychiatric Nursing.	Systematic on-going review of service improvements.	No funding applications.
Q-Mapping computer software package to facilitate quality improvements throughout the Trust.	External process to other staff groups. Domestic Services O.T's Day Unit Human Resources Department.	Funding in place. Improvements through internal resources.

6. SUPPORTING PROGRAMMES - EFFECTIVE AND EFFICIENT ORGANISATIONS (continued)

Planned Quality Initiatives	Objectives	Agreed Funding
BS 5750	Catering services work towards procedures for registration in 1993. Identifies other services to incorporate in process.	No funding implications
Trust Quality Group, comprises representatives from Service Users. Carers, C.H.C., Non-Executive Purchasers.	Establish group to monitor Quality Assurance across the Trust. Structured systematic approach results in reports to staff/Managers with recommendations and positive feedback. Reports also to the Trust Board.	No funding implications
Medical Audit	Review use of Section 5 (2) Mental Health Act.	No funding implications
Medical Audit	Monitor and evaluate Care Programmes and After Care orders (Section 117).	No funding implications
Medical Audit	Review of G.P. referrals to identify protocol development.	No funding implications

28

7. ACTION PLAN FOR 1993/1994

MAIN OBJECTIVES	KEY TASKS	LEAD	TIMESCALE
Resettle remaining 26 LD residents to district of origin	1. Agree dates and individual plans for community placements 2. As residents leave, maintain level of service, dependent on clinical need		April 93 onwards On-going - complete by December 93
Relocate LD residents of Park Road West	1. Identify Housing/Capital requirements 2. Obtain purchaser agreement 3. Develop individual plans for residents 4. Agree incremental programme of change		July 93
Establish Community Support	1. Agree treatment/admissions model for people with a LD and an additional mental illness 2. Plan type of service		April 93
Relocate "Snoezelen" Therapeutic facility to a community site	1. Identify suitable location in the Southport & Formby area 2. Agree organisation/management of the facility		November 93
Relocate EMI services to SGI & Hesketh Centre	1. Commission 2 Wards at SGI (42 beds). 2. Agree provision of day care facilities and include in scheme		May 93

29

7. ACTION PLAN FOR 1993/1994

MAIN OBJECTIVES	KEY TASKS	LEAD	TIMESCALE
Relocate Paterson Unit to community facilities	3. Agree alternative accommodation for remaining 11 residents Ward 14		May 93
	1. Identify location for 8 bed community unit		April 93
	2. Agree arrangements with NSF for 13 places for longer term rehab.		
Relocate Acute MH services to Hesketh Centre	1. Commission 1 ward at HC		July 93
	2. Identify supporting day hospital facility and include in scheme		
Develop Community MH Team	1. Identify manpower		April 93
	2. Agree operational model		
Establish Consultant Out-Patient clinic in Formby	1. Identify site		May 93
	2. Agree clinical and medical record support issues		
Achieve maximum space utilisation of Trust premises	1. Produce and agree plan for transfer of remaining services on GH site		August 93
	2. Identify suitable space at HC and community clinics		April 93
	3. Investigate lease/rent of property in Southport in addition if there is insufficient space		May 93

7. ACTION PLAN FOR 1993/1994

MAIN OBJECTIVES	KEY TASKS	LEAD	TIMESCALE
Centralise services for children	Commission Children's Centre at 52 Hoghton Street subject to final funding agreement		July 93
Expand existing computerised system to include all items used on loan basis	1. Identify equipment on loan used in all services 2. Develop a plan for inclusion in existing Home Loan software package 3. Include a system and site for storage of items 4. Include clerical support issues		November 93
Centralise information services	1. Review all existing services identifying responsibilities and manpower implications for finance, clerical activity, medical records, out-patient clinics, medical secretaries, community services 2. Develop and implement a plan 3. Identify a central base		May 93
Develop a corporate marketing function	1. Produce a strategy and implement a plan 2. Establish links with contracting team 3. Work in parallel with Business Planning process		April 93 May 93 On-going

31

7. ACTION PLAN FOR 1993/1994

MAIN OBJECTIVES	KEY TASKS	LEAD	TIMESCALE
Achieve efficiency savings	1. Develop 2% CIP 2. Plan 3% service development fund for 1994/95		April 93 on-going
Trust & Pay Reward strategy	1. Conclude design of package based on job evaluation moving away from Whitley to single pay spine 2. Extend performance improvement schemes for individual and group incentives to achieve the business objectives 3. Link efficiency saving plan to more flexible use of staff to increase efficiency and generate funds for service development		On-going
Benefits to staff and patients	1. Implement the commitments stated in the Trust application		April 93
Continue a corporate strategic manpower review	1. Identify remaining manpower issues for services and implications of retraction and locality development 2. Develop and implement a skill mix issues and workforce reprofiling review plan		May 93

7. ACTION PLAN FOR 1993/1994

MAIN OBJECTIVES	KEY TASKS	LEAD	TIMESCALE
Develop locality model management and provision of community services	3. Implement a training plan which focuses on staff development and reorientation to new patterns of service provision		April 93 - June 93
Establish Trust Contracting process to meet expanding contracting requirement	1. Produce and implement a plan that incorporates managerial, geographical and clinical issues.		April 93 onwards
	1. Develop role and objectives of Contracting Team		
	2. Involve clinicians/managers in process.		
	3. Link to marketing strategy		

33

ADDITIONAL FUNDED DEVELOPMENT FOR 1993/94

DEVELOPMENT	AGREED FUNDING
Dental Health Education Post To target Dental Health education and support General Dental practitioners	FHSA
Clinical Psychologist- Child & Family Health Services	Purchaser agreement
Crossroads Care Scheme	joint funding Sefton Social Services (Health)
3rd MacMillan Nurse	Cancer Relief
"Open" screening sessions for children during school holidays	Will be achieved within existing resources
Asthma Nurse Nutritionist	Health gain monies Health gain monies
Extension of centralised open appointment system for Chiropody to all clinics	Will be achieved within existing resources
Increase therapy time in Stroke Team Speech Therapy - 0.4 wte Occupational Therapy - 0.8 wte	Purchaser agreement Purchaser agreement
P.T. Clinical assistant Mental Health Day Care facilities	Purchaser agreement
Community Physiotherapy Learning Disabilities	Purchaser agreement

ADDITIONAL FUNDED DEVELOPMENT FOR 1993/94

DEVELOPMENT	AGREED FUNDING
Co-ordinator for Childrens Centre	from within existing resources
Speech therapy support group *Childrens Centre *Adult treatment clinic, 2 Church Street	Will be achieved within existing resources
Support for Paramedics	Purchaser agreement
Development of a local Audiology Service 0-5 year age group to reduce dependencies on Regional resource	No additional cost implications
Outreach worker AIDS/HIV (6 months)	(non-recurring) (National Aids Initiative Fund)
Treatment room Nurse Churchtown clinic	FHSA support
Continence Service - increase in demand	& (non-recurring)
Community Dentistry - E Grade 4 sessions	Purchaser agreement
Enhancement of Marie Curie service	Purchaser agreement, awaiting further top-up support

PROPOSALS FOR DISCUSSION WITH PURCHASERS 1993/94

SOURCE OF FUNDING TO BE IDENTIFIED/AGREED	
Establish a computer based clinical management system/database for Child Medical Services	Medical Audit monies bid, awaiting confirmation re: National Funding
Family Planning - GP practices	awaiting Purchaser/FHSA pick-up
Terminal Care Team Home Care support workers	Hospice awaiting purchaser agreement to pick up on-going costs for current scheme. Central funding issue.
Chiropody. Expansion of services with General Practice to include all client groups	part waiting list monies, G.P. Health Promotion issue.

36

8. REVIEW AND MONITORING

The key to the success of a Business Plan lies in a commitment to its objectives and the mechanism for its implementation. Sufficient flexibility must exist for the Plan to be modified in response to changing circumstances, this is particularly important as the Trust is undergoing a major service change from hospital to community based services.

Objectives for individuals, teams and services will be set through the normal management process.

In addition, reports on progress will be submitted to the Trust Board on a quarterly basis.

Clinical service and management meetings will include progress with the Business Plan as a regular agenda item.

Business Planning Workshops are planned to raise staff awareness and to develop expertise in this process in preparation for the next year's plan.

The Business Plan will be widely publicised internally and included in communication briefings.

A summary will be produced for external publication.

External monitoring will be carried by the North West Outpost on a monthly basis for the first six months and later at quarterly intervals.

37

APPENDIX A   SOURCE AND APPLICATION OF FUNDS

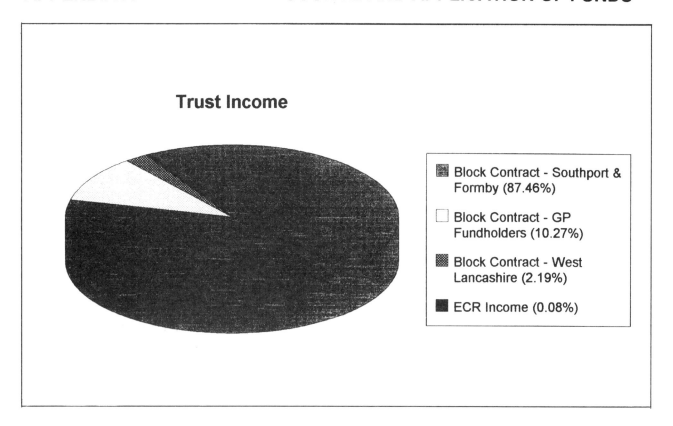

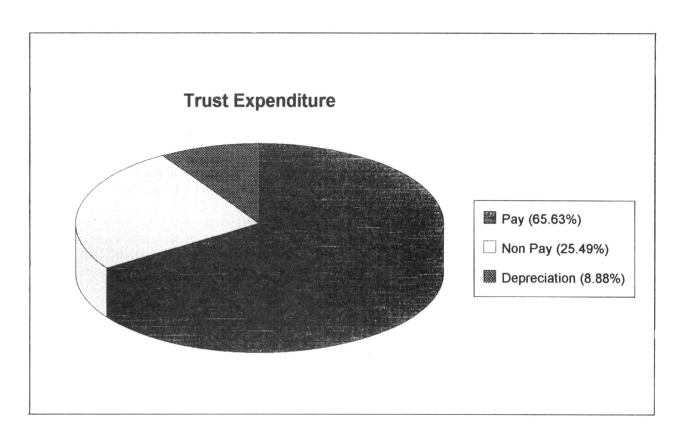

STAFF PROFILE

APPENDIX B

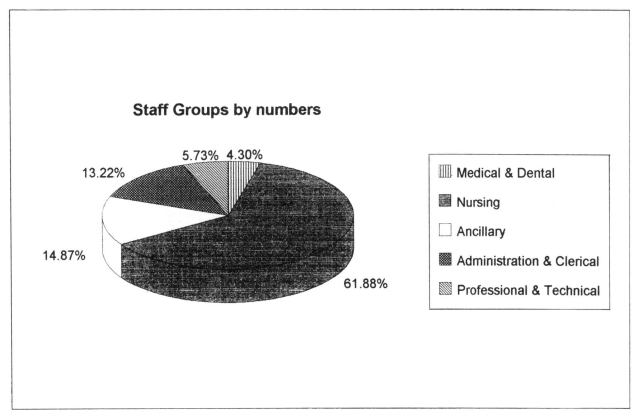

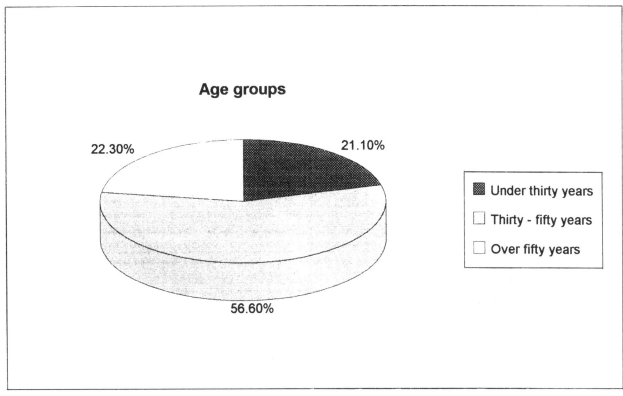

EXISTING BLOCK SERVICE AGREEMENTS 1992/93

Contracting arrangements for 1993/94 under negotiation

PURCHASERS			
SOUTHPORT & FORMBY H.A.	**WEST LANCASHIRE H.A.**	**GPFH EXISTING 1992**	**GPFH TO JOIN SCHEME 1993**
Mental Health - Acute Rehab.,Continuing Care and Respite Alcohol Drug Abuse Child/Adolescent Psychiatry	Mental Health - Long stay Acute Admissions Elderly	& Partners & Partners & Partners	&) Partners) &) Partners) & Partners
Learning Disabilities	Learning Disabilities - Long Stay	& Partners	
District Nursing Health Visiting Terminally Ill Nursing Cervical Cytology Well Woman Well Men Family Planning Continence Community Child Health Community Dental Community Diabetic Chiropody Speech Therapy Home Loan Supply Wheelchair Service Stroke Team Health Promotion		Community Nursing/HV Learning Disabilities Chiropody Mental Health Paramedical Out Patient Services/D.V.'s	

ADDITIONAL EXISTING CONTRACTUAL ARRANGEMENTS 1992/93

ECR's	Dental Services - cost per case
	Community services
FHSA Scheme GP Health Promotion Fee	Chiropody - cost per case
	O.T. Stress Management - cost per clinic

Health promotion fee - Recent guidance states that the existing scheme will cease to be applicable from July 1993.

Service and financial implications are being negotiated with Sefton FHSA and Purchasers.

41

APRIL 1993 PROPERTIES OWNED BY THE TRUST 　　　　**APPENDIX D**

PROPERTY	LAND AREA (HECTARES)	GROSS FLOOR AREA (SQ. METRES)	CAPITAL VALUE 1992 REVAL. £000's	USE
Hospital: Greaves Hall				Leased from D.H.A. retracting MI/LD Hospital with supporting paramedical and admin. services including cook/freeze production and district laundry.
Community Hospital : Hesketh Centre				Mental illness ward, day hospital, out-patient facilities, day unit, supporting patient services dept. Major part of the Trust's admin. functions.
Community Clinics: Church Street				Community services admin, offices,clinic
North Road				Clinic
Churchtown				Clinic
Poulton Road				Clinic
Hoghton Street				Clinic
Hampton Road				Clinic
Lincoln Road				Clinic
Sandbrook Road				Clinic
Formby				Clinic
L.D. Community Homes				
18 Park Road West				12 place community home
141 Rufford Road				4 pl. com. home 1 child adm. bed
Lincoln Road/Bungalow				5 place community unit
TOTAL				

SUMMARY OF SERVICES PROVIDED BY SPECIALITY

MENTAL HEALTH	LEARNING DISABILITY	COMMUNITY
In-patient facilities	Admissions/Assistant	District Nurses
Day Care	Continuing care	Health Visitors
Liaison and Domiciliary	Community Teams	Specialist Nurses: Terminally ill
Out-patient clinics	Day Care	Hospital liaison Diabetes
Respite and Family Support	Family Support	Stoma Continence
	Residential	Aids/HIV prevention Family Planning
	Out-patient clinics	School nurses Well Woman/Man
	Liaison and Domiciliary	Health Promotion
		Clinical Medical
		Child and Family Therapy
		Dental
		Chiropody
		Wheelchair/Home Loans
		Stroke Team
		Registration of Nursing Homes

Professional support services from Physiotherapy, Occupational Therapy, Speech Therapy, Psychology across the Trust.

43

HEALTH OF THE NATION TARGETS   APPENDIX F

Summary of Action for 1993/94

1.   **Coronary Heart Disease and Stroke (Southport & Formby)**

Age Group	Actual 1990	Target 2000
Under 65	58	35
65-74	113	76

The reduction of death rates among the under 65's is to be achieved by lifestyle changes i.e. stopping smoking, healthy diet and physical activity.

Cardiac support group

School based health education

5K Family Fun Run in conjunction with Southport Running Club

Support to Primary Health Care Teams - workshops

Annual Treasure Walk in conjunction with Community Clinics

"Look after yourself" health & fitness programme of courses

Annual Cycle for Health with Southport Road Cycling Club

Workplace health promotion
Lay course at Smedley Hydro

Health Education resources distribution and production

Smoking, school based education

"Look after yourself" Smoke Stop course for general public and NHS staff

Review of Priority & Family Services Smoking Policy - develop action plan

Nutritionist post

Campaigns planned for women and smoking and pregnant women and

smoking

44

HEALTH OF THE NATION TARGETS   **APPENDIX F**
                                          (continued)

Summary of Action for 1993/94

2.   **Cancers (Southport & Formby)**

Age Groups	Actual 1990	Target 2000
Breast Females 50-60	8	6
Cervical average per year 1983-87 Total female population	17	14
Lung Males under 75 Females under 75	42 23	30 20
Skin - Actual registrations 1983/7 (Excluding malignant melanoma of skin) Male Female	208 228	- -

School-based smoking education

"Look after yourself" Smoke - Stop course

Cervical Cytology, targeting of low uptake groups. Young women 19-24 & 50-64 year olds

Skin cancer campaign

Smoking and women, targeting particularly Harrington Ward and pregnant women

Mammography screening, develop support programme

Menopause support group

45

HEALTH OF THE NATION TARGETS   **APPENDIX F**
                                                       (continued)

Summary of Action for 1993/94

3.   **ACCIDENTS (Southport & Formby)**

Age groups	Actual 1990	Target 2005
Children under 15	2	1
Young people 15-24	3	2
People 65+	16	11

Cycle for health   Henry Newt alcohol awareness campaign

Accident Prevention Forum   Health Promotion Bulletin

"Look After Yourself" over 55 classes   Target the elderly and under 15's age groups

4.   **MENTAL ILLNESS (Southport & Formby)**

	Actual 1990	Target 2000
Suicide	8	7
Suicide and Injury undetermined	12	11

Mental Health promotion group, steering group formed with Health Promotion Service, Schools, Psychology and Learning Disabilities staff.

Crisis Helpline linked to facilities in the Community Mental Health Teams and supported by the Core In-Patient service. To publicise the Helpline and evaluate the benefits.

5.   **HIV/AIDS AND SEXUAL HEALTH (Southport & Formby)**

	Actual 1990	Target 1995
Gonorrhoea incidence	24	21

Sex education in schools, Advice and Information room at Southport College.

Drug Prevention Campaign aimed at under 16 and 16-20 year olds.

46

CIPFA

BUSINESS PLANS

A Compendium

HEALTH

Staffordshire Ambulance Service NHS Trust

Strategic Direction and
Business Plan 1993 - 1996

*This document sets out the strategic direction for the
period 1993 to 1996 and incorporates the Business Plan
for the financial year 1993/94.*

Note:

Annexes detailing projected activity and contracts for services 1993 to 1996; major expenditure programme 1993 to 1996 and manpower planning targets 1993-96 are not reproduced.

STAFFORDSHIRE

AMBULANCE SERVICE

NHS TRUST

ADVANCE WITH CARE

STRATEGIC DIRECTION
&
BUSINESS PLAN
1993 TO 1996

Chairman: C R M Boote TD, DL   **Tel: 0785 53521**

Chief Executive: R C Thayne OBE   **Fax: 0785 46238**

Headquarters: 70 Stone Road, Stafford, Staffordshire ST16 2RS

CONTENTS

ADVANCE WITH CARE

EXECUTIVE SUMMARY

This document sets out the Strategic Direction for the Staffordshire Ambulance Service NHS Trust for the period 1993 to 1996 and incorporates the Business Plan for the financial year 1993/94.

The document details the mission and the core values of the Trust and is based on key assumptions made as a result of a strategic analysis of the market and environment in which we operate.

The Trust strategy takes full account of the national, regional and local purchasers' requirements, priorities and initiatives, with an emphasis on achieving the targets of the Health of the Nation, paramedic provision and the development of the North West Midlands Trauma System Pilot Scheme.

The Trust appreciates that it can best develop its services and provide value for money through close alliance with its purchasers and with local authorities and voluntary agencies.

Quality standards, targets and objectives have been set for our Operational Services.

We recognise that without increased capital funding the Trust will not be able to maintain either its current vehicle fleet or its estate and reviews are in progress on both. Our working methods will continue to be reviewed in order to keep costs down whilst maintaining quality. The financial climate, over the next three years, is unlikely to allow our purchasers to significantly increase revenue, in real terms, in order to support developments. The successful generation of additional income from the expansion of our operational services into the private sector, particularly in the area of first aid training, will be a key factor in achieving cost efficiency targets and securing development funding.

The quality of service provided by the Trust is heavily dependent on the ability and morale of our front line staff. We recognise that is essential that we constantly seek to improve the management and leadership skills of all our managers to provide a highly motivated, dedicated and professionally qualified workforce.

The changes introduced to the Trust executive and senior management levels should ensure improved resource management and efficient development of our estate assets.

In summary: The strategy of the Trust is to achieve, through close partnership with our purchasers, improvement in the healthcare provided to the population we serve. Our principal objectives are twofold: The maintenance and steady improvement of our ORCON standards; and, the provision of a paramedic to each emergency ambulance by 1996.

This document is aimed at as wide an "audience" as possible.

ADVANCE WITH CARE

STRATEGIC DIRECTION 1993 TO 1996 AND BUSINESS PLAN 1993/94

FOR THE STAFFORDSHIRE AMBULANCE SERVICE NHS TRUST

PART ONE - BACKGROUND

1.   The Staffordshire Ambulance Service, previously directly managed by Mid Staffordshire District Health Authority on behalf of the three Staffordshire Health Authorities, became a Trust on the 1st April 1992. The Trust provides emergency and non-emergency patient transport to the resident and transient population of Staffordshire, the non-emergency patient transport for Wolverhampton Health Authority, together with courier transport and lease car services to NHS units within Mid Staffordshire. The Trust provides its services from a Headquarters and Central Ambulance Control in Stafford and 15 separate locations throughout the County. It operates 57 emergency and 85 non emergency ambulances plus 34 support vehicles.

2.   The Trust recognised from its inception that its transition from a directly managed status would provide a number of challenges that would require changes in culture and operation, whilst building on the inherent strengths of the Service. The Trust Board decided, therefore, to complete a thorough Review of its management and operating procedures to:

     a.   Identify inefficient use of resources and cost savings.

     b.   Provide effective and responsive management structures with responsibility for decisions and financial management devolved to the lowest practical level; and,

     c.   develop long term operational, financial, business development and human resources strategies for the service.

3.   The first Phase of this Review has been successfully completed and has resulted in changes to the Trust executive and senior management structure and responsibilities. It has identified the following three key areas where significant action is required:

     a.   A review of operational procedures to reduce Trust estate requirements to the minimum required to provide a quality service;

     b.   reduction of high sickness levels; and,

1

c.   improved management skills at all levels with the emphasis on improvement in staff confidence and trust.

4.   Action in these three key areas will form the basis for the continuance of the Review to the following programme:

a.   **Phase 2 -FY 93/94**. Review of middle and junior management structures and operating procedures.

b.   **Phase 3 -FY 94/95**. Completion of implementation of revised operational procedures throughout the Trust.

5.   This document will form the basis for discussions on development of the Trust, for three years, through partnership with the purchasers of our core services. The detailed objectives and financial projections for FY 93/94 are contained within the Business Plan.

AIM

6.   The aim of this document is to define the strategic direction of the Staffordshire Ambulance Service for the years 1993 to 1996.

SCOPE

7.   The subsidiary aims of this Direction are to:

a.   Determine the long term direction of the Trust.

b.   Determine the scope of the Trust's activities.

c.   Match the activities of the Trust to the environment in which it operates.

d.   Match Trust activities to its resources.

e.   Allocate or reallocate resources within the Trust.

f.   Identify implications of change.

ADVANCE WITH CARE

PART 2 - MISSION AND CORE VALUES OF THE STAFFORDSHIRE AMBULANCE SERVICE NHS TRUST

MISSION STATEMENT

8.   The mission of the Staffordshire Ambulance Service is to:

" Provide the highest standards of pre hospital treatment and patient transport care, within the resources available in agreed contracts/service agreements with purchasers."

PRINCIPAL OBJECTIVE

9.   The principal objective of the Trust is to:

" provide professional standards of pre-hospital and non-emergency care that are within the financial limitations of our purchasers and that provide a 6% return on net capital assets to allow the Trust to break even, after interest, and remain within the External Financing Limit".

CORE VALUES

10.   The core values of the Trust are:

a.   NHS. That we remain an integral part of the NHS.

b.   Patients. The interests and well being of the patient remains paramount.

c.   Access To Services. We acknowledge the right of access of duly authorised medical practitioners to Ambulance services for patients under their care.

3

d.   <u>Relationship To Purchasers</u>. We recognise that the resources available to the NHS purchasers are limited and that it is our responsibility to maximise the benefit derived from their investment in our services. We also recognise the need to make information readily available on our activity and performance to allow purchasers to monitor the provision of such services.

e.   <u>Integration With Other Providers</u>. We accept the importance of integrating the services provided into the care regimes and protocols of our partners in the delivery of high quality care to the patient.

f.   <u>Quality</u>. Inherent in our provision of services is the constant search for improvement in quality.

g.   <u>Voluntary Aid Societies</u>. We recognise the contribution made by the Voluntary Aid Societies in the delivery of care to the patient and will continue to actively seek to develop their close relationship with the Trust.

h.   <u>Accountability</u>. The Trust recognises its duty, as a public service, to be accountable to the community it serves and that it will strive to inform the general public of the performance and developments of the Ambulance Service, not least through close links with its Community Health Councils.

ADVANCE WITH CARE

PART 3 - KEY ASSUMPTIONS

11.   The following assumptions have been made as a result of a strategic analysis of the market and environment within which we operate. They form the underpinning to the Trust's Strategic Direction.

OPERATIONAL SERVICES AND ACTIVITIES

12.   **A&E Ambulance Service**. Competitive tendering for this service will not be authorised by the NHSME before 1996, but remains a future possibility.

13.   **Non emergency (Patient and Courier Transport) Service**. All our current purchasers will move to competitive tendering for this service by 1995. The creation of Trusts and the merger of Mid and South East Staffs Health Authorities will provide further opportunities for the Trust to assume responsibility, through contracts, for the provision of Non Patient Transport Services to NHS units and to the Health Authority.

14.   **Information Technology and Communications**. It will be essential for the development of our core services that the Trust develops its information technology resources to provide both effective tasking and control of the operational transport fleet together and to easily extract accurate cost and activity information. There are opportunities, primarily within the NHS in the County, of utilising the Trust IT and communications capabilities to generate income to reduce costs and fund necessary developments.

15.   **Contract Car Service**. Although there may be a decline in the use of contract cars if personal taxation increases, any such volume decrease would not have a major implication on Trust resources committed to this activity. There is a market within NHS units in Staffordshire to extend our current purchasers.

16.   **Income Generation Through Training**. The strict enforcement and development of Health & Safety at Work and similar regulations to safeguard the public will maintain the demand for professional training in First Aid and Safety procedures.

FINANCE

17.   NHS income provided from core NHS contracts is not likely to rise in line with forecast inflation. There will be increasing pressure to achieve annual cost efficiencies whilst maintaining and improving quality. Purchasers are likely to expect significant cost/activity savings in order to achieve national activity targets. This will entail stringent value for money and management audit of both financial and performance data.

18.   Cost improvement programmes and additional income generation will need to provide the sources for meeting shortfalls in inflation funding, efficiency targets and development funding.

HUMAN RESOURCES.

19.   Personnel will continue to command the major share (currently 75%) of Trust revenue expenditure. The effective management and utilisation of human resources will be the key factor for the continued viability of the Trust.

20.   **Training**

    a.   Current and future managers, at all levels, will require training to develop the necessary skills if they are to provide the necessary leadership and management expertise to achieve Trust objectives.

    b.   The Trust will be expected to meet the national target of one paramedic per emergency ambulance by 1995.

    c.   National vocation qualifications will be introduced for all ambulance service qualifications, which will radically alter training methods and assessment.

SUPPORT SERVICES

21.   **Sales, Marketing, Internal Communications and Public Affairs**. The retention and development of core NHS contracts and the development of additional income from the NHS and private sector will be dependent on our ability to identify customers and their requirements and supply our services as a quality and value for money product.

22.   **Vehicle Fleet Management**. Our customers will increasingly expect our vehicle fleet to be within NHS age and mileage standards. However, they will be unable to provide the full amount of the increased capital funding required to replace aged vehicles and the increased revenue to meet capital charges. A high proportion of funding for replacements will have to be found from within Trust resources and through income generation, with capital charge increases being absorbed through reduced operating costs.

23.   **Supply**. The increased treatment capability of all ambulance crews, together with the availability of sophisticated pre hospital treatment and monitoring equipment, will necessarily result in an increase in the resources allocated to front line ambulances. It will be essential that the procurement of such resources reflects value for money and that their use is closely monitored. Stock levels must be maintained at the minimum safe levels. The retention of the NHS supplies organisation to meet the Trust requirements will be kept under review and the Trust is prepared to undertake its own procurement organisation if this proves to be cost-effective.

ADVANCE WITH CARE

24.   **Estate Management**. The Trust has insufficient income to meet the maintenance and repair costs of its current estate; neither is it likely to generate, from its existing customer base, the capital required to provide the development necessary. It is recognised that the historical siting of the estate operational bases does not, in all cases, assist the provision of an efficient service. A Review is in hand to determine the future configuration of the Estate.

PART 4 - NATIONAL, REGIONAL AND LOCAL PURCHASERS' REQUIREMENTS, PRIORITIES AND INITIATIVES

25.   This Strategic Direction takes into account the following policy guidance:

a.   **National Policy**.

(1)   Implementation of "Health of the Nation" with emphasis on the reduction of deaths due to Coronary Heart Disease/Stroke and Accidents.

(2)   The national target for all Ambulance Services to provide a paramedic on every emergency ambulance by 1995.

(3)   Development of the Patient's Charter Standards for Emergency and Non-Emergency Ambulance Services.

(4)   Direction for purchasers of non-emergency patient transport services to competitively tender for such services in the future.

b.   **Regional Priorities and Policy**.   West Midland Regional Health Authority - Priorities and Planning Guidance 1993/94.

c.   **Purchasers Strategy and Priorities**.

(1)   North Staffs Health Authority - Health Strategy and Business Plan 1993/94 and 1994/96 with emphasis on the development of the National Trauma System Pilot Scheme.

(2)   Mid Staffs Health Authority - Strategy for Health - 1993 to 2005.

(3)   The proposed merger of Mid and SE Staffs Health Authority to form a single purchasing authority for South Staffordshire during FY 1993/94.

(4)   The stated intention of purchasers of the non-emergency patient transport services in North Staffordshire to competitively tender for the future provision of such services for the period FY 1993/95.

ADVANCE WITH CARE

HEALTH OF THE NATION

26.   The Trust will aim to contribute its particular expertise, in cooperation with purchasers, to the achievement of purchasers' targets to reduce deaths due to Coronary Heart Disease/Stroke and Accidents, and to play its part in developing a healthy workplace for Trust employees and the patients we transport.

27.   **Coronary Heart Disease/Stroke**.

   a.   To improve protocols and monitoring equipment to provide improved pre hospital care for patients suffering from Coronary Heart Disease who require emergency assistance.

   b.   To increase the provision of Cardio-Pulmonary Resuscitation (CPR) first aid training of the public, with emphasis on the relatives of patients suffering or at risk from Coronary Heart Disease/Stroke.

   c.   To provide a 12 lead ECG monitoring service, linked using telemetry, direct to specialist hospital departments, for use on emergency ambulances and for GP clinics.

   d.   To provide a blood pressure measurement service for purchasers and GPs.

28.   **Accidents**.

   a.   To provide information for purchasers on the person, location, time and occurrence of serious accidents.

   b.   To increase the provision of public first aid training with emphasis on schoolchildren and the over 65s.

   c.   To work closely with Local Authorities on the development of joint action and sharing of information to reduce accidents on the road, at home and at work.

29.   **Healthy Workplace** To provide a healthier workplace by:

   a.   Improving physical fitness.

   b.   Reducing the number of staff who smoke, at work, by:

      (1)   10%. - FY 93/94.

      (2)   25%. - FY 94/95.

      (3)   50%. - FY 95/96.

ADVANCE WITH CARE

c.   Reduction of "wastage" as a result of accidents and sickness from 8% to:

    (1)   7%. - FY 93/94.

    (2)   6%. - FY 94/95.

    (3)   5%. - FY 95/96.

THE ACHIEVEMENT OF THE NATIONAL PARAMEDIC TARGETS

30.   The Trust aims, with the support of purchasers, to train, over the next three years, a further 90 paramedics to achieve a total establishment of 156 qualified personnel. This will allow one paramedic per A&E ambulance, together with the necessary qualified supervisors and instructors.

31.   In order to achieve these targets we will require to work closely with our purchasers to provide the funding necessary through both internal cost efficiencies and additional revenue allocations.

SER	DATE	SUBJECT	NORTH STAFFS HEALTH AUTHORITY	MID STAFFS HEALTH AUTHORITY	SOUTH EAST STAFFS HEALTH AUTHORITY	TOTALS
(a)	(b)	(c)	(d)	(e)	(f)	(g)
1.	FY 93/94	Numbers	24	12	12	48
		Trg Costs	160,800.00	80,400.00	80,400.00	321,600.00
		Revenue Cost	43,200.00	21,600.00	21,600.00	86,400.00
		Total Cost	204,000.00	102,000.00	102,000.00	408,000.00
2.	FY 94/95	Numbers	12	6	6	24
		Trg Costs	80,400.00	40,200.00	40,200.00	160,800.00
		Revenue Cost	21,600.00	10,800.00	10,800.00	43,200.00
		Total Cost	102,000.00	51,000.00	51,000.00	204,000.00
3.	FY 95/96	Numbers	9	5	4	18
		Trg Costs	60,300.00	33,500.00	26,800.00	120,600.00
		Revenue Cost	16,200.00	9,000.00	7,200.00	32,400.00
		Total Cost	76,500.00	42,500.00	34,000.00	153,000.00
4.	Total	Numbers	45	23	22	90
		Trg Costs	301,500.00	154,100.00	147,400.00	603,000.00
		Revenue Cost	81,000.00	41,400.00	39,600.00	162,000.00
		Total Cost	382,500.00	195,500.00	187,000.00	765,000.00
5.	1996 +	Revenue Cost	140,400.00	70,200.00	70,200.00	280,800.00

Notes:
(1)   Amounts do not include:

    (a)   An uplift for inflation.
    (b)   Revenue costs of existing trained staff which are estimated to total £118,800 at the start of FY 93/94.
(2)   Costs are based on a 100% pass and retention rate.

11

NORTH WEST MIDLANDS TRAUMA SYSTEM PILOT SCHEME.

32.   The "trauma system area" includes Staffordshire, Shropshire and South East Cheshire, a radius of some 50 miles, a population of some 2 million people and including six "peripheral" Hospitals each with Accident & Emergency (A&E) Departments. The system relies on the Staffordshire, Shropshire and Mersey Ambulance Services and the Air Ambulance Service of West Midlands Ambulance Service for provision of pre-hospital care and delivery.

33.   The Trial aims to prove the effectiveness of a "critical care system" that provides, dependent on the severity of illness or injury, direct transportation and admission to a main A&E department for a given area which is permanently manned by A&E and Anaesthetic Consultants with access to resuscitation, intensive care departments and specialist surgical and medical treatment facilities.

34.   A key element of the system is the development of the capabilities of the ambulance services to identify those patients who should be moved direct to the Centre, and not to the nearest A&E facility, through "trauma scoring" and the extended (paramedic) skills to provide sustaining treatment during the lengthy ambulance journey. It is considered vital that a capability exists to move the most critically injured and ill patients by air ambulance.

35.   In addition to the ability to move patients direct to the Trauma Centre, there must also be a capability to provide high quality transfer of patients, following resuscitation, from one of the "satellite" Hospitals within the Trauma System catchment area to the Centre itself.

36.   **Specific Objectives for the Ambulance Service**. The Ambulance Services play a key role in the success of the Trauma System Trial as they are responsible for the pre-hospital care and delivery of patients to the Trauma Centre. The Trust will aim, in consultation with purchasers, to meet the following objectives:

   a.   **Air Ambulance Support**. Maintenance of an air ambulance service for at least 40 hours per week through direct funding subsidised by public subscription.

   b.   **Trauma System Ambulance Liaison Group**. The formation of a liaison group comprising the Mersey, Shropshire and the Staffordshire Ambulance Services to coordinate the improvement of pre-hospital care and ambulance tasking protocols within the System area.

ADVANCE WITH CARE

PART 5 - ESTABLISHMENT OF HEALTHY ALLIANCES

37.   The Trust appreciates that it can best develop high quality services and provide value for money through alliances with other agencies, internationally, nationally and locally both within the NHS, Local Authorities and Voluntary Agencies.

38.   The principal alliances will be with the Staffordshire Health Authorities, our major purchasers, NHS Units and Trusts, the FHSA, GPs and GP Fundholders, the Police, Fire & Rescue Services, Community Health Councils, neighbouring Ambulance Services and the Voluntary Aid Societies.

EXCHANGE SCHEME WITH THE JOHANNESBURG EMERGENCY MANAGEMENT SERVICES

39.   The Trust has established an exchange scheme with the Johannesburg Emergency Management Services, who provide a similar-sized ambulance service linked to a Trauma System. The exchange will be open to one Ambulance Officer/paramedic per year from each Service for a six week period and will provide valuable experience in acute trauma pre hospital care for our operational staff.

LIAISON WITH THE CLEVELAND AND THE AVON AMBULANCE SERVICES NHS TRUSTS

40.   The Trust is developing a close liaison between Board members and senior managers of both the Cleveland and Avon Ambulance Service Trusts to provide solutions to common problems and to share ideas for future development.

HEALTH AUTHORITIES

41.   The Trust aims to work closely with the District Health Authorities to develop and improve the Accident and Emergency Ambulance Services and to identify areas where the Trust can assist the Authorities in achieving their objectives in commissioning healthcare for the improvement of their populations' health and well-being.

42.   **The Staffordshire Ambulance Service Medical Advisory Group**. The Trust will continue to be guided by the Medical Advisory Group in determining the clinical protocols and practices adopted by the Trust. The Group is composed of senior clinicians and nursing staff nominated by the purchasers and GPs nominated by the FHSA. The Chairman of this Group reports to the Trust Board and acts as the clinical spokesman of the Trust.

ADVANCE WITH CARE

ACUTE, COMMUNITY AND MENTAL HEALTH UNITS

43.   The Trust will aim to continuously improve the A&E Ambulance Service through close liaison with management and clinical staff in Acute units.

44.   The Trust will also work with purchasers of the non emergency patient transport service to closely tailor the service provided to the units' needs and requirements.

FAMILY HEALTH SERVICE AGENCY, GPs AND GP FUNDHOLDERS

45.   The Trust will liaise closely with the FHSA to:

    a.   Encourage the development of a British Association of Immediate Care (BASICs) organisation throughout the County of Staffordshire.

    b.   Ensure that GPs are aware of the improved capabilities of the Ambulance Service.

    c.   Continue to maintain close cooperation over the pre-hospital care of their patients.

    d.   Maintain the current Courier Transport Services provided to the FHSA and to extend such services to the whole of the County.

POLICE AND FIRE & RESCUE SERVICES

46.   The Trust will maintain a close relationship with the other Emergency Services, including the County Emergency Planning Department, to develop joint operating protocols at incidents and to maintain and test emergency plans.

47.   We will explore the potential for the joint provision or shared use of the following resources to reduce costs:

    a.   Communications systems.

    b.   Training.

    c.   Estate.

COMMUNITY HEALTH COUNCILS

48.   The Trust recognises the legitimate rights of, and the key role played by, the three Community Health Councils in Staffordshire, to both represent the general public and to the Trust itself. The three CHCs in Staffordshire, each send a representative to monthly Trust Board Meetings as observers and have right of access to visit all Ambulance Stations on request. We intend to consolidate these links in the future.

STAFFORDSHIRE BRANCHES OF THE BRITISH RED CROSS SOCIETY AND ST JOHN'S AMBULANCE ASSOCIATION

49.   The Trust will form a Joint Ambulance and First Aid Committee during 1993 with the following objectives:

    a.   To improve liaison within the three organisations.

    b.   To formulate plans for the use of BRCS and StJAA resources in a major incident.

    c.   To provide practical training experience for voluntary ambulance crews.

    d.   To coordinate public first aid training programmes.

THE RESIDENTS OF STAFFORDSHIRE

50.   The Trust is keen to inform the residents of Staffordshire and Wolverhampton of the performance, skills and developments of their Ambulance Service and to learn of their views. We aim to achieve this objective through a range of activities, including:

    a.   Initiatives through the local media.

    b.   Ambulance Station Open Days and public first aid and CPR training initiatives.

    c.   Rapid investigation of complaints with follow-up personal visits wherever possible.

ADVANCE WITH CARE

PART 6 - OPERATIONAL SERVICES PROVIDED BY THE TRUST

ACCIDENT AND EMERGENCY (A&E) AMBULANCE SERVICE

AIM

51.   To provide a timely and high quality accident and emergency service within Staffordshire that delivers, to agreed protocols, pre-hospital treatment and in-transit care which maintains life and reduces to the minimum any deterioration in a patient's condition and delivers patients, without unnecessary delay, to the most appropriate NHS facility for specialist medical care.

QUALITY STANDARDS

52.   **Personnel**.   To provide a minimum crew of two trained and qualified Ambulance Technicians, one of which will hold a minimum of one year's experience and have received additional training in cardiac care, and to progressively ensure that one member of the crew has received extended "paramedic" training.

53.   **Ambulances**. All A&E ambulances will be less than seven years of age and have covered a total mileage of less than 140,000 miles and will be equipped with sufficient medical equipment, including a cardiac monitor and defibrillator, stores, drugs and intravenous fluids and lifting and carrying equipment to provide high quality care for patients.

54.   **Reaction Times - ORCON Standards**.

a.   **Emergency Requests**.   The Service will react to requests made by any member of the public requesting immediate assistance and operate to the ORCON Standards for rural areas, now incorporated in the Patient's Charter, to meet the following "rural area" standards for all areas in which the Trust operates:

(1)   **Activation**.   An ambulance will be tasked and mobile within 3 minutes of the request being received in 95% of all cases.

(2)   **Response**.   An ambulance will arrive at the location where assistance was requested:

(a)   Within 8 minutes of the initial request in 50% of all cases.

(b)   Within 19 minutes of the initial request in 95% of all cases.

b.   **Urgent Requests**.   The Service will also react to all requests from Doctors, Dentists and Midwives to take urgent action to move or transfer patients requiring skilled in-transit care to Hospital within the following standard in 95% of all cases:

    (1)   Not more than 30 minutes earlier than the agreed time.

    (2)   Not more than 30 minutes after the agreed time.

TARGETS

55.   **Cost Efficiency Targets**.   The A&E service is tasked to achieve 2% cost efficiency savings, each financial year through:

a.   Reduction in sickness rates.

b.   Strict control of overtime.

c.   Improved operational deployment and utilisation of assets.

d.   Absorption of increased activity without additional resources.

56.   **Quality and Performance Targets**.

a.   **ORCON Standards**.   Increase performance under the ORCON Standards by 1%, above the minimum for each standard, each year for the next three years subject to the purchasers' agreement and that the real value of contracts for A&E ambulance services being maintained.

b.   **Paramedics**. Subject to agreement on funding with our purchasers:

    (1)   Provision of a paramedic on each ambulance during peak operating times, 1100 to 2300 hours daily, by April 1994.

    (2)   Provision of a paramedic on each ambulance deployed by April 1996.

    (3)   Provision of a paramedic trained officer to directly supervise A&E operations by April 1996.

c.   **Improved Communication with Hospitals**.

    (1)   The phased resiting of ambulances, where practical, to Hospital A&E departments, minor injuries clinics and suitable primary care facilities by September 1996 to improve activation and communication between the A&E ambulance service and clinicians.

(2)   Transmission of data between ambulance control, hospital A&E departments and ambulances to improve notification of casualty arrival and improve transmission of advice from clinicians to ambulance crews.

d.   **In-Transit Care**. Introduction of single cot ambulances and Intensive Treatment facilities to improve in-transit care capabilities.

e.   **Air Ambulance Service**. The continuation of the Regional air ambulance service.

f.   **Equipment Enhancements**. The provision of the following essential equipment enhancements to ambulances:

(1)   Pulse oximeter - by 1995.

(2)   Enhanced communication capability to allow crews to communicate when away from ambulance - by 1996.

57.   **Income Generation Targets**. To progressively generate net income from non-core NHS purchasers to £10K by FY 1995/96.

PRINCIPAL OBJECTIVES

58.   Maintain and develop the service provided in partnership with both our purchasers and providers of primary, secondary and tertiary acute medical care.

59.   Provide the A&E Service for the Seisdon Peninsula of Staffordshire, through agreement with purchasers, by FY 94/95.

60.   Examine the possibility of expansion, by FY 95/96, to Wolverhampton Health Authority area.

61.   Develop close cooperation with bordering Ambulance Services, with emphasis on Mersey and Shropshire Services, whose area also includes part of the Trauma System, to provide economical and efficient coverage through sub contracts or service agreements by FY 94/95.

62.   In consultation with purchasers, provide a comprehensive county first-line medical major incident and specialist task capability to meet likely scenarios.

63.   Develop the use of A&E resources in the private sector to produce resources for development of the service and cost efficiency targets.

64.   Improve the quality of performance and efficient use of resources, both to release funds for development and to meet cost efficiency targets.

PATIENT & COURIER TRANSPORT SERVICE

AIM.

65.   The Patient Transport Service aims to provide purchasers with a total transport service providing reliable, timely and quality movement of non emergency patients within Patient Charter standards, from or to any location in the United Kingdom. The Courier Service provides a personnel and freight transport service tailored to meet the requirements of NHS units. Both Services provide a vital first line reinforcement in support of the Emergency Service in the event of a major incident and provide necessary skills training for personnel who progress to Technician and Paramedic employment.

QUALITY STANDARDS

66.   **Personnel**.   All personnel will wear the uniform of the Staffordshire Ambulance Service. Care Assistants will receive advanced first aid, handling and lifting and driver training. All voluntary car drivers will be screened and supervised by the Trust.

67.   **Ambulances**. The Trust aims to ensure that all PTS ambulances will be less than seven years of age and have covered a total mileage of less than 140,000 miles by the year 2000. All new ambulances will be fitted with forward facing seats and be capable of carrying up to two stretchers and two wheelchairs. All existing ambulances will be equipped with:

    a.   First aid equipment.

    b.   Lifting and carrying equipment.

    c.   A radio.

68.   **Voluntary Cars**. All cars used by the voluntary car service will be inspected annually by the Trust vehicle mechanics and such cars will provide comprehensive insurance covering patients transported.

69.   **Same Day Service**. The Service will aim to meet all unforeseen requests within the times requested by purchasers.

TARGETS

70.   **Cost Efficiency Targets**. The Patient & Courier Transport Service is tasked to achieve 2% cost efficiency savings, each annually through:

    a.   Absorption of 2% increased activity without additional resources.

b.　　Strict control of overtime.

c.　　Improved operational deployment and utilisation of assets.

d.　　Reduction in sickness rates.

71.　**Patient's Charter**. The Trust will aim to work closely with purchasers to achieve, by 1995, the Patient Charter standards for the non-emergency ambulance transport which meet the following parameters:

a.　　**Collection of Patients from Residence**. Not more than 30 minutes earlier or 60 minutes later than the agreed time.

b.　　**Arrival for Appointments**. Not more than 30 minutes early or later than the appointment time.

c.　　**Collection from Hospital or Other Centre**. Within 60 minutes of being declared ready for collection.

d.　　**Length of Time of Patients on Ambulances**. No patient to spend more than 60 minutes on an ambulance where the journey is within a single Health Authority area.

72.　**Courier Transport Service**. To extend, where appropriate, the CTS service to the remainder of Staffordshire and in other areas where we provide a patient transport service.

73.　**Income Generation Targets**. To progressively generate net income from non core NHS purchasers to £10K by 1995/96.

PRINCIPAL OBJECTIVES

74.　　To retain current contracts with purchasers in Staffordshire and Wolverhampton. No further major expansion of the Patient Transport Service, is envisaged, outside existing areas of operation, within present resources.

75.　　To develop the capability to provide a comprehensive transport service to all NHS purchasers in Staffordshire and Wolverhampton.

76.　　To develop, in cooperation with bordering Ambulance Services, the provision of a more economical and efficient service for purchasers through sub contracts or service agreements.

77.　　To fully incorporate current resources into the Service major incident and specialist task capability.

ADVANCE WITH CARE

78.   To improve the quality and efficient use of resources to release funds for development and cost efficiencies.

79.   To develop the use of P&CTS resources in the private sector to provide income for development and cost efficiencies.

80.   To maximise the economical use of the Voluntary Car Service.

AMBULANCE CONTROL, COMMUNICATIONS AND INFORMATION TECHNOLOGY STRATEGY

AIMS

81. The aims of the Control, Communications and Information Technology department of the Trust are as follows:

    a. **Ambulance Control**. To provide an efficient message receipt and ambulance tasking service.

    b. **Communications**. To maintain radio voice communications with all ambulances operated by the Trust.

    c. **Information Technology**. To provide rapid access to information on Trust activity, performance, resources and costs.

QUALITY STANDARDS

82. **Requests for Emergency Assistance**. To ensure that all requests for emergency ambulance support are acknowledged, recorded and an ambulance tasked within 90 seconds of a call being received by the Service.

83. **Provision of Information**. To provide purchasers, by the tenth day of each month, with information on activity and performance of the Trust for such purchasers for the previous month to the detail agreed in contracts.

84. **Data Protection**. To ensure that protection of information stored electronically meets the requirements of the Data Protection Act.

TARGETS

85. **Identification of Key Information**. To determine the key information requirements of the Trust and Purchasers and the structuring of our IT software to meet the requirement by 1994.

86. **Income Generation**. To progressively generate net income from non-core NHS purchasers to £10K by FY 1995/96.

PRINCIPAL OBJECTIVES

87. To develop hardware, software and operator skill to provide effective operational ambulance and transport tasking and control, financial, personnel and resource management that allows rapid access to detailed information on costs, activity and

resources for both external customers and internal management.

88.   To provide an efficient and cost-effective electronic communications system for Trust mobile and static locations, both for voice and data which is linked to the main computer and records key messages.

89.   To improve quality and efficient use of IT resources to release funds for development.

90.   To develop the use of IT and communications' resources and skills within the NHS and the private sector to provide income for development and cost efficiencies.

CONTRACT CAR SERVICE

AIM

91.   To provide a lease car service, with professional advice on choice of vehicle and maintenance and repair, to NHS employees in Staffordshire.

TARGETS

92.   To progressively generate net income from this Service to £15K by FY 1995/96.

OBJECTIVES

93.   To develop the capability to provide a comprehensive contract car service to all NHS units throughout Staffordshire and Wolverhampton.

ADVANCE WITH CARE

PART 7 - TRUST INTERNAL SUPPORTING SERVICES

FINANCIAL STRATEGY

DEVELOPMENT OF FINANCIAL SYSTEMS

94.   The Trust has purchased a Financial System which will become operational from April 1993. An independent payroll system is planned to be installed by April 1994. The new system will also be linked to provide timely advice to all Executives and Managers on the performance of their budgets. Such detailed and up-to-date information will be required to enable the Finance function to be proactive, rather than reactive, to realise financial improvements and/or efficiency benefits.

MARKET APPRAISAL/COMPETITOR PRICE ANALYSIS

95.   Pricing to the non NHS market will be as dictated by the market forces and competitor activity. We ensure that we can be competitive in areas targeted for additional income generation, wherever possible, without initial capital investment.

96.   We are confident that our quality of service, together with our local knowledge, unique ability to meet same day requests for patient movement and the current level of purchasers satisfaction will make it difficult for our competitors in other Ambulance Services and the private sector to secure our current business through competitive tendering. However, we will take action to reduce capital charges for Trust estates if we are to retain a competitive edge.

RISK MANAGEMENT/CONTINGENCY PLANNING

97.   Risk and uncertainty are minimised by ensuring that major decisions are taken after risk analysis and sensitivity analysis has been completed.

98.   The pricing strategy of the Trust is such that it allows for the recovery of full costs allowing for depreciation and the generation of the 6% return on net assets. Costs and services, including the appropriate overheads, are allocated to individual contracts. This enables sensitivity analysis to be carried out on a contract by contract basis. Pricing of spare capacity, where currently available, is calculated at marginal cost.

99.   The cash releasing element of the cost improvement programme allows for a reserve to be held to deal with risks such as inflation above that originally funded.

100.   The Trust has retained all its current core NHS contracts for FY 1993/94 but has yet to obtain agreement on paramedic training.

101.   The Trust considers that the principal risks, over the next three years are:

     a.   Retention of the non-emergency Patient Transport contracts.

     b.   Maintenance of the Trust Estate to the standard required under current legislation.

102.   **Retention of Non Emergency Patient Transport Contracts**.

     a.   The securing of the Wolverhampton contract for non-emergency patient transport services, together with the increasing employment of staff in this service on part-time, fixed term contracts, has enabled the Trust to be more flexible in adapting quickly to increases or downsizing of activity.

     b.   A key facing the Trust is that although the PTS Ambulance Fleet has an average age of 5.3 years, only 39 of the 87 ambulances are below the 7 year age maximum of the NHS recommended standard. Current allocations of block capital are inadequate to maintain both the emergency and non emergency ambulance fleets. Indeed, as priority will continue to be given to the emergency ambulance fleet, it is estimated that the average age of the non emergency fleet will deteriorate to 6.5 years by 1996 unless corrective action is taken.

     c.   The Trust is aware, from the current non-emergency competitive tendering process in the Region, that purchasers are moving towards a requirement for vehicles to meet a standard of being under 7 years old and less than 140,000 miles.

     d.   To meet such a requirement the Trust would require a capital injection of £1.4M to bring all vehicles within the minimum standard and an annual increase in block capital allocation of 25% to maintain such a standard.

     e.   There is little doubt, that without such a capital uplift, if purchasers were to stipulate ambulance provision to minimum NHS standards, the Trust could face great difficulty in retaining all of its current PTS contracts.

     f.   Necessarily, for the Trust, such investments in support of long term developments would require longer term commitments through contracts.

103.   **Maintenance of the Trust Estate**. It is freely acknowledge that the Trust does not generate sufficient revenue to meet the current maintenance requirements of the Trust estate. Purchasers are not likely to meet increased charges and indeed the Trust would likely to become uncompetitive if such additional revenue charges were made. It is essential that the Trust adopts a more flexible operating system, in order to reduce dependence on individual Ambulance Stations to allow it to rationalise the estate assets. Any income realised from such rationalisation should fund necessary improvements in the Trust Ambulance Fleet. As noted previously, the Estates review is now tasked to address that issue.

ADVANCE WITH CARE

LONG TERM FINANCIAL PLANNING

104. The overall Financial Management strategy of the Trust is the recovery of the full cost of provision of the service to our customers who, in the main, have defined and limited resources available for the purchase of Ambulance Services.

105. The Trust recognises that external factors affect both the amounts of funding available and the demands placed on these funds in a changing national and local environment for the provision of Healthcare.

106. These factors are leading the Trust to evaluate, on an ongoing basis all the likely scenarios that may emerge. The Trust proposes to continually evaluate the worst case scenario to ensure that the Trust remains a viable and financially strong organisation for the provision of Ambulance Services to both Purchasers and Patients.

107. The current block capital allocation is inadequate to achieve the recommended vehicle fleet standards. Action will be taken to expand this allocation in FY 93/94 together with an initial injection of capital to bring the complete Fleet, to the standards expected by purchasers, by FY 95/96.

108. **Capital Programme** The priorities of the Trust capital expenditure programme are:

    a.   To maintain the Emergency Ambulance Fleet within the recommended age and mileage standards.

    b.   To improve the Non Emergency Ambulance Fleet.

    c.   To fund improved communication and IT developments.

    d.   To replace medical equipment and to fund enhancements.

INCOME GENERATION

109. It is planned that income generation will grow significantly, during the next 3 years, through the exploitation of appropriate and available resources, to develop the areas where initial progress has been made. Such additional income will be essential for the Trust to meet its cost efficiency targets and to meet shortfalls anticipated in capital and revenue required for future developments.

FUND RAISING

110. The Ambulance Services have traditionally received support from the public to purchase equipment not normally available through normal revenue funding. The total annual income from this source is approximately £150K.

ADVANCE WITH CARE

111. The Staffordshire Heartstart Fund, founded in 1989, has contributed over £300K to date, to the provision of defibrillators, pulse oximeters, and a variety of other equipment and training aids.

112. Contributions within Staffordshire towards the Regional Air Ambulance are likely to reach £100K by the end of FY 92/93.

113. The Trust intends to continue supporting initiatives to priority need including:

    a.   The regional air ambulance.

    b.   The provision of pulse oximeters to all emergency ambulances.

    c.   The introduction of 12 lead ECG equipment with telemetry links to acute hospitals.

    d.   Public CPR training.

STRATEGY FOR A FINANCIAL FRAMEWORK FOR THE FUTURE

114. The Trust recognises the need to have a depth of finance skill and expertise within its organisation. It will support the NHSME initiative "Framework for the Future" which aims to provide for the development of financial staff at all levels.

115. The Finance Director has been tasked to work closely with the Director of Human Resources to ensure that there are clear job specifications for all financial appointments, that training needs for all financial are determined and plans made to implement them.

116. The Trust will also provide financial training for all budget holders.

COST IMPROVEMENTS AND EFFICIENCIES TO ACHIEVE VALUE FOR MONEY

117. The cost improvement strategy aims to achieve value for money and cash-releasing cost improvements. Detailed plans include :

    a.   Reduction in Operational vehicle fleet.

    b.   Introduction of more efficient operating procedures within core services.

    c.   Rationalisation of the Trust estate.

    d.   Reduction in overtime and sickness rates.

    e.   Reviewing Trust charges and ensuring that they remain competitive.

    f.   Reducing management costs as a proportion of the total (revenue) costs.

118. **Audit**. The internal and external audit of the Trust will be used to:

a. Maintain and evaluate systems which safeguard the Trust's assets.

b. Ensure "value for money" (VFM) exercises are initiated and completed continuously.

c. Review management systems and methods to ensure effective working practices.

d. Ensure that systems are such that external audit costs are reduced to a minimum.

KEY CONSTRAINTS

119. Key constraints are :

a. Without increased capital funding the Trust will not be able to maintain the level of either its current estate or vehicle fleet. The Trust will have to consider the reorientation and rationalisation of its capital to meet current requirements to enable it to expand its business and customer base in new market areas.

b. Inflation above contracted levels. Working methods will be constantly reviewed in order to keep costs down whilst maintaining quality.

c. Pressure on purchasers over the next three years is likely to be such that there will be little opportunity to increase revenue in order to support developments.

PROJECTED ACTIVITY, INCOME AND EXPENDITURE - 1993 TO 1996

120. An outline of the projected activity, income and expenditure is at:

a. **Annex A**. Projected Activity and Contracts for Services - 1993 to 1996.

b. **Annex B**. Major Expenditure Programme - 1993 to 1996.

c. **Annex C**. Manpower Planning Targets - 1993 to 1996.

PRINCIPAL FINANCIAL OBJECTIVES

121. Ensure the future financial viability of the Trust.

122. Maintain and develop a Trust budgetary system, both in terms of activity and resources, that devolves responsibility and accountability and allows for accurate and timely monitoring and reporting.

123.   Provide and develop an accurate, flexible and timely costing system for all Trust activities.

124.   Create an ongoing cash-releasing, cost improvement programme as a reserve against inflation and to provide for developments/improvements in service delivery.

125.   Maintain a strict internal audit system which provides safeguards for trust assets and which also allows for "value for money" exercises and management review.

126.   Maintain regular risk assessment procedures and activities.

127.   Maintain detailed trust financial plans for three years in advance and long term costing plans for major developments ten years in advance.

128.   Design and implement throughout the Trust a staff development and education strategy in financial management.

HUMAN RESOURCES STRATEGY

129. The Human Resources Strategy includes the strategies for:

   a.   Personnel Management.

   b.   Health, Safety and Welfare.

   c.   Training and Training Development.

130. The quality of service provided by the Trust is heavily dependent on the ability and morale of our staff. It is essential that we constantly seek to improve the personnel management and leadership skills of all our managers to retain a dedicated and highly motivated workforce.

AIM

131. The aim of the Trust's Human Resources Strategy is to provide the highest standards of personnel management and training and to ensure that we provide a healthy and supportive environment for all our employees.

PARTICIPATION IN NATIONAL HUMAN RESOURCES INITIATIVES

132. **Investment in People**. The "Investors in People" initiative, promoted by the Training Enterprise Council, provides a national standard for effective human resource management. This Trust Board intends to make a commitment that the Trust will train and develop individuals on recruitment and throughout their employment, continually reviewing and assessing achievements against business objectives.

133. **Equal Opportunities**. The Trust is an equal opportunity employer, and has introduced a policy to substantiate that fact. The aim of the policy is to ensure that no job applicant or employee receives less favourable treatment on the grounds of sex, marriage status, physical disability, race, colour, creed, ethnic or national origins or sexual orientation or social background or is disadvantaged by conditions or requirement which cannot be shown to be justifiable. Selection criteria and procedures are to be frequently reviewed to ensure that individuals are selected, promoted and treated on the basis of their relative merits and abilities. All employees are given equal opportunity and encouraged to progress within the organisation. The Trust is committed to an ongoing programme of action to prove this policy is fully effective.

134. **Opportunity 2000**. This initiative which aims to ensure that women are given opportunity to play a full role in management is strongly supported by the Trust. Women already make up 40% of our Non Executive and 50% of Executive posts on the Trust Board. Women are similarly well represented in Trust general management posts and

within the management of the Patient Transport Service. We do recognise that there are currently no women managers within the A&E ambulance service and we are committed to improving that situation over the next three years.

TARGETS

135. **Post Proficiency Training**. The Trust does not currently meet the requirement to provide post proficiency training for all A&E staff every 3 three years, but has plans to do so by FY 1995/96.

136. **External Training - Income Generation Targets**. Targets for net income generated from external training are projected to rise from £25K in FY 1993/4 to £75K by FY 1995/6.

PRINCIPAL OBJECTIVES

137. **Personnel Management**.

a. Develop and maintain effective manpower planning processes to ensure use of the minimum appropriate resources to meet the tasks required.

b. Develop and maintain effective selection, recruitment and retention procedures to reduce wastage and conserve initial training resources.

c. Develop the capability to negotiate directly with all staff on terms and conditions of service.

d. Monitor performance to identify employment potential and training requirements of all staff.

e. Provide clear lines of progression for all cadres of staff.

138. **Health, Safety and Welfare**.

a. Ensure compliance with Health & Safety legislation providing for the employment of staff in the workplace.

b. Introduce measures, within available resources, to reduce sickness and absence levels of employees to minimal levels.

c. Develop a welfare and counselling service for all employees.

d. Establish and encourage the development of the Ambulance Service Retirement Association.

139. **Training and Development**.

a.   Develop a training needs assessment to all categories of work and all cadres of employment.

b.   Introduce formal training for all managers.

c.   Provide a trained cadre of 156 operational paramedics by 1996.

d.   Develop the capability and introduce the NVQ method of training for all Trust personnel.

e.   Increase the provision of training in first aid and related safety procedures within the NHS and the private sector.

SUPPORT SERVICES STRATEGY

AIM

140.   To provide timely, cost effective and efficient support to the individual Directorates of the Trust to enable them to meet their agreed objectives in the areas of:

    a.   Sales & Marketing.

    b.   Public Affairs and Internal Communications.

    c.   Estates.

    d.   Vehicle Fleet.

    e.   Supply.

TARGETS

141.   **Contracts With Core NHS Purchasers**. To move to the provision of three year contracts with all our NHS purchasers by FY 1995/96.

142.   **Income Generation**. To identify and secure, through active sales and marketing of Trust capabilities to secure net income generation for the Trust, additional to core NHS contracts, of £40K in FY 1993/4 rising to £150K by 1995/96.

143.   **Estate**. To complete the rationalisation of Trust estate assets to meet operational requirements and Estatecode standards by 1996.

144.   **Vehicle Fleet**. To maintain, subject to purchaser specifications, the NHS recommended standard for the Trust Vehicle Fleet of a maximum age of 7 years or maximum mileage of 140,000 for all Emergency Ambulances and to adopt the standard for Non Emergency Ambulances by the close of FY 95/96.

PRINCIPAL OBJECTIVES

145.   To play a lead role in the promotion of the Trust in customer relations and marketing in order to consolidate and develop existing contracts and to meet the principal priorities of customers in both the NHS and non-NHS market sectors.

146.   To ensure that both external and internal audiences are informed of the objectives and achievements of the Trust.

ADVANCE WITH CARE

147.   To develop a long-term estate ownership programme that meets the operational needs of the Trust within the resources available through capital acquisition and the funding capabilities of Purchasers.

148.   To ensure that the Health & Safety and Firecode obligations are met within the Trust estate.

149.   To purchase, maintain and manage the vehicle fleet, meeting the requirements of Purchasers and Operations and providing value for money in their initial purchase, operation and resale.

150.   To provide and maintain an improving procurement, supply and accounting system for all Trust purchases which is both cost effective and efficient.

151.   To achieve a 2% cost efficiency saving each year through the reduction in sickness and overtime rates, improved utilisation of Trust assets and the absorption of increased activity without increased resources.

152.   To identify, research and develop new, net income from non-core services in the public, private and voluntary sectors to provide additional income for development.

ADVANCE WITH CARE

CONCLUSIONS

153.   The Staffordshire Ambulance Service is justifiably proud of its achievements in its first year as a Trust and particularly the relationships that it is developing with its staff and the Community Health Councils of Staffordshire.

154.   We have set robust targets and objectives for the Trust to achieve over the next three years. We have done so conscious of the limited availability of our additional funding to support developments. Great emphasis has therefore been placed on the constant improvement in internal efficiency and the development of open relationships with our purchasers.

155.   The Trust's unique achievement in securing the non-emergency ambulance contract for the Wolverhampton Health Authority demonstrates to our current purchasers and our potential competitors the quality of our service and capability of our dedicated staff.

156.   Our Plans outline a radical approach to the provision of emergency ambulance services in the future, which will work closer with the primary care sector and the providers of acute hospital treatment.

157.   We look forward to our "advance with care" with confidence.

ANNEXES

A. Projected Activity and Contracts for Services - 1993 to 1996:

B. Major Expenditure Programme - 1993 to 1996:

C. Manpower Planning Targets - 1993 to 1996.

37

CIPFA

BUSINESS PLANS

A Compendium

HEALTH

**West Dorset Mental Health
NHS Trust**

Business Plan 1993/94

Note:

Appendices detailing current service provision; management structure; activity analysis and current service investments are not reproduced.

WEST DORSET MENTAL HEALTH NHS TRUST

BUSINESS PLAN

1993/4

February 1993

WEST DORSET MENTAL HEALTH NHS TRUST

BUSINESS PLAN 1993/94

CONTENTS

Successful mental health services rely on a flexible workforce whose skills include the ability to network across agency boundaries and respond effectively to primary care demands.

WEST DORSET MENTAL HEALTH NHS TRUST

FOREWORD

The West Dorset Mental Health Trust is at the forefront of development for mental health services, in working towards meeting patient needs in a community setting. The business plan reflects the continual learning process and management of change, which is involved in building high quality services for the people of West Dorset.

The strategic direction of the Trust is focused in working with primary health care to provide specialist support for those with a mental illness or learning disability. The Dorset Health Commission shares this objective and supports the continued development of community mental health services.

A key priority for 1993/94 is the need to remain financially viable. The organisational review undertaken at the end of 1992 will be implemented in April 1993, enabling the Trust to be responsive and flexible to external influences, while having a clear direction and improved management structures. We look forward to 1993/94 with continued confidence that the Trust will be able to meet the challenges that all who work in the NHS will face in the next few months and years.

ALISTAIR HOWIE
Chief Executive

1.   EXECUTIVE SUMMARY

The West Dorset Mental Health NHS Trust faces many challenges in the coming year, but is confident that it will continue to build on the reputation for innovation and excellence, which has been achieved by the closure of two large institutions and the development of high quality community services.

*   A fundamental review of the activity and management arrangements of the Trust was undertaken in the autumn of 1992, to address inappropriate managerial systems and a growing financial deficit. The review has resulted in improved management and organisational structures, which are being implemented in April 1993, and a financial recovery plan, which has been agreed with the Dorset Health Commission and the Management Executive.

*   With a clearer strategic direction and robust management structure, the Trust will be well placed to address the many national and local priorities, in partnership with other agencies. The successful implementation of care in the community remains a prime objective, building on working relationships and joint planning arrangements.

*   Developing links with general practitioners will have major benefits for service delivery, in terms of improved responsiveness to GPs' needs, the provision of expertise and advice in developing new service models.

*   New opportunities and strategies will continue to be explored in the interests of patients and carers, and the Trust will be working closely with Dorset Health Commission in the development of services. The Trust is ready to respond and adapt to the rapidly changing health care environment, working in partnership with primary care providers, in developing specialist treatment for those with mental health problems and learning disabilities, in the most appropriate environment.

2.   MISSION AND VALUES

The Mission Statement of the Trust is:

"The business of the West Dorset Mental Health Trust is to provide a full range of high quality specialist hospital and community services which are accessible and responsive to the needs of individuals with a psychiatric disorder or learning disabilities and their carers."

The mission statement will be reviewed in consultation with staff and other agencies by September 1993, to ensure that the Trust's values are fully owned by those who work in providing its services.

To enable the Mission Statement to be achievable, the following primary aims have been adopted:

*   to provide a high quality personalised service which responds swiftly, is responsive to the individual's need and which at all times seeks to foster the individual's independence, dignity and responsibility;

*   to involve patients, residents or clients and their families or carers as much as possible in the pattern of care for an individual;

*   to provide the service through a balanced provision of central and local facilities so as to maintain patients, residents or clients in the setting of an ordinary life whenever possible;

*   to strive, through the provision of professional support in the community, to promote and encourage any practice which will lead to a more positive approach to mental health and the prevention of mental illness, or which will enhance the status of people with a learning disability;

*　　to work in positive partnership with Dorset Social Services and other statutory agencies, and relevant voluntary organisations to ensure that a 'seamless' service is provided against a background of the shared philosophy, standards and goals that have been set out in the joint planning agreements and joint service specifications

The Business of the Trust

The Trust provides a range of specialist services for people in West Dorset with mental illness and learning disabilities including diagnosis, assessment and treatment. The underlying service philosophy is to provide acute, rehabilitative and continuing care in an appropriate environment to enable each individual to lead as independent a life as possible in a domestic setting.

The Trust ensures that all provisions of the Mental Health Act 1983 and any subsequent amendments are met.

The following services are provided by the Trust:

- **Acute Mental Illness:** the strategic aim of the service is to improve support in the community for people with acute mental illness and provide alternatives to inpatient admission where possible

  Inpatient beds are available at Forston Clinic and Blackdown for intensive care

- **Long–term mental illness:** six multi–disciplinary community teams established jointly with Dorset Social Services provide increased support for the mentally ill in the community and their carers. Day care is offered at seven centres, and outpatient clinics are held weekly in Weymouth, Bridport, Dorchester, Sherborne, Blandford and Shaftesbury. A limited range of educational and employment facilities are provided.

- **The Elderly:** inpatient beds are provided at Forston, Blandford, Weymouth and Bridport (Greenfields opening April 1993). Local resource centres offer day and respite care for the elderly mentally frail, with support for carers.

  Multi–disciplinary community teams specialising in supporting the elderly mentally ill with dementia and their carers, are based in Weymouth, Dorchester, Bridport, Sherborne, Blandford and North Dorset.

- **Learning Disabilities:** a range of support services is provided including community based residential care, (in conjunction with Dorset Residential Homes) specialist day care, respite care and community mental health teams. Specialist services are provided for those with challenging behaviour.

- **Services for Alcohol and Drug Abuse:** confidential services are provided for those with drug and alcohol problems, including counselling, advice and support. Services are based in Dorchester with outreach centres in Bridport, Weymouth and North Dorset, and are managed by the Trust in collaboration with two voluntary organisations.

- **Services for Mentally Disordered Offenders:** Consultant Psychiatrists provide a service to the Magistrates' Courts and the Crown Prosecution Service including admissions via the Courts under the Mental Health Act.

The 'MenDos' scheme provides opportunities to divert offenders from criminal justice courts. The scheme involves close liaison with the Probation Service, social workers, the police and the courts, and is based on a multi–disciplinary panel including a Community Psychiatric Nurse.

Corporate Objectives

The Trust's Corporate Objectives for 1993/94 provide the framework for the business plan and incorporate the management agenda for the next year. They are based on the need to achieve improved management of resources and increase organisational effectiveness. The corporate objectives will be reflected in individual managers' objectives to ensure that they can be delivered, and are underpinned by the strategic aim of continuing to develop care in the community in preference to hospital treatment.

9

WEST DORSET MENTAL HEALTH NHS TRUST

KEY CORPORATE OBJECTIVES

Strategic Objective	Key Tasks/Critical Success Factors
To provide specialist mental health and learning disability services, supporting the aim of primary care as the principal focus for the delivery of health services	To collaborate with Dorset Health Commission in reviewing the provision of mental health services throughout Dorset
	To develop closer working relationships with GP practices, by ensuring that every GP practice is linked to an area service organisation.
	To develop area based service organisations which relate strongly to primary health care, with multi–disciplinary management
	To implement improved management structures following internal reviews
To develop community based services in response to the external environment which maximise available resources, increase access, and meet patient needs.	To increase the involvement of users and carers in planning and reviewing services, and ensure that management arrangements are responsive to local needs.
	To support the development of the West Dorset Mental Health Forum.
	To continue to shift resources from hospital to community care, strengthening community support and communications systems.
	To develop counselling services and forensic psychiatry services.
To ensure the continued viability of the organisation.	To implement the financial recovery programme, develop contracting, costing mechanisms and ensure the timely and accurate production of financial management information.
	To maintain stringent financial control and achieve improved value for money

10

WEST DORSET MENTAL HEALTH NHS TRUST

KEY CORPORATE OBJECTIVES

Strategic Objective	Key Tasks/Critical Success Factors
To develop services for learning disabilities, including residential care	To agree and implement a strategy for delivery of services for learning disabilities.
	To review the provision of residential care.
	To support recommendations contained in a national review of services
	To develop and agree a strategy for challenging behaviour services.
	To develop proposals in collaboration with other agencies for day services for learning disabilities.
	To develop services for respite care.
To ensure that public confidence is maintained following the development of services in the community	To develop well defined policies and procedures and communicate these through an open management style.
	To develop public awareness through the promotion of the needs of those with mental illness
To work increasingly with and through other agencies to improve community support services and the health status of the local population.	To further develop partnerships involved in the Health of the Nation and other national and local initiatives.
	To network with other agencies to ensure the effective implementation of community care and the Criminal Justice Act.
	To stimulate the development of support strategies for people with con-tinuing mental health needs which will enhance their quality of life.

11

WEST DORSET MENTAL HEALTH NHS TRUST

KEY CORPORATE OBJECTIVES

Strategic Objective	Key Tasks/Critical Success Factors
To develop a Human Resources strategy which supports the Trust's strategic objectives.	To appoint a Director of Human Resources.
	To review the skills necessary for changing patterns of service delivery and enhance by means of training programmes if appropriate.
	To develop and implement a communications strategy, for both internal and external communications.
To continue to develop the quality assurance strategy and programmes, improving standards of service and outcome of care	Identify and implement the action required to rectify problems affecting the quality of services.
	Identify outcomes of care
	Continuous assessment to ensure services are delivered within available resources and to agreed standards.
	Continued development and definition of standards of care for all areas.
To continue to evaluate and develop service innovations	The dissemination of good practice to other service providers and purchasers.
	The establishment of local training courses for the management of institutional closures.
	To collaborate with other agencies in the development of social policy in mental health.

12

Strategic Development

The West Dorset Mental Health NHS Trust has a unique position at the leading edge of developing community–based mental health services, having closed Coldharbour Hospital in 1990/91 and Herrison Hospital in 1991/92. The underlying philosophy of providing specialist supportive care services has been recognised nationally, and past achievements provide a strong base from which to further develop services. An internal review, undertaken in the autumn of 1992, will enable the Trust to develop the decentralised management model necessary to realise the objective of further enhancing services in the Community.

- The proposals agreed by the Trust Board provide a clear strategic direction underpinned by a vision and values, together with a multi-disciplinary management structure responsive to a changing health care environment.

- The Trust recognises that efficient and effective services to patients depend on a partnership between professional staff, patients and managers as well as within the wider community. A community development model based on a multi–disciplinary approach with Social Services, primary health care providers, voluntary and other agencies, will improve access to services and user involvement.

- The Trust recognises the importance of primary health care and will seek to work in partnership with primary health care providers, while strongly maintaining the promotion and delivery of specialist services which the Trust provides.

13

- The Trust is committed to developing further specialist treatment in the home and the community, including a home based service for those in crisis.

- The Trust continues to promote an improved quality of life for those with mental illness and learning disabilities and the provision of services for patients as near as possible to where they live. Organisational arrangements are being established which relate directly to primary health care provision.

Organisational Development

● **Financial Recovery Plan**

The review provided the basis of the financial recovery process, and enabled the establishment of new management arrangements. A significant financial deficit had been identified in 1991/92, as the contract with Dorset Health Commission did not fully take into account some of the costs incurred by the Trust.

A recovery plan has been agreed with the Health Commission which means the Trust having to meet a large part of the deficit from within the organisation. Plans have been drawn up to try and minimise the impact on services and staff.

● **Service Development**

Revised management arrangements will be implemented from April 1993 following an internal review. It is planned to:

* establish Service Area Organisations, based on FHSA medical practice areas, for three localities – North Dorset, Dorchester and Bridport, and Weymouth and Portland

* provide a local management structure for the delivery of the specialist mental health services, including a crisis support service, and continuing support services

* provide the management structure for community mental health teams, staff employed in residential homes and specialist services.

Staff will be encouraged to become actively involved in service developments including suggestions for improvements in service provision.

15

- **Management Team**

A multidisciplinary management team will be responsible for:

- the management, planning and development of services, with service profiles established as part of the contracting process.

- the delivery of the contract agreed with the purchaser and the monitoring of standards.

- the establishment of strong working relationships with general practitioners

The management team will comprise a minimum of five people – a nurse, a medical consultant, a psychologist, an occupational therapist and a manager. A manager from the Social Services District Teams may also be included following consultation, and the involvement of the voluntary sector will be considered.

- **Management Arrangements**

The three service managers will be directly accountable to the Chief Executive, with responsibilities for:

- delivering the mental health and learning disability services in accordance with the agreed contract. All staff in each area will be accountable to the relevant service manager.

- budget management, including the ability to vire to meet service needs.

16

The objective of the new arrangements is to establish a decentralised management system, with strong links to primary care. Services will be agreed through the contracting process, based on clinical advice from the multidisciplinary team, and with local decision making on service priorities.

● **Corporate Development**

The role of the senior management structure is:

–   to implement policies, develop procedures and strategic overview to ensure effective management.

–   to promote the vision and values of the organisation, and ensure that operational arrangements are discharged

–   to implement the Trust's strategy and promote developments .

17

MAP OF THE AREA COVERED BY WEST DORSET MENTAL HEALTH NHS TRUST

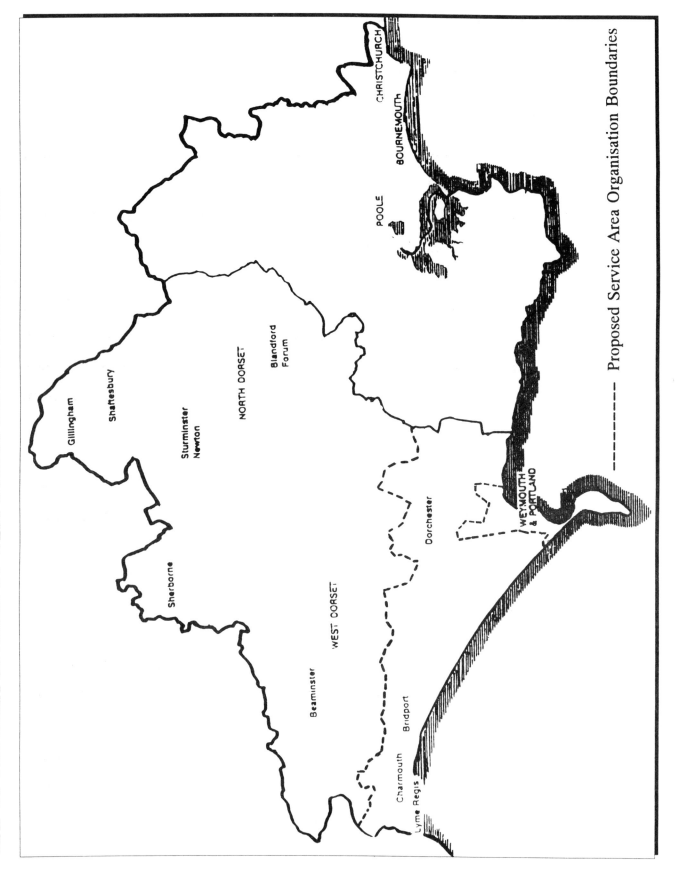

Gillingham

Shaftesbury

Sturminster
Newton

NORTH DORSET

Blandford
Forum

CHRISTCHURCH

BOURNEMOUTH

POOLE

Sherborne

Beaminster

WEST DORSET

Dorchester

WEYMOUTH
& PORTLAND

Charmouth

Bridport

Lyme Regis

———— Proposed Service Area Organisation Boundaries

3.   ENVIRONMENTAL ANALYSIS

Local Health Needs
---

*   The County of Dorset is relatively affluent compared to the rest of England and Wales, with 75.7% of the population owning their own homes and 83.9% with exclusive use of a bath or shower, inside WC, and with central heating.

*   The resident population for Dorset is 647,245 (1991 census), with distribution ranging from densely populated urban areas to sparsely populated rural areas. West Dorset is characterised by market towns interspersed by small villages, and a coastline which attracts many thousands of visitors every year.

*   There are no major industries in West Dorset, but there is a well established tourist industry centred mainly on the coastal resorts of Weymouth and Lyme Regis. The major employers are service industries, the Armed Forces, County Council and NHS. Farming is the major occupation in rural areas.

*   The population of West Dorset served by the West Dorset Mental Health Trust is 200,807, and is estimated to be 220,000 by 2001. There is a large population of pensioner households in Dorset (17.8%), with 24.1% in West Dorset. The numbers of those aged 75 years and over is predicted to increase rapidly in the next ten years, with important implications for future health service provision.

19

* Transport facilities and road links are relatively poor in parts of West Dorset, leading to problems of accessibility to health services. Housing is relatively expensive in West Dorset compared to the average for England and Wales.

* Weymouth and Portland has the highest proportion of lone parents (2.1%), children under 16 years, and unemployed young adults (11.3%).

* Although unemployment in West Dorset has generally been lower than the national average, the number of unemployed is rapidly increasing due mainly to the effects of the recession. In the 1991 census, 6.9% of males were unemployed in West Dorset and 3.4% of women.

  Unemployment is acknowledged to be associated with an increased risk of ill–health including depression, suicide and other mental illnesses. The proposed closure of Portland Naval Base in 1996 will further exacerbate the situation.

* The standardised mortality ratio (SMR) takes into account the age and sex structure of the population in comparing mortality rates. The SMR for Dorset in 1990 was 86 in comparison to the regional figure of 91 and 100 nationally. The rate for suicides is above the national average at 109 for men and 111 for women.

Purchaser Priorities

The major purchaser for services provided by the Trust is Dorset Health Commission, which accounts for 90.7% of Category A and B (patient) income. The Health Commission was formed to bring together the purchasing intentions of Dorset Health Authority and Dorset Family Health Services Authority. The aim of the Health Commission is:

–   to integrate primary and secondary care to secure the best possible delivery of health services within the resources available. The Trust works in close partnership with the Health Commission to achieve these aims and is strongly guided by the Health Commission's Strategic intentions. The Health Commission is reviewing its policy for the purchase of mental health services in 1993/94.

The following three priorities have been identified by the purchaser in relation to mental health services:–

*   **The five year rolling average death rate for suicide for males to be reduced by 25% by the year 2000;**

*   **75% of general practitioners should offer psychology or counselling services to patients on their premises by 1995;**

*   **The suicide rate of severely mentally ill people to be reduced by at least one–third by the year 2000.**

Mental Health is one of ten health gain areas identified by the Health Commission, to improve significantly the health and social functioning of people with mental illness and the promotion of positive mental health.

21

4. MARKETING STRATEGY

The provision of health services will become increasingly competitive as the effects of the internal market become more pronounced. The Trust recognises the need to develop new markets and services with other purchasers, as the reliance on one major purchaser makes it particularly vulnerable.

The marketing strategy of the Trust is to actively identify areas of unmet need and discuss with purchasers the development of new services following an analysis and appraisal of the external environment. The Trust's values will continue to underpin all proposed service developments, which will be based on the individual needs of patients and carers.

Existing Position

The Trust has gained a national reputation for expertise and innovation by becoming one of the first health providers in the country to close its institutions for mental health and learning disabilities and develop services in the community which are cost effective and efficient.

As a first wave NHS Trust, the organisation faced many new demands which have resulted in an improved management structure and better utilisation of staff skills, including increased involvement of clinicians in management. The Trust has shown that it is responsive to change, and the new management structure will enable services to be moved even closer to primary care.

The facilities currently used to provide services together with present and projected activity levels are detailed in Appendix 1.

Competitive Position

The West Dorset Mental Health NHS Trust is one of three Trusts in Dorset providing community health services in collaboration with primary care teams and Social Services. Dorset Healthcare NHS Trust provides community and mental health services to residents in East Dorset, and West Dorset Community Health NHS Trust provides community services in West Dorset.

Dorset Healthcare has developed a different model for the delivery of mental health services with greater dependence on hospital care. The development of two distinct service models will need to be addressed by the main purchaser, together with the provision of county wide specialist services.

No other providers are currently perceived as a direct threat to the financial viability of the Trust, although there are other Trusts across the county borders in Devon, Wiltshire and Somerset and other providers may enter the market following provider mergers or reconfigurations. There is expected to be an application for 'fourth wave' NHS Trust status from a Mental Health provider in Yeovil. The health care market will continue to be actively monitored to assess any current or future threats or opportunities.

23

Opportunities in the Market

● **Dorset Health Commission**

The Health Commission will continue to be the major purchaser of services for the next five years, and requires the Trust to apply for 'preferred provider' status.   There are areas, however, where extra services could be developed, particularly for highly specialised services. These services, such as semi–secure accommodation, are presently provided as Extra Contractual Referrals outside Dorset. The Trust will review the resources necessary to provide such services on a county–wide basis in response to any future requests from the Health Commission. The Health Commission is gradually building up a knowledge base of the health care needs of its residents, and a number of services have been identified for possible future investment, including:

*   head injuries rehabilitation
*   services for eating disorders
*   forensic specialist services.

The feasibility of developing such services will be the focus of continuing discussions with the Health Commission and other NHS Trusts in Dorset.

● **Primary Care**

Two GP practices in West Dorset are fundholders, at Sherborne and Shaftesbury, with list sizes of 5,900 and 12,200 respectively. From April 1993 they will be able to purchase community nursing care and other services which the Trust could provide.

24

The Trust will need to develop relationships with GP fundholders and monitor purchasing plans to ensure responsiveness to their needs, particularly offering advice and support, such as the development of service specifications. West Dorset is unusual, however, compared to the rest of the Wessex Region, as less than 1% of the population is covered by GP fundholders (25% in Dorset as a whole).

Two general practices in Lyme Regis and Charmouth will also be able to purchase services from the Trust in 1993/94 as part of the Lyme Community Care Project, to directly provide a range of services for patients including community psychiatric nursing.

A structured approach to discussions with GPs about service developments will be implemented by the Trust to include:

*   all GPs visited annually by service manager and consultant
*   a communications strategy with GPs involving regular visits, feedback and support
*   close liaison with GP fundholders to discuss their purchasing intentions.

As the key objective of the Health Commission is establishing primary care as the principal focus for health and health care, the Trust is well placed to improve its responsiveness to GPs' needs and will be working closely with GPs in developing models for delivery of mental health services through primary care. GPs have requested access to counselling services for their patients, and the Health Commission has agreed targets that 75% of GPs should offer such services on their premises by 1995. The Trust will be supporting this aim by either developing counselling services under the management of the clinical psychology service or advising GPs on procurement of a service.

● **Other Purchasers**

Wessex RHA contracts with the Trust for the provision of Old Long Stay places, which forms 8.7% of patient income. This is likely to reduce over the next five years through natural wastage, and will have to be replaced by other contracts for the Trust to remain viable, although there are options to reconfigure services.

Other opportunities for development include:

*   the provision of new services for those with mental illness or learning disability under the provisions of the Criminal Justice Act,
*   the provision of medical services to the four penal establishments in Dorset.

The Trust provides a counselling service to Dorset Police Force, which is expected to continue in the near future. The securing of contracts to provide services commissioned by Dorset Social Services is also under consideration.

The remainder of the Trust's patient income (0.6%) emanates from other health authorities and commissions outside Dorset, for patients living near the county boundary, those residing with their families in Dorset but whose home address is elsewhere, and those referred for specialist services. The Trust will continue to monitor the provision of specialist services with a view to extending services to meet local needs and attracting referrals from outside the county.

The Trust is planning to develop a training and consultancy package for other service providers and purchasers in the management of closure programmes. The Trust's expertise has been recognised nationally and can be built upon to develop market opportunities.

A further scheme under discussion is the training and service provision related to 'post traumatic stress syndrome'.

● **Growth**

For 1993/94 the Wessex Regional allocation will increase by 1.48% above inflation, the highest growth rate amongst the 14 English RHAs. Dorset Health Commission has allocated a 1.17% growth above inflation from the £244 million budget in 1993/94. These figures represent a potential for new developments, and the Trust will be discussing several possible investment options including a business case for a PAS (Patient Administration System), as this will be critical in developing a home treatment service.

5. **NATIONAL AND LOCAL PRIORITIES**

The following national priorities will be incorporated in the services provided by the Trust.

> **National Priorities**

● **Health of the Nation**

Mental Health has been identified as one of five key areas for health gain in the White Paper. Mental illness is acknowledged as a leading cause of illness and disability, accounting nationally for 14% of certificated sickness leave, 14% of NHS inpatient costs and 23% of NHS drug costs. The main targets are:

– To improve significantly the health and social functioning of mentally ill people

– To reduce the overall suicide rate by at least 15% by the year 2000

– To reduce the suicide rate of severely mentally ill people by at least 33% by the year 2000

■ The Trust will actively seek ways of reducing suicide rates and will continue to develop multi–disciplinary audit of all suicides (and undetermined death) of people in contact with the Trust's mental health services.

■ Community mental health services and family intervention strategies will also be strengthened and suicide risk will be assessed in collaboration with other agencies

■ A register of vulnerable people has already been established based on the Care Programme Approach

28

■   A criminal justice diversion scheme (MenDos) has been developed to provide an alternative to custody for mentally disordered offenders. A clinical psychologist will be appointed in 1993/94.

The concept of health alliances is supported, and the Trust will continue to work with other agencies in support of the targets in the White Paper. The Trust has continued to support the work of the Community Alcohol and Drug Advisory Service (CADAS) with the proposals for an appointment of a probation officer to work with the service, for implementation in 1993/94.

●   **Care in the Community**

The Trust recognises that the future success of community care depends upon collaborative partnerships with other agencies to ensure the continued development of appropriate services in the community, including Learning Disability services.

*   For mental illness services, a locally based response service for crisis intervention will be developed including the provision of home–based crisis services.

*   The support for people with long–term mental health problems and their carers will be strengthened, based on care management principles.

*   The Health Commission has also supported proposals to improve facilities at Blackdown in Weymouth, supported proposals to develop psychology services and the establishment of a mental health team base in Blandford.

29

*   The establishment of local resource centres for the elderly confused and their carers will offer day and respite care:

–   The Greenfields Unit in Bridport will operate a service from April 1993 to improve support and respite facilities for carers including at night and weekends.

–   A service based at the Yeatman Hospital is also being planned with the support of the Health Commission.

● **Patient's Charter**

The Trust has developed its own Patient's Charter in line with the national Patient's Charter initiative. The further development of the Charter nationally, particularly the Priority Care Charter, will influence the Trust's Charter. Local standards have been developed, including the right of outpatients to be given an appointment within 4 weeks of referral.

The Trust will continue to develop services in direct response to patients' and carers' needs by fully involving service users in the planning and reviewing of services. The national Patient's Charter initiative will continue to influence the Trust's quality assurance programme.

● **Opportunity 2000**

The Trust introduced an Equal Opportunities Policy in 1989 and has developed action plans for ensuring equality of opportunity which incorporate the Opportunity 2000 initiative. Regular monitoring takes place on:

–   career progression based on gender, and the identification of barriers to progress

30

–   the ethnic origin of staff and the numbers of registered disabled who are employed by the Trust

Positive employment policies and practices have been implemented to meet the requirements of the Opportunity 2000 initiative.

The profiles of women members of the Trust Board and women in senior posts will be highlighted as role models.

●   **Junior Doctors' Hours**

The Trust employs associate psychiatrist grade staff who work an average of 74 hours per week (including on call duties). Guidance is awaited as part of the EC directive on this issue, which will be addressed in 1993/94 if necessary.

> **Local Priorities**

● **Mental Health Services**

The strategy of the Dorset Health Commission is to promote mental well–being and the prevention of mental illness as well as to secure comprehensive services which provide primary care, acute care, rehabilitation and continuing care for adults of all ages with mental illness.

The following prime objectives and priorities have been identified:

- to contain and reduce psychiatric morbidity;

- to secure a positive approach to mental health through the establishment of a health promotion service;

- to secure a service which can respond swiftly through settings which are as domestic as possible;

- to procure a range of high quality hospital and community based services for the care of people with acute mental illness;

- to procure services for the care of elderly severely mentally ill people (ESMI) in their local communities wherever possible;

- to provide support and encouragement to other statutory and voluntary agencies who care for people with mental illness;

- to secure the development of community services for those requiring specialist mental health care, including nursing, psychology and occupational therapy services.

In shaping the strategy for mental health services, the Trust wishes to play an active role in advising the Health Commission, and in participating in joint planning arrangements and strategic planning. The Trust fully endorses the

32

strategic direction of the Health Commission in establishing primary care as the focus for the delivery of health services.

To realign services to meet this objective, Service Area Organisations will be developed to strengthen mental health services.

The Trust is working with the Health Commission to plan specialist services locally in response to GP needs, including counselling services and an eating disorders service. Work is also continuing with GPs towards the development of good practice guidelines for the assessment and management of common psychiatric conditions and for protocols for the use of the Mental Health Act.

● **Learning Disabilities**

The strategy of the Health Commission is:

*   to ensure that the individual needs of people with learning disabilities are identified and met through a comprehensive range of appropriate community–based services with the aim of enabling people to achieve maximum levels of independence and quality of life

*   to ensure, in collaboration with other agencies, the provision of suitable housing for people with learning disabilities which should, as far as possible, be ordinary housing in the community

*   to support and develop educational training and employment opportunities for people with learning disabilities

*   to work closely with the voluntary sector in joint planning and needs assessment in order to ensure the provision of a comprehensive integrated service

33

The Trust is committed to developing services for people with learning disabilities, and extending the availability of respite care. Specialist services are provided for those with challenging behaviour and special needs.

A learning disabilities strategy group has been established by the Trust on a multi–disciplinary basis to promote discussion and good practice and develop services. The Trust will implement the strategy and assess the feasibility for extending the provision of residential care, and support the advocacy programme being developed by the Dorset Health Commission and Social Services.

6. RESOURCES

> **Human Resources**

The future success of the Trust is dependent on developing an effective organisation which is responsive to change. **A key objective in the achievement of this aim is the development of a human resources strategy which will result in a caring, well motivated, cost effective and productive workforce within the context of the Trust's business plans. The staff who work for the Trust are its most important asset, and will continue to be valued and cared for by the Trust.**

The development of skills necessary to deliver high quality services in the community is a key priority of the Trust.

It is anticipated that a Human Resources Director will be appointed in April/May 1993, following which a review will be undertaken of the skills necessary for the changing patterns of service delivery. A communications strategy will be developed and implemented to ensure effective communications both internally and externally.

35

● **Staffing Profile**

An analysis of manpower resources as at 1 April 1993 is set out below:

Staff group	WTE
Psychiatric Staff	6.00
Other medical staff	6.64
Nursing Staff:	
– Qualified	211.52
– Unqualified	206.26
Occupational Therapy	19.62
Other rehabilitation staff	30.93
Psychology	9.00
Management	10.00
Administration	53.66
Ancillary Support Staff	34.13
TOTAL	587.76

N.B.   New developments have not been included

The turnover rate for the period 1 January 1992 to 31 December 1992 was 13.74%, which includes the closure of Herrison Hospital. The predicted turnover for the year ending 31 March 1993 is 8.16%, highlighting the difficult external economic conditions.

Overall sickness rates are low compared to surrounding NHS employers, and the national NHS figure of 6%. The sickness absence level for 1 April – 30 November 1992 was 4.27%, a reduction of 0.43% for the same period last year. Sickness rates are monitored and management action taken where appropriate.

● Training and Development

The Training Strategy developed in 1992/93 will continue to be implemented with priorities being identified on a 6 monthly basis. The following areas will be addressed:

- further health and safety training to comply with EC workplace regulations
- skills training for crisis support in the community
- management development training for staff at middle to junior management levels
- training for challenging behaviour service
- general skills development for professional staff

It is planned to establish a Training Strategy group to co–ordinate training programmes and review ongoing training needs.

The Trust recognises the need to develop advisory systems and support for professional advice and development.

● Job Evaluation

A skills–based job evaluation scheme has been implemented to ensure the appropriate skills are in place for the changing patterns of service delivery and the provision of one common pay and grading structure. The target is to complete the evaluation by the end of 1993/94, followed by an annual review of skills for all staff. It is envisaged that the new structure will be based on the competencies required for each job, with the appropriate reflection in pay.

● Performance Management

Individual performance assessment will be introduced by the end of the financial year and monitored mid–way through 1993. Individual performance review for senior staff will also be reviewed.

● **Terms and Conditions**

The Trust has developed a single pay spine for all staff on Trust terms and conditions. The target is to retain all staff on Trust terms and conditions by 1997/98. As at the end of January 1993, 30% of employees were employed on Trust terms and conditions.

● **Equal Opportunities**

Action plans have been developed for ensuring equality of opportunity, and these are continuously monitored. The targets outlined in Opportunity 2000 have been incorporated in the action plans, and places have been reserved on the 'Springboard' programme to develop non–managerial female employees.

● **Implications of the Hospital closure programme**

The closure of Herrison and Coldharbour Hospitals poses a number of long–term implications:

■ the continued payment of long–term protection, the majority of which will continue until 1995/96 with a few extending to 2002.

■ the surplus of qualified nursing staff following skill–mix reviews, particularly at Forston Clinic, although this is being partially addressed with the closure of Kingston Ward in March 1993.

■ short–term protection concerning the redeployment of hospital staff will cease by the end of the current year.

■ the need to address the financial disincentive in hospital closure as a result of the Management Executive's Efficiency Index initiative which does not adequately reflect the costs involved.

● **Information Systems**

From April 1993 the Trust will take on full responsibility for its payroll and manpower information systems.

● **Healthy Employer Initiatives**

The Trust endorses the Health Commission's 'Healthy Employer' initiative, and encourages staff to have regular health checks. The Charter for Staff Support, published by the Association for Staff Support, is also endorsed.

Finance and Information

● **Financial Viability**

The Trust Board agreed a Recovery Programme in December 1992, which will ensure that the Trust has a sound financial basis for the future and is able to meet its three financial targets in 1993/94:–

– breakeven

– 6% return on capital

– meet its EFL, £1,298,000

Detailed Financial Plans are contained in Annex 1 to the Business Plan.

The Dorset Health Commission has underlined its confidence in the Trust, earmarking £497,000 in its Health Investment Plan for 1993/94 to support and develop mental health services. Specific developments for 1993/94 include:

* ESMI resource centres in Sherborne and Weymouth

* Melstock House, Dorchester

* Psychology

* Counselling Service

The Trust will manage a Capital Programme of £1,639,000. Details of the Trust's capital investments for the next three years are set out in the table on Page 48.

Total turnover for 1993/94 will exceed £13 million.

To ensure continued financial viability six financial objectives have been set for 1993/94:–

FINANCIAL OBJECTIVES 1993/94

1. Achieve more efficient management of resources through improved efficiency and value for money	4. Implement a robust information strategy
2. Ensure effective financial control	5. Resolve ongoing financial problems in relation to the hospital closure programme
3. Implement Audit Commission reports	6. Achieve value for money in capital investments

Short term financial management targets include:–

* achievement of the 3 Trust financial targets

* 2.5% activity gain

* 2.0% efficiency gain

* creditor payments below eight weeks

● **Managing Change**

The closure of Herrison Hospital in the first year of Trust status, following on from the closure of Coldharbour in 1990, has resulted in significant problems both in managing the changes operationally and financially.

The management of change has only been possible with the support of the Dorset Health Commission, formerly West Dorset Health Authority, and the

41

Wessex Regional Health Authority. In addition to the substantial bridging funds received in 1991/92, the Trust has been successful in securing funding from the Regional Mental Illness/Learning Disabilities Project to meet the continuing costs of moving services out of institutions and into the Community. The £340,000 received in 1992/93 will meet the costs of skill–mix, protection of grades, retraining of staff, excess travel payments, and redundancy.

Regional funding is imperative if the Trust is to effectively manage these changes, while ensuring that the contract prices of services are competitive. It is envisaged that a further bid will be made in 1993/94 from the Project Fund with the Health Commission's support.

The cost of change was highlighted in 1992/93 when it was discovered that the use of 62.9% of water (77.2% of electricity) supplied to the Herrison site, could not be accounted for. This risk will be met in full by Wessex Regional Health Authority in 1993/94.

● **Finance Department and the Market**

Significant resources have been invested in the Finance Department to ensure that it can effectively respond to the changes in the NHS market. The Department has been reorganised to improve the quality of financial management and a strategy implemented to ensure:

* the development of staff through professional qualifications and NVQ (National Vocational Qualifications)
* the investment in computerised financial systems, including payroll, purchasing and Capital Charges

New technology has not only resulted in more accurate and timely financial data, but improvements in efficiency and productivity have resulted in a reduction in staff from 15.0 to 11.5 WTE. Management Accounts has been strengthened and integrated with the new service organisations and budgetary responsibility decentralised.

Priorities for 1993/94 include:

*   the integration of activity data and costs
*   developing costing mechanisms
*   identifying appropriate contract currencies
*   replacement of the existing P.A.S.

43

PROJECTED INCOME BUDGET 1993/94

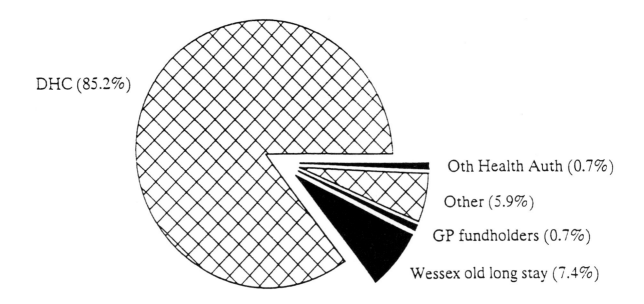

PROJECTED EXPENDITURE 1993/94

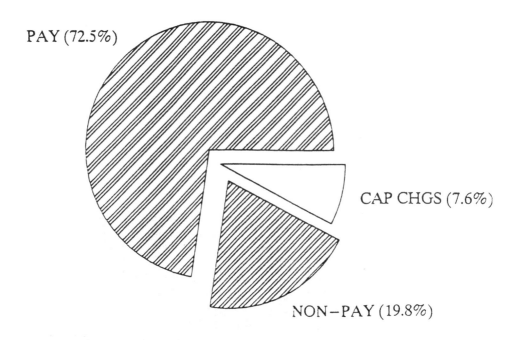

PROJECTED PAY BUDGETS 1993/94

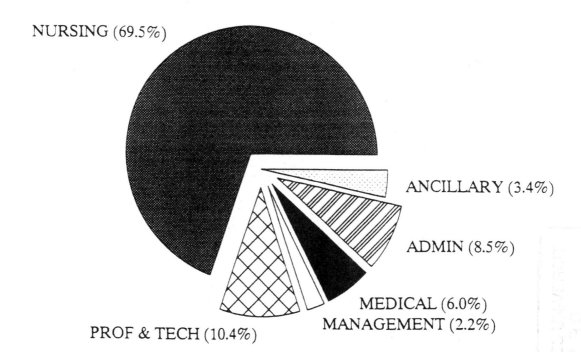

NURSING (69.5%)

ANCILLARY (3.4%)

ADMIN (8.5%)

MEDICAL (6.0%)
MANAGEMENT (2.2%)

PROF & TECH (10.4%)

PROJECTED NON–PAY BUDGETS 1993/94

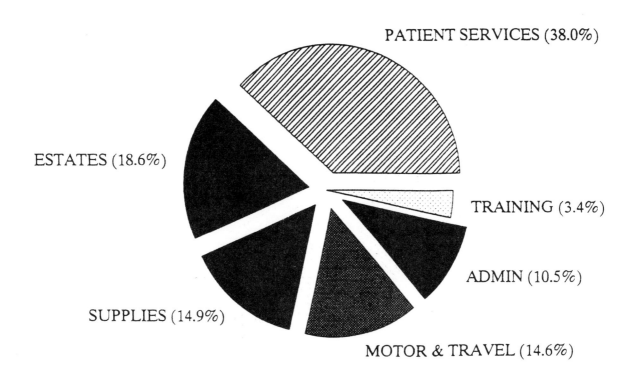

PATIENT SERVICES (38.0%)

ESTATES (18.6%)

TRAINING (3.4%)

ADMIN (10.5%)

SUPPLIES (14.9%)

MOTOR & TRAVEL (14.6%)

● **Activity**

The Trust will be unable to meet its activity target, derived from the Management Executive's 'Efficiency Index' of 2.5%. The index is a disincentive to the transfer of hospital based services to the Community and an ineffectual measure of the Trust's performance.

As the Trust moves further towards the support and treatment of clients in their own homes rather than inpatient admissions, the support services become difficult to measure and accurately capture, particularly when using the Körner activity measures.

A good example of the difficulty of client support and the capture of activity for Körner and the Efficiency Index is Blackdown Hospital. Blackdown not only provides traditional outpatients' clinics and day care, it also provides drop–in facilities and an emergency support service. The emergency support service is akin to inpatients, but does not include the stay in a bed overnight. It is not daycare or a daycare in terms of Körner.

The capture and classification of activity will form a part of the Trust's Resource Management Project and it is also the current subject of much national debate.

Resource Management

The Trust is progressing a Resource Management Project funded by Wessex Regional Health Authority. A Steering Group has been established to develop a Project Plan.

The Resource Management Project will have the following objectives:

* to provide information which enables professional staff to manage their resources more effectively, thereby improving clinical care

* to establish new workload measures which reflect the Trust's mainly community-based services

* to introduce a new 'currency' for the Contract with Dorset Health Commission

* to establish an information system which is easily accessible, meaningful, and improves utilisation of resources and management information

The workload measures currently in use are inadequate for effective contracting and it is therefore considered essential to develop more meaningful and accurate information. An initial allocation of £20,000 was made by Wessex RHA for 1992/93 to support the project, and a further £20,000 has been requested in 1993/94. It is planned to develop new workload measures and pilot these in one locality in the spring of 1993, with full implementation by the end of 1993.

Capital and Estates

The Trust's portfolio of property ranges from a five resident community home to the 66 bed Forston Clinic. The two large ex–Psychiatric Hospital sites at Herrison or Coldharbour are owned by Wessex RHA.

The District Valuer revised the valuation of the Trust's assets in April 1992, from £7.5 million to £9.1 million, an increase of 20.5% after allowing for work in progress. In addition to the revised valuation of property the remaining life of a number of properties was significantly reduced, and the classification of assets changed, substantially increasing the Trust's depreciation charges in 1992/93, and consequently the price of services offered to the purchaser.

The portfolio is generally in good repair and the Trust has benefited from the closure of the two ex–psychiatric hospitals in West Dorset, as many of the community residential homes have either been built or converted in the last decade. Adequate resources must be ring fenced to maintain the fabric of this property.

Work already identified for 1993/94, includes Coldharbour houses redecoration, 32 St Andrews Road external repairs, 3 Prince of Wales Road wall replacement and Blackdown improvement to facilities. Major repairs and minor improvements of this nature are met from the Trust's block capital allocation.

● **The Estate**

Acute mental illness beds are provided at Forston Clinic, Melstock House and Blackdown. Forston Clinic is a two–storey building set in 9 acres of land, north of Dorchester. Built in 1958, it has undergone a £1 million uplift between 1990–1992. The property was valued at £3,705,300 (April 1992). The Clinic provides a service to the whole of West Dorset.

Melstock House will open in September 1993, at a cost of £622,000. It will provide twelve acute beds in an improved setting, in the grounds of Forston Clinic.

The Trust has nineteen residential homes, providing continuing care to residents with mental illness or learning disabilities. Eight homes have been leased to Dorset Residential Homes, in a partnership to provide care for 143 residents.

Linden was built in 1983, on the outskirts of Weymouth. Surrounded by large gardens, it provides nursing care for elderly, confused residents. It has twenty beds available, and also provides respite care to meet the needs of carers and day care.

Rawleigh House in Sherborne provides care for eleven residents with learning disabilities and profound physical handicaps.

The Albany Unit, consists of three detached modern buildings in Sherborne, each providing residential care for five clients with severe behavioural problems.

Greenfields is the first of the Trust's new ESMI Resource Centres, providing a base for the Bridport (Elderly) Community Team, respite, assessment and day care. Undergoing conversion in 1992/1993, it will open in April 1993.

● **Capital Investment**

The Trust's Capital Programme since 1991 has been preoccupied with the run-down of Herrison Hospital and the reprovision of services in the Community. The Trust recognises the need to develop a Capital Investment Strategy, a framework within which Managers can research, develop and plan capital investment to meet the Trust's long–term requirements for capital, to ensure value for money is achieved and investment meets both short and longterm objectives. The Strategy will be developed in 1993/94, following a review of the Strategic Direction, to inform the 1994/95 business planning cycle.

The Capital Investment Strategy will take into account the continued movement of services into the Community.

DRAFT CAPITAL INVESTMENT FRAMEWORK

	1993/94 £'000	1994/95 £'000	1995/96 £'000
Sherborne – ESMI Resource Centre	384		
Horticultural Centre – Dorchester	213		
Residences reprovision	62		
Dorchester Day College	288		
Blackdown Alterations	92		
Blandford CMHT Base	170		
Patient Information System		250	
Gillingham – ESMI Resource Centre	180	179	
North Dorset Mental Health Base			165
Weymouth/Portland Mental Health Base		165	
Blandford ESMI Day Centre			
Provision of Service Area bases	50	150	
Block Capital	200	300	300
	1639	1044	465

7.   QUALITY

During 1993/94 the Trust will continue to develop the Total Quality Management approach to quality assurance which has been implemented as part of a national initiative over the last 3 – 4 years.

The Trust is committed to:

*   a high, measurable standard of care and service

*   systematic quality assurance as the main method of ensuring a high standard of care and services

*   demonstrable improvement in the process and outcome of care and services year by year.

Within this policy framework the quality assurance strategy and programmes will continue to be developed, strengthening service delivery in relation to standards and outcome of care.

A Total Quality Management Plan will be prepared for 1993/94 which will include planned activity for standards definition, audit, outcomes and service review. The Trust has an effective system of standard setting and monitoring, covering all areas including management and support services.

● **Medical and Clinical Audit**

Medical and clinical audit are currently undertaken independently of each other but with the strategic aim of incorporating both systems.

● **The Quartz System**

This quality review system will be implemented in April 1993. It involves the identification and training for the review of services with local teams, based on staff participation. Twelve service areas will be reviewed in 1993/94.

49

- **Training**

  An annual training and communications plan for quality issues will be prepared for 1993/94.

- **Community Health Council**

  Close liaison with West Dorset Community Health Council will continue to ensure the continued provision of high quality services and the monitoring of service standards.

SL/AW/25.2.93

bus9394.rep

CIPFA

BUSINESS PLANS

A Compendium

HEALTH

**The Business Plan of an
NHS Trust Finance Department**

FINANCE DEPARTMENT

BUSINESS PLAN

---

1   **MISSION STATEMENT**

The purpose of the Finance Department is to harness the finances of
for the benefit of patients.

2   **CORE PURPOSES**

2.1   To advise the Board on financial structure and strategy.

2.2   To maintain financial control.

2.3   To contribute towards achieving economy, efficiency, and effectiveness.

2.4   To compile the accounts and make reports to outside agencies.

2.5   To specify, provide and review financial systems within the organisation.

2.6   To provide information and advice to those managing services.

3.   **WAYS OF WORKING**

-      **Senior Managers**

Working Together

*   Closer Integration with related Senior Managers
*   Awareness within Department of what each other is doing
*   Working within objectives

Systematic

*   Develop systems
*   Operate systematically

Communications

*   With their own staff
*   With top Managers
*   In a defined and notified way
*   Management by walking about is a useful way of communicating

Development of services

*   Minor developments and changes will be instigated
*   Implement developments where appropriate
*   Revise development in relation to changing requirement

Top and Senior Managers will work with the values established for Health

Patient Centred

*   Right to Quality Service
*   Involvement
*   Effectiveness for patients
*   Communication

Financial Integrity

*   Income dependant
*   Understand costs
*   Intolerant of waste and inefficiency
*   Contain expenditure within income

Dynamic

*   Solve problems
*   Take opportunities
*   Flexible and innovative

Customer Responsive

*   Services our customers want
*   Relationship with purchasers

Focused on Services

*   Constant search for improvement
*   Specify activity and quality
*   Integrate other providers
*   Effective Working Together

Staff

*   Involve staff
*   Multi-disciplinary approach
*   Match profession/organisational objectives
*   Enable staff to provide a good service
*   Value our staff
*   Open and honest communications

Top Managers in Finance will:

* Ensure that responsibilities are clearly defined
* Resolve Conflicts
* Promote and develop the finance function

4. STATEMENTS OF SERVICE

- Financial Management

* Develop the experience and expertise of Financial Management staff
* Provide sound and effective management control information
* Support managers in costing and business planning
* Work to ensure   Health NHS Trust stays within its target financial and fiscal limits.

- Accounting

* Provide NHSME returns in an accurate and timely fashion
* Ensure accountancy standards.

- Treasury Services

* Monitor the Capital Programme in conjunction with other top managers.
* Operate payroll and pension services to agreed quality standards
* Provide a seamless payments service operating within flexible creditor policies
* Reimburse expenses at levels of agreed "customer" service having regard to cost constraints.
* Maintain debtor control within specified targets.

- Internal Audit

* Provision of internal audit services to at least Mandatory Minimum Audit Standards.

* The give assurance on the integrity of activities of   Health and NHS Trust. ie., to objectively examine, evaluate and report upon the adequacy of internal controls as a contribution to the proper economic, efficient and effective use of resources.

* To assist the various levels of management in discharging their duties and responsibilities by carrying out appraisals and making the necessary and appropriate recommendations to mangement for operations under its control.

* To give added value.

* To ensure that the activities of   Health and NHS Trust conform to laid down policies and legal requirements.

Objectives for 1993/94

* Achievement of the Annual Audit Plan to the required mandatory minimum audit standards.

* Provision of the Audit Service within agreed costs and agreed manday levels within the terms of the Service Level Agreement.

* The appraisal and monitoring of key controls and procedures to ensure that internal control is maintained.

* Provision of a service to management.

Departmental Structure Statement

Chief Internal Auditor	-	Evaluates adequacy of systems and procedures
	-	Verifies integrity of financial and operational systems
	-	Ensures sound internal controls
	-	Provides an independant appraisal activity

5.   **STRATEGIC DIRECTION**

The strategic direction of the department was established in late 1991. The key aims within the strategic plan are:

* to maintain the operation of the basic finance functions within Health;

* to develop finance professionals;

* to establish the financial operation required for Trust Status;

* to develop financial management with particular emphasis on costing and integration with the business planning process;

* to contribute to improvements in value for money throughout Health.

The only proposed change to these aims are:

* to improve the department's own value for money.

6. OBJECTIVES FOR 1993/94

- ### Finance Director

Specific Responsibilities

* Formulates all necessary financial policies and strategies - for agreement with the Chief Executive - to support the shaping, maintenance and development of all services in the Trust.

* Ensures the systematic development of the financial functions of management accounting, treasury management, financial accounting, financial services and internal audit.

* Set an appropriate structure, defines the roles and assigns responsibility to finance top managers - that are compatible with health's organisational arrangements - for the provision of the finance functions including the Trust's statutory financial responsibilities.

* Provides policies and strategies which achieve improvements in cost performance.

* Ensures that the implementation of agreed financial policies and strategies is co-ordinated and monitored comprehensively across both groups and all departments and functions.

* Ensures appropriate training and development in conjunction with the Director of Personnel on non-specified managers and other professionals in the field of finance (and also ensures the proficiency of the finance functional staff).

* Provides financial advice, information and analysis to the Chief Executive to assist him in maintaining overall financial control and in monitoring the performance of the Groups and the Directorates.

* Provides leadership to professionally qualified staff in the Directorate and within the Groups.

Specific Objectives

None at present.

- **Director of Financial Planning**

- **Financial Management Function**

  - Support Business Planning
  - Support the Trust Reporting Systems
  - Develop Costing Support
  - Develop Activity/Income Management System
  - Monitoring of implementation of VFM studies

- **Group Management Accounting (Medicine)**

- **Group Management Accounting (Surgery)**

- **Group Management Accounting (Headquarters)**

  1. Consolidation of present reporting arrangement into monthly Trust income and expenditure report.

  2. Instigate system on monthly reconciliation of Group expenditure budgets into overall Trust income expectations thus consolidating roll over of block contracts with purchasers. Assist in the establishment of minimum costing standards within   in order to improve the costing and contracting process.

  3. Implement system of contract income monitoring within IRIS reporting mechanisms in order to conform with 1) and 2) above.

  4. Support MAP implementation within Estates and Headquarters.

  5. Consolidate activity statistics within reports in order to supplement IRIS reporting.

  6. Establish a system of trading accounts within specific areas.

- **Financial Projects**

  General Index

  1. MAP/ABC/Costing System
  2. Contracting/Pricing - All relevant aspects
  3. Systems - General and Specific
  4. Ad-Hoc Projects

  Specific Objectives

  <u>MAP</u>

  Devise a set of principles and procedures on the MAP project in order to establish a controlled and consistent approach. Project-manage MAP and produce an agreed timetable. Carry out pilot studies on xxxxx departments and when complete, implement remainder of MAP according to the agreed timetable.

Contracting/Pricing

Financial assistance in setting, negotiating, finalising and monitoring Trust prices/contracts. Establish methodology on pricing for contracts with the aim of introducing more accurate and reliable specialty prices for the 1994/95 contracting process.

Value for Money

Assist Deputy Director of Finance on developing and implementing VFM issues and other initiatives in order to produce cost benefits, savings and enhance the quality of services throughout the organisation. Issue quarterly newsletter.

Risk Management

Involvement in extension of risk management culture to all areas of Trust.

Systems - General and Specific

Provide objective appraisal on current financial and information systems and suggest possible solutions. Assistance on new General Ledger implementation.

Staff Officer Role to Deputy Director of Finance

Act as staff officer/support role to the DDF

Ad-Hoc Projects

Assist and/or project-manage any ad-hoc projects that may arise.

- **Director of Treasury Services**

- **Financial Services**

Customer Responsive Focused Services

* Establish service level agreements with customer areas

* Develop internal performance indicators to support/monitor service level agreements (includes production of quality manual).

* Placing accountability back into appropriate parts of   Health.

Working Together

*   Provide input to cash forecasting system from all sections

*   Examine space utilisation

*   Development of quality circles

Development of Systems

*   Implement CASE Travel Expenses systems in Income Section

*   Implement Invoice Registration and Creditors Ledger system and revise processing techniques in Payments Section

*   Input Acquisition details to Britannia

*   Develop Departmental Procedure Manuals

Financial Integrity of the Trust

*   Become Income driven (ie., actively seeking payment of amounts due)

Financial Integrity of Financial Services

*   Understand costs associated with Health and Safety issues

*   Optimize use of resources (eg., training in the use of equipment)

Valuing Staff

*   Establish staff objectives and appraisal systems for Level 2 and other staff.

*   Identify staff training needs

*   Implement procedures regarding Health and Safety issues and educate staff in the issues.

*   Undertake reprofiling of Payroll Section

-     **Trust Accounts**

1.   Cash and Treasury Management

a.   Implement and maintain adequate systems to control and forecast cash flows.

b.   Implement and maintain adequate systems to control the investment of surplus funds, and loans to meet borrowing requirements.

2.   Monthly Management Reporting

Provide accurate, timely reports on a monthly basis to the Director of Finance and update EIS with Key Indicator information.

3.   External Agency Reporting (NHSME)

Provide accurate and timely reports on a quarterly basis, or as required, to the Outpost.

4.   Business Planning

To provide input to the business planning process with regard to:

a.   Medium and long term financial projections

b.   Capital projects requiring a business case to be submitted to the NHSME

5.   Capital Asset Management

a.   Implement systems to support the Britannia asset register.

b.   Maintain an up to date asset register.

c.   Provide capital chargers forecast information and quantify the effects of capital schemes.

d.   Provide information regarding the finance of capital assets.

7.   Income Monitoring

a.   Implement and maintain adequate systems to monitor the contract income of the Trust.

b.   Provide information of income variance to the Director of Service Agreements.

8.   Technical Accounting Compliance

Provide technical guidance on new accounting regulations and standards which effect the Trust.

-    **Internal Audit**

*   The 1993/94 internal audit plan is attached.

6.   DEPARTMENTAL STRUCTURE

The Top Management posts within Finance can be defined in these terms as:

Finance Director
- Financial advice within the board
- Operational pacing
- Ensure finance operation is appropriate and complete

Director of Financial Management
- Provides financial information to the board in relation to in-year monitoring in relation to plan
- Ensures that systems are in place to advise those managing resources
- Develop financial projects

Director of Treasury Services
- Provides information for financial justification to outside agencies (ie., the accounts)
- Assists in providing strategic advice (eg., capital structure)
- Ensures that financial services systems exist and work

Chief Internal Auditor
- Reviews financial systems

The Senior Management posts with Finance responsibilties can be defined as:

Group Management Accountants (Medical and Surgical)
- Budgetary Monitoring
- Costing
- Advice to Group General Managers, delegated budget holder, consultants
- Provision of finance information within Finance

Central Management Accountant
- Group Management Accountant roles in relation to Estates, Support and Headquarters
- Support to Director of Financial Management
- Accounts for Reservces

Financial Projects Manager
- Mainly costing and pricing projects

Trust Accountant
- Accounting and Reporting
- Balance Sheet Management

Financial Services Manager   -   Payroll, Payments, Income, Cash and other Financial Services

Internal Audit   -   Audit of Financial Systems.

to report to   et al.

7.   **RESOURCES REQUIRED**

CIPFA

BUSINESS PLANS

A Compendium

HOUSING ASSOCIATIONS

Canmore Housing Association

Business Plan 1993

CANMORE HOUSING ASSOCIATION

BUSINESS PLAN
· 1993 ·

I N D E X.

1.

Section 1.1

SUMMARY OF DOCUMENT

This is the Association's fifth Business Plan. It has the following purposes:

a. It gives information on the nature of the Association, its history and its broad objectives.

b. It outlines the areas where the Association operates now and wishes to operate in the future.

c. It gives information on the housing needs in the proposed operational areas and the opportunities for meeting these needs.

d. It details the Association's Rent Policy.

e. It gives information on the Association's organisation and track record, particularly as a developer and manager of housing.

f. It summarizes the Association's financial position demonstrating that this is sound and provides a satisfactory base for future development and management initiatives.

g. It outlines the Association's development strategy, with emphasis on partnership and the orientation of the Association's organisation towards achieving its goals.

2.

Section 1.2

SUMMARY BID - 1994/95

The Association is confident of its ability to further expand its development programme in both geographical and purpose terms.   It has a sound financial base, an excellent housing management structure and a positive approach to development opportunities. The Association recognises that HAG resources are limited and that Private Finance will play an increasing part in its development funding.   It also recognises that flexibility, partnership with the public and private sectors, and the provision of new types of accommodation, reflecting changing needs and economic circumstances are the keys to the future and the basis of its planning.

1.   The Association is making bids for HAG funding for projects in Edinburgh, West Lothian and Fife.   A variety of developments is envisaged housing the single, elderly and families on both a rented and shared ownership basis.   In one scheme, there is provision of workspaces as well as houses.

The bids for **HAG** are summarised as follows:

	1994/95	1995/96	1996/97
Edinburgh District Office	£4,157,000	£3,537,000	£2,420,000
Lothian and Borders District Office	1,787,000	555,000	705,000
Fife District Office	100,000	89,000	-

The figures for 1995 and beyond are necessarily indicative at this stage.

In respect of all the proposed rented accommodation, HAG is calculated meantime on the basis of 70% of total scheme costs, the remainder will be borrowed privately.

2.   The Association is making a bid for **New Powers funding** as follows:-

	1994/95	1995/96
Gorgie Goods Yard Workshops	£35,000	-

3.   The Association is making a bid for **SNAPS** as follows:-

	1994/95	1995/96
	£14,000	£30,000

3.

Section 2.1

THE ASSOCIATION

The Association was constituted in April 1975 as a Limited Company not trading for profit. It operates under the Model HSA(Scotland)Rules. It is registered with Scottish Homes and under the Industrial & Provident Societies Act 1965.

Section 2.2

HISTORY

In 1975, Councillor Duncan Drummond Young and six others interested in promoting the improvement of housing, were given the opportunity of acquiring properties in a newly declared Housing Action Area in Newton Street, in the Gorgie area of Edinburgh. The Housing Corporation encouraged them to register as a Housing Association which would carry out comprehensive improvements in Housing Action Areas declared in Gorgie and Dalry. With the aid of HAG, the Association commenced to acquire and improve many properties, providing housing for rent for those in low incomes. It also provided a service to owner-occupiers participating in comprehensive tenement improvements in the Housing Action Areas.

The Association has improved well over 700 properties and assisted nearly 500 owner-occupiers. In addition, it has built 160 new dwellings and has a further 270 units, including provision for Special Needs, under construction or in course of preparation. Most recently, it has acquired 92 improved flats from Livingston Development Corporation for letting on Assured Tenancies. Nearly 100 houses have been sold to tenants under the Right-to-Buy arrangements.

In 1990, the Association changed its name from the Gorgie Dalry Housing Association to Canmore Housing Association and widened its geographical operational area to include, for example, the whole of Edinburgh and West Lothian. Within this area, the Association seeks to provide homes for a wide variety of needs.

The Association employs a full complement of in-house staff working from a new office which is owned by the Association.

The Association has over 100 members from whom the Committee of Management is elected each year.

Details of current stock are shown in Annex A.

4.

Section 2.3   Organisational Summary

The organisation of committee and staff is as follows:-

COMMITTEE   STRUCTURE. *

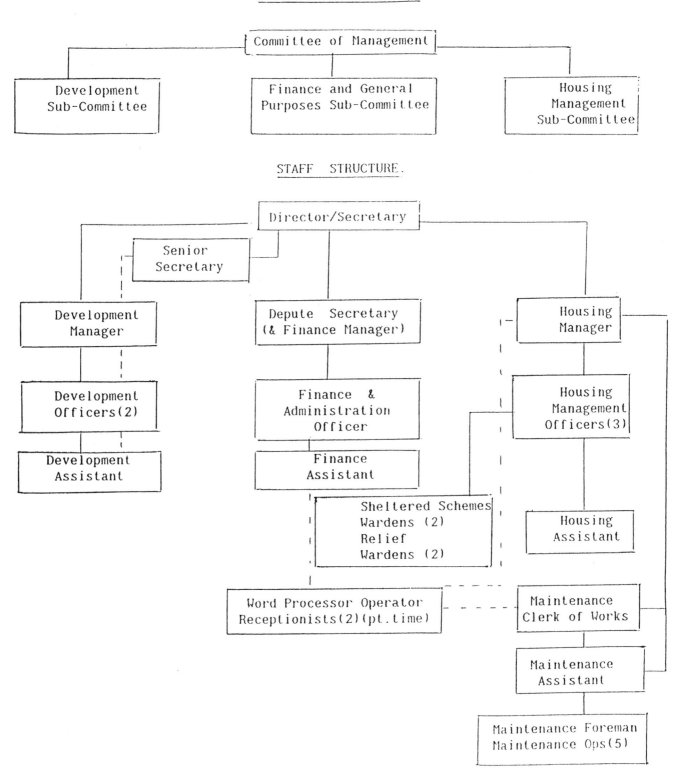

STAFF   STRUCTURE.

Line management _____
Service function - - - - -
* Under Review

5.

Section 2.4

WHAT THE ASSOCIATION DOES

The Association currently owns and manages over 800 houses, providing for a wide range of housing needs. A comprehensive Tenant Survey just carried out indicates that most tenants are well satisfied with the management of these houses.

The Association takes initiatives, for example, it introduced the first conversion of a tenement to provide full sheltered accommodation; the first Mid-Rent development for those with low incomes but not requiring the normal HAG subsidy; and the first development project which gave unemployed young people both work experience and subsequent accommodation. Other new projects cover a wide range of needs, including "very sheltered" housing.

The Association works closely with a variety of voluntary agencies, and Lothian Social Work Department in respect of the provision of housing for a range of individuals requiring supported accommodation.

The Association provides the highest possible standard of service to its tenants while at the same time ensuring that its financial performance is sound. One of the keys to its success is its in-house maintenance team which provides an effective response, for the most part within 24 hours, to tenants' maintenance requests.

While applications for housing far outstrip its restricted supply, the Association ensures a speedy response to all applications and a clear statement of the applicant's position within a month of receipt of an application.

6.

Section 2.5

THE ASSOCIATION'S OBJECTIVES

a. The Association's principal aim is to provide barrier-free
    housing for those with low incomes and to manage these
    houses to the highest standards and in the best interests
    of its tenants

b. The Association is aware that demand for such houses out-
    strips supply and will seek in co-operation with Scottish
    Homes and others to provide additional housing, meeting a
    wide variety of needs wherever possible within a sensible
    range of the Association's operational base.

c. The Association recognises the financial and social climate
    within which it operates.   It will be customer driven, in-
    novative and will work in close partnership with both the
    public and private sectors.

d. The Association's key resource is the skill and commitment
    of its staff. Staff will be fully involved in the develop-
    ment of objectives to which they will commit their skills.
    A positive personnel policy will be implemented which will
    reward achievement, encourage initiative and develop the
    staff skills and knowledge.

7.

Section 3.1

AREA OF OPERATION

Edinburgh and West Lothian Districts are considered in this Plan. Dunfermline District is also considered though in less detail, pending a conclusion to discussion at present under way with Scottish Homes about the Association's involvement in Fife.

EDINBURGH

Although the population of Edinburgh is stable, the number of independent households is forecast to increase,while the average household size decreases (Table 1)

Table 1 - Edinburgh's Population

Year	Population	No. of Households	No. of Single Person Households	Average Household Size
1992	431,912	189,660	59,820	2.21
1997	432,073	196,350	64,842	2.12

There is an increasing proportion of single person households relative to the total number of households within the City (1992- 31.7%, 1997- 33%).Edinburgh District Council's Housing Department estimate, however, that two-apartment properties constitute only 18.3% of all housing types within Edinburgh. There is, therefore, a severe imbalance between the needs of the population and the existing housing provision.

However, careful consideration is required in the planning and provision of future housing types, for the general population estimates disguise a variety of differing needs.

Population projections to 1996 indicate that the number of individuals within the 25-44 year age bracket will increase by 0.3%, while the 16-24 year age band will decrease by 11.3%. As a result, an adequate provision of appropriately located single person and family accommodation, suited to cater for the needs of the next family forming generation require to be made available. This provision will be required for both those relying on benefit of various sorts and for those who are economically active but whose incomes are relatively low.

8.

Section 3.1 contd.

Although there is likely to be a slight decline in the number of people over retirement age,the proportion of over 85 year olds will increase by some 14% between 1992-1997.   While the majority of elderly people are able to sustain independent life styles within their own homes,increasing numbers are likely to require either specialist housing types in the form of sheltered, amenity or very sheltered housing, or, adaptations made to their existing homes which will enable them to maintain an independent lifestyle.

TENURE

Edinburgh has the highest rate of owner-occupation of any district in Scotland, the lowest proportion of public sector housing and a rapidly de-clining privately rented sector (Table 2).

Table 2 - Edinburgh's Housing Stock by Tenure (1992)

	No.	%
Owner-occupied	137,355	69%
District Council	40,432	20%
Scottish Homes	1,377	1%
Private Let	10,770	5%
Housing Associations	7,945	4%
Unestablished	3,245	1%

The high proportion of owner-occupation is likely to increase, partly as a consequence of further Local Authority and Scottish Homes' house sales. The private rented sector will continue to decline, in keeping with recent trends.   Housing Associations such as Canmore are, therefore, ever more im-portant as providers of rented housing for those with lower incomes.

As a consequence of Edinburgh's unique tenure pattern, those individuals and families unable to consider owner-occupation or the expense and insecurity of the privately rented sector, and confronted with the reducing Local Authority stock, have little option but to apply to one of the Housing Associations established within the City in their search for secure, affordable housing.

WEST LOTHIAN DISTRICT

West Lothian possesses a range of housing problems.   These vary throughout the District but have much in common with Edinburgh.

Canmore Housing Association recognise that West Lothian District and Livingston has many unmet needs and is prepared to participate in resolving some of them.

LIVINGSTON

Livingston Development Corporation in West Lothian is beginning to contem-plate its wind up towards the end of the decade.   Canmore has already acquired 92 rehabilitated houses from the Corporation and is prepared to negotiate the acquisition of further properties in the New Town, in order that these can be maintained in the "Social Rented" sphere.

9.

Section 3.1 contd.

POPULATION

The most recent population forecast (Table 3) suggests that the population of West Lothian is likely to increase by 3.4% from 144,437 (1992) to 149,316 (1997). The proximity of the District to Edinburgh, results in West Lothian accommodating significant numbers of commuters who take advantage of the District's comparatively low cost housing.

Table 3 - West Lothian Population

Year	Population	No. of Households	Average Household Size
1993	148,574	56,708	2.62
1995	150,839	56,239	2.59
1997	153,231	59,856	2.56

It is anticipated the average household size will decrease from 2.62 (1992) to 2.56 (1997), the higher proportion of single person and smaller family households placing considerable strain on the District's existing housing resources.

It is forecast the proportion of those over retirement age will increase significantly until the turn of the century, the proportion of over 65 year olds increasing by 13.3%, 75 year olds by 15.9% and over 85 year olds by 34.9%.

West Lothian District Council has identified serious shortages and inadequacies in the provision and geographical distribution of specialist housing provision, suited to the needs of its ageing population.

TENURE TYPE

(Table 4) gives the most up-to-date information available on the tenure pattern within West Lothian District.

Table 4 - West Lothian Housing Stock by Tenure (1992)

	No.	%
Private Sector	28,000	49.9
Local Authority	17,400	31.0
Livingston Development Corporation	7,585	13.5
Housing Associations	628	1.1
Scottish Homes	2,092	3.8
Unknown	383	0.7
	56,088	100%

The marked increase in the proportion of owner-occupation which occurred has been at the expense of Local Authority Stock, 3,922 of the 8,936 new owners established between 1980-1988 being Local Authority or Livingston Development Corporation tenants who had exercised their Right-to-Buy.

10.

Section 3.1 contd:

West Lothian District Council anticipates losing further houses leaving a total stock of approximately 14,000 properties in 1994. This decline in stock availability is having a profound effect on the Authority's ability to cater for the needs of an expanding population and its statutory obligations.

As with Edinburgh District, there exists a mismatch between future household size and current stock,a situation made more acute by the continued reduction in the availability of privately rented accommodation. As a consequence of diminishing public sector housing stock, and past escalation in house prices those in low paid work are likely to rely increasingly on Housing Associations.

DUNFERMLINE DISTRICT COUNCIL

Dunfermline District Council is experiencing population trends and increasing housing demands from a variety of client groups, similar to both Edinburgh and West Lothian District Councils.

With an expanding population and increasing proportions of single person and elderly households, the District's current housing stock displays a mismatch in terms of size and distribution between what is required and that which is presently available. The most recent Housing Plan (1990-1995) indicates that an additional 2,785 dwellings are required throughout the District to accommodate anticipated needs.

As in other Districts, there is a need for additional sheltered and amenity housing, as well as the establishment of provision to accommodate disabled persons, homeless people,the mentally ill and handicapped, as well as victims of domestic violence.

Reducing Council stock within the District is likely to make it increasingly difficult for those on low incomes to secure suitable accommodation. Canmore Housing Association is willing to play it's part in meeting the housing needs of those with low incomes if Scottish Homes so wishes.

11.

Section 3.2

HOUSING NEEDS ANALYSIS
Introduction

The Association's analysis of housing needs are drawn from a number of sources:-

1. Our own experience of housing demand and the variety of individuals seeking assistance who contact the Association.

2. The assessment of need provided by the Local Authority's Housing Plan.

3. Forecasts and assessments provided by specialist voluntary or statutory agencies involved in caring or providing practical assistance to a wide variety of special needs groups.

4. The recently published Lothian Community Care Plan 1992-95.

Section 3.2(i) EDINBURGH.

The demands for housing facing Canmore Housing Association are very similar to those experienced by Edinburgh District Council's Housing Department and other Housing Associations within the City.

During the second half of 1992, Canmore Housing Association received a total of 616 applications for General Needs Housing, the characteristics of these applicants being detailed in **Table 5.**

Table 5

Client Group	No.	%
Single People	319	51.8
Couples	78	12.7
Couples with 1 child	29	4.7
Couples with 2 or more children	27	4.4
Lone parents with 1 child	95	15.4
Lone parents with 2 or more children	66	10.7
Related Adults	2	0.3
	616	100%

Applicants Housed During 1992

Client Group	No.	%
Single People	79	71.0
Couples	15	13.9
Couples with 1 child	8	7.1
Couples with 2 or more children	1	0.8
Lone parents with 1 child	5	4.5
Lone parents with 2 or more children	3	2.7
	111	100%

Single people and lone parents constitute the greatest source of demand for housing within the City. Edinburgh District Council indicate that in July 1991, 42% of those on their waiting list were single people, while 24% were lone parents with dependent children. The need for suitably located secure, affordable accommodation is becoming increasingly evident.

While there is a clear trend towards smaller household sizes overall it is still necessary to enhance the provision of family accommodation, particularly within the inner City, in an endeavour to retain a balanced population structure, while addressing the problem of acute homelessness.

HOMELESS

During 1992, Canmore Housing Association provided accommodation to 90 in-dividuals from its Allocation List of whom 64% were homeless in that they did not possess independent secure accommodation. This feature is borne out by evidence provided by the Scottish Statistical Bulletin (May'91) which indicated that Edinburgh had more persons assessed as statutorily homeless and in priority need than in any other district in Scotland.

SPECIAL NEEDS HOUSING

In keeping with Canmore Housing Association's objective of assisting in the maintenance of balanced communities, the Association provides for a variety of Special Needs Groups and promotes Community Care initiatives.

The provision of accommodation to those groups detailed below frequently requires a commitment from Canmore Housing Association to work in conjunction with statutory or voluntary agencies or involves the Association in providing a variety of support and care services. Canmore Housing Association therefore uses funds made available via the Special Needs Allowance Packages(SNAPS).

THE ELDERLY

Consideration of population projections for Edinburgh covering the periods 1991-2001 indicates that the number of over 65 year olds will decrease from 73,274 to 71,273 (a net decline of 2.7%), however, there will develop in the same period a 2.8% increase (33,932 to 34,374) in the number of people over 85 years of age. These groups are major users of services for older people and there is an urgent need to prepare for these additional demands as the proportion of elderly people living in the community increases.

13.

While many elderly people are capable of living within their homes with very little support, increasing numbers are likely to require specifically designed or adapted accommodation which will enable them to sustain independent lifestyles for as long as practicable. To this end, Canmore Housing Association will in its long-term planning of developments, consider and react to the housing requirements of the elderly, as set out in SDD Circular 8/91 (Community Care in Scotland; (Housing and Community Care) which established the following guidelines:-

Very sheltered housing	20 dwellings per 1000 elderly
Sheltered housing	46 " " " "
Medium dependency housing	80 " " " "

Applying this criteria to West Central Edinburgh there should exist 58 very sheltered, 134 sheltered and 234 medium dependency properties. At present there are 7 very sheltered, 33 sheltered and 9 medium dependency flats.

Careful design and the adoption of barrier-free concepts in future newbuild schemes will enable the Association to cater for a wide variety of those needs experienced by the elderly, enabling them to remain within familiar communities.

MENTAL ILLNESS

Edinburgh District Council has identified a City wide requirement for an additional 60 bedspaces per year, for each of the next 10 years, to cater for the needs of those with mental health problems who, with support, could successfully live in the community.

Although the provision of housing for this client group may take a variety of forms, the important factor remains that tenants are housed in secure independent environments and that support services cater for their needs.

MENTAL DISABILITY

The Lothian Community Care Plan (1992/95) identified a marked shortfall in the provision of community services to meet the known needs of those with mental disability, there existing an over-reliance on largescale institutional hospitals to accommodate individuals with mental problems.

The Joint Planning Group for people with mental disability recommends the provision of 1 place per 1000 in the community, thus requiring a total of 750 bedspaces, which implies an existing shortfall of some 400 bedspaces within Lothian Region at the present time.

14.

DISABLED PERSON HOUSING

Edinburgh District Council's housing plan indicates that there are between 1500 and 1900 physically disabled people within Lothian Region between the ages of 16 and 65 who require suitably adapted housing.

The Scottish Office's standard recommendation for the provision of disabled person housing is that 1% of the housing stock should be suitable for wheel-chair use and 10% for ambulant disabled use. Based on these recommendations, Edinburgh as a whole falls far short of catering for the needs of the disabled Some centrally located areas which might otherwise prove particularly suitable for the needs of those with mobility problems, in terms of access to public transport, shops, employment and recreation facilities lack any specifically designed provision whatsoever, an imbalance which Canmore Housing Association would where practically possible wish to redress.

FURNISHED TENANCIES

An increasing proportion of those applying to Canmore Housing Association have almost no resources with which to furnish their homes. This can result in new tenants failing to sustain their tenancies, or, occasionally result in tenants incurring unmanageable debts.

Canmore Housing Association like Edinburgh District Council, has already identified and reacted to this problem by providing some partially furnished accommodation.

Future partially furnished tenancies will irrespective of age, be targeted to-wards the most vulnerable tenants, that is:-

- Homeless people with few possessions and resources

- Those leaving institutional care

- Those being rehoused from furnished bedsits or bed
  and breakfast establishments.

OTHER TENURES

Canmore is prepared to provide Shared Equity and Shared Ownership housing where it sees the need for this type of accommodation, particularly in "single tenure" locations within its operational area.

CONCLUSIONS

The housing needs identified by Canmore Housing Association are similar to those encountered by Edinburgh District Council's Housing Department and are being addressed by the Association within Edinburgh. These are:-

1. Provision to meet the increasing level of demand for single person accommodation, particularly amongst homeless people.

2. Provision to meet the continuing demand for family-sized sized accommodation within the City centre areas.

3. Provision of increased numbers of suitably located amenity, sheltered and very sheltered housing. Expansion of community alarm schemes and the adaption of existing homes to suit the needs of elderly tenants and others with special needs. In addition, future new build developments will conform to barrier-free standards, enabling increased movement and independence for tenants who have mobility problems.

4. Increased provision of supported accommodation for those with mental health problems and mental handicap.

5. Increased provision of accommodation suited to the needs of the disabled and wheelchair bound.

6. Provision of partially furnished accommodation, particularly catering for the needs of young single people and those leaving institutional care or privately rented furnished accommodation.

7. Provision of Shared Ownership and Shared Equity housing for those on lower incomes.

Section 3.2.(ii)

WEST LOTHIAN

SINGLE PEOPLE

The increasing number of single people on the West Lothian District Council Waiting List is indicative of the requirement for more suitably sized accommodation. However, the needs of single people are varied and encompass a range of provisions including independent and shared tenancies, furnished accommodation, supported accommodation or property specifically designed for a particular special needs client group.

FAMILIES

New families on low incomes have been adversely affected by the high proportion of West Lothian District Council Stock lost under the Right-to-Buy provisions. The restricted opportunities available to West Lothian District Council to accommodate families is best illustrated by the Authority's difficulty in re-settling families occupying temporary homeless persons' accommodation and the subsequent difficulty this creates in the acceptance of new potentially vulnerable homeless families.

SPECIAL NEEDS

West Lothian District Council believes, as does Canmore Housing Association, that Special Needs Housing in whatever form should be integrated with mainstream provision.

THE ELDERLY

The District Plan forecasts a deficiency of 463 Very Sheltered Flats, 532 Sheltered and 1,509 Amenity flats by 1993, a shortfall it is anxious to remedy. West Lothian District Council wish to ensure that a proportion of Housing Association resources are channelled towards this provision.

PHYSICALLY DISABLED

There exists only 138 properties within West Lothian suited to the varied needs of the physically disabled. Based on the premise that disabled housing should form 1% of the area's entire housing stock, West Lothian has a current shortfall of some 397 units.

MENTALLY DISABLED

West Lothian District Council is keen to establish locally-based mainstream and hostel provision with suitable support services to cater for the varied needs of the 391 individuals suffering from various forms of mental handicap.

MENTAL HEALTH

Research indicates that there are presently 26 places available within the community for those suffering from various forms of mental illness. A further 58 people have been identified if appropriate housing provision can be found.

LCHO

West Lothian Housing Department would welcome the provision of shared owner-ship housing throughout the District as one means of providing suitable accom-modation for those on low incomes, particularly those establishing homes for the first time.

CONCLUSIONS

The identified housing needs of West Lothian are as follows:-

1.   The provision of both single person and family accommodation to remedy existing shortfalls.

2.   Provision of suitably designed, accessible housing for the elderly, particularly amenity housing.

3.   Provision of suitably designed accommodation catering for the needs of the physically disabled.

4.   Provision of housing for the mentally ill and mentally handi-capped.

5.   The provision of shared ownership accommodation to assist those on modest incomes.

6.   The provision of partially furnished accommodation, to cater for the needs of young single homeless people and those leaving institutional care or privately rented furnished accommodation.

18 .

Section 3.3

OTHER PROVIDERS

This sub-section indicates alternative sources of accommodation for the Association's client groups. Again consideration is given to (1) Edinburgh and (ii) West Lothian.

EDINBURGH.

OWNER OCCUPATION

The predominant tenure within Edinburgh is owner-occupation (69% of all households). Those in low paid work or without work, i.e. the Association's clients, whose opportunities to become owner-occupiers are limited find it difficult to obtain "affordable" rented housing.

LOCAL AUTHORITY HOUSING

The 1992/97 Edinburgh District Council Housing Plan indicates that there are 40,302 Council properties within the City, a total which has been reduced by 14,379 (25%) as a result of house sales under the Right-to-Buy provisions.

The reduction in the number of Local Authority homes has been most evident amongst the 3-4 apartment types 90.9% of all houses sold by EDC have been of this form. 19.3% of Local Authority stock is now of 1 or 2 apartments while 5.5% comprises 3 apartments and 23% of 4 or more apartments.

Considerable public investment is currently being channelled towards Edinburgh's priority peripheral estate areas, as a means of improving homes and the quality of life for some residents within these areas.

PRIVATELY RENTED ACCOMMODATION

Despite the Government's supposed desire to increase the role of the private rented sector, house prices and the restrictions imposed by the Rent Registration Offices in respect of housing benefit subsidy, has reduced the proportion of privately rented accommodation available within the City. It is estimated that the number of rented bedspaces in multiple occupation dwellings within Edinburgh decreased by 37% since the introduction of the Housing (Scotland) Act, 1988. Many presently occupying privately rented accommodation feel insecure and would like access to either Housing Association or Local Authority stock.

HOUSING ASSOCIATIONS

As at 31st March,1991, there were 34 Housing Associations operating within the Edinburgh area renting 7,945 houses (34.8% special needs, 65.2% mainstream). A high proportion of the Housing Associations' stock consists of small flats in rehabilitated tenements,73.6% being of 1 and 2 apartments. Although Edinburgh Housing Associations' forecast a stock increase of 1,730 properties during the period 1989-1992, much of this will be as a result of development in the community programme in peripheral estates and further special needs provision. The net stock increase is therefore significantly less.

19.

Other Providers

WEST LOTHIAN

Owner Occupation
The proportion of owner-occupation within West Lothian increased markedly between 1988 and 1989 (an increase of 13.6%) as a result of a buoyant housing
market, Local Authority, Scottish Homes and Livingston Development Corporation
house sales.

Local Authority and Livingston Development Corporation
Both West Lothian District Council and the Livingston Development Corporation
witnessed marked reductions in their housing stock during the 1980's.   As a
direct result of this depletion,fewer opportunitites exist to provide suitable
accommodation for those in housing need or who require special provision.

Housing Associations
The involvement of Housing Associations has increased markedly since 1980
and 1989.

West Lothian District Council wish Housing Associations to provide both
mainstream housing and housing for those with special needs.   Canmore Housing
Association which has experience of managing a wide range of housing
provision, has its base only 15 minutes from the West Lothian border and is
well placed to make a practical contribution to the housing needs of the
District.

20.

Section 3.4

OPPORTUNITIES FOR DEVELOPMENT/GROWTH

Based on this Association's analysis it is our intention, in conjunction with Scottish Homes and the relevant Local Authorities, to cater for those in housing need, and we have identified the following development areas:-

i). **Provision for the housing needs of single people and families requiring mainstream housing.**

ii). **Provision for the elderly, particularly amenity but also sheltered and very sheltered housing. The Association also wish to develop initiatives which will enable existing elderly tenants to continue to occupy their existing homes, leading independent lives.**

111). **Provision in conjunction with external agencies of supported accommodation to meet the needs of the mentally ill and those with mental handicap.**

iv). **Provision within all new schemes of barrier-free housing and the establishment of suitably located wheelchair access housing for those with mobility problems.**

v). **Recognition and participation in programmes designed to house those suffering from AIDS and HIV related illnesses.**

vi). **Provision of partially furnished accommodation for those who require such provision.**

vii). **Provision of shared ownership and mid rent housing as a means of aiding economic expansion and widening housing choice for those on lower incomes throughout the operational area.**

viii). **Provision of work spaces related to new housing.**

21.

Section 4.1

RENT POLICY

The Association at present operates a rent setting system capable of catering for all housing types.

The Association's rent policy aims to ensure that:-

1.   Assured Tenancy Rents are as affordable to tenants as is in the Association's power to make them.

2.   The rents are consistent i.e. rents for existing property must bear a relationship to rents for new properties.

3.   Rents must reflect the value and amenities of the property concerned.

4.   Rents must fully cover the Association's Management-Maintenance, Major Repairs and Borrowing Costs.

5.   The rent policy must be simple to administer and as far as practicable understandable and justifiable to tenants.

The system is based upon a formula which, starting with a base rent for all properties, makes a specific charge for each feature and facility. It allows for value to be attributed in respect of both the age and the amenity enjoyed by the property and meets the criteria outlined above.

In devising this mechanism care has been taken to ensure that the rent levels produced are affordable to those Association tenants in work.

Analysis indicate that the average gross weekly income of those Canmore house-holds in work and not in receipt of Housing Benefit during 1993, was £164.64. Based on the average figure, Canmore Housing Association rents will represent between 18 and 30% of net income depending on the size and age of the property Most tenants' incomes fall below the average, however, in which case they are eligible for Housing Benefit.

Canmore Housing Association seeks to reduce, as far as possible, any disparity which exists between re-registered fair rents, new assured tenancy rents and annually reviewed assured tenancy rents.Fair Rent re-registration applications and rents proposed in bids to Scottish Homes for HAG, for new projects, are based on the use of our Rent Formula.

Fair Rent re-registrations in respect of older rehabilitated property have largely conformed to the Association's Rent Policy, the average rents in these cases being approximately £1,489 per annum (£28.63 per week).

Annex "B" illustrates present and future rent levels.

22.

Rent Policy(contd)

The present rent system has been flexible enough to cater for the wide range of housing types owned by the Association. The Association is, however, undertaking a wholesale review of its rent setting arrangements as a more sophisticated approach, incorporating detailed estimates of repair and main- tenance costs over the life of the properties, is now required. To this end, a survey of the Association's properties is being carried out and the results will be used to introduce a revised rent structure with effect from 1st January 1994. The basic policy with regard to affordability will, however, remain the same. The new rent structure is not expected to require radical or unacceptable increases across the board, though changes are likely.

An addendum to this Business Plan, giving full details of the new Rent Structure and Rent Setting arrangements will be available by January 1994.

Section 4.2

COMPARABLE MONTHLY RENTS -

Property Types	Canmore H.A.	Edinvar H.A.	Castle Rock H.A.
One Bedroom - (Edinburgh)	£143.00.p.m.	£138.54.p.m	£155.00.p.m.
Two Bedroom - (Edinburgh)	£166.33.p.m.	£156.00.p.m.	£176.00.p.m.
Three Bedroom - (Edinburgh)	£183.33.p.m.	£170.83.p.m.	£188.00.p.m.
One Bedroom - (West Lothian)	£143.00.p.m.	£127.38.p.m.	£140.00.p.m.

23.

Section 4.3

CANMORE HOUSING ASSOCIATION

Rent Setting Formula 1993

1.	Base Rent	£1150
	Bedrooms	
2.	Single	75
3.	Double	130
	Additional Bedrooms	
4.	Single as second bedroom	120
5.	Double as second bedroom	200
6.	Single as third bedroom	185
7.	Double as third bedroom	260
8.	Boxroom/dark bedroom	65
	Kitchen	
9.	Recessed kitchen	35
10.	Separate kitchen	130
11.	Kitchen/Dining-room	200
12.	No separate kitchen area	25
	Bathroom - Toilet	
13.	Bathroom	85
14.	Shower-room	65
15.	Separate toilet	30
	Amenities	
16.	Maindoor property	65
17.	Full house heating	120
18.	Absence of door entry system	-20
	Bedsit/Shared Accommodation	---
	Age of Property	
19.	Built/modernised less than 5 years ago	+ 10%
20.	Built/modernised between 5-10 years ago	+ 5%
	High-Low Amenity	
21.	High amenity	+ 5%
22.	Low amenity	- 5%
	Parking	
23.	Private off-street parking related to property	£55.

24.

Section 5.

STRUCTURE AND SKILLS

This should be read in conjunction with the Organisational Summary on Page 4.

The Association's Full Committee meets at least five times a year to establish policy, decide any issues deemed sufficiently important to be brought before the Full Committee,and to ratify decisions taken by the three Sub-Committees.   The Chairman, Kenneth Boal,is a High School Teacher with eight years service on Canmore's Committee of Management.

The Development Sub-Committee meets at least four times a year to receive and approve reports on work in progress, pipeline schemes, construction issues and to authorise relevant expenditure.   The Convenor, Gordon Fraser, is a Development Company Director and Quantity Surveyor and has extensive practical experience in all aspects of the construction business.

The Finance & General Purposes Sub-Committee meets at least five times a year to exercise financial control generally and specifically to approve and supervice budgets and accounts, salaries establishment and staffing issues. The Convenor is Kenneth Miller, a Bank Manager, with practical experience of financial control issues.

The Housing Management Sub-Committee meets at least four times a year to establish housing policies, priorities for applications, rent structures and to receive reports on new housing initiatives, rent arrears and maintenance issues.   The Convenor is Miss Nan White, former Chairman of the Gorgie Dalry Community Council and a retired Health Board Official.   She is a long time member of the Association with wide experience of tenant related issues.

The Committee of Management is at present reviewing its structure and operations with a view to considering whether even more effective arrange- ments are necessary.

The Association's Director and Secretary is Alan Brown (53),who formerly held senior posts with the Housing Corporation and Scottish Homes.   He has wide experience of housing association development and financial control issues and takes responsibility for the Full Committee.

The Association's Depute Secretary and Financial Manager is Arthur Cockburn, ACEA,(38). He was appointed Depute Secretary in 1990 having been Financial Manager since 1986.   He takes responsibility for the Finance and General Purposes Sub-Committee.

The Housing Manager is Graeme Russell,(BA.Hons),MRTPI,MIH, DipH. (35) who was appointed three years ago after seven years experience as Housing Officer. He has a Diploma in Housing Studies and takes responsibility for the Housing Management Sub-Committee.

The Development Manager is Mrs Susan Napier, BSc. ARICS, (37) who had eleven years experience of development work with another Housing Association before joining Canmore in January 1991. She takes responsibility for the Development Sub-Committee.

Section 5.1

CONTROL OF CONSULTANTS, CONTRACTORS AND AGENTS

Consultants are selected individually for all types of projects. All Consultants appointed must be on the Association's List of Approved Consultants, which is submitted for approval to each Development Sub-Committee. The criteria for successful inclusion is:-

a). Previous successful work completed for the Association.

b). Satisfactory references from other relevant clients.

On the conclusion of a successful feasibility study, a formal appointment will be made and fees will then be negotiated to secure the best value for money consistent with service to the Association.

Tenders will be sought, or contracts negotiated, with Contractors on the Association's List of Approved Contractors. The criteria for successful inclusion is:-

a). Satisfactory examination of latest annual audited accounts and annual reports.

b). Satisfactory banker's reference.

c). Satisfactory past performance either with the Association or relevant other clients.

The Design Team and Contractor on any development project must work within the Association's Development Procedures and Design Brief. The Association is provided with a programme of work from the Contractor, and Monthly Progress Reports from the Design Team, with progress related to the programme and anticipated variations of cost. All increases to the contract sum must be explained and, if possible, compensated for by equivalent savings The Design Team is expected to be particularly vigilant on slippage in the programme which might lead to claims for Loss & Expense from extensions to the contract period.

The Association ensures that routine and extraordinary maintenance items and office supplies are obtained at the most competitive prices. It is recognised that substantial economies can be made if attention is paid to systematic reviewing of procurement policies for revenue as well as for capital items.

26.

Section 6.1

PERFORMANCE INDICATORS	1.	HOUSING MANAGEMENT

MANAGEMENT.	1991	1992
Application Form Requests	1050	998
Application Forms Received	905	616
Active Waiting List Numbers	127	211
Home Visits	189	192
Tenancies Terminated	52	68
New Tenancies Commenced .	52	68
New Tenancies Created (new projects)	116	22
Total Houses in Management	695	722
Average Time to Relet	12	13

ACCOUNTING	1991	1992
Total Rents Receivable	789,153	1051561
Total Rents Received	770,950	1069178
Rents Received as % of Rents Receivable	98.69%	101.67%*
Voids/Bad Debts	19,614	12386
Voids as % of Rents Receivable	2.49%**	1.18%
Gross Cumulative Arrears(current tenants)	26,669	18632
Gross Cumulative Arrears(former tenants)	3,836	2383
No. of Tenants more than £100 in arrears	40	74
Housing Management costs as % of allowances	98.48%	91.5%

Last Update of Tenants' Handbook		1991
Date of last Tenant Satisfaction Survey		1993

* Exceptional repayment of arrears.

** Temporary increase in consequence of large number of Transfers moving into new property.

27.

Section 6.2

PERFORMANCE INDICATORS	2.	DEVELOPMENT

FINANCE	1991/92	1992/93
Scottish Homes Business Plan Bid	3,590,000	7,889,000
HAG Cash Planning Target	1,785,000	1,877,387
HAG Allocation		3,252,448
% CPT spent in year	97.12%	173.24%

OTHER GRANTS		
	-	-

	1991	1992
PRIVATE LOANS	1,249,535	1,885,528

CAPITAL RECEIPTS	-	-

INCOME GENERATED:Development Alowances	50,685	112,826
Clerk of Work Allowances	-	-

SURPLUS/(DEFICIT)ON DEV. ADMIN.	6,072	2,675
DEVELOPMENT COSTS AS % OF DEV.INCOME	88%	98%

UNITS		1991	1992
Unit	Completions	138	36
Unit	Acquisitions	20	83
	Approvals Acquisitions	8	83
	Approvals Tender	20	47

Section 6.3

28.

PERFORMANCE INDICATORS	3.	MAINTENANCE

REACTIVE MAINTENANCE	1991	1992
Job Orders	2,540	2980
% Response Times Achieved	81%	82.71%
Average cost/dwelling/annum	£312	£297
% cost under allowances	96.6%	95.2%
Overheads as % of total reactive maintenance costs	33%	39%

CYCLICAL MAINTENANCE	1991	1992
Average cost/dwelling/annum	117	148
% cost under allowances	54%	68%
Overheads as % of total Cyclical maintenance costs	27%	26%

There is a life cycle costing system in course of preparation.

29.

Section 6.4

PERFORMANCE INDICATORS	4.	FINANCE

INCOME AND EXPENDITURE	1991	1992
INCOME		
Net Rents	677857	923912
Net Service Charges	83682	115263
Clerk of Works	–	–
Development	50685	112826
Commercial Rents	–	–
Investments	129717	137421
Other Income	979	120784
TOTAL	942920	1410206
EXPENDITURE		
Residual Loans	95259	211025
Service Costs	76334	108459
Maintenance Costs	171199	218127
Staff Costs	216618	268119
Office Overheads	100833	159070
Other Expenses	112134	226483
TOTAL	772377	1191283
SURPLUS	170543	218923

Section 6.5

PERFORMANCE INDICATORS	5.	CONTROL & ACCOUNTABILITY

MEMBERSHIP	1991	1992
* Total Membership Numbers *	99	123

THE ASSOCIATION HAS IN OPERATION, THE FOLLOWING	Tick or Name
*1. Membership Policy *	Yes
*2. Tenant Participation Policy *	Yes
*3. Equal Opportunities Policy	Yes
*Equal Opportunities Targets *	No
*4. Open Access Policy	Yes
*Open Access Monitoring *	Yes
*5 Staff Conditions of Employment *	Yes
*6 Staff Appraisal System *	Yes
*7 Training Programme and Budget *	Yes
*8 Participation in Outside Bodies	Yes

31.

Section 7.

Summary of Financial Information
The Association has established a sound financial base and presently has over £1.25m of uncommitted reserves with a forecast to achieve £1.44m of un-committed reserves by December 1993. The Annual Revenue Surplus, generated mainly by Investment Interest is predicted to be £197,276.

Close attention is paid by the Association to its financial performance by the analysis of its Management Accounts every quarter. Deviations from budgeted performances are analysed and corrective action, if possible, is taken. The Annual Budget is prepared each November for the following financial year and contributions and responsibilities for the various items within the budget are delegated to the appropriate Managers/Directors of the Association.

The following financial statements outline past performance and the forecasts of future performance.

Section 7.1

SUMMARY OF FINANCIAL INFORMATION

Summary of last 3 years results
(i) Income & Expenditure

		1992		1991		1990
PROPERTY REVENUE ACCOUNT						
Total Income		1039175		761539		578592
Less:						
Property Management Cost	182960		164728		135113	
Property Maintenance Costs	321052		272009		229868	
Service Costs	116459		83634		59133	
Loan Repayments	211025	(831496)	95259	(615630)	53631	(477745)
PROPERTY REVENUE ACCOUNT SURPLUS		207679		145909		100847
DEVELOPMENT ACCOUNT Surplus/(Deficit)		2675		6072		(32366)
OTHER INCOME(Gross Interest on Investments less tax		242015		85182		145632
RENT SURPLUS FUND TRANSFER		(132159)		(66620)		(32657)
TRANSFER TO RESERVES		(101287)		-		(190569)
TOTAL SURPLUS/(DEFICIT) FOR THE YEAR		218923		170543		(9113)

32.

Section 7.1

(ii) Balance Sheet.

	1992	1991	1990
FIXED ASSETS Housing Property at Cost	19399593	16644938	13755128

Less:						
Property Equity	16994548		14886791		10388560	
Depreciation	44018	17038566	18884	14905675	16096	10404656
		2361027		1739263		3350472

	1992	1991	1990
OTHER FIXED ASSETS	799206	392346	569514
TOTAL NET FIXED ASSETS	3160233	2131609	3919986
CURRENT ASSETS (Investment & Cash)	1739051	1315957	733215
CURRENT LIABILITIES	(143467)	(182274)	(55077)
PROVISIONS	(607883)	(513478)	(472961)
	4147934	2751814	4125163

Financed By:-

	1992	1991	1990
Scottish Homes/Private Lenders	2273780	1692924	3245949
Share Capital	123	99	74
Non Housing Loan	567479	-	-
Sales Reserve	26280	25977	21414
Other Reserves	33080	4545	-
Accumulated Surpluses	1247192	1028269	857726
	4147934	2751814	4125163

Section 7.2

FORECAST RESULTS

(i) Projected Income and Expenditure (000's)

	1993		1994		1995		1996	
PROPERTY REVENUE ACCOUNT								
Total Income		1264		1524		1777		2036
Less:								
Property Management Costs	236		254		297		353	
Property Maintenance Costs	392		447		496		589	
Service Costs	130		142		156		172	
Loan Repayments	305	1063	409	1252	540	1489	631	1745
Property Revenue Account Surplus		201		272		288		291
Development Account Surplus		43		79		5		5
Sales Account		4		3		3		3
OTHER INCOME AND EXPENDITURE		68		65		68		71
RENT SURPLUS FUND TRANSFER/MAJOR REPAIRS		(119)		(143)		(172)		(206)
Total Surplus for the year		197		276		192		164
		===		===		===		===

Section 7.2 (contd)

(ii)   <u>Projected Balance Sheet (000's)</u>

	1993		1994		1995		1996	
<u>FIXED ASSETS</u>								
Housing Properties		24892		27670		32001		38868
Less:								
Property Equity	20654		22594		25622		30427	
Depreciation	<u>56</u>	<u>20710</u>	<u>76</u>	<u>22670</u>	<u>106</u>	<u>25728</u>	<u>146</u>	<u>30573</u>
		4182		5000		6273		8295
Other Fixed Assets		788		793		798		803
TOTAL NET FIXED ASSETS		4970		5793		7071		9098
Current Assets		1592		1928		2180		2404
Current Liabilities		(100)		(105)		(110)		(115)
Provisions		(<u>732</u>)		(<u>792</u>)		(<u>852</u>)		(<u>912</u>)
		5730		6824		8289		10475
		====		====		====		====
<u>FINANCED BY</u>:-								
Private Loans and Mortgages		4182		5000		6273		8295
Sales Reserves		26		26		26		26
Accumulated Surpluses		<u>1522</u>		<u>1798</u>		<u>1990</u>		<u>2154</u>
		5730		6824		8289		10475
		====		====		====		====

Section 8.1

STRATEGY

The Association's principal aim is to provide housing for those in acute housing need and to manage these houses to the highest standards. The Association is aware that the demand for such housing outstrips supply and will seek, in co-operation with Scottish Homes and others, to provide additional housing within the operational range of the Association's base.

The Association must be customer driven, innovative and will need to work in close partnership with both public and private sectors. The uncommitted financial reserves of the Association will be used to pump prime new housing opportunities where necessary.

The commitment and skill of the Association's staff is its key resource and the highest priority will be given to staff development.

The key elements of the strategy for the Association over the next 18 months will be:-

- The pursuit by the Association of its chosen goals and opportunities.

- The continued effective management of existing and new stock and retention of the Association's local credibility while pursuing new goals.

- The continuing adjustment of the management of the Association so that it takes full account of the changed financial climate and much more competitive atmosphere in which Housing Associations generally operate.

- The requirement to market the Association as a good developer and manager of houses to the widest possible range of clients, and partners.

PROGRAMME OF ACTION

To achieve this broad strategy, the Association has adopted a programme of action with four key objectives.

    i. To promote the Association's initiative and services in a competitive market.

    ii. To provide an appropriate range of services and housing developments to meet the growing housing demand in the Association's operational area.

    iii. To secure the present development pipeline.

    iv. To provide cost effective management and financial in-formation systems in support of new initiatives.

36.

Section 8.2

Business Plan Bid 1994/95 for HAG

Schemes in order of Priority	No.Flats	HAG 94/95	95/96	96/97	97/98
Under Construction 94/95					
Morrison Street	75	1770000			
Gorgie Goods Yard,Slateford Rd.	69	1000000	701000		
507 Gorgie Road,Chesser.	61	750000	1206000		
Misc. Commons	9	127000			
TENANTS' INCENTIVE SCHEME	4	40000	40000	40000	40000
Site Purchases 94/95					
Morrison Street	12	200000	130000		
101 Gorgie Road	6	70000	160000		
Harrison Road	20	200000	300000	270000	
Under Consideration 94/95					
West End Place	12		150000	110000	200000
Caledonian Distillery,Dalry Rd.	40		400000	750000	390000
Ferranti Site,Robertson Ave.	40			400000	750000
Pentland Annexe,Gorgie Rd.	40			400000	750000
40 Balcarres Street	24		300000	200000	425000
Longstone Street	15		150000	200000	225000
Phase 5 Caledonian Cres.Env.				50000	
TOTAL EDINBURGH		4157000	3537000	2420000	2780000

Section 8.3

	No.Flats	HAG 94/95	95/96	96/97	97/98
Under Construction 94/95					
Torphichen - Site 2 The Loan	14	292000			
Bathgate - Sth. Bridge Str.	27	276000			
Blackburn - Mosside Rd.	25	600000			
Stoneyburn - Main Street	18	374000			
Site Purchases 94/95					
Linlithgow - Preston Rd	9		70000	180000	
Under Consideration 94/95					
Linlithgow - Colthill - LCHO	20		225000	225000	
East Calder	20		150000	480000	
TOTAL - WEST LOTHIAN		1612000	555000	705000	

	No.Flats	HAG 94/95	95/96		
Site Purchases 94/95					
MUSSELBURGH	5	175000			

	No.Flats	HAG 94/95	95/96		
Site Purchases 94/95					
DUNFERMLINE - Headwell Rd	6	100000	89000		

37.

Section 8.4

SUBMISSION FOR TENANT INCENTIVE SCHEME FUNDING
Canmore Housing Association wishes to apply for four Tenant Incentive Scheme
Grants as a means of freeing much needed accommodation for re-letting.

Housing Stock Analysis/Needs Assessment
Although our 1-2 person two apartment properties become available on an
irregular basis, such is the level of demand, particularly from one and two
person households (64.5%) of applicants accepted to the Allocation List) that
we can house only a small proportion of those in need.   Similarly 3-4 apartment family housing is greatly in demand both amongst existing over-crowded
tenants and applicants admitted to our Allocation List.

During the second half of 1992, the Association received a total of 616
applications of which 271 were accepted to our Allocation List.   During
the whole of 1992, 90 properties became available for letting.

Any mechanism which would encourage existing tenants, capable of sustaining
owner-occupation, to relinquish their tenancies, would enable us to re-house
from our Allocation or Transfer Lists individuals deemed to be in need.

Tenants' Interest
A number of tenants, currently occupying a variety of house types have
indicated a desire to become owner-occupiers outwith our traditional area of
operation, but have been discouraged by the costs involved.   It would be our
intention to approach such tenants with a view to offering T.I.S. Grants.

Likely Grant Requirements
We would envisage targeting four existing tenants (occupying 2 or 3 apartment
property) as a means of releasing the property for re-letting to those on our
Transfer or Allocation List.

Prioritising Applicants
It would be our intention to target T.I.S.Grants towards tenants who had:-

    i)   Previously indicated a desire to relinquish their tenure
        and move from our area.

    ii)   Considered purchasing their present home.

but who had been restrained by the costs involved.

Monitoring
It would be the intention of the Association to monitor the scheme
in conjunction with the regular reviews undertaken of applicant demand, in
order to target the Grants to tenants occupying those properties most in
demand.

Section 8.5

PUBLIC SECTOR STOCK TRANSFERS
While Canmore Housing Association is not prepared to become involved in competitive bidding, it is prepared to negotiate directly with Public Sector
Housing Authorities (and their tenants) wishing to transfer stock to alternative ownership.

Section 9.

ANNEX A:

Housing Stock as at 31st August 1993.

Apartment Size	Newbuild	Rehabilitated	Total
1	20	3	23
2	86	491	577
3	72*	133	205
4	22	16	38
7	1	—	1
	201	643	844
	===	===	===

(* including 20 shared-ownership properties).

Inclusive Special Needs Provision

	Newbuild	Rehabilitated	Total
Amenity	16	3	19
Sheltered Housing	19	14	33
Very Sheltered Housing	7	-	7
Wheelchair Access	2	1	3
Furnished Tenancies	8	3	11
Hostels	3	-	3
Shared Flats	-	2	2
	55	23	78
	===	====	===

ANNEX B: TO BE COMPLETED & ATTACHED TO BUSINESS PLANS: RENTAL FRAMEWORK

HOUSING ASSOCIATION .... CANMORE .... BUSINESS PLAN FOR PERIOD COMMENCING (FINANCIAL YEAR) ....1994........

Illustrative rent levels based on rental policy incorporated in the Business Plan and applied to the various project types planned for cost plan and design and/or tender approval in the following year (fill in the applicable boxes only)

HOUSE SIZE	ILLUSTRATIVE ASSURED TENANCY ANNUAL RENT LEVELS, BASED ON CURRENT YEAR RENTAL POLICY				ESTIMATED ASSURED TENANCY ANNUAL RENT LEVELS, BASED ON CURRENT YEAR + 1 (ie YEAR 1 OF BUSINESS PLAN) PROJECTED RENTAL POLICY			
	NEW BUILD	REHABILITATION (pre 1919)	COMO (modernisation of post 1919 ex public sector stock)	OTHER (specify)	NEW BUILD	REHABILITATION	COMO	OTHER (specify) students
Hostel Bedspace	£1150	£1150			1196	1196		1500
1 Person	£1716	£1544			1784	1605		
2 Person	£1776	£1598			1847	1662		
3 Person	£1908	£1717			1984	1785		
4 Person	£1996	£1796			2075	1867		
5 Person	£2200	£1980			2288	2059		
6 Person	£2282	£2053			2373	2135		
7 or more persons								

Note: (i)   If the housing association intends to cater for a mix of client groups for whom significantly different rents are proposed, and/or to cover a range of locations in which significantly different rents are proposed, please append separate details or use the "Other" column (and specify).

(ii)   The assumptions on which current rents are projected for the following year should be clearly stated within the Rental Policy in the business Plan.

Certification (1)   The above rental proposals are calculated on the basis of the rent policy set out in the association's Business Plan.

(2)   The association will amend these proposals in accordance with any variation in rental policy which may be agreed following appraisal by and consultation with Scottish Homes.

Signed .... Date

BUSINESS PLANS

A Compendium

HOUSING ASSOCIATIONS

**Cynon Tâf
Housing Association Ltd**

Corporate Plan 1992 - 1995

*This plan is due to be revised and updated
in the near future.*

Note:

Appendices 5, 6 and 7 (staffing structure; senior staff details; committee of management details) are not reproduced.

CYNON TÂF
HOUSING ASSOCIATION LTD

CORPORATE PLAN
1992 – 1995

CYNON-TAF HOUSING ASSOCIATION LIMITED

CORPORATE PLAN

1992 — 1995

Cynon-Taf Housing Association Limited is the largest of the indigenous housing associations operating in the South Wales Valleys.

It was founded in 1978 by a group of people in Cynon Valley who were concerned at the deteriorating housing situation within their Borough. Operations actually commenced in July 1979 since which time some 931 homes have been provided within the communities of the valley. This has primarily taken place through the medium of the rehabilitation of older properties although, since the implementation of the mixed funded regime the emphasis has, of necessity, swung toward new build. Special needs have not been forgotten and provision has been made for ex-psychiatric patients, people with learning difficulties and women who have been subjected to domestic violence as well as sheltered housing for the older members of society.

The Association is fully independent, is recognised as a charity by the Inland Revenue and is registered with Housing For Wales. This is the body that administers Housing Association Grant throughout Wales on behalf of central government. Housing associations are thus able to purchase land and develop accommodation for those in greatest need.

Cynon-Taf Housing Association Limited is active within the Welsh Federation of Housing Associations and as such conforms in all respects to its Code of Conduct for Housing Associations.

There follows a report of the Association's Corporate Plan for the period 1992 to 1995. It lays down the aims and values that are necessary in addressing the current housing needs of the communities that we serve, and the measures that will be necessary in this next period in the Association's development.

D H LEWIS
DIRECTOR

SEPTEMBER 1992

1

INDEX

SECTION ONE

ORGANISATIONAL OBJECTIVES

OUR PURPOSE IS:

1.1   TO   develop and manage good quality rented accommodation (and other low cost tenures) for people in necessitous circumstances upon terms that are appropriate to their means, particular attention being given to those in low paid employment.

OUR INTENTIONS ARE:

1.2   TO   develop and manage good quality rented accommodation (or other low cost tenures) designed or adapted to meet the specific disabilities and requirements of the aged, disabled, handicapped and chronically sick persons.

1.3   TO   provide services, advice or assistance to aged, disabled, handicapped and chronically sick persons in need of arranging or carrying out works of improvement, repair or maintenance to houses occupied by them, at terms appropriate to their means.

1.4   TO   operate fair, open and accountable policies to ensure that housing is let to those in greatest need thereof.

1.5   TO   provide an effective, efficient, economic and participative housing service to all tenants.

1.6   TO   contribute to and participate in wider aspects of housing, urban regeneration, environmental improvements, training/employment initiatives and community activities and encourage participation and consultation with residents and the community.

1.7   TO   be fully accountable for all our activities to our tenants, the appropriate statutory authorities and the general public.

1.8   TO   ensure that we are able to honour current and future capital and revenue commitments through the prudent management of our financial affairs.

1.9   TO   provide the highest possible standards in the design and construction of our housing, having particular regard to long term maintenance obligations and the cost of use to our tenants.

1.10   TO   be a fair employer and offer staff training openings and career advancement against a background of continuing commitment to equal opportunities in respect of employment and access to services.

1.11   TO   develop positive partnerships with other housing associations, funding bodies and statutory/voluntary agencies to ensure our primary objectives are successfully secured.

SECTION TWO

FUTURE DIRECTIONS

2.1 The Association will continue to focus its housing services and investment over the next three years in the Borough of Cynon Valley. This will include the rehabilitation of existing houses, wherever the funding arrangements allow, as well as selected new build schemes.

2.2 The Committee of Management will consider proposals for investment outside of the above area based upon the following criteria:-

- it is consistent with its aims and objectives

- effective and accountable services can be provided

- local authority support is obtained

- the activity does not detract from the pursuance of development opportunities and existing commitments within our traditional area.

2.3 Consideration will be given to the diversification of activities on the understanding that such work is consistent with the Association's permitted objects. Such areas of activity can be summarised as follows:-

- support for Cynon Valley Home Improvement Agency in recognition of the need for such a service given the high number of elderly and disadvantaged owner occupiers in Cynon Valley who suffer inferior housing conditions.

- co-operation with Merthyr and Cynon Groundwork Trust in bringing about environmental improvements within the communities that we serve

- assisting the efforts of Cynon Valley Housing Co-operative in establishing co-operative tenure in Cynon Valley

- encouragement of Cynon Homes in their efforts to widen housing choice

- support for Shelter (Wales) in their effort to provide an effective housing advice service in Mid Glamorgan.

- links with any other organisation operating within the Borough or having an impact in it, where the aims and objectives of that organisation are sympathetic to, or in keeping with, those of the Association.

2.4 The Association recognises the moves within Housing For Wales to concentrate the development activities of housing associations with the assumption that better value for money can be achieved.

Against this background it is vital that the Association's performance in all respects achieves targets established by Housing For Wales, funding bodies, Cynon Valley Borough Council and those it establishes for itself. An important factor in this process is to ensure prudent financial management and development control to minimise the Association's exposure to risk. However, over the next three years, the Association is prepared to consider proposals to work with or for other associations to secure mutual development objectives.

2.5 Any proposal for development rationalisation and its impact on the Association will be dealt with professionally and proposals thoroughly examined based on the following criteria:-

- the independence and identity of the Association is not threatened

- it will result in an increase in the provision of good quality accommodation for those in greatest need

- high standards of provision and services are not diluted

- tenants and relevant statutory and voluntary organisations are fully consulted

- the interests of the Association's staff are properly considered

- accountability to tenants and communities can be secured

- voluntary member control and executive delegation are clearly defined

- activities are not undertaken which are contrary to the Association's permitted objects.

At all times, the primary concern of members and senior staff must be to protect the best interests of the Association, its tenants and staff.

2.6 Stock transfers or management agreements with other associations to more adequately recognise existing and future areas of activity will be considered. This should be supported in conjunction with the Welsh Federation of Housing Associations and Housing For Wales.

2.7 The Association does not envisage being involved in any local authority stock transfers or management agencies whether by way of tenants choice legislation or other mechanisms. Provision of new homes must be the priority and stock transfers or management agencies could only be considered on the basis of the following criteria:-

- a clear majority of tenants specifically request or vote for Cynon-Taf's involvement

- local authority support is obtained

- sufficient capital and revenue resources are available to enhance existing provision and services to tenants

- the long term management of stock is consistent with the Association's Management Plan.

2.8   In all its activities the Association will strive to implement and develop good practice and conduct itself in a manner consistent with an organisation in receipt of public funding and within guidelines established by the Welsh Federation of Housing Associations and Housing For Wales.

2.9   Many significant challenges face the Association in the coming years, however, with the skill and dedication of Committee Members and staff, the aims will be acheived through the objectives it has set itself. Irrespective of its external profile the Association must never become complacent but continually review its policies and practices so they adequately reflect its responsibilities.

SECTION THREE

GROWTH PROFILE

3.1   Based on the known capital allocations from Housing For Wales for our stock will increase by 259 units in the next three years. There is no indication of possible allocations beyond that date, but there may be a possibility of extending this figure through rehabilitation undertaken with local authority renovation grants.

3.2   The projected figures for units in management, excluding the rehabilitation possibility, at the 30th September in each year are as follows:-

1992	963
1993	1074
1994	1157
1995	1222

This is indicated in Appendix I attached.

3.3   The average level of growth throughout this period is not untypical of previous years. However, in this changing world, Committee members and senior staff will have to acquire further skills to cope with new emphases and approaches successfully.

3.4   As a greater proportion of our stock is subject to the mixed funded regime, the tensions between rent levels, standards, viability and risk management will become more critical and could undermine our best intentions. Resolving these problems will probably be a dominant feature of future years.

3.5   Many important factors, outside of our direct control, will also influence progress. Actual capital allocations, subsidy levels, the cost of loans, definitions of affordability, market forces, letting rates, further changes in the funding regime, the adaptability of the system toward rehabilitation and pressures on the existing structure of the voluntary housing movement in Wales could encourage or frustrate us in reaching our goals.

3.6   It is essential, therefore, that we use the annual review of the Management Plan as a dynamic process to review targets and ensure that change is managed effectively based on our established long term objectives.

3.7   The following sections highlight measures that should be taken to ensure the impact of future change is successfully managed and controlled.

SECTION FOUR

FINANCIAL PROFILE

4.1   Prudent financial management over previous years has placed us in a very strong position to face the future. We have an accumulated surplus approaching £2 million and substantial provisions for cyclical maintenance and major repairs sinking funds.

4.2   The cash flow position is extremely healthy with the prospect of a significant build up in sinking funds and reserves in future years.

4.3   The profile of housing stock shows an increasing level of new build developments and in assured tenancies with their self-determined rents increasing from forty-six to fifty-six percent. of the total.

4.4   Our ability to secure private funds in support of the development programme and manage their use in a prudent way, that adheres to all accounting requirements and internal control procedures, will play a major part in determining our success, or otherwise, in achieving long term objectives.

4.5   Rent setting will obviously have a considerable effect on financial plan-ning and our ability to meet development targets, whilst ensuring appropriate housing management and maintenance services are properly resourced. Internal financing to meet the shortfall between the rents and actual costs, including prudent provisions for future liabilities, will need to be carefully controlled to avoid excessive strain on the Associa-tion's cash flow and reserves.

4.6   It would now appear that the plan to abolish the Rent Surplus Fund has been abandoned for the time being. Should it be revived then it will be of great assistance in allowing rent pooling to be a reality and thus spreading the impact of growth more evenly across the housing stock. In saying that it must be remembered that it would bring increased responsibilities for maintaining homes to a high standard as all future building failures would have to be self financed. Consideration will be given to offset part or all of this potential liability through insurance cover for defects via Housing Association's Property Mutual.

4.7   The longer term trend on mixed funded schemes is illustrated in the appendices. Appendix II shows the projected results of pipeline mixed funded developments. Whilst all future schemes may not be financed in this way it does give an indication of the underlying position including the need to generate sinking funds. After the first six years progress is made toward the healthy surpluses that can be expected by nature of conventional loan finance.

4.8   In Appendix III, projected cash reserves are indicated assuming that all development period funding is provided from our own resources. The moving average is fairly steady throughout the three years and thus indicates a very satisfactory situation, particularly since additional expenditure due to higher staffing levels and new office accommodation has been included. Should development finance be obtained from other sources then these reserves would show considerable growth.

4.9   Irrespective of the essentially healthy nature of these projections and the undoubted stability of the organisation, it is essential that appropriate financial disciplines and procedures are adhered to at all times. To this end a balanced portfolio of loans should be aimed at with the intent of allowing maximum flexibility coupled with minimum risk.

4.10 Our capital adequacy, or the long term equity in our stock, will be an important factor in ensuring that we are disciplined in the approach to development aspirations and risk management. Combined with the projections of future financial stability, we can convince potential lenders that Cynon-Taf has more than adequate security for loans and is implementing sound techniques for money management.

4.11 A number of items will need to be addressed within the three year cycle to ensure continued financial success. Among other matters these may include:-

-   review of financial and related regulations;

-   enhancement of internal audit and control procedures;

-   procedure guides covering all aspects of the financial function;

-   development of cost centred management;

-   greater attention to money management in the light of future capital and revenue commitments and the requirement to maximise investment income;

-   improved systems to more accurately assess scheme costs and cash flows with resulting development and long term funding requirements;

-   review of the Risk Management Policy (see Appendix V) and increased sophistication in the preparation of viability studies;

-   a property audit and whole life cost analysis to more adequately forecast the investment required to maintain current and future stock to a high standard;

-   continued scrutiny of the criteria used to set and amend rent levels;

-   re-evaluation of the policy on the use of internal funding to resource development;

–   development of policy on the basic level of free reserves
         necessary to under-pin development and long term risk and that
         available to subsidise current and future rent levels.

4.12   The Association has a particularly good record in the management of its
         financial affairs.   However, we must not under-estimate the necessity
         for consistent review and improvement in procedures that enable the
         Committee of Management and senior staff to exercise proper control
         over the significant responsibility that the future will bring.

4.13   Fundamental to this approach will be our ability to minimise risk, accur-
         ately assess costs and develop a borrowing strategy and loans portfolio
         that affords us maximum flexibility.

SECTION FIVE

DEVELOPMENT STRATEGY

5.1 Indications suggest that we should produce a minimum of 75 new homes every year, although this may need to be radically increased should the local authority place greater emphasis on urban renewal. In either case we must achieve cash limited allocation targets and harness private sector resources against a background of sound financial management and tight control of the development programme and its attendant risks.

5.2 We must examine development projects and opportunities within a clear strategy which sets the priorities to be observed and identifies the most cost effective methods of bringing about objectives.

5.3 There has been a significant trend, in recent years, away from our traditional rehabilitation role towards new build projects and this is likely to continue for the foreseeable future. This development has not been part of any planned approach and is deplored by both the Association and the strategic housing authority alike, however, it is the natural consequence of the disincentives that are inherent in the financial regime for such work and its unknown qualities which can adversely affect risk exposure.

5.4 It is our intention to continue to focus activity within the Borough of Cynon Valley. In doing so due cognisance will be given to the specific needs and objectives identified within the housing authority's Housing Strategies and Investment Programme.

5.5 Within these local authority corporate objectives, we will seek to encourage small scale developments targeted to agreed priority need groups.

5.6 As indicated by the local authority and our own observations, rehabilitation remains an essential ingredient in ensuring a balanced programme. Given the difficulties previously mentioned further discussion will take place with Housing For Wales and investigation will be undertaken as to whether the local authority renovation grants could be effectively used in this regard.

5.7 Development of special needs housing should not be by specifically designed projects with voluntary organisations acting as management agents. Rather, we should seek to use conventional stock with packages of support provided by appropriate statutory/voluntary agencies under-pinned by the Special Needs Management Allowance arrangements.

5.8 The outcome of the Housing For Wales consultation on their document, "Improving the Effectiveness of Housing Association Development and Management", will have a considerable effect on procurement methods along with design specification and standards. Within any imposed constraints we will endeavour to maintain the highest standards of provision whether through our own organisation or some other agency. As far as it remains possible we will seek to:

–   choose the contractual arrangements for procurement on the basis of their suitability for particular projects and their merits in achieving maximum development control and minimum risk;

–   provide definitive guidance on new build and rehabilitation projects, to consultants on the space standards and specification materials that are known to work and take due account of long term maintenance obligations and the cost in use for tenants;

–   maintain enhanced technical records of schemes that are in progress so as to facilitate highest possible degree of development control;

–   regularly review the approved panels of consultants and contractors to ensure that capacity and performance is appropriate to the on-going programme and the standards we set ourselves.

5.9   Irrespective of the systems that are eventually adopted or imposed, a comprehensive procedure guide will be prepared to allow for internal/external audit and staff induction.

SECTION SIX

HOUSING MANAGEMENT & MAINTENANCE SERVICES

6.1 The move in emphasis to new build and the general requirements of the mixed funded regime has considerable impact on the style and effectiveness of the management and maintenance services provided to tenants.

6.2 The ability to continue to deliver high quality services will depend on the standards of homes produced and the resources available to manage and maintain our stock effectively.

6.3 Housing management policies will be regularly reviewed to ensure that they comply with current best practice guidance and with the requirements of the law, Tenants' Guarantee and Performance Standards.

6.4 Every effort must be made to ensure that future methods, whether adopted internally or imposed from outside, allow for housing management and maintenance staff to be fully consulted and be able to influence the design and specification of new homes.

6.5 Rent setting should fully recognise the need to properly resource future management responsibilities and make prudent provisions for long term maintenance obligations, particularly bearing in mind the age of our stock and the disappearance of funding for Grant Aided Repairs.

6.6 Affordability and rent levels will need to be monitored to ensure that they remain within reach of those in low paid employment, thus ensuring high letting rates, low voids and arrears levels that do not escalate and thereby undermine our financial stability.

6.7 Alternative methods of rent collection will be investigated while, at the same time, ensuring our computerised rent accounting system has sufficient capacity and flexibility to cope with the increasing demands that will be placed upon it.

6.8 Considerable effort will be put into encouraging tenant participation at all levels of the Association's activity. In particular a high quality information service for tenants must be maintained as a vehicle to full consultation and specific measures should be taken to obtain feedback from tenants of our homes.

6.9 The computerisation of maintenance records and administration will be completed and further developed to ensure the identification of problem areas, materials and design. This will include a review of the systems whereby tenants are notified of orders placed and certify their satisfaction with the work carried out.

6.10 A more systematic approach to property inspections should be introduced to form a more reliable data base for cyclical and planned maintenance programmes. This is particularly important as the need to develop whole life costing and the resulting financial provisions becomes more pressing with the curtailment of Grant Aided Repair funding and the need to prudently manage sinking funds.

13

6.11   Development must be needs led. This requires Housing Management to take a more pro-active role in forward programmes to ensure that informed decisions are made in the light of historical letting trends and identified future priorities.

6.12   Further review of service charge setting and accounting methods should be undertaken. This must ensure that charges are fair and reasonable and that specific and general income and expenditure data on services is easily obtained.

6.13   During the next year, a review will take place of the capacity of the Association to undertake part or the whole of its own repairs. This will examine the effectiveness of the present systems and consideration of whether the service could be improved through direct labour.

6.14   It is intended that a Common Waiting List and Lettings Policy, with Cynon Valley Borough Council, will be put in place early in the life of this Plan. While this will account for the majority of applicants and tenants, further intensive discussions on nomination arrangements and level of provision will take place, with the strategic housing authority, regarding special needs, the homeless and the poorly housed.

6.15   Procedure guides will be established to facilitate induction training for new staff, external/internal audit and accountability.

SECTION SEVEN

STAFFING PROFILE AND STRUCTURE

7.1   There tends to be a significant level of commitment and teamwork within our staff. Most have an intimate understanding of, and identify strongly with the Association's work. Our approach to staff management and general personnel functions is an important ingredient in ensuring that we do not loose these advantages, but bring everyone along with us. The senior management team has an important role to play in this regard.

7.2   In the past twelve months there have been a number of significant changes and additions to the staff. These are not encumbered with idealist dreams of the past and so can and do play an important part in planning and realising a dynamic future for the organisation.

7.3   Several changes in staffing policies and procedures have already been made and further recommendations will be considered to address the need for a more consistent approach to personnel and related matters.

7.4   As part of an induction programme for new staff and to regularise the position with existing, a Staff Handbook must be completed. This should incorporate information on all staffing policies and provisions particularly equal opportunities, health and safety, paternity leave and training as well as general supplementary information to the Contract of Employment.

7.5   The Contract of Employment will be examined to identify any changes that may be necessary as the Association further develops its personnel and staffing policies.

7.6   As a result of the staff appraisal system, a more comprehensive annual training plan will need to be developed in recognition of the enhanced and new skills that will be necessary for the future.

7.7   Consideration will be given as to how staff can be best encouraged and assisted towards career advancement through further and/or higher education.

7.8   Moves have been made away from a general administrative backup to a position where these services are more closely related to individual sections. This will be further developed since it enables staff to become familiar with sectional priorities and enhances the team based approach.

7.9   Proposals for an increased level of tenant participation and consultation will require additional staff. In addition, further consideration will need to be given to the size and spread of our housing stock, the effects of the implementation of the Common Waiting List and to whether area based housing management responsibilities should be allocated.

15

7.10   In order that our commitment to a more systematic approach to cyclical and planned maintenance can be accomplished and the day to day maintenance service enhanced, a total restructure of this function is needed.   At the very least this will involve the appointment of a section controller and the provision of administrative support.

7.11   The great imponderable in determining the future staffing structure is the outcome of the consultation process on their document, "Improving the Effectiveness of Housing Association Development and Management". This could result in all the Association's development programme being undertaken by someone else, however, it does not follow that the services of the whole of that section could then be terminated.   Some technical input would still be required to monitor schemes and ensure our best interests, as well as providing support on major repairs and securing private finance.

7.12   A review of the salary structure and related benefits will be undertaken which may include consideration of the appropriateness of the introduction of a performance related pay scheme.   This should recognise the need to retain and attract high calibre staff, however, care must also be taken to ensure that the N.J.C. spinal column scales and the nationally negotiated cost of living awards are matched by our resources and are an appropriate mechanism.

7.13   Taking the above factors into account, Appendix VI illustrates the staff changes that are necessary in the coming year.

7.14   Actioning the objectives we have set will depend on how we motivate, train and reward the staff who are our most important resource.   This should take place within a framework of good employment practice based on equal opportunity principles.

16

SECTION EIGHT

OFFICE ACCOMMODATION

8.1 It has been evident for some time that the Association's office accommodation is unsatisfactory to its needs through size, position and the facilities provided. Future plans with their accompanying expansion in staff numbers can only make the situation worse. The provision of new offices has therefore become essential.

8.2 Basically, there are two approaches that we can adopt:

i) an office for central services is acquired, or built, to accommodate financial, development, technical and administrative functions. This would be combined with area offices for housing management and maintenance services in close proximity to stock. Initially such offices would be in Aberdare and Mountain Ash.

ii) an office is acquired, or built, in Aberdare to accommodate all staff. Area offices would then be considered, at a later date, for Mountain Ash and other areas, probably within a "one stop" facility in partnership with the local housing authority.

8.3 At present centralised housing management could only be justified on a part-time basis in any one location and is perhaps best pursued through the one stop option mentioned above. It is therefore likely that the first option is, at best, premature.

8.4 The second option is the one that should be pursued based upon the following criteria:

- must be near the town centre to facilitate easy access for tenants and the general public;

- floor area of at least 6,000 square feet with the potential for expansion should future growth and resources justify;

- a secure reception area with proper interviewing rooms and disabled access;

- separate access to a Committee Room which could possibly be hired out for community group use;

- all senior management should have easy access to each other and their departments, which will be primarily open plan;

- parking facilities to meet staff needs and planning requirements.

8.5 Proposals being discussed include:

- a site in Duke Street is being considered in partnership with Cynon Valley Borough Council and the Welsh Development Agency;

17

–　　　the former Black Lion Hotel is under investigation;

–　　　enquiries are being made with regard to the South Wales Electrical Discount premises in Whitcombe Street

–　　　Several empty shops and showrooms are under active investigation

8.6　　It remains to be seen whether progress can be made on any of these proposals or indeed if they all prove to be suitable for the development that we would prefer, however, a definite project will need to be firmed up by the Spring of 1993, for occupation in early 1994.

SECTION NINE

COMMITTEE OF MANAGEMENT

9.1 In fulfilling the set agenda, Committee Members have a key role to control, monitor, motivate and be accountable for the public resources that are available to the Association.

9.2 Over recent years, the Committee Members' job has become more complex, indeed it is a daunting task. However, with vision, clear objectives and sustained commitment, the Committee will tackle the obstacles that face them and achieve their shared goal; increased provision for those in need at rents they can afford with high quality services that are accountable to users and the general public.

9.3 Of paramount importance will be shared confidence between Committee Members and senior staff that they have the necessary skills and financial acumen to succeed.

9.4 Membership of the Committee of Management will require constant review to ensure it has the necessary knowledge and capacity available to it in the light of its increased responsibilities. This should be done without undermining the balance of the Committee so that its community base is not diluted or lost. Indeed, strenuous efforts will be made to extend this through the greater participation and involvement of the Association's tenants.

9.5 Training of Committee Members, whether by in-house packages, or by the Welsh Federation of Housing Associations/Housing For Wales will be fundamental to this process.

9.6 The delegation by the Committee of Management to Sub-Committees and their related terms of reference are well defined, but will be reviewed to take into account recent changes in rules and practices. A considerable responsibility rests with senior staff to translate the tasks and performance measures outlined in this Plan into reports that are decisive and easily understood.

9.7 Ultimately, the control and development of policy within Cynon-Taf rests with the Committee Members. They, therefore, need to be properly resourced to undertake their role, a fact that the organisation must fully recognise. This does not involve payment, as it would undermine the voluntary ethic, but ensuring that professional guidance and training is made available to support their active citizenship.

SECTION TEN

PERFORMANCE EXPECTATIONS AND INDICATORS

10.1 Accountability is a fundamental issue for housing associations given their use of public resources and their role as the main provider of new homes in the social housing sector.

10.2 The development of performance expectations and indicators against which we can be judged and held accountable is therefore to be welcomed.

10.3 Housing For Wales has adopted a more dynamic approach to performance audit than did the former Housing Corporation toward monitoring and has provided a significant opportunity to examine our policies and practices and ensure that they are robust enough for the challenges that lie ahead.

10.4 A full range of performance audit visits have now been made to this Association and a number of recommendations put forward. Corrective action on these matters is currently being undertaken on a priority basis. It is expected that all items will be completed within the time-scale suggested by Housing For Wales.

10.5 Irrespective of the performance indicators that have been set or any negotiations concerning these that may take place between the Welsh Federation of Housing Associations and Housing For Wales, it is incumbent upon us to establish our own and reflect these in standard reports for monitoring by the Committee of Management.

10.6 Suggested indicators are attached. This is not an exhaustive list and will require review from time to time to reflect particular concerns that may arise. However, they do provide a series of 'bench marks' against which Committee Members and senior staff can judge if performance is achieving the standards that are necessary to meet long term objectives.

SCHEDULE OF INTERNAL PERFORMANCE INDICATORS

A. Capital adequacy compared to investment programmes. Long term equity growth in housing stock.

B. Measures of compliance with the Risk Management Policy such as accuracy of contingencies for development period risk.

C. Accuracy of budget forecasting and resulting management accounts.

D. Performance on investment income generation and general cash flow forecasting and management.

E. Percentage take up of cash limited allocations against forecasts.

F. Percentage cost and time overruns on development projects.

G. Rental impact resulting from improved housing management and maintenance efficiency.

H. Percentage variances against forecasts of development and long term funding requirements.

I. Efficiency in resolving post contract defects and final account processing periods.

J. Tenant satisfaction returns on repairs.

K. Percentage of current and former tenant arrears compared to the projected annual rent roll.

L. Percentage of voids and bad debts compared to the projected annual rent roll.

M. Percentage of offers of accommodation refused on criteria such as rent levels, condition, location and amenities.

N. Monitoring of equal opportunity issues on access to housing.

O. Waiting list management and percentage of performance against any declared nomination targets agreed with the local authority.

P. Percentage property inspections to stock on an annual basis.

Q. Percentage response times to repair requests within targets set.

R. Comparative analysis of day to day maintenance expenditure by stock type and location.

S. Percentage against set budgets for day to day and cyclical maintenance targets.

21

T.   Monitoring ability to identify and implement the major repairs and planned maintenance programme.

U.   Percentage tenant dissatisfaction with design and specification standards.

V.   Percentage variance between project viability studies and sensitivity analysis against outturn costs.

SECTION ELEVEN

RELATIONSHIP WITH OTHER ORGANISATIONS

11.1 A vital feature of our future progress will be a positive partnership with the various organisations with whom we work.

11.2 High standards of presentation and the quality of the material we produce will be an important factor in this process. Everything from letters, Annual Reports, tenant information, finance applications and our Corporate Plan should be professionally presented with clear and concise language being used at all times.

11.3 A positive and collaborative working relationship must be formed and sustained with Housing For Wales. Honesty of approach is an important factor in this and we should not in any way change our message for their consumption. Accountability criteria demands a vigorous debate on investment priorities, subsidy/rent levels, capital costs and proper legal and administrative arrangements.

11.4 We must never confuse their dual functions as an investment agent and a supervisory body. Whilst conflicting messages can sometimes arise, we must act at all times within the objectives that we have set for ourselves and in the best interests of the Association, its tenants and staff.

11.5 As the strategic housing authority, Cynon Valley Borough Council can have a considerable influence on many of the initiatives we wish to progress. The good relationship that currently exists across all departments should continue. We will maintain our support, advice, encouragement and practical input to the formation and attainment of realistic strategic targets in the provision of social housing within the valley.

11.6 The confidence that we have about the future should form the basis of an open relationship with other housing associations so that we can share knowledge, skills and experience in pursuit of the aims we have in common.

11.7 It is essential that we recognise and support the Welsh Federation of Housing Associations as the only legitimate representative body that acts in the best interests of all housing associations in Wales. They can provide invaluable assistance with training, policy development and guidance on good practice. The affiliation fees and staff resources expended in this regard should be judged on the value obtained from continuing support for the Federation's sole objective, which is to act in the best interests and further the role of housing associations in the social rented sector in Wales.

11.8 An integral part of our requirement to be accountable is the need to work with community groups within our area of operation. We must seek to inform and assist so that shared objectives can be realised.

11.9 Much of what we do requires a sophisticated network of formal and informal relationships with statutory and voluntary agencies. We should seek to harness their support and use every opportunity to highlight the work of Cynon-Taf and how it complements their own efforts to provide a safe and supportive environment for a variety of individuals and families.

11.10 How we market ourselves and the profile we establish, will do much to harness the support of private sector lenders and the many other organisations with whom we have dealings. This does not require arrogant displays of one off projects, but a consistent approach which is based on quality presentations and an honest appraisal of our strengths and weaknesses. Cynon-Taf can only be successful if it sets long term objectives for itself that are of merit, and is constantly willing to challenge and review its policies and practices.

APPENDICES

1.   PROJECTED UNITS IN MANAGEMENT

2.   PROJECTED RESULTS OF PIPELINE MIXED
           FUNDED DEVELOPMENT
           (incl. provision for sinking funds)

3.   PROJECTED CASH RESERVES
           (incl. self financed development periods)

4.   RISK MANAGEMENT POLICY

25

PROJECTED UNITS IN MANAGEMENT

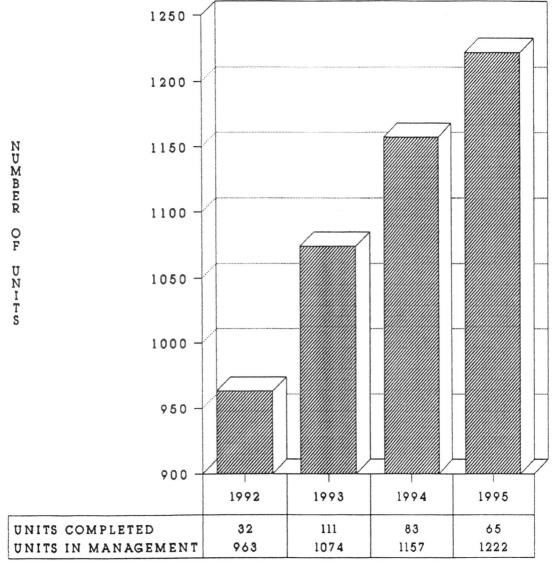

	1992	1993	1994	1995
UNITS COMPLETED	32	111	83	65
UNITS IN MANAGEMENT	963	1074	1157	1222

YEAR

UNITS IN MANAGEMENT

APPENDIX 2

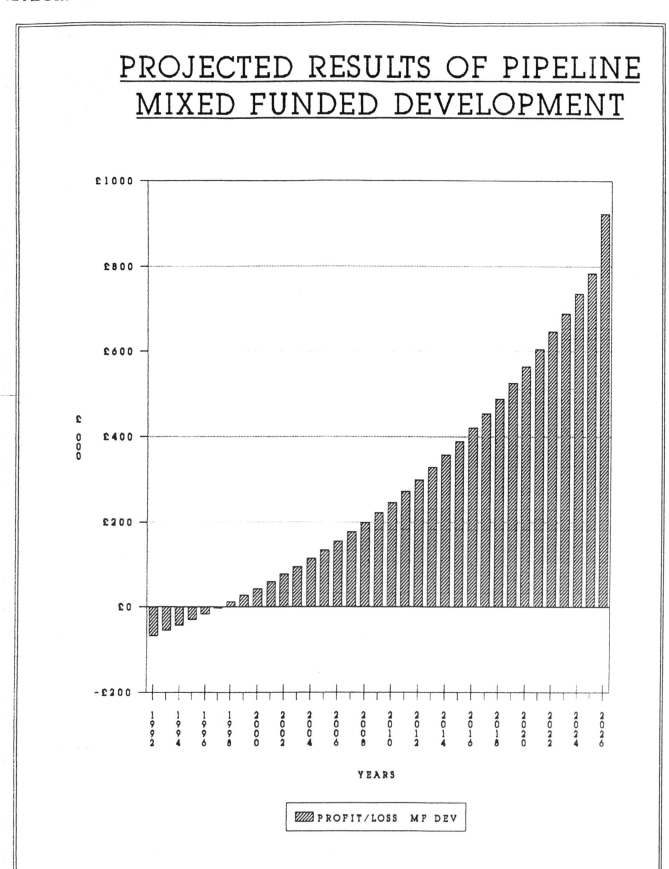

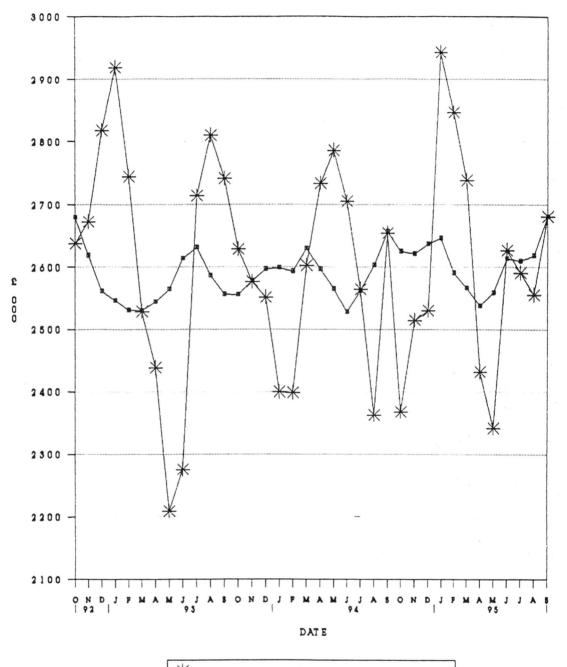

APPENDIX 4

CYNON-TAF HOUSING ASSOCIATION LIMITED

RISK MANAGEMENT POLICY

1. ### INTRODUCTION AND SCOPE

   1.1   This policy seeks to ensure that an effective system exists for the efficient management and administration of the Association's services, both now and in the future.

   1.2   The Risk Management Policy applies to all mixed funded schemes.

   1.3   The principal aims of the policy are:-

   to make proper provision for the acknowledged risks that are inherent in the mixed funded finance regime;

   to identify, quantify and minimise both the long term and short term risks inherent in the development and management of mixed funded housing schemes;

   to ensure that should any such risk come to fruition the full effect can be contained within the Association's reserves.

2. ### PRE-CONTRACT RISK MANAGEMENT

   2.1   At the initial identification of a project, a feasibility study will be prepared to assess the apparent viability of the scheme. Should this exercise produce satisfactory projections, meeting all necessary criteria for acceptance by the Association (need, design standards, etc.), a detailed scheme appraisal should be prepared, by the Management Accountant, using current interest rates, reasonable estimates of contract period and costs, consultants' fees, costs of borrowing and H.A.G. rates. The project should be viable within the Association's cash limited allocation.

   2.2   At this stage approval of the scheme must be obtained from the Business Facilities Sub-Committee. The report to the Sub-Committee should contain all relevant sensitivity analysis to identify and highlight the main areas of risk in the project and the estimated maximum financial effect.

   2.3   Each project will be judged both individually and together with all current schemes, under development, to give the Sub-Committee the overall picture of the Association's exposure to development risk.

   2.4   Written indication will be given by the Projects Controller to the Management Accountant of any specific undertakings with regard to the cost of any item relevant to the scheme appraisal. Estimates should be provided showing a maximum total cost likely to be incurred both pre and post contract.

1

2.5   The level of pre-H.A.G. costs and how those costs are to be financed will be considered by the Business Facilities Sub-Committee at its approval of the appraisal.   Initial considerations of development and long term financing will also be considered at this time.

2.6   The form of contract to be used can minimise financial risks. Conventional J.C.T. Contracts are to be preferred for design reasons but may be subject to cost and time over-runs.   To counteract this, a ten percent. contingency, based on estimated works costs, should be included in appraisals.   While Design and Build contracts give a more reliable estimate of the out-turn figure, there is still some risk of cost and time over-runs.   A three percent. contingency should therefore be included.

2.7   All contracts will contain provisions for liquidated and ascertained damages of a level sufficient to reimburse the Association for the loss of income or increased expenditure due to time over-runs on the contract.

2.8   Sensitivity analysis will cover the possible effects of:

Interest rate variations (both during development and long term);

contract time over-runs;

cost inflation;

variation in the assumed level of void losses.

2.9   Before any contractor is selected from the Association's approved list, either to be placed on a tender list, or to enter into negotiation for the placing of a contract, full financial and quality references will be taken up and assessed by the Projects Controller. The contractor's capacity to manage the contract should also be taken into account.

2.10   No submission for funding will be made to Housing For Wales without full approval of the appraisal by the Business Facilities Sub-Committee.

2.11   Before any contract is accepted, a firm and acceptable offer of finance from a private lender should be in place, the appraisal being amended to reflect the actual terms offered.

3.   **CONTRACT PERIOD RISK MANAGEMENT**

3.1   Adequate performance bonds and collateral warranties consistent with best practice, from contractors and consultants involved in the scheme, will be in place before signing the contract.   Public liability and professional indemnity insurances should be examined for all parties involved in the scheme.

3.2 Progress against approved costs will be monitored, by the Business Facilities Manager, on a monthly basis and reported to the Director. Reports will also be presented to each meeting of the Business Facilities Sub-Committee. Projected out-turns shall also be calculated monthly and variations over five percent. above approved figures reported back to the Sub-Committee for their specific approval.

3.3 Monthly consideration of the overall exposure to development risk must be made and reported to the Director. Each meeting of the Business Facilities Sub-Committee must also receive the exposure report.

3.4 Progress on take-up of C.L.A. is required monthly by Housing For Wales and these figures should also be reported to the Business Facilities Sub-Committee as required by the Programme Management Procedures.

Where a shortfall of H.A.G. seems likely, provision should be made to meet this by use of cash balances and/or short-term borrowing. This strategy should be approved by the Business Facilities Sub-Committee.

3.5 On practical completion, the rate of letting units and resulting void losses should be calculated and included in the appraisal.

3.6 At final account, a report should be made to the Business Facilities Sub-Committee showing total actual costs against the originally approved appraisal and giving explanation of any significant variances.

4. LONG TERM RISK MANAGEMENT

4.1 Generally no scheme should be undertaken where estimated rental income, based on the Association's rental policy, is insufficient to meet estimated running costs (mortgage repayments, repairs and maintenance, management costs, voids, major repairs provisions, etc.). However, when a conventional mortgage is needed to finance the long term liability, deficits may occur during the early years of the project as long as these are contained within the limits agreed, from time to time, by the Committee of Management. In all cases, projects must be showing a positive cashflow.

4.2 Analysis should be carried out to discover how sensitive the scheme is to variations in interest rate, excessive voids, inflation rises in the cost of management and maintenance, and possible rent increases less than the rise in R.P.I.

4.3 The Business Facilities Sub-Committee should receive a quarterly report with the management accounts showing the progress against approved figures of all mixed funded schemes, highlighting any individual schemes where variance is significant.

4.4 The Business Facilities Sub-Committees should be made aware of the implication of the form of borrowing used on a particular scheme (conventional, deferred interest, etc.).

4.5 The method of rent review in tenancy agreements should be examined to ensure that increases in rent may mirror increases in mortgage costs when using low-start finance.

CIPFA

BUSINESS PLANS

A Compendium

HOUSING ASSOCIATIONS

Keniston Housing Association

Business Plan: A Three Year Plan,
April 1992 to March 1995

KENISTON HOUSING ASSOCIATION

Business Plan

A three year plan

April 1992 to March 1995

Keniston Housing Association is committed to providing well managed rented housing for people in need in London and the South East. Like other housing associations it helps those who would otherwise have great difficulty in securing a suitable home - particularly those on low incomes. It manages 600 homes in six local authorities, 60 of which are owned by a sister organisation Keniston (Second) Housing Association.

Keniston is ultimately run by a management committee. The members of this committee, which is equivalent to a board of directors, give their time without pay to overseeing, planning and monitoring the association's work.

In providing its services, the organisation takes the views of its residents seriously. Consultations about the level and quality of services are made and information gathered is used to refine the delivery of housing management and maintenance services. There have been significant improvements in both the level of service provided and the satisfaction of our residents.

Great sums of money are required in order to carry out substantial repairs to Keniston's properties. These major repairs to our existing homes are funded by a system of grants from the Housing Corporation. The money available to carry out these repairs is restricted and Keniston has to compete with many other housing associations for it.

Keniston's future lies not only in continued improvements in service delivery and securing funds for major repairs but also in growth in the number of homes it manages. This business plan sets out the objectives of the organisation for three years from April 1992 which are keys to the organisation's future success.

Why meet housing need?

In a world where many are sheltered from the effects of poor housing and homelessness it is important to remember that there are many who have great difficulty accessing decent homes. In spite of the efforts of housing associations and local authorities across the country the problem continues to grow.

Official homelessness doubled in the ten years from 1980. In 1990 local authorities recorded 145,800 households which probably represents over 400,00 individuals. These people fell within the statutory classification of homelessness and where housing departments of local authorities had an obligation to rehouse.

Unrecorded homelessness adds to the scale of this problem but is extremely difficult to estimate. The statutory classification excludes nearly all single people who find themselves without a home. Shelter estimates that as many as 7,000 people are sleeping rough across the country of which some 2,000 to 3,000 are in London. The London Housing Unit estimates that there are a further 60,000 single homeless people in London. Centrepoint estimates that as many as 50,000 of the single homeless in London are between the ages of 16 years and 19 years.

Keniston is pleased to work in partnership with other organisations in contributing to meeting housing need. It works with local authorities, particularly in targeting homeless people; it also works with referral agencies which provide advice and help for those with housing problems and who cannot generally get help through housing departments.

The purpose of Keniston is   **The purpose**

    1   to meet housing need

    2   to provide good quality well managed homes and

    3   to provide the service tenants want

in an innovative way.

Values

Keniston is a social landlord and in every respect people are important. Customer care is a fundamental principle and residents need to be able to get access to the services provided when they need them. The standards of service are high and there are systems for monitoring whether our targets for delivering on time are being met.

It is extremely important that the decisions Keniston makes are fair and therefore the principles of Equal Opportunities are applied at every level in service provision and employment.

The committee and staff recognise that in managing homes the people who live in them have an important role in the decision making process. Therefore mechanisms are being developed which will enhance their involvement so that it becomes effective. Good communication is essential at all levels of the organisation.

The Association is keenly aware of its wider responsibilities and has developed a green policy which reflects this.

Keniston is essentially a charitable organisation with a firm commitment to ensuring efficient and effective management and achieving sound financial practices.

Keniston has worked hard to develop many areas of its work. Some of the important achievements of 1991/92 are as follows.

What has Keniston achieved so far?

1   *A smooth transition from being a region of a larger housing association to being an Association in its own right.*

2   *Major reviews of important policy areas including,*
        Selection and Allocation
        Rent Setting
        Complaints
        Code of Practice
        Accountability
        Performance Expectations
        Equal Opportunities
        Personnel and Staff Handbook

3   *The commissioning of an extensive report by the Tenant Participation Advisory Service on developing the involvement of tenants in the association's work.*

4   *The successful implementation of job sharing.*

5   *A second home made available for people with learning difficulties.*

6   *The success of an assured shorthold tenancy scheme for potential first time buyers.*

7   *Take up of 161% of allocation of funding for major repairs made at beginning of the financial year by the Housing Corporation.*

8   *A thorough investigation of the potential of merging with another housing association which concluded that Keniston was sufficiently strong and capable to continue independently.*

9   *Excellent scores in the monitoring process which the Housing Corporation carries out periodically. Keniston scored six grade 1's out of a possible eight.*

This is a sound background for the 1992/95 business plan.

What does the business plan set out to achieve?

The business plan is a framework within which the Association will operate over the next three years. It provides clear direction and requires the ongoing commitment of members of the committee and staff.

It hangs upon seven extremely important objectives which are essential to the successful future of the Association. Success is measured by meeting our targets for meeting housing need, high standards of service and improved financial performance. It requires a measure of investment in order to be achieved but will produce long term financial benefits which are otherwise unobtainable.

It is not cast in tablets of stone. If a major opportunity presents itself which is not anticipated in the plan, a thorough review will be necessary.

In the normal course of events progress against the plan will be reviewed annually.

The seven objectives which have been agreed as essential for Keniston's future have been fully discussed by the management committee and staff in order that there is full commitment to the direction of the Association.

The objectives

Objective 1
To increase the number of people whose housing need has been met by 5% per annum.

Objective 2
Maintain the professional and high standards of operation which have been established.

Objective 3
To manage an additional 100 units within three years.

Objective 4
To increase tenant satisfaction with services by 10%.

Objective 5
To develop a structure for tenants to be represented in a meaningful way in the management of the organisation.

Objective 6
Bring the Property Revenue Account into surplus in Keniston Housing Association in three years.

Objective 7
To have secured an investment plan for the long term maintenance of the organisations' portfolio of property.

These objectives are considered in more detail in the following pages.

Objective 1

To increase the number of people whose housing need has been met by 5% per annum.

Meeting housing need is Keniston's main objective. More ways need to be found to make homes available for people in housing need. The creative use of empty property and opportunities available for housing mobility can provide more scope for meeting tenants' aspirations for their homes.

Strategies

In order to increase the number of people who are housed, Keniston will

◆   *promote mobility schemes*

◆   *promote home ownership schemes*

◆   *consider new housing schemes.*

Objective 2

Maintain the professional and high standards of operation which have been established.

Good progress has been made in improving service delivery and in formalising and updating policies and procedures. This has provided a sound starting point for the Business Plan. The momentum of organisational review needs to be maintained to keep standards high.

Strategies

In order to ensure continuing high standards, Keniston will

◆   *implement and review all policies and procedures*

◆   *maintain equal opportunities issues with a high profile*

◆   *implement personnel policies to ensure that staff are motivated*

◆   *provide training wherever necessary*

◆   *continue to promote the principles of customer care*

◆   *adhere to guidance issued by the Housing Corporation, Department of the Environment, National Federation of Housing Associations, Institute of Housing, Commission for Racial Equality and other relevant bodies*

To manage an additional 100 units within three years. **Objective 3**

The historical problems that faced the Association prevented it from carrying out new development of housing from 1980 onwards. However the management committee are very keen to further the Association's main objective of meeting housing need by developing more homes and ways will be sought to do this.

As the organisation is now strong, opportunities for management of other stock will also be sought. This may involve considering merging with other associations.

Strategies
In order to increase the management portfolio, Keniston will

◆   *seek and create opportunities for growth*

◆   *seek and create opportunities for management.*

To increase tenant satisfaction with services by 10%. **Objective 4**

Recent surveys have shown that there have been significant increase in satisfaction with the repair service and that 90% of tenants are generally satisfied with Keniston as their landlord. The Association will continue to seek to improve its services.

Strategies
In order to improve levels of satisfaction, Keniston will

◆   *identify areas of dissatisfaction and take appropriate action*

◆   *carry out major surveys of satisfaction every three years*

◆   *introduce monitoring systems on performance*

◆   *involve tenants more*

◆   *publish positive publicity.*

Objective 5

To develop a structure for tenants to be represented in a meaningful way in the management of the organisation.

Keniston is committed to taking account of its residents views because they are the main recipients of the services that the Association offers. Keniston wants to achieve increasing levels of satisfaction amongst its tenants; by asking them about how they wish to see the services provided, agreeing new standards and then achieving them, tenant satisfaction will increase.

Keniston also wants to develop more formally its accountability to those whom it serves and the structure for tenant involvement will contribute to this. Previous surveys of tenants views shows that there is significant support for this approach.

Strategies
In order to achieve an agreed structure for tenant representation, Keniston will

◆ *continue to survey tenants' opinions on ideas for such a structure*

◆ *consult on the consequent proposals*

◆ *introduce a structure for tenants to be represented in the organisation.*

Objective 6

Bring the Property Revenue Account into surplus in Keniston Housing Association in three years.

In order to fund the management of an organisation which can fully meet the expectations of the Housing Corporation while only managing comparatively few properties, and without the benefit of development allowances, balancing the Property Revenue Account has been very difficult. This is exacerbated by the problems of providing a maintenance service when the allowable income is so low.

Steps have been taken to improve the revenue position, including an organisational review in 1990. The momentum for financial efficiency needs to be maintained for the future strength of the Association.

Strategies
To improve the revenue position, Keniston will

◆ *dispose of the north London office mortgage*

◆ *bring new units into management*

◆ *make revenue savings*

◆ *introduce planned maintenance.*

To have secured an investment plan for the long term maintenance of the organisations' portfolio of property.

Objective 7

Keniston has a responsibility to its tenants to ensure that its properties are maintained to the highest standard. This means having an effective responsive repairs service on a day to day basis, and taking account of the longer term aspects of maintenance and how to resource them effectively.

As previously mentioned, there are problems arising from design defects which require substantial investment. Housing associations have not been able to make provision for long term repairs until 1988; previously associations would request the original public funding authority for a further grant in the event of a major repair becoming necessary. Although the responsibility for these repairs is being transferred to housing associations at present, Keniston will continue to need such grants from the Housing Corporation in the foreseeable future.

Strategies
In order to secure a satisfactory future for the housing stock, Keniston will

◆　　*reduce the commitment for major repairs*

◆　　*achieve a real increase in maintenance allowances over 91/92 levels*

◆　　*devise a programme of cost effective planned maintenance*

◆　　*consider options for swapping housing stock with other associations*

◆　　*review options for private finance for the repairs.*

Each of these objectives have implications for the direction of work in each department. The following pages show the targets for each department.

TARGETS: Directorate finance and administration		
	Target	To be completed by
Objective 1: To increase the number of people whose housing need has been met by 5% per annum.		
None		
Objective 2: Maintain the professional and high standards of operation which have been established.		
2.1	A policy on committee accountability.	September 1992 Review 1994
2.2	Set up a programme of staff training on Association policies.	December 1992
2.3	Review staffing structure	December 1992
2.4	Review Auditors	December 1992
2.5	Review performance monitoring	Each March
2.6	Finance policy and procedure guide	March 1993
2.7	Review committee reporting	March 1993
2.8	Revuiew customer care training	March 1993
2.9	Review rent policy	March 1993
2.10	Review computer provision and service	September 1993
2.11	Review salary levels	September 1993
2.12	Review insurances	September 1994
2.13	Review equal opportunities policy	December 1994
2.14	Review personnel policies, procedures and staff handbook	March 1995
2.15	Prepare new business plan	March 1995

Objective 3: To manage an additional 100 units within three years		
3.1	Complete 30 new units	March 1995
3.2	Manage 100 additional units	March 1995
3.3	Have an ongoing development programme of at least 30 units per year	March 1995
Objective 4: To increase tenant staisfaction with services by 10%		
4.1	Survey tenant satisfaction	December 1994
4.2	Programme action to improve performance	March 1995
4.3	Programme positive publicity	March 1995
Objective 5: To develop a structure for tenants to be represented in a meaningful way in the management of the organisation		
5.1	Consult tenants on a proposal for tenants to be represented in the Association	September 1992
5.2	Programme implementation of TPAS recommendations	September 1992
5.3	Introduce a structure for tenants to be represented in the organisation	March 1993
5.4	Make future AGMs open events which tenants can attend	June 1993
5.5	Review the structure of tenant participation	March 1995
Objective 6: Bring the property revenue account into surplus in Keniston Housing Association in 3 years		
6.1	Redeem the north London office mortgage	March 1993
6.2	Review all areas of revenue expenditure and income	March 1993
6.3	The property revenue account to be in surplus	March 1995
Objective 7: To have secured an investment plan for the long term maintenance portfolio of property		
7.1	Achieve a programme of funding for major repairs of at least £1.5 millions per year	September 1993
7.2	Achieve a real increase in maintenance allowances	December 1993
7.3	Reduce the commitment for amjor repairs by £6 millions	March 1995

TARGETS: Housing Services		
Objective 1: To increase the number of people whose housing need has been met by 5% per annum.		
1.1	Increase the number of TIS completions by 2 per year	Each March
1.2	Increase the number of people being housed by 5% per year	Each March
Objective 2: Maintain the professional and high standards of operation which have been established		
2.1	Complete the review of the tenancy agreement and handbook	September 1992
2.2	Develop a policy for relationships with local community groups	March 1993
2.3	Complete housing management policy	March 1993
2.4	Review the performance in homelessness, equal opportunities and standards of service	Each March
2.5	Review selection and allocation policy	March 1994
2.6	Review standards of service	June 1994
2.7	Review racial harassment policy	December 1994
Objective 3: To manage an additional 100 units within three years		
3.1	Take on management of additional property	As required
Objective 4: To increase tenant satisfaction with services by 10%		
4.1	Monitor complaints and take action	Ongoing
4.2	Identify areas of dissatisfaction in TPAS survey and programme action	September 1992
4.3	Introduce monitoring of satisfaction with communal services	December 1992
4.4	Review communications with tenants	March 1993
4.5	Complaints received from less than 5% of tenants	Each March
4.6	An increase of 10% in satisfaction with communla services recorded in next major survey	December 1994
4.7	Programme action following next full survey	March 1995

Objective 5: To develop a structure for tenants to be represented in a meaningful way in the management of the organisation		
5.1	Hold at least 3 tenants' meetings a year at each development	Ongoing
5.2	Programme implementation of TPAS recommendation	September 1992
5.3	Review the effectiveness of tenants involvement	March 1995
Objective 6: Bring the Property Revenue Account into surplus in Keniston Housing Association in 3 years		
6.1	Review expenditure in housing services department	March 1993
6.2	Reduce arrears to 4%	March 1995
Objective 7: To have secured an investment plan for the long term maintenance of the organisations' portfolio of property		
None		

TARGETS: Repair Service		
Objective 1: To increase the number of people whose housing need has been met by 5% per annum		
None		
Objective 2: Maintain the professional and high standards of operation which have been established		
2.1	Complete maintenance policy	March 1993
2.2	Review contractors' performance	Each March
2.3	Review the approved list of contractors	Each March
2.4	Increase repairs done on time to 95%	March 1995
Objective 3: To manage an additional 100 units within three years		
None		
Objective 4: To increase tenant satisfaction with services by 10%		
4.1	Tenant satisfaction surveys recording less than 5% of surveys returned	Each March
4.2	Increase in 5% of satisfaction with the repair service recorded in next full survey	December 1994
Objective 5: To develop a structure for tenants to be represented in a meaningful way in the management of the organisation		
5.1	Programme TPAS recommendations	September 1992
5.2	Review the major repairs code of conduct	March 1993

Objective 6: Bring the Property Revenue Account into surplus in Keniston Housing Association in three years		
6.1	Review expenditure in repair service team	March 1993
6.2	Ensure expenditure is within budget	Each March
Objective 7: To have secured an investment plan for the long term maintenance of the organisations' portfolio of property		
7.1	Review the cost effectiveness of the repair service	September 1992
7.2	Complete specification of materials for major repairs	March 1993
7.3	Make recommendations for a cost effective planned maintenance programme	March 1993
7.4	Achieve cash planning targets set by the Housing Corporation	Each March

Revenue Appraisal

Surplusses in rental income have previously been clawed back by the government through Grant Redemption Fund (GRF). This was phased out after the 1988 Housing Act; financial regulations which followed this act facilitated housing associations making long term provisions for major repairs. GRF became RSF (Rental Surplus Fund) and instead of all the rental surplus being clawed back by the government, a percentage was retained by each association for building up its long term major repair sinking fund for stock already in ownership.

From the financial year 1992/93 the amount for the sinking fund is 80% of the rental surplus, while the remaining 20% is retained by the association. Further changes are also being proposed at the time of writing the business plan.

There are a number of ways in which the financial health of an association can be measured. Some of these are the profit and loss account, expenditure against allowable income ("allowances"), and the Property Revenue Account.

The most obvious measure of revenue performance is by reference to the income and expenditure account as in the current statutory form of accounts: does this show a surplus for the year?

However expenditure against allowances can also be considered. This measures expenditure against the sums per property which the DOE deem an association should be spending to manage and maintain its tenants and property. It should be easier for larger associations to achieve expenditure within these sums on the basis of economies of scale; associations which have active development programmes may also find it easier to achieve because they have to apportion less overheads to housing management and maintenance. Keniston neither benefits from size nor a development programme at present. Of course, using this indicator begs the question whether the allowances which the DOE set are reasonable.

Forward projections have been made on the 1992/93 budget to look at the factors which would achieve keeping expenditure within allowances. The projection shows that housing stock would have to increase by 140 units before current levels of expenditure can be contained within the current allowance structure.

Cuts in revenue expenditure sufficient to make a significant impact on costs, after the organisational review in 1990, would almost certainly result in reduced standards of service - a price which the association is not prepared to pay. The long term aim must therefore be to achieve these extra 140 units. The target of increasing stock by 100 units in three years is very ambitious. It would be unrealistic to set a target in excess of this number but, if 100 units can be achieved in three years, it is reasonable to assume that an additional 140 units could be brought into management in 5 years.

The following extracts from the 1992/93 budget and forward projections show the changes that take place in the revenue position with increases in managed stock.

REVENUE ANALYSIS: KENISTON HOUSING ASSOCIATION

(£s)	1992/93	+ 100 units	+ 140 units
Income			
Rents and Service Charges	1,135,234	1,395,234	1,499,234
Other	168,480	169,471	169,471
Total Income	1,303,714	1,564,705	1,668,705
Expenditure			
Overheads	698,995	678,495	678,495
Mortgage repayments	370,624	598,113	639,700
Transfer to major repair provision	199,844	235,844	250,244
Transfer to general reserve	48,347	48,347	48,347
Total Expenditure	1,317,811	1,560,799	1,616,786
Net surplus	(14,096)	3,906	51,919
Housing management costs	203,457	202,911	202,911
Housing management allowances	170,926	194,426	203,826
Repair and maintenance costs	254,388	224,661	225,471
Repair and maintenance allowances	194,744	222,716	230,438

Assumptions

All costs at 1992/93 levels.
North London office mortgage redeemed by 31/3/93
Real increase of day to day repair allowances of 11%
Major repair programme of £1.5 millions (contract value)
Major repair provision at 0.8% of build cost
Additional work absorbed within current establishment
Transfer to general reserve as in RSF calculation

This is the first Business Plan that Keniston has prepared and it is important for the Association's future. It has the support of the committee and staff and there is anticipation about the opportunities that achievement will bring.

Any further information about Keniston can be obtained by contacting the Office Administrator at the Association's offices. In particular, policies, a performance statement and a full set of accounts are available.

If you are interested in becoming a member of the Association please write to the Secretary of the Association.

Keniston Housing Association Ltd
Keniston (Second) Housing Association Ltd
Keniston Homes Ltd
13 Artington Close
Farnborough
Kent BR6 7UL

Tel 0689 850319

CIPFA

BUSINESS PLANS

A Compendium

HOUSING ASSOCIATIONS

**Penge Churches
Housing Association Limited**

Business Plan

Note:

Appendices E and F (Performance audit report; Chartered surveyor's report on future repairs liability) are not reproduced.

**Penge Churches
Housing Association
Limited**

BUSINESS PLAN

A MEMBER OF
National Federation
of Housing Associations

INDEX

1. **Executive Summary**
2. **The Association**
3. **Present/Future Stock**
4. **Rent Policy**
5. **Organisation**
6. **Track Record**
7. **Development Strategy**
8. **Appendices**

    A.   Notes on cashflow forecasts

    A1. Cashflow forecast: No development @ 3.5% inflation

    A2. Cashflow forecast: 5 year development @ 3.5% inflation

    A3. Cashflow forecast: 5 year development @ 5% inflation

    B.   Rental income forecast

    C.   Mortgage repayment/major repairs forecasts

    D.   Routine maintenance/cyclical maintenance forecasts

1. EXECUTIVE SUMMARY

The demise of the small housing association has been greatly exaggerated. Not only are we alive and kicking but we are looking to the future with optimism and anticipation. Planned growth, prudent financial control and good management are the key to our success.

We perform our job well and provide a vital service in the heart of the community. The needs perceived by our founders are as relevant today as they were in 1969. We are faced with new challenges and new systems to master. Change itself is not new to associations, the shifting sands of housing policy have always existed.

It has been estimated that nationally we need to build 100,000 homes per year to have any significant effect on the homeless situation. The provision of social housing has to expand to meet that need. In our small way we intend to be part of that projected expansion.

We believe that as a small housing association we provide an efficient service to our customers. We deliver a cost effective service within a caring framework. It is rare to find such a combination of sound fiscal control linked with a genuine concern for customers' welfare.

This is, in fact, the unique quality that the small housing association movement brings to social housing. The vast majority of associations are small and the good reputation that associations enjoy would not exist without us. We fully realise the changes that are taking place. We intend to remain at the 'cutting edge' of that change. Our tenants need us. They would not forgive us if we decided to rest on our laurels. Our plan demonstrates the way forward for the Association over the next decade. We look forward to the opportunities that the future will bring us.

2. THE ASSOCIATION

Penge Churches Housing Association Ltd. was set up by members of the Penge Council of Churches in 1969 with the objective of providing rented accommodation for people in housing need locally. There was then, and remains today, an acute problem of homelessness within London and consequently within our local area. The Association's range of operation is within the London Borough of Bromley specifically the areas of Penge, Beckenham, Sydenham and Upper Norwood. The Association has a strong local base at 99 Maple Road, the Registered Office, which was opened in 1973. The Association is community based with a high concentration of local people involved in its Committee structure.

The majority of the Association's units are located within a two mile radius of the office. The Association currently consists of 165 units in management with a further 28 units expected to come into management in the next two years. It is small in that it has under 250 units in management. The need to house the homeless however remains a priority and the Association will continue to meet that need.

As a developing Association, it is important to realise the need to grow. Growth is the key both to satisfying the high demand for new homes and also for us as an Association to deliver higher standards of service to our established and new tenants. We anticipate that the market for rented homes in five years' time is likely to be as high as ever but expectations of quality and service are rising also. We have to ensure that the quality of our stock and our delivery of service meets the rising demand of consumers.

Quality goes hand in hand with care. One of the major strengths of our organization is its social welfare concern. Our Association was founded on a Christian caring ethos and it is important that this remains and that we maintain strong links with the churches while at the same time developing a business ethos with an emphasis on quality in terms of service delivery and provision of high quality homes to our tenants.

3. PRESENT/FUTURE STOCK

The present stock consists of 165 units. We own one hostel for people recovering from mental illness together with six units that have been adapted for wheelchair users. The hostel consists of ten bedspaces. The remainder of the Association's stock consists of mixed general purpose housing of variable quality. 75% of our vacancies are offered to Local Authority nominees, the majority of whom are statutory homeless. The concentration on funding going to house the statutory homeless is likely to increase in the future, particularly as funding institutions favour supporting Associations with increasing allocations, provided that the Association is concentrating the main provision at this particular group. The local Authority at present has a priority for two-bed type of accommodation. The Association has therefore concentrated on bidding with this need as a priority.

The Association has been very successful in terms of attracting Housing Corporation funding in the face of increased competition. We have received an allocation in 1992/3 for 12 units of newbuild accommodation and a pre-allocation for a further 16 units in the year 1993/4. Thus our target for expansion in the first three years is 10/20 units annually but we would hope to increase this depending on our success rate in the first five years. The Association should however look at the possibility of expansion into other areas, which should include:—

i) The possibility of gaining resources, and new developments in the Lambeth and Croydon area. We should therefore make contact and establish relations with these boroughs with this in mind;

ii) The provision of homes for other needs e.g. special needs. As we have a hostel for mentally ill people, we should look at the expansion of this provision, perhaps in conjunction with the Health Authority;

iii) Acting as agents for other smaller Associations in the provision of services/management/development. This would both increase income and improve financial viability.

4. RENT POLICY

In our budget predictions we have assumed an overall increase in rent levels. The rents set consist of three categories: –

 i) Existing secure tenancies;

 ii) Re-lets of existing secure tenancies;

 iii) New assured tenancy lets.

a. Existing Secure Tenancies

Rent levels for existing secure tenants are determined independently of the Association by the fair rent Officer. Increases have to be applied for every two years. Current increases are decided by comparison with similar properties in the same area. Current increases are well above inflation, coming in at 25/30% for a two year period. Thus rent increases on this type of tenancy are between 12.5/15% per year and have been set in the forecast at 11%.

b. Relets of Existing Secure Tenancies

If a securely tenanted property becomes vacant and it is relet to a tenant from outside the Association, then the new tenant becomes an assured tenant. The Association then fixes the rent at a level of 50% above the existing secure rent level. From that point on, the Association determines the rent level. Once set, the rent level will rise at the rate of inflation at the time of the increase plus 2%. This will take place on an annual basis.

c. New Assured Tenancy Lets

The rents determined on new developments under mixed funding are calculated according to the total cost of the scheme, taking into account the costs of servicing private finance loans plus interest. Rents on such developments will take into account sinking fund costs for major repairs, maintenance costs, management costs etc. The scheme will not go ahead unless the Association agrees that the rent set is affordable. A detailed scheme appraisal, including all costs, will be examined at the earliest stage before the Association commits itself. The rents once set will increase by the rate of inflation plus 2% in line with our policy for relets of existing assured tenancies. However, in the event that inflation fell to zero, rents on such properties would rise by a rate no lower than 5%.

5. ORGANIZATION

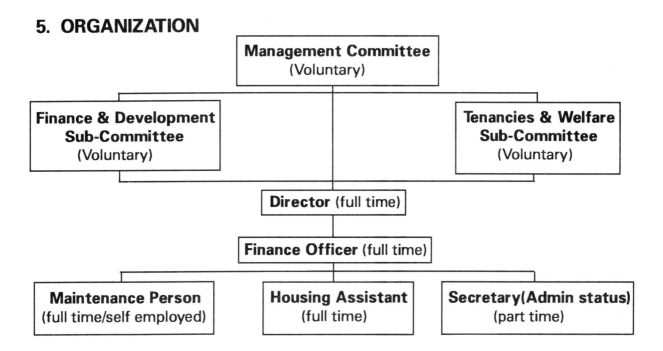

The Association is governed by its Committee which includes a wide range of local people who possess a variety of expertise in different areas. Their occupations include: – A civil engineer; civil servants; Area Housing Director; Hostel Co-ordinator; local councillor; clergymen etc.

The main Management Committee is serviced by two Sub-Committees. The Tenancies & Welfare Sub-Committee deals with all matters relating to tenants (arrears, allocations etc.). The Finance & Development Sub-Committee deals with all financial matters and new developments and projects. Meetings are held regularly during the year and full reports are given and discussed at these meetings. The reports are prepared by the Director with assistance from other staff members.

The Association has three full-time members of staff and one part-time. The Director has delegated powers from the Committee of Management. He is assisted by the Finance Officer. There is also a full-time Housing Assistant and a part-time secretary, the latter acting as a personal assistant to the Director, providing general administrative support.

In addition the Association employs a self-employed builder who undertakes the bulk of routine maintenace tasks. This allows the Association to have an extremely good response time and promotes good relations with tenants.

In view of its size, the relationship between staff is good and we do not suffer the problems which can beset larger organizations e.g. inter-departmental rivalries and friction. The staff show a high level of commitment to tenants and to the Association.

6. TRACK RECORD

Over the last two years the Association has enjoyed a considerable improvement in its financial situation. Three years ago we were in a position of having an overdraft in excess of £40,000. At present we have reserves in excess of £100,000. We therefore have a liquid reserve to cover financial risk in the new economic climate where mixed funding is seen as a priority for funders.

Three years ago we were involved in potentially expensive litigation which has now been dealt with. Indeed, we have recovered considerable sums from this period which were causing us cashflow problems at that time. We no longer have any litigation pending and our last two schemes have been completed on time. within budget, and within T.C.I. cost limitations.

The experience of running a tight ship in difficult circumstances has had a positive effect. It has strengthened the Association and given the staff and Committee experience on which to draw. This should ensure that the same mistakes are not repeated. We have gained the respect and support of the Local Authority and the Housing Corporation over the last two years. The recovery and turn-round in the financial position of the Association has meant that we have received pre-allocations for 1993/4. We have proved that we can deliver the units and we fully expect to build on that success. We intend to increase our development programme which will strengthen our financial position.

Our statistical returns also indicate an improved position and compare favourably with other organisations. Over the last three years we have worked to a situation where we have eliminated our voids, which three years ago were in excess of 8%. Arrears are currently 6% which again compares favourably with other Associations, particularly when it is noted that 2.5% of arrears are due to late Housing Benefit payments. Our rent collection is also good, in that 99.4% of rent receivable was collected in 1991/2. Repairs are carried out promptly, 95% being done within the target time.

We are proud of our record as managers but realise that there is always room for improvement. While committed to improving service delivery we wish to maintain our emphasis on care for the customer.

7. DEVELOPMENT STRATEGY

During the last year we have developed two units i.e. a three-bed house and one four-bed unit. Both have been finished to a high standard including uPVC double-glazing, gas central heating and carpeting throughout.

These two units have been developed through our Agent, Croydon Churches Housing Association. They have been developed within cost limits, contract time and T.C.I. On the strength of these two developments − and in line with our performance generally − we have been given pre-allocations for 12 units of new-build for 1992/3 .

Our strategy for the present is to continue to use Croydon Churches H.A. as development agents for the next two/three years and thereafter to employ our own development officer. We are currently looking for 16/20 new units in 1993/4 and 20 + new units each year from 1994 onwards. By the end of the financial year 1997/8 we therefore have a projected growth to 253 + units. We would anticipate growth to be at least 20 units per year after the first five years, however.

One of the most significant factors to note is the growth of free reserves. The reserves will be in the region of £1m. by the end of the ten year period.

As the Association grows, we see the need to strengthen the staffing support available. As previously indicated we anticipate employing our own Development Officer from 1995. From the administrative point of view we see a need for a full-time secretary/personal assistant and for a receptionist/clerical assistant.

One of the time consuming aspects of our work is the social welfare role which comes in as part of our relationship with tenants. As the number of units increase there will be a place for a social worker.

At present we rely on the vehicles owned by the Director and the maintenance worker for the transport required to travel around our properties. The Association should give serious consideration to purchasing its own vehicle. This could be of service for management, maintenance and the welfare needs of tenants.

Major Repairs/ Cyclical Maintenance/ Routine Maintenance

Our development aspirations do not just depend solely on the development of new units. We are also concerned about our older stock and potential repairs obligations. We aspire to improve the quality of our older units and to bring the standard closer to that of our new units. We have recently undertaken a complete ten year stock survey of all our properties. This indicates our repairs obligations for the next ten years. These costs plus inflation have been worked out in our budget calculations. Although we are able to claim major repairs funding from the local authority on our pre-HAG (Housing Association Grant) funded properties, in practice this has been difficult to obtain. However, we have reduced our major repairs liability from £292,000 at the end of 1990 to nil at April 1992. This has been achieved through different methods:–

i) The use of Local Authority HAG to rehabilitate existing units;

ii) The use of charitable funds to carry out major repairs;

iii) The sale of properties for which funding was not available.

For future major repairs, cyclical repairs and routine repairs on existing stock we have used Clarke Wilson's figures. Our budget predictions illustrate that all of these liabilities can be undertaken within our budgeted costs. We have added inflation at 3.5% and 5% per year to Clarke Wilson's figures. For all new properties we have included a provision – to be backed by cash reserves – of 0.535% of the initial build costs. All other costs have been included, based on present allowances for the particular type of dwelling.

From 1990 all new developments undertaken have to have a sinking fund provision for major repairs. On such developments, major repairs funding cannot be claimed at a later date from the Housing Corporation. We can still however make applications for major repairs on our pre-1990 stock both to the Housing Corporation and the Local Authority. We would see this as a bonus as our major repairs liability can be funded from our existing resources. Our projected budget should allow us to improve some of the older units, to include such improvements as:–

i) Additional heating where appropriate;

ii) Provision of carpet to communal areas;

iii) Replacement of old kitchen units;

iv) Redecoration/improvement of vacant properties (between lets);

v) Service contracts for central heating systems;

vi) Move towards preventive maintenance.

Growth/Competition/ Development Risk

As a small Association in competition with others we have done well to achieve the level of allocation resources we will receive over the next two years. Although this is to our credit we have to recognise the limitations placed on growth by the combined perceptions of the Local Authority and the Housing Corporation, together with increasing competition for sites and resources. The key to future success and increased allocations in the face of such competition is twofold: –

a) Concentrating on continuous improvement with regards to quality of stock together with strengthening the internal structures of the organisation;

b) Delivering the existing allocations within target times, on cost, and giving value for money;

If as a policy we concentrate on these two areas, this success should equate to increased allocations and further growth. While directing our energies towards growth, we should remember two essential points: –

a) To retain the unique position of an Association with a local community base. Our small size allows us to deliver a personal service with close contact with our tenants and a high profile within the local community – we would strive to preserve this;

b) As we grow, we should retain enough of a cash-backed reserve to ensure the Association can cope with financial risk.

APPENDIX A

Notes on Cash Flow Forecasts

Throughout these forecasts annual increases have been made at the assumed rate of inflation. The notes specify where other elements are included.

Rents - Other Income - Income from Hostel – TSNMA

Rent Losses	at 4%
Staff Costs	Provision for an additional member of staff in 1995.
Management Costs	Increased by £357 per unit for each new development.
Interest Received	Inflation + 2% on Free Reserves.
Insurance	Increased by £1.000 for each new development and by 5%.
Miscellaneous	1993 £ 12,000 Provision for computerisation
	1994 £ 4,000 Provision for computerisation
	£20,000 Provision for association vehicle
	1995 £ 4,000 Provision for computerisation
L.G. Subsidy	Assumed to be constant.
Development Income	Income from Tenants Incentive Scheme. In the event that a development officer is employed from 1995 then the income here will increase given continued development.
Sinking Fund	Based on Housing Corporation allowances for major repairs.

N.B. 1. It is assumed that when developments take place they are completed within costs.

2. With inflation at 3.5% in 10 years time £1.14 million would be worth only £808,000 in terms of today's values.

£1.3 million would be worth £922,000.

At 5% inflation £1.59 million would be worth £975.000.

APPENDIX A1

Cashflow forecast: No Development @ 3.5% inflation

	92 TO 93	93 TO 94	94 TO 95	95 TO 96	96 TO 97	97 TO 98	98 TO 99	99 TO 00	00 TO 01	01 TO 02	02 TO 03	TOTALS
INCOME												
RENTAL INCOME	278651	309294	339888	373522	410501	451157	495856	545003	599040	658456	723786	5185154
SERVICE INCOME	6579	6809	7048	7294	7550	7814	8087	8370	8663	8967	9280	86461
RENT LOSSES	-11146	-12372	-13596	-14941	-16420	-18046	-19834	-21800	-23962	-26338	-28951	-207406
L.G. SUBSIDY	8500	8500	8500	8500	8500	8500	8500	8500	8500	8500	8500	93500
OTHER INCOME	1000	2336	2418	2502	2590	2681	2774	2872	2972	3076	3184	28405
TOTAL INCOME	283584	314567	344257	376878	412720	452105	495384	542945	595214	652660	715799	5186114
EXPENDITURE												
MANAGEMENT EXPENSES	102894	109995	113845	137829	139548	144433	149488	154720	160135	165740	171541	1550167
INSURANCE	4000	4200	4410	4631	4862	5105	5360	5628	5910	6205	6516	56827
MISCELLANEOUS	5760	17962	30170	10386	6843	7082	7330	7587	7852	8127	8412	117512
ROUTINE MAINTENANCE	49000	44445	31340	46031	85763	72868	76741	77239	55099	61985	105200	705711
CYCLICAL MAINTENANCE	45335	32479	15180	19502	12060	59690	46325	17093	22224	13382	69955	353226
SERVICE COSTS	8880	9191	9512	9845	10190	10547	10916	11298	11693	12103	12526	116701
MORTGAGE PAYMENTS	87630	87812	88002	88202	88412	88633	88865	89108	89363	89631	89913	975571
TOTAL EXPENDITURE	303499	306083	292459	316426	347679	388357	385025	362673	352277	357174	464062	3875714
SUB TOTAL	-19915	8484	51798	60451	65041	63748	110358	180272	242938	295487	251737	1310400
OTHER INCOME AND EXPENDITURE												
INTEREST RECEIVED	4664	2951	1944	3263	5190	8098	9873	15545	21647	33757	48604	155534
DEV. INCOME	800	828	857	887	918	950	983	1018	1053	1090	1128	10514
TOTAL OTHER	5464	3779	2801	4150	6108	9048	10856	16562	22700	34847	49732	166048
SURPLUS/DEFICIT	-14451	12264	54599	64601	71149	72796	121215	196835	265638	330334	301470	1476448
DEDUCT PROVISIONS	16680	30573	30628	29568	18268	40524	18091	85886	45463	60381	45744	421807
SURPLUS/DEFICIT AFTER PROVISIONS	-31131	-18310	23971	35033	52881	32271	103123	110949	220175	269953	255726	1054641
RESERVES B/FWD	84792	53661	35351	59322	94355	147236	179507	282630	393579	613755	883708	84792
RESERVES CARRIED FWD.	53661	35351	59322	94355	147236	179507	282630	393579	613755	883708	1139433	1139433
PROVISIONS												
MAJOR REPAIRS	15160	29000	29000	27883	16524	38719	16223	83952	43461	58309	43600	401831
SINKING FUND	1520	1573	1628	1685	1744	1805	1868	1934	2002	2072	2144	19976
FOR NEW PROPERTIES												
TOTAL PROVISIONS	16680	30573	30628	29568	18268	40524	18091	85886	45463	60381	45744	421807
ACCUMULATED PROVISIONS	16680	47253	77881	107450	125718	166242	184334	270219	315682	376063	421807	421807

APPENDIX A2   Cashflow forecast: 5 Year Development @ 3.5% inflation

	92 TO 93	93 TO 94	94 TO 95	95 TO 96	96 TO 97	97 TO 98	98 TO 99	99 TO 00	00 TO 01	01 TO 02	02 TO 03	TOTALS
INCOME												
RENTAL INCOME	278651	347701	433407	540756	657904	785621	848717	917271	991783	1072800	1160919	8035529
SERVICE INCOME	6579	6809	7048	7294	7550	7814	8087	8370	8663	8967	9280	86461
RENT LOSSES	-11146	-13908	-17336	-21630	-26316	-31425	-33949	-36691	-39671	-42912	-46437	-321421
L.G. SUBSIDY	8500	8500	8500	8500	8500	8500	8500	8500	8500	8500	8500	93500
OTHER INCOME	1000	2336	2418	2502	2590	2681	2774	2872	2972	3076	3184	28405
TOTAL INCOME	283584	351438	434034	537423	650227	773191	834130	900322	972247	1050430	1135446	7922474
EXPENDITURE												
MANAGEMENT EXPENSES	102894	109995	119757	151597	158609	164160	169906	175853	182007	188378	194971	1718126
INSURANCE	4000	5200	6460	7783	9172	10631	11162	11720	12306	12922	13568	104925
MISCELLANEOUS	5760	17962	30170	10386	6843	7082	7330	7587	7852	8127	8412	117512
ROUTINE MAINTENANCE	49000	49750	44151	68762	119093	117510	122946	125061	104595	113213	158220	1072301
CYCLICAL MAINTENANCE	45335	32479	15180	19502	12060	59690	46325	17093	22224	13382	69955	353226
SERVICE COSTS	8880	9191	9512	9845	10190	10547	10916	11298	11693	12103	12526	116701
MORTGAGE PAYMENTS	87630	110978	144758	190363	240376	295125	305682	316766	328404	340624	353455	2714161
TOTAL EXPENDITURE	303499	335554	360089	458239	556343	664745	674267	665377	669082	688749	811108	6196951
SUB TOTAL	-19915	15884	64047	79184	93883	108446	159863	234945	303165	361681	324338	1725522
OTHER INCOME AND EXPENDITURE												
INTEREST RECEIVED	4664	2960	2140	3608	5648	8803	11252	17835	25118	38710	55378	176114
DEV. INCOME	800	828	857	887	918	950	983	1018	1053	1090	1128	10514
TOTAL OTHER	5464	3788	2997	4495	6566	9753	12235	18853	26171	39800	56507	186628
SURPLUS/DEFICIT	-14451	19672	67044	83679	100449	118199	172098	253798	329336	401481	380845	1912150
DEDUCT PROVISIONS	16522	34586	40349	46589	43089	73670	52397	121392	82212	98416	85111	694333
SURPLUS/DEFICIT AFTER PROVISIONS	-30973	-14914	26694	37089	57360	44529	119701	132406	247125	303065	295734	1217818
RESERVES B/FWD	84792	53819	38905	65599	102689	160049	204578	324279	456685	703810	1006875	84792
RESERVES CARRIED FWD.	53819	38905	65599	102689	160049	204578	324279	456685	703810	1006875	1302610	1302610
PROVISIONS												
MAJOR REPAIRS	15160	29000	29000	27883	16524	38719	16223	83952	43461	58309	43600	401831
SINKING FUND	1362	1410	1459	1510	1563	1618	1674	1733	1793	1856	1921	17899
FOR NEW PROPERTIES		4176	4322	4473	4630	4792	4960	5133	5313	5499	5691	48990
			5568	5763	5965	6173	6389	6613	6844	7084	7332	57732
				6960	7204	7456	7717	7987	8266	8556	8855	63000
					7204	7456	7717	7987	8267	8556	8856	56043
						7456	7717	7987	8267	8556	8855	48838
TOTAL PROVISIONS	16522	34586	40349	46589	43089	73670	52397	121392	82212	98416	85111	694333
ACCUMULATED PROVISIONS	16522	51108	91457	138046	181135	254805	307202	428594	510806	609222	694333	694333

APPENDIX A3

Cashflow forecast: 5 Year Development @ 5% inflation

	92 TO 93	93 TO 94	94 TO 95	95 TO 96	96 TO 97	97 TO 98	98 TO 99	99 TO 00	00 TO 01	01 TO 02	02 TO 03	TOTALS
INCOME												
RENTAL INCOME	278651	347807	439736	556235	686160	830826	909977	997082	1092978	1198587	1314935	8652973
SERVICE INCOME	6579	6908	7253	7616	7997	8397	8816	9257	9720	10206	10716	93466
RENT LOSSES	-11146	-13912	-17589	-22249	-27446	-33233	-36399	-39883	-43719	-47943	-52597	-346119
L.G. SUBSIDY	8500	8500	8500	8500	8500	8500	8500	8500	8500	8500	8500	93500
OTHER INCOME	1000	2336	2453	2575	2704	2839	2981	3130	3287	3451	3624	30382
TOTAL INCOME	283584	351639	440353	552677	677914	817329	893876	978087	1070766	1172801	1285178	8524202
EXPENDITURE												
MANAGEMENT EXPENSES	102894	111539	123114	157141	166964	183990	193190	202849	212992	223642	234824	1913138
INSURANCE	3500	4675	5909	7204	8564	9993	10492	11017	11568	12146	12753	97821
MISCELLANEOUS	5760	18048	30350	10668	7350	7717	8103	8508	8934	9380	9849	124668
ROUTINE MAINTENANCE	49000	50394	45258	71457	125638	125564	133315	137560	116524	128002	181786	1164498
CYCLICAL MAINTENANCE	45335	32878	15479	20147	12478	63741	50058	18374	24326	14539	79986	377339
SERVICE COSTS	8880	9324	9790	10280	10794	11333	11900	12495	13120	13776	14465	126156
MORTGAGE PAYMENTS	87630	110978	144758	190363	240376	295125	305682	316766	328404	340624	353455	2714161
TOTAL EXPENDITURE	302999	337835	374658	467260	572164	697463	712739	707569	715867	742109	887119	6517783
SUB TOTAL	-19415	13804	65695	85417	105750	119865	181136	270518	354898	430692	398059	2006419
OTHER INCOME AND EXPENDITURE												
INTEREST RECEIVED	5935	3880	2673	4587	7602	12333	16005	25763	37059	57993	84314	258144
DEV. INCOME	800	840	882	926	972	1021	1072	1126	1182	1241	1303	11365
TOTAL OTHER	6735	4720	3555	5513	8574	13354	17077	26889	38241	59234	85617	269510
SURPLUS/DEFICIT	-12680	18524	69249	90930	114324	133219	198213	297407	393139	489926	483676	2275929
DEDUCT PROVISIONS	16680	35772	41907	47857	46744	80760	58809	136039	94077	113912	100316	772871
SURPLUS/DEFICIT AFTER PROVISIONS	-29360	-17248	27343	43074	67581	52459	139404	161368	299063	376015	383361	1503058
RESERVES B/FWD	84792	55432	38184	65527	108601	176181	228640	368044	529412	828475	1204489	84792
RESERVES CARRIED FWD.	55432	38184	65527	108601	176181	228640	368044	529412	828475	1204489	1587850	1587850
PROVISIONS												
MAJOR REPAIRS	15160	30000	30000	27682	17503	41598	17688	92862	48741	66309	50333	437876
SINKING FUND	1520	1596	1676	1760	1848	1940	2037	2139	2246	2358	2476	21594
FOR NEW PROPERTIES		4176	4385	4604	4834	5076	5330	5596	5876	6170	6478	52525
			5846	6138	6445	6767	7106	7461	7834	8226	8637	64461
				7673	8057	8459	8882	9327	9793	10283	10797	73270
					8057	8460	8883	9327	9793	10283	10797	65600
						8460	8883	9327	9794	10283	10797	57544
TOTAL PROVISIONS	16680	35772	41907	47857	46744	80760	58809	136039	94077	113912	100316	772871
ACCUMULATED PROVISIONS	16680	52452	94359	142216	188959	269720	328529	464567	558644	672556	772871	772871

APPENDIX B   Rental Income

Old Stock. The rent on "Secure rent" properties is set every two years by the Fair Rents Officer. Currently rent increases on these properties are in the region of 30%. Assured rents are being increased at the rate of inflation + 2% annually. These have produced an overall average increase of between 10.5% and 14.5% over the last five years.

1992 & 1993. These figures are based on projected rents property by property.

1994 onwards. Based on an annual increase of 10% with 3.5% inflation and 11.5% if inflation is at 5%.

New Stock. Since these will all be Assured Tenancies the rent increases are based on inflation + 2%. Overall the rental income figures are at a conservative level.

RENTAL INCOME 3.5% INFLATION

	1992	1993	1994	1995	1996	1997	1998	1999	2000	2001	2002	
OLD STOCK	271579	301833	332016	365218	401740	441914	486105	534716	588187	647006	711706	
1992 NEW STOCK + 5.5%	7072	7461	7871	8304	8761	9243	9751	10287	10853	11450	12080	
1993 NEW STOCK + 5.5%		38407	40519	42748	45099	47580	50196	52957	55870	58943	62185	
1994 NEW STOCK + 5.5%			53000	55915	58990	62235	65658	69269	73079	77098	81338	
1995 NEW STOCK + 5.5%				68571	72342	76321	80519	84947	89620	94549	99749	
1996 NEW STOCK + 5.5%					70971	74874	78992	83337	87921	92756	97858	
1997 NEW STOCK + 5.5%						73455	77495	81757	86254	90998	96003	
5 YEAR DEVELOPMENT	278651	347701	433407	540756	657904	785621	848717	917271	997783	1072800	1160919	8035529
NO DEVELOPMENT	278651	309294	339888	373522	410501	451157	495856	545003	599040	658456	723786	5185154

RENTAL INCOME 5.0% INFLATION

	1992	1993	1994	1995	1996	1997	1998	1999	2000	2001	2002	
OLD STOCK	271579	301833	336544	375246	418400	466516	520165	579984	646682	721050	803971	
1992 NEW STOCK + 7%	7072	7567	8097	8664	9270	9919	10613	11356	12151	13002	13912	
1993 NEW STOCK + 7%		38407	41095	43972	47050	50344	53868	57639	61673	65990	70610	
1994 NEW STOCK + 7%			54000	57780	61825	66152	70783	75738	81039	86712	92782	
1995 NEW STOCK + 7%				70573	75513	80799	86455	92507	98982	105911	113325	
1996 NEW STOCK + 7%					74102	79289	84839	90778	97133	103932	111207	
1997 NEW STOCK + 7%						77807	83253	89081	95317	101989	109128	
5 YEAR DEVELOPMENT	278651	347807	439736	556235	686160	830826	909977	997082	1092978	1198587	1314935	8652973

SERVICE INCOME

	1992	1993	1994	1995	1996	1997	1998	1999	2000	2001	2002
3.5% INFLATION	6579	6809	7048	7294	7550	7814	8087	8370	8663	8967	9280
5.0% INFLATION	6579	6908	7253	7616	7997	8397	8816	9257	9720	10206	10716

APPENDIX C

Mortgage Payments

Although there will be some changes in the payments on present properties as interest rates vary these have been assumed to be constant.
On new properties the figures on the projection of deferred mortgage repayments have been used.
These are based on an annual increase of 5%.

MORTGAGE PAYMENTS	1992	1993	1994	1995	1996	1997	1998	1999	2000	2001	2002	
	84000	84000	84000	84000	84000	84000	84000	84000	84000	84000	84000	
	3630	3812	4002	4202	4412	4633	4865	5108	5363	5631	5913	
		23166	24324	25541	26818	28158	29566	31045	32597	34227	35938	
			32432	34054	35756	37544	39421	41392	43462	45635	47917	
				42567	44695	46930	49277	51740	54327	57044	59896	
					44695	46930	49276	51740	54327	57043	59896	
						46930	49277	51740	54327	57044	59896	
5 YEAR DEVELOPMENT	87630	110978	144758	190383	240376	295125	305682	316766	328404	340624	353455	2714161
NUMBER OF PROPERTIES	165	177	193	213	233	253	253	253	253	253	253	
NO DEVELOPMENT	87630	87812	88002	88202	88412	88633	88865	89108	89363	89631	89913	975571
NUMBER OF PROPERTIES	165	165	165	165	165	165	165	165	165	165	165	

Major Repairs

Major repairs on older properties should be funded by the Local Authority.
However, we feel it to be prudent to make our own provision in case the necessary funding is not forthcoming.
Again based on Clarke Wilson's projections but distributed more evenly over the years 93 to 95.

Major repairs provision for new properties appears under the sinking fund.

MAJOR REPAIRS	1992	1993	1994	1995	1996	1997	1998	1999	2000	2001	2002	
CLARKE WILSON	25300	43450	13200	15000	14400	32600	13200	66000	33000	42780	30900	
INFLATION @ 3.5%	25300	44971	14137	16635	16524	38719	16223	83952	43461	58309	43600	401831
	15160	29000	29000	27883	16524	38719	16223	83952	43461	58309	43600	401831
INFLATION @ 5.0%	25300	45623	14553	17366	17503	41598	17688	92862	48741	66309	50333	437875
	15160	30000	30000	27682	17503	41598	17688	92862	48741	66309	50333	437876

APPENDIX D

Routine Maintenance

Clarke Wilson have produced a 10 year forecast of the Routine Maintenance requirements on present properties (Line 1 and these have been increased by the rate of inflation (Line 2).

For new properties the figures included are based on the Maintenance costs allowances and include Cyclical Decoration (Line 3).

Line 4 shows the accumulated figures as new properties come on line incremented by the rate of inflation for 5 years of development.

The projected expenditure will be the sum of Line 2 and Line 4 for 5 years of development.
However, we expect to spend £49000 in the current year and that figure has been used for 1992.

ROUTINE MAINTENANCE	1992	1993	1994	1995	1996	1997	1998	1999	2000	2001	2002	
CLARKE WILSON FORECAST	32985	41955	28275	40520	73720	60365	61455	59735	40850	44490	73570	557920
INFLATION @ 3.5%	32985	43423	30283	44937	84631	71696	75528	75983	53799	60640	103807	677711
NEW PROP.	987	5305	7321	9471	9803	10146						
ACCUM + INFL	987	6327	13869	23825	34462	45814	47418	49078	50795	52573	54413	379562
92 DEV + INF	987	1022	1057	1094	1133	1172	1213	1256	1300	1345	1392	12971
5 YEAR DEVELOPMENT	49000	49750	44151	68762	119093	117510	122946	125061	104595	113213	158220	1072301
NO DEVELOPMENT	49000	44445	31340	46031	85763	72868	76741	77239	55099	61985	105200	705711
CLARKE WILSON FORECAST	32985	41955	28275	40520	73720	60365	61455	59735	40850	44490	73570	557920
INFLATION @ 5.0%	32985	44053	31173	46922	89644	77026	82350	84047	60335	69004	119838	737377
NEW PROP	987	5305	7426	9746	10233	10744						
ACCUM + INF	987	6341	14084	24535	35994	48538	50965	53513	56189	58998	61948	412094
5 YEAR DEVELOPMENT	49000	50394	45258	71457	125638	125564	133315	137560	116524	128002	181786	1164498

Cyclical Maintenance

Based on Clarke Wilson's projections on present stock plus £5000 per year from 1993 for the general improvement of properties.

CYCLICAL MAINTENANCE	1992	1993	1994	1995	1996	1997	1998	1999	2000	2001	2002	
CLARKE WILSON FORECAST	45335	26550	9505	13080	6150	46035	33625	9505	13080	6150	46035	303226
INFLATION @ 3.5%	45335	27479	10180	14502	7060	54690	41325	12093	17224	8382	64955	353226
PROPOSED	45335	32479	15180	19502	12060	59690	46325	17093	22224	13382	69955	
INFLATION @ 5.0%	45335	27878	10479	15147	7478	58741	45058	13374	19326	9539	74986	327339
PROPOSED	45335	32878	15479	20147	12478	63741	50058	18374	24326	14539	79986	377339

CIPFA

BUSINESS PLANS

A Compendium

HOUSING ASSOCIATIONS

A Large Housing Association (Over 6,000 units)

Three Year Plan 1993 - 1996

Note:

Appendices containing financial projections for the budget and balance sheets are not reproduced.

HOUSING ASSOCIATION LIMITED

THREE YEAR PLAN

1993 - 96

CONTENTS

Chapter 1

CHAIRMAN'S INTRODUCTION

This is the first three year plan since   undertook a major management restructuring in 1991. It reflects the confidence and strength of the new   and builds on the solid financial achievements of the last eighteen months. This Three Year Plan exemplifies the business disciplines and financial control techniques that are now embedded in the Association's management culture. For the first time there are well developed performance standards for the key objectives as well as detailed departmental plans. This document is necessarily a summary of a management control framework that, at its most detailed level, sets personal targets and performance standards for every member of staff of the Association.

       remains true to its social and charitable objectives, but these now have a sharper focus and are reconciled with effective business disciplines. The housing association world is set for another period of change. Public resources are under substantial pressure and the Housing Corporation is likely to focus its support on fewer associations. New opportunities and threats will arise over the next three years to which this Association will be able to respond quickly and decisively.

I am confident that this Three Year Plan provides a framework within which a strong committee and an understanding management team can grow, prosper and secure its objectives.

Housing Association Limited is a "charitable" housing association registered under the Industrial and Provident Societies Act 1965   and with the Housing Corporation

Chapter 2

PROFILE OF

RANGE OF ACTIVITIES

owns and manages approximately 7,000 homes and aims to provide a comprehensive range of accommodation in a variety of tenures to meet local needs.

The Association started life in 1974 as   Housing Association with the aim of providing low cost housing in   for those in need.   HA expanded rapidly and formed two subsidiary companies;   Housing Association in   and   Housing Association in   In 1991 the three associations merged and consolidated their activities under   Housing Association Limited.

In addition to the core activity of purchasing general rented housing at affordable rents,   provides shared ownership and other low cost home ownership initiatives.
is also a substantial provider of homes for people with special needs. Services for the elderly encompass sheltered housing, residential homes for the frail elderly, and a 'staying put' scheme to assist elderly owner occupiers. One third of   tenants are elderly. There are fifty supported housing schemes and hostels, managed in conjunction with specialist voluntary organisations, which provide accommodation for younger single people needing transitional housing or housing with care.

The Association's Emergency Housing Service provides Over 800 temporary homes through leasing and hostels, as an alternative to the use of bed and breakfast hotels by local Councils.

STOCK PROFILE

All the Association stock was developed during and after 1974. Although the older stock, particulars the conversions, are needing upgrading this is a smaller problem for   than many other   associations.

About 60% of the rented stock is rehabilitated and converted dwellings and 40% new building. Almost all the shared ownership housing is new build - there are a few exceptions to this in

Table 1
Stock by type

Rented	4,597
Shared Ownership	1,204
Freehold Ownership	202
Managed for others	170
Emergency Housing	808
Total	6,981

The make up of   stock is much more complex than that of many large associations. The Table below shows the stock by geographical area.

Table 2
Stock Size by Local Area

	3,679
	873
	888
	598
	209
	196
	170
	368
Total	6,981

DEVELOPMENT PIPELINE

Development Activity

The Association is one of the larger spenders of Housing Corporation funds in the London North West region.

Part of our business activity is carrying out development work on property that will remain in ownership but a large part is also involves on development agency work for smaller and specialist associations.

At any point in time there is considerable development work in progress and set out below is a profile of the work in hand at lst April 1993 divided between   and agency activity.

Table 3
Properties in Pipeline

	Units proposed for others	Units Proposed for
Land with Terms Agreed	44	201
Land bought	32	64
Land with works in progress	102	144
Existing Properties with Terms Agreed	-	6
Existing Development bought and tendered	-	65
Existing Developent with works in progress	-	2
Total units in pipeline	178	482
Grand Total		660

AREA AND NEEDS PROFILE

General Review

     has its main activities currently in North West London but takes its area of business operation as London north of the Thames and district councils close to the edge of this segment of London. There is and will remain great housing need in this area.

Most housing need studies have looked at London as a whole and concluded that there remains a severe shortage of affordable housing to rent. In a detailed study published in July 1991, Christine Whitehead of LBE Housing concluded that over 20% of the existing stock is either unfit or in need of substantial repair. In terms of the number of households and potential households on one side and the availability of suitable housing on the other, there will be a shortfall of some 420,000 adequate housing units by 1995. Even given some positive assumptions this would require a programme of 50,000 units per year in order to meet the needs in the capital by the year 2000.

Some would disagree with these specific figures but there remains little difference of view about the still considerable need for new social housing provision over the next decade.

Social housing provision will be spread through temporary housing, affordable rented housing and shared ownership.   is well placed to provide all of these.

Housing Association Grant (HAG) Availability

Although by no means all of   activity relies on HAG, its availability in the Association's area is of crucial importance. Local authorities are able to offer HAG but its availability from this source is very limited. The main provider of HAG is the Housing Corporation and set out in Table 4 is the 1993/4 HAG allocation by borough within 'core' Local Authority areas. Also shown in the table is the HAG received by   in 1993/4 and the percentage of HAG for each borough that was achieved.

Table 4
HAG Distribution in Borough 1993/4

Local Authority	Total HAG £m	£m	% to
	30.3	9.15	30.2
	29.5	5.13	17.4
	5.4	0.2	3.7
	12.5	0.1	0.8
	1.8	1.61	89.4

It can be seen that the Association has a high market share in   but has little or no programme for HAG spending in 1993/4 in other area.   However HAG programmes do occur from time to time in   The Association is also actively seeking to expand its geographic area of opperations .

The total cash available from the Housing Corporation is set to follow the trend outlined in Table 5 over the next three years and   is in a good position to increase the total HAG available to it because of low unit cost of production and interest from other local authorities in our work.

Table 5
Housing Corporation Cash Limit

	1993/4 £m	1994/5 £m	1995/6 £m
London NW	268	284	274
London NE	276	275	269

Set out below are short descriptions of the housing issues of the main lead authorities in whose area   is active.

FINANCIAL STRENGTH

There are different methods of valuing assets. The balance sheet at 31 March 1992 shows a value based on costs. Set out in Tables 5 and 6 are values on our main stock which have been obtained through external valuers. The value for 1993, and future years will be publsihed with our annual accounts.

Table 6
Open Market Value - 31 March 1992

Rental Stock	£259m
Shared Ownership	£ 25m
Development sites at cost	£ 15m
Total	£299m

Table 7

Cash flow value - 31 March 1992

Rental Stock	£68m
Shared Ownership	£25m

The annual rent roll totals £14m and the cash spend on on our development activity in 1992/3 was £19m. During 1992/3 the cash flow was robust enough to avoid using, to any significant degree, the development loan facilities agreed with our lenders.

STAFFING PROFILE

The Association employed 260 staff at the beginning of April 1993 and the Table below sets out some further detail.

Table 8

Staff employed by Department -

Housing	134
Property Services	15
Development	13
EHS	40
Finance & Central Services	36
Temporary cleaners/pt	22
Total	260

This is large staff for a 7,000 unit association but reflects the high level of staffing required in our elderly persons care homes and in the hostels and short stay housing.

Three Year Plan

Chapter 3

MANAGEMENT CONTROL

COMMITTEE OF MANAGEMENT

The Committee of Management has overall responsibility for the direction, policy and performance of the Association. It s the equivalent of the Board of Directors of a Companies Act company.

The Committee meets every eight weeks and is supported by three sub committees as set out below:

<u>Management Committee</u>

| Tenants Advisory Committee | Finance Sub-Committee | Joint Staff Committee |

The Committee has nineteen members with a wide range of experience covering all of the areas of the Association's operations. A brief profile of each Member is set out below:

MANAGEMENT TEAM

Executive day to day responsibility for the Association's operations rests with the Chief Executive and Management Team. There is a total staff complement of   The senior management staff structure is set out below:

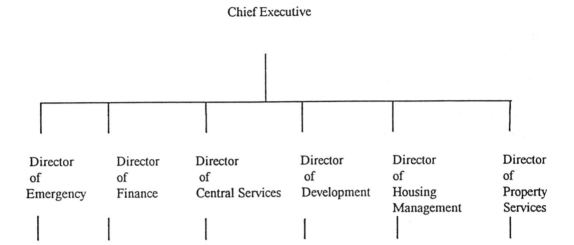

Chapter 4

THINKING AHEAD

In this section of the Plan there is a review of initiatives being worked on by   which do not form part of the firm plans of the Association at present but which are actively under review and will probably form the basis of new initiatives during the Three Year Plan period. Because of their uncertainty no financial projections have been made.

The Management and Maintenance of Council Housing Stock on Contract

In advance of Compulsory Competitive Tendering (CCT) for housing management a number of local authorities are looking at negotiating or tendering their housing management services.   is discussing each of these opportunities with the local authority as they arise. Westminster and Brent are 'pilot' authorities under the CCT arrangements. Close contact has been maintained, but no satisfactory arrangement has emerged as yet. However, tentative ideas for working with existing local authority staff groups to win a tender and then to use this core group as the basis of a team to extend this type of work are being discussed.

Taking Voluntary Transfer of some existing housing from local authorities

      is willing to work with local authorities on small scale voluntary transfers and has responded positively to such initiatives. Particularly within northwest London, the Association is well equipped to take on such activities.

The Development of "Tax Break Housing"

Although   has not yet carried out a BES (Business Expansion Scheme) development , it has looked in detail at several opportunities and is well placed to carry out such schemes on a partnership basis with local authorities.

      hopes that when BES is no longer available some other form of Tax Break Housing will be available to add to the options to meet housing need.

Group Structures and partnership with small associations

      is in discussion with several small associations about the best way for it to help them take forward their work. As a large association,   is in a position to support their development work and to support them with financial services. A possible group structure is being developed to facilitate these partnerships.

Work Training Related Housing

Recognising that the housing work of   is often set in an inner city environment where many needs have to be met, the Association has taken an interest in providing housing for young single people in association with work training and has been developing ideas for taking this forward including providing, a Foyer type housing scheme.

Further work will be undertaken on each of these initiatives and as any of them are developed to a quantifiable stage they will be integrated into the action plans and the financial consequences integrated into the appropriate commentary and appendices.

Care in the Community

At present the financial framework for providing this type of housing is too volatile but it must improve over the next three years or the existing policies will flounder.   has the experience to undertake this work and indeed it will help by enabling the association to develop a greater management strength in this field.

Chapter 5

KEY OBJECTIVES AND PERFORMANCE INDICATORS

The Association adopted a set of objectives in 1991 but felt that it was essential that these be underpinned by realistic performance targets and indicators.

Set out below are each of the objectives and a range of indicators. The indicators are by no means the full range used by the Association, but by regular reporting against the key Performance Indicators the Committee can seek to ensure that the Association's objectives are achieved and progress made in appropriate areas. They do help to monitor the achievement against the objectives and prevent them being simply statements of good intent.

1.   **To keep available good quality affordable housing in North West London and adjacent home counties for people who cannot afford to meet their needs through owner occupation, with priority to those in greatest need.**

Performance Indicators	1993/4	1994/5	1995/6
1. Total units owned/managed at end of year	7,084	7,247	7567
2. Voids as % of lettable stock (ex-sales)	1.25	1.25	1.%
3. % LA nominations housed	50%	50%	50%
4. % homeless housed	35%	35%	35%
5. % hostel "move on" lettings	10%	10%	10%
6. Turn round times for voids (ex-sales) days	13	11	10
7. Average rent	£ 44.35	£47.65	£ 51.22

2.   **To produce as many good sound homes as we can whether by improving older properties or by new building.**

Performance Indicators	1993/4	1994/5	1995/6
1. Number of units to be completed in year	188	215	310
2. Allocation of new HAG	£16m	£19m	£24m
3. Number of units below 'standard brief' quality	75%	75%	75%

3. **To provide our tenants with a responsive management service to enable them to obtain maximum enjoyment from their homes.**

Performance Indicators	1993/4	1994/5	1995/6
1. % Management Committee who are tenants	16%	16%	16%
2. No. of newsletters p.a.	2	2	3
3 Service satisfaction levels from surveys	80%	85%	87%
4. % arrears to annual charge (target end of year)	7%	6%	5.5%
5. % of cash collected in period (the year)	100%	105%	101%
6. % of lettings to transfers (target for year)	35%	35%	35%

4. **To provide our tenants with a responsive maintenance service to repair and improve the housing stock and to protect the Association's investment.**

Performance Indicators	1993/4	1994/5	1995/6
% of work completed within target by category			
24 hours	90%	92%	95%
7 days	90%	92%	95%
14 days	80%	82%	85%
28 days	80%	80%	80%
Average	80%	80%	80%

Performance Indicators	1993/4	1994/5	1995/6
% of work inspected			
Pre-inspection 15%	15	12	10
Post- inspection 10%	10	11	12

Performance Indicators	1993/4	1994/5	1995/6
Spend against budget	£,000	£,000	£,000
Cyclical	965	982	1,168
Responsive	730	751	688
Major repairs	500	1,000	1,255

18

5. **To make specific provision for people with special needs either by direct provision of homes or by management partnerships between the Association and specialist agencies.**

Performance Indicators	1993/4	1994/5	1995/6
1. Hostels bedspaces owned (end of year)	539	519	569
2. Hostel bedspaces - completion target	24	-	50
3. "Move on" units completion target	26	35	20
4. Number of tenants covered by 'High Care Housing Manager' (end of year)	7.1%	7.2%	7.3%

6. **To promote equal opportunities for both sexes, all races and those with disabilities in the provision of housing and employment.**

Performance Indicators	1993/4	1994/5	1995/6
1. % lettings to ethnic minority groups	47%	48%	48%
2. % ethnic minority staff target	35%	38%	38%
3. % disabled staff target(long term 3%)	1%	1.5%	2%
4. % ethnic minority members on Committee	16%	25%	33 %
5. % women members on Committee target	16%	25%	33%

7. **To work in co-operation with local authorities, other housing associations, health authorities and private and voluntary agencies in order to benefit the local communities and their environments.**

Performance Indicators	1993/4	1994/5	1995/6
1. Satisfaction levels on annual Chief Executive visit to appropriate organisations 1= v.dissat 5=v.sat	3	4	5

8. **To maintain a sound financial and administrative base to promote 1 to 7 above.**

Performance Indicators	1993/4	1994/5	1995/6
1. Brought forward surplus	£3.298m	£4.482m	£4.762m
2. Ratio of current asset/Current liabilities (end of year)	2.78	2.86	2.94
3. % Training Budget to payroll	4%	4%	4%
4. % days lost through sickness/ absenteeism	3.8%	3%	2.5%
5. % Housing Management cost against allowance.	100 %	98 %	95%

Three Year Plan

Chapter 6

DEPARTMENTAL PLANS

6.1   Development

Housing Corporation Programme

The development of new homes for rent with the benefit of Housing Association Grant (HAG) allocations from the Housing Corporation, in   traditional areas of operation, will continue as the departments core activity.

This will be supplemented by share equity projects as the Housing Corporation's policy to accelerate this type of initiative comes further into play.

Work is being undertaken to expand from the Association's geographic area over the currency of the plan. This will widen the scope for grant funding in the future.

In co-operation with a partnership of associations   has led a bid to obtain a 'Volume Programme' from the Housing Corporation . This involved working with two contractors to build a minimum of 600 new homes and up to 1200, having the benefit of discounts for the large volume of work. Although this does not so far seem to have been successful, despite offering a significantly cheaper option to the Housing Corporation, the associations and its partners are looking at ways of entering the agreement with the builder/developer in the confident belief that between us we will be able to get the volume of work through their ordinary programmes.

This would put each association in a good position to gain significant allocation in 1994/5 and 1995/6.

The total programme envisaged takes some regard to this but hopefully the benefits will be even greater.

Table 9

Housing Corporation Committment HAG Main Programme Forecast

1993/4	£16m
1994/5	£19m
1995/6	£24m

Table 10 outlines the new programme HAG that   expects to gain for each of the three years of the plan. 1993/4 is confirmed. Roughly 35% of the new programme will be on behalf of other smaller or specialist associations.

DEVELOPMENT CLIENTS - HAG PROGRAMME

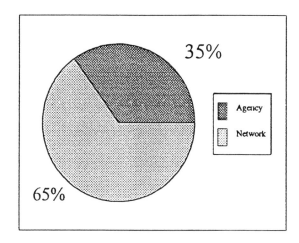

PARTNERSHIPS WITH STATUTORY AGENCIES

Partnership arrangements with local housing authorities and other statutory agencies in the health and social service field provide the opportunity to undertake development in new areas of need and new geographical areas.

A substantial initiative with   Council will start to come to fruition during the period of the plan. The proposal is that the Council will transfer unimproved sheltered housing for the elderly to   at nil cost. They will be refurbished using private finance raised against the rental stream and retained in   ownership.

Table 10

Sheltered Housing Initiative	1993/4	1994/5	1995/6
Units transferred	-	60	60
Units refurbished	-	-	60

Council has also awarded   a contract to manage Women's Aid services in the borough. The development aspect of this initiative include refurbishment of one refuge and acquisition and conversion of a second both with HAG support.

Three Year Plan

COMPLETED UNITS - HAG PROGRAMME

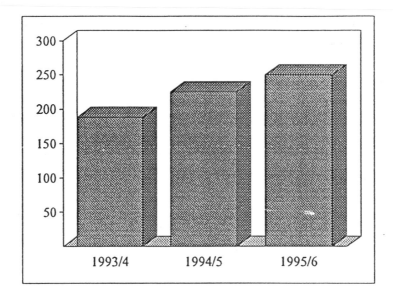

The Development Department also manages a Staying Put Scheme in   which assists elderly owner occupiers with repair and improvements to their homes. Statutory sources of funding are maximised but other voluntary funding is needed as this service runs at a deficit and will need to be phased out in 1994/5 unless further funding is forthcoming.

CITY CHALLENGE

In 1993/4 Ministerial decisions on City Challenge will be an important influence on how resources are directed, both through the funding committed during Round One, and for new programmes which are likely to include up to twenty new areas. The London Borough of   has been successful in acquiring funding during Round One, and it would be our intention to secure funding from this source for a housing scheme. Should other Authorities in any of our current or proposed areas of operation show an interest in putting together a City Challenge bid, we will seek to secure an involvement at an early stage.

ESTABLISHMENT

The Development Department will budget to work within development fee income over the three year period. To support the increased programme, the establishment of the department will grow by two in 1993/4 and two in 1994/5.

MAJOR REPAIR

The responsibility for   HAG repair programme will transfer to the Property Services Department during 1993/4.

6.2   Housing Management

tenants are highly represented amongst the most disadvantaged households in our local communities. The Housing Department will operate within Management Allowances throughout the three year term of the plan.   Within this financial constraint, the Housing Department will aim to maximise the cost effectiveness and quality of its service to tenants.

Service quality initiatives will include:

-    A "Tenants' Charter" to guarantee service delivery on a wider range of issues.

-    A programme of Tenant Participation initiatives.

-    A customer care / total quality orientation.

KEY DEPARTMENTAL TARGETS

Table 11

Rent Arrears and Void Property

1. Rent Arrears:	
1993/4	7% of Annual Charge
1994/5	6% of Annual Charge
1995/6	5.5% of Annual Charge
2 Void Property	
1993/4	1.25%
1994/5	1.25%
1995/6	1.00%

Three Year Plan

LETTINGS

Property available for letting can arise from a number of sources:

A.   New programme
B.   Other initiatives (eg DIY Shared Ownership, Tenants Incentive Scheme)
C.   Transfers of existing tenants
D.   Other reasons, eg death or notice by tenant

aims to meet the "Partners in Housing Need" target of providing 75% of new lettings to family units and 50% of smaller homes to local authority nominees.   also aims to offer 25% of smaller homes as "move-on" accommodation to residents in its special projects.

ANTICIPATED LETTINGS

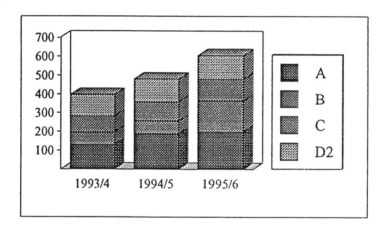

SALES

The Association needs to sell a portfolio of vacant units to raise money to rebuild brought forward surpluses. Throughout the first half of 1993/4, sales will continue at a rate of 60 units p a and the net annual value of sales will approximate to £0.8 million.

Following the completion of this programme, limited sales will continue to fund major repairs and improvements to   stock.

Table 12
Void Sales

	1993/4	1994/5	1995/6	1995/6
Units sold	60	45	30	30
Net receipt	£1.0m	£0.75m	£0.5m	£0.55m

The sale of the remaining 35 units from the former Shared Ownership Housing Association portfolio will be completed.

ELDERLY PERSONS HOUSING

has three sheltered housing schemes in the development pipeline . New sheltered housing transferred from   Council will be relet in 1995/6.

Table 13

	1993/4	1994/5	1995/6
New sheltered housing units	98	35	60

One existing scheme may be transferred out to another registered housing association with a specialist interest in the client group.

SPECIAL PROJECTS

A programme of new special needs housing is contained within the development portfolio:

Table 14

	1993/4	1994/5	95/96
New shared housing units	24	35	20

The transfer out of around 20 units is envisaged over the period, as registered housing associations amongst our special project agencies seek transfer of ownership of the schemes they manage.

. will undertake a new contract with   Council to provide Women's' Aid Refuge services in   Provision of 100 bedspaces in four properties is anticipated.

GENERAL RENTED HOUSING

The Associations sales programme will concentrate on general rented housing. The net growth in general rented housing is:

Table 15

	1993/4	1994/5	1995/6
New general rented units	66	145	230
Sales	45	30	30
Net growth	21	120	200

RENT POLICIES

. will seek to move towards a harmonised rent policy where rent differentials between fair rent and assured tenancies and mixed funded scheme rent are reduced. Target increases are:

Table 16

	1993/4	1994/5	1995/6
Fair Rent	10%	10%	8%
Assured Relet	7%	7%	7%
Mixed funded assured	0%	0%	5 %

LEASEHOLD / SHARED OWNERSHIP TARGETS

- Gross receipts from staircasing of shared ownership property of over £200k p.a..

- New shared ownership leases in management

- New DIYSO leases in management

- Tenant Incentive Scheme (TIS) vacations agreed.

Table 17
Shared Ownership

	1993/4	1994/5	1995/6
New and shared ownership leases in management	0	8	70

Table 18

	1993/4	1994/5	1995/6
TIS vacations completed	65	65	65

- Mortgage rescue scheme of 20 acquisitions.

- Agency management work to remain unchanged at 170 units.

- 20 new HAG funded shared ownership homes in 1994/5.

STAFFING / ESTABLISHMENT

Overall stock increases in 1993/4 are relatively small, and activity on property sales reduces in 1993/4. No staffing increase is anticipated in this period, except for the finalisation of recruitment of 30 staff to manage the residential home opening in the first quarter of 1993/4.

Overall stock will increase by 143 in 1993/4 and 190 in 1994/5 and 280 in 1995/6. One additional post will be required in 1995/6.

6.3   Property Services

Property Services undergone a comprehensive reappraisal in 1992/3. The aim has been to consolidate a good responsive service for day to day repairs, but also to concentrate on maximising the upgrading elemental renewal of the housing stock to protect the asset value for the Association and the amenity level for tenants.

- Introduction of new departmental structure headed by the Property Services Director

- The Department started to work towards BS5750/IS9000 registration in January 1993, with the aim of securing registration in 1993/4.

- The responsive maintenance computer system went live in November 1992 and a new schedule of Rates system will be introduced in mid 1993.

- A stock survey will be carried out in 1993/4 at an approximate cost of £100,000.

- The Department will relocate to new offices in 1994/5.

- A detailed appraisal of the potential to become involved in compulsory competitive tendering in conjunction with Housing Management.

- The Department negotiated new service level agreements for EHS, Leasehold and Special Projects starting from January '93.

REVENUE EXPENDITURE

The Department will maintain its expenditure on works costs and overheads within the allowances for day to day and cyclical repairs.

Table 19
Planned Expenditure

	1993/4	1994/5	1995/6
EXPENDITURE ON:	£K	£K	£k
DAY TO DAY REPAIRS	730	751	688
MAJOR REPAIRS	500	1,000	1,255
CYCLICAL REPAIRS	965	1,100	1,180
TOTAL	2,195	2,733	3,111

HAG FUNDED REPAIRS

During 1993/4 this responsibility for administering HAG funded major repair schemes will be transferred from the Development Department to the Property Services Department.

Table 20
HAG Repair

1993/4	£410,000
1994/5	£500,000
1995/6	£700,000

ASSOCIATION FUNDED REPAIRS

In the second half of 1993/4, the Association will start a limited programme of property disposals to finance an internal programme of major repairs and reimprovements.

1993/4 : £500,000
1994/5 : £500,000
1995/6 : £555,000

STAFFING/ESTABLISHMENT

To resource the expanding programme, meet service commitments, and act as lead department in relation to BS5750, the staff establishment will increase to 15 during 1993/4.

6.4 Emergency Housing

The Emergency Housing Department's core activity is to provide, in partnership with local authorities, temporary accommodation for homeless households. Temporary homes are provided in two main ways:

- "Permanent" structures, such as hostels developed and owned by

- Procurement and management of Short term leased accommodation with private sector landlords.

In addition to the service benefit of providing good quality temporary accommodation for the "statutory" homeless, the activities of the Emergency Housing Department provide a range of benefits to the Association:

- EHS will budget for surpluses (although reducing) for the benefit of the Association's overall activity

- EHS activities in new geographical areas can "open the door" to the Association, in particular in relation to development

- EHS is well placed to attract financing to develop new services, for example for the non-priority single homeless.

SHORT TERM LEASING/MANAGING AGENTS SCHEME

The Department's activity in providing short term housing will continue to grow throughout the period of the plan. However, the legal and financial arrangements with local authorities will change with amendments to the local authority subsidy system. Whilst most homes are currently provided through Private Sector Leasing (PSL) arrangements, all new homes are acquired on the basis of Assured Shorthold Tenancies either within Housing Association Managing Agents or Housing Association Leasings Scheme. In some cases financial support in setting up new schemes with L.A's will be provided by the Housing Corporation.

Table 21

	1993/4	1994/5	1995/6
PSL leases ended	160	330	280
New AST programme	200	250	250
Hostel bedspaces	20	-	50
Net increase	60	(80)	20

The Association will enter AST Programme agreements with two new London Boroughs ( ) and a "procurement only" arrangement with a third ( ).

The Association's small Mobile homes programme came to and end in December 1992.

HOSTELS

- All existing hostels will continue in management throughout the period of the plan.

- A 20 unit hostel scheme for homeless households will be provided for DC in 1994/5. On site late 93/94.

- The Department will aim to start a 50 bed "Foyer" initiative for young single people in the west London area in 1993/4, and start a 20 unit hostel for the non-statutory homeless in 1994/5.

STAFFING / ESTABLISHMENT

To meet the projected growth in programme, an additional 6 staff will be required over the three years. Two will be for the homeless hostel and four in the Foyer.

The Department will start preparing for BS5750 in 1993/4 with the aim of securing registration in 1994/5.

6.5   Central Services

The Central Services provides personnel, office management and related support services to the Association.

WORK PROGRAMME

The Department has a programme of strategic initiatives throughout the terms of the plan.

Current activities include:

-       the introduction of new staff appraisal scheme for all staff.

-       a comprehensive programme of customer care training

-       co-ordinating the Association's P/R. strategy.

Planned initiatives for 1993/4 and 1994/5 include:

-       Co-ordination of the organisation's progress towards Total Quality Management and BS5750.

-       Piloting a performance related pay scheme for senior staff.

-       Computerisation of Personnel systems.

-       Ensuring compliance with EC directives on Health & Safety.

STAFFING/ESTABLISHMENT

Given in particular the significant growth in   staff group and the co-ordinating role of the Department in quality/customer care issues, an additional post in 1993/4, and a further post in 1994/5 will be required.

Chapter 7

FINANCIAL COMMENTARY

has transformed its balance sheet in less than two years following the loss of over £2m arising from the transfer of engagements with the former subsidiaries. While this transformation reflects the underlying value within the organisation this dramatic change has been achieved by a programme of void sales and by a detailed appraisal of reserves and provisions.

strength is rooted in its sound approach to financial control within an innovative environment. Its financial policies minimise risk and enhance the value of the entire business.

Over the past three years, despite the organisational trauma, we have with the support of the Housing Corporation, local authority clients and our funders continually grown and successfully expanded into new markets. Our key corporate objective, for the next three years, is to build on our reconstruction with a period of consolidation and sustainable growth. This requires the continuation of financial services of the highest quality.

We shall seek to make the most effective use of our accounting, private finance, special needs accounting and internal audit staff and to offer our expertise to the many other associations with whom we work in partnership.

PRIVATE FINANCE

Housing Association has a long history of working with funders to provide social housing. In recent years we have developed a close working relationship with our principal lender which has seen the Society's commitment to us expand alongside our reconstruction.

Our borrowing strategy is to move towards long term conventional finance and to replace individual loans with consolidated loan portfolios. We have achieved this objective with our two major private lenders and are now wish to seek similar arrangements with our other existing private finance partners. We will continue to cultivate an appropriate environment for our lenders to be confident about our ability to deliver their requirements within a partnership for social housing. We will also seek to develop the borrowing opportunities for the smaller associations with whom we work

Table 22

Our Major Funders at 31 March 1993

Facilities agreed

The projected falling grant rates will place pressure on traditional lending arrangements. We will explore opportunities to secure the release of locked equity in our housing stock by seeking to refinance some old, and relatively expensive local authority loans as part of new consolidation arrangements with private lenders.

We shall seek new arrangements for the funding of new shared ownership housing schemes.

The Association's policy has been to ensure that long term funding facilities are in place before schemes commence on site. Facilities to fund the HAG funded rental allocation for 1993/4 are already in place and we intend to continue with this policy as far as practical over the next three years. Our estimated borrowing requirements over the next three years are set out below. We intend over this period extending our existing business partnerships with major lenders as the principle means of raising finance. Should appropriate consortium stock issues or similar opportunities become available then they will be considered, but it is not our intention, given our existing involvement in stock issues, to overtly seek to use this method of raising finance in the next 3 years.

Three Year Plan

Table 23
Borrowing Requirements - New HAG allocations

	£m
1993/4	0.5
1994/5	8.61
1995/6	2.66

Notes

1993/4	Shared ownership only
1994/5	Plus the refinancing of some local authority loans
1995/6	Plus refinancing of a leased scheme £2.3m

PERFORMANCE CRITERIA

has a long history of successfully raising private finance for social housing. The Association is highly geared compared to other associations. Our approach to lending is to ensure that revenue streams for individual schemes remain adequate to service debt. We believe that this is the real test of an association's performance. However the Association will aim to ensure that its gearing ratio (as defined by the Housing Corporation) is contained within the published target. Where possible internal cash resources will be used to reduce the level of external borrowing. Similarly the Association will pursue financial policies which aim to ensure the achievement of published financial performance criteria where this does not fundamentally conflict with other strategic objectives.

FINANCIAL CONTROL

The Association's strategy is to ensure that all cost centres should break even after a fair and reasonable allocation of central charges. The Association does not wish to establish a pattern of cross subsidy between services. This will be achieved by a rigorous programme to ensure that costs are controlled through cost effectiveness reviews. Where it is not viable to continue with a service alternative methods of financing will be achieved.

Managerial and budgetary accountability will be emphasised and improved by the increasing use of new technology to ensure that management information is immediately accessible.

The balance sheets have been prepared in traditional form. These do not reflect the underlying value of the business. This issue is dependent on the outcome of the debate on stock valuation and the details of teh SORP. The Association is committed to an annual valuation of its stock to support our balance sheet information.

Our projected Balance Sheet also demonstrates the growth in the Rent Surplus Fund. This is particularly difficult to project but is expected to add to the overall financial strength of the business.

TECHNOLOGY

The Association is committed to the expansion of technology through our computer strategy. Over the next two years the Association will be installing Local Area Networks in its main offices and connecting these to the main computer system. This will provide us with an essential hardware infrastructure to enable technology to be harnessed for all our, and our clients needs. Central systems, such as word processing will be devolved to the local users to create additional capacity on the central mainframe. The association will, by 1996, seek to put in place a programme for the replacement of its mainframe computer. This will involve a transfer of systems onto the LAN. We are already working with our software house to ensure that our existing systems have a natural upgrade path to a PC LAN network.

The Association continues to invest in software developments designed to increase our productivity and to improve our service to clients.

FINANCIAL PROJECTIONS

The attached budgets Appendix 1 - 3 for the three years 1993 to 1996 together with the projected balance sheets for the year ends (Appendix 4) reflect the policies and strategies set out in this plan. The financial projections emphasise that the Association will be working through a period of consolidation. Our financial performance will be linked to the overall economic position and in particular the level of inflation. The financial projections assume that inflation will be as follows :-

	93/4	94/5	95/6
General price inflation	3.4%	4%	4%
Pay inflation	2%	5%	5%

Naturally these key assumptions play a significant part in our planning and our projections are dependent on the economy performing to these assumptions.

The sales programme designed to rebuild our reserves will come to an end in 1993/4 but a modest level of void sales will continue to provide additional finance for improving our housing stock. The Association will rigorously pursue major repair HAG but in order to deliver an appropriate service to our customers we feel that we must supplement this provision through a modest programme of void sales.

A key element of our financial strategy has been to tackle loss making services. The financial projections reflect this approach to our business. The Association is expected to have an accumulated surplus of over   by March 1994 and over   by 1996. This is considered reasonable to provide the financial stability to the organisation.

The Financial projections demonstrate the need for effective financial control as we will be entering an era with modest projected annual surpluses arising from a diverse set of activities.

The balance sheets have been prepared in traditional form. These do not reflect the underlying value of the business. This issue is dependent on the outcome of the debate on stock valuation and the details of the SORP. The Association is committed to an annual valuation of its stock to support our balance sheet information.

Our projected Balance Sheets also demonstrate the growth in the Rent Surplus Fund. This is particularly difficult to project but is expected to add to the overall financial strength of the business.

(L332.38)

CIPFA

BUSINESS PLANS

A Compendium

LOCAL AUTHORITIES

Bexley London Borough

Guidance for the Production of Business Plans

Legal Services Business Plan 1993/94

Note:

Legal Services Business Plan 1993/94 Appendix 1 is not reproduced.

Guidance for the Production of Business Plans

BEXLEY LONDON BOROUGH
GUIDANCE FOR THE PRODUCTION OF BUSINESS PLANS

The Council's organisational strategy encompasses the concept of the enabling Council under which a range of agencies will be used to fulfil Council objectives and deliver services. A key feature of the strategy is to devolve management and accountability to the most appropriate level of the organisation and in a form which most suits the particular services being provided. This can be achieved in a number of ways to meet differing circumstances including trading units, cost centres and practice accounts. Where appropriate some of these internal units could be 'externalised' by transfer to the private sector.

An essential pre-requisite of these developments is to place provider units on a more business-like footing and the starting point for this is the preparation and publication of a Business Plan. The purpose of this guide is to set out a model format for a Business Plan which can be tailored to the needs of business managers.

It should be emphasised that the production of a Business Plan should not be seen as a mechanical process simply to meet Council requirements. The value of a soundly based Business Plan comes from the processes which lead up to its production. This process – business planning – is a continuous management process which involves setting objectives and standards, monitoring activity and responding to changing circumstances and opportunities. The Business Plan is derived from this process and is a comprehensive analysis of the business situation at a particular point in time. The Business Plan should not be seen to be set in tablets of stone. Planning for the future is notoriously difficult and unforeseen circumstances may require revision and updating of the plan before the next annual review.

In a commercial context the Business Plan would be used in the following ways:-

  i)   to demonstrate the viability of the business to potential investors or lenders;

  ii) to assure potential customers of the reliability of the business and its ability to deliver services to the standards required; and

  iii) as a management tool to communicate common goals, values and objectives to employees.

Most important of all the Business Plan should not be seen as an end in itself but as a means of planning for business success.

The completed Business Plan will normally be submitted to Members for approval. In some respects however it may be desirable to produce business planning information which is too detailed for Members. Where this occurs it is suggested that this information be prepared in the form of supplements for internal use only.

1

The remainder of this document sets out the suggested model format for a Business Plan with the following elements:-

1. Overview.
2. Objectives of the Business.
3. Action Plans.
4. Resource Plans.
5. Performance Standards.
6. Outlook for the Future.
7. Separate Supplements
   (i)   Project plans for each Action Plan item
   (ii)   Monthly profile of anticipated staffing levels
   (iii)   Monthly income and expenditure profile for each sector.
   (iv)   Anticipated workloads and performance targets for each sector

The model format can be adjusted and tailored to meet individual needs. It should not be regarded as prescriptive nor should it be used as a standard pro forma with blank spaces to be completed. Managers at all levels of the business should be involved in its preparation and production if the benefits of proper business planning are to be derived. Where appropriate suggested methods of business analysis are put forward but it should be emphasised that this document is not intended as a definitive guide to business planning as a management tool. Users of this guide may therefore wish to obtain alternative guidance on the various methods of business analysis which could be used in the formulation of their Plan.

For further information on Business Plans or Business Planning contact:

Mike Ellsmore, Assistant Financial Controller (Audit & Technical) Extension 3035

or

Mark Harrison, Assistant Management Secretary. Extension 2028

BEXLEY LONDON BOROUGH
BUSINESS PLAN – MODEL FORMAT

1. OVERVIEW

1.1 Purpose of the Business Plan

This Section should explain the purpose of the Business Plan
using (perhaps) some of the statements contained in the
introduction to this guide. It should make reference to the
period covered by the Plan and the format which the Plan
takes.

> *Examples*
>
> *This Business Plan identifies the main issues affecting
> the   business in 1993/94 and highlights the key
> areas requiring attention during the year.*
>
> *Its purpose is to establish the profit target for the
> year and to identify the key action areas which need to
> be addressed in order to maintain/improve profitability.*

1.2 Context

It is useful to remind readers of the history of the
business and the context within which the Business Plan is
being produced including

- decisions leading up to the creation of the unit
- reasons for the creation of the unit
- the current position of the unit in terms of its creation
  and development and where it expects to be at the end of
  the period

1.3 Nature of the Business

This section should describe the essential features of the
business and its core values possibly by reference to the
following sub headings:-

Characteristics

- what is the size of the business eg no. of employees, no.
  of jobs, value of contracts
- what is the main purpose of the business
- what are its major objectives
- what are its main products/services

Example

The primary purpose of the   business is to
.
It has a turnover of £   pa.
It employs   permanent and   temporary staff
The main business activities are   .

Customers

- who are the main customers for particular services
- what standards do they expect

Examples

Our main customers are   though we also undertake
work on behalf of   .
The contract specification requires us to   .

Environment

- what is the present business environment
- what local factors influence the business and its local
  customers
- what services will be tendered for in this/next year
- what are the market factors affecting these services
- who are the main competitors.

Examples

The contract for   will be re-tendered in 19
Our main competitors are   (describe nature, size,
experience etc).

Economic Situation

- what is the national economic climate like
- how might this affect business

Examples

Business is likely to increase/decline in 19   as a
result of
Opportunities for growth will be limited to   .

2. ## OBJECTIVES OF THE BUSINESS

2.1 Operational Objectives

This section should contain the operational objectives and
should relate to the efficiency of the business and the way
in which products and services will be provided.

What are the operating outputs and how could they be
improved? How could an improvement in efficiency be
achieved?

4

Examples

To provide an efficient and effective service within the specification of the customer.

To manage all our resources within the business plan targets.

To increase the number of chargeable hours per fee earner.

To improve operator performance.

2.2 Financial Objectives

This section should comprise a succinct statement of the overall financial target of the business. What should the financial targets be related to, turnover or profit? Are there statutory requirements? Has the Council set its own local targets? Is there a profit sharing scheme which needs to be taken into account? Can profit margins be improved?

Examples

To achieve a   % return on turnover.

To meet the statutory target.

To achieve a   % return on capital employed.

To improve gross profit margin.

2.3 Personnel Objectives

This section should outline the objectives of the business in relation to staffing and personnel issues. It should contain a statement of the key employment policies relating these to the main issues or problems facing the business. Are there any major staffing or personnel problems? How do terms and conditions compare with those of competitors? Is the management structure appropriate for current/future business needs? Are staff/management appropriately skilled and trained for their jobs.

Examples

To reduce staff turnover.

To maintain sickness absence below 3%.

To streamline the management structure.

To introduce terms and conditions of employment which increase flexibility and improve efficiency.

To ensure that the whole of the workforce is appropriately trained.

2.4 Qualitative Objectives

These should relate to products or services delivered and how the client/ customer is to be treated. Is a definition of quality set out in contract specification? What business reputation do you aspire to? Do contract specifications include service penalties and rectification notices?

Examples

To provide services to the highest professional standard.

To treat the client/customer fairly.

To meet in full the client's service specification.

To be the best_____(insert type of business) contractor in Bexley.

To be responsive to our customer's needs.

To minimise the number of penalties or rectification notices received.

2.5 Marketing Objectives

These should relate to the markets within which the business operates. Given the constraints of Cross Boundary Tendering this will be restricted to within Bexley. However, some business units will have a mixture of internal and external customers (e.g. the public). What are the current markets in which the business operates? Do they include the public and local schools? Are there opportunities to increase market share? What initiatives can be proposed? How might the service be developed?

Examples

To win all Bexley London Borough contracts.

To market our services to the public (where statutory constraints allow).

To increase our customer base.

To concentrate on marketing our core services.

3. ACTION PLANS

3.1 General

This section should reflect the objectives set out in Section 2 and explain the main action points which need to

be addressed during the year. Particular reference should
be made to any specific requirements set by the client eg
achievement of BS5750. What problems are anticipated? What
solutions might be examined and what objectives can be set?
Which areas of the business might be reviewed to improve
efficiency/profitability? Where possible a detailed project
plan should be prepared for each Action Plan item and
included as a supplement to the Plan this should set out the
timetable for completion/implementation of each project.

3.2   Site by Site, Sector by Sector

This section should examine the performance of each site,
sector or profit centre identifying those areas which
present the greatest opportunities for business development
or pose the greatest threat to profitability or overall
business performance.

The strengths and weaknesses of each sector should be
examined. Measures should be set out to build on strengths
so as to develop and enhance the business. Proposals should
be put forward to address weaknesses by reference to
specific Action Plans. Particular attention should be paid
to:-

- the relationship between income and costs
- profit in relation to turnover
- measures to control the costs of labour/materials/
  overheads
- customer's demands/expectations
- financial and management information systems
- quality control systems
- staff training motivation and commitment

Each of these topics should be examined in depth and where
appropriate action plans identified for the year ahead.

Examples

*Activity in the   sector has declined by   % over
the past 12 months making it necessary to
There is scope to increase income/reduce expenditure at
     by
Problems arose at   in 19   because of a lack of
adequate/up to date monitoring information. To combat
this it is proposed to   .*

3.3   Personnel

This section should build on the personnel objectives set
out in section 2.3 by identifying specific courses of action
designed to implement business objectives or address
identified problems.

Examples

Sickness absence averaged over 4% in 19 .
In order to reduce this and maintain absence below 3% it
is proposed to

Terms and conditions of employment no longer meet business
needs. A full scale review will be carried out during the
year.

A management development programme will be introduced to
improve managers understanding of business practice.

An employee profit sharing scheme will be introduced as a
means of increasing the motivation and commitment of
staff.

3.4 Product or Service Development

This section should examine existing products/services; the
extent to which they meet the present/future demand; and
anticipated areas of growth or decline. It should also
examine opportunities to expand the business base both in
terms of new products/services and new markets. It may also
include reference to market research which may have been, or
is proposed to be carried out to identify opportunities for
product development.

- Which activities have been growing/declining in recent
  years
- What evidence is there to suggest future trends
- How are customers needs likely to change in the future
- What market research has been or should be carried out to
  identify future trends

Examples

Workloads in the   sector are likely to decline/grow
over the next   years as a result of   .

Market research in the field of   suggests that there
is scope to increase business in the   activity.

4. RESOURCE PLANS

This section should reflect the contextual statement at the
beginning of the Business Plan together with the primary
objectives of the business and the action plans already set
out.

4.1 Staffing Plans

The expected employee levels at the beginning and end of the
plan period should be stated together with the assumptions
or eventualities which underpin these numbers. A separate
supplement should indicate staff numbers on a sector by

sector or site by site basis and by reference to numbers of core staff/temporary employees/agency staff. Where work is seasonal the supplement should be accompanied by a detailed period profile showing the number of staff anticipated to be in employment on a monthly basis over the period as a whole.

Attention should also be paid to the skills/competence of staff currently employed, their training/development needs and proposals to address any perceived shortcomings.

4.2 Financial Plan

The financial plan should translate the businesses objectives and action plans into a financial statement. It is a key element and will provide the benchmark against which the performance of the business will be monitored. The management structure of the business can be looked upon as a series of profit centres which may equate to individual sites, centres, functions or operating divisions dealing with specific services. The financial plan should reflect these profit centres and specific financial targets should be set for each one. It is essential that the plan is constructed in a way which allows the business to be monitored. The Plan for the forthcoming financial year should be structured as follows:-

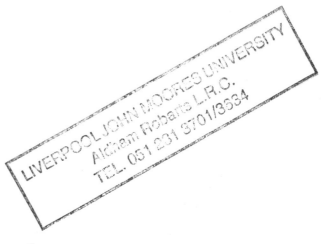

Financial Plan for Year   /

£'000

| | PROFIT CENTRES | | | | TOTAL |
	A	B	C	D	
Income – Bexley 　　　 – Other					
Total Income					
Operating Costs – Labour – Materials – Transport – Etc					
Total Operating Cost					
Operating Profit					
Overheads –　Management –　Service Level 　　　Agreements –　Insurance –　Etc					
Total Overheads					
Trading Profit					
Profit Required to 　meet Statutory 　Requirements					
Operating Cost as a % of Income					
Overheads as a　% of Income					
Trading Profit as a　% of Income					

The Financial Plan should include a statement of assumptions covering for example:-

- the basis on which pay and price inflation has been calculated.

- the basis on which central overheads have been allocated.

A commentary should also be included on the figures set out in the Plan. This should highlight major areas of risk. For example, if a large contract is due for renewal the impact on trading profit should be stated in the event of the contract being lost. If the effects are significant a second more pessimistic plan should be included.

In order to provide a basis for monitoring the Plan a set of monthly profiles should be included as separate supplement.

4.3 Capital Investment Plan

The Capital Investment Plan will include those large items of plant and equipment for which it is not appropriate to make a provision in the Financial Plan. For most business units it is unlikely that there will be any significant capital investment. However, there may be a requirement to provide for the replacement of vehicles, plant and equipment and computer hardware.

The Plan should cover a 3 year period and should identify the profit centre for which the expenditure is planned or purchased. The items should be categorised into those which can be financed through an operating lease and those which will be financed by either capital receipts or loan. (For advice on the method of financing please contact the Finance Department).

Example

Capital Investment Plan (£'000)

	199-/9-	*199-/9-*	*199-/9-*

Leasing
Profit Centre A
  Vehicles
  Equipment			

Loan *Profit Centre B* *Purchase of Premises*			

11

5. <u>PERFORMANCE MONITORING</u>

This section should include a general statement (on a sector by sector basis where appropriate) of the performance standards required to meet Business Plan objectives. In addition to the general statement a more detailed supplement should be prepared setting out the anticipated workloads and the targets against which performance will be monitored. This will include a combination of performance monitoring information drawn from the clients service specifications together with targets set by the business itself. Where appropriate performance targets should be stated as business objectives for example by reference to the numbers of rectification notices or penalties incurred. Progress against each of the Action Plans set out in Section 3 should also be monitored against individual project plans. The Business Plan should also include a statement of the forms of performance monitoring which may be used for example:-

- monthly monitoring against budget profiles
- achievement of client/end-user specifications
- sectional performance objectives on both quantitative and qualitative bases.

6. <u>OUTLOOK FOR THE FUTURE</u>

This should cover the main opportunities and threats facing the business over a three year planning period. Are there any major pieces of legislation which may affect the business environment? Which activities are likely to expand or decline? What are the future prospects for the business? Are the market trends upwards or downwards? What contracts are due for re-tendering? Are there any national economic trends which will affect the business markets? Are there any areas of the business which would benefit from review or restructuring?

This section should also include a 'budget preview' of the following year. This should identify any significant changes which may arise and any particularly sensitive assumptions.

<u>T:\GEN\GEN1.MH</u> (July 20, 1993)

LEGAL DEPARTMENT - PRACTICE ACCOUNT AND BUSINESS PLAN APPENDIX

BEXLEY LEGAL SERVICES

BUSINESS PLAN 1993/94

Overview

1.   PURPOSE

This Business Plan identifies the main issues which affect Bexley Legal Services in fulfilling its role as the Council's provider of Legal Services and highlights key areas requiring attention.

Not only is this the first business plan for Bexley Legal Services ("BLS") but this is the first occasion when the Legal Department, as such, will not be funded centrally. It now has the responsibility of operating on commercial principles through a practice account and of meeting a profit target of 5%.

The purpose of the Plan therefore is to set out the way in which BLS will operate its financial and manpower plan and an Action Plan which addresses the key issues facing the Service.

2.   NATURE OF THE BUSINESS
As a practice, BLS provides a wide range of legal services to all departments of the Council. Those legal services not provided by or through the practice are generally (a) where outside firms of Solicitors are appointed to act from time to time and which are generally financed from client departments own budgets and (b) in certain instances (such as magistrates court proceedings to enforce the collection of local taxes and of off street parking) where departments may deal direct.

BLS comprises   F. t. e. staff who are divided into three profit centres plus management and administrative support. The three profit centres, which are each headed by a Principal Solicitor, comprise Property Planning and Development, Family and Common Law and Education Employment and Competition. A structure chart is set out at Appendix 1. The Controller of Legal Services and the Principal Solicitors are responsible for servicing individual Directorates.

BLS is geared to meet the needs of the Council and its Departments. These are reflected in the Action Plan targets and Work Plan which identify between them volume work commitments and corporate priorities. (The Action Plan priorities for 1993/94 are contained at Appendix 5 to this plan.) The Department also responds to the

1

specific work demands of client departments which may not be formally identified in these planning processes. For instance, the practice always ensures that child protection work on behalf of the Social Services Department is a first priority.

Although the BLS services the whole Council, departmental usage naturally varies depending on the subject area. General advice, personnel and contract work are undertaken on behalf of all client departments from time to time. An indicative list of the different areas of work undertaken is set out in Appendix 2.

3.   ENVIRONMENT

The present environment of BLS is stable and has been so for some years. In response to changing client demands however, the practice has primarily been restructured every four or five years. The last restructuring was in 1989.

The main influence affecting the provision of services is the move towards CCT of Council services as part of Government policy and the pursuit by the Council of a division between enabler and provider roles. This affects BLS in three ways: -

(1)   Central to the Council's review of its basic organisational structure is the development of a number of management models which have increased the demand and pressure on legal services. Examples include the creation of new management arrangements for BTS and the Music Centre and also the present review of strategic housing options.

(2)   If the move to externalise services becomes extensive, there will eventually be a noticeable diminution in demand as provider initiatives take service provision outside of the Council. Although there will be increased contract type work from within the Council the severe restrictions imposed on the provision of legal services to bodies outside of the Council will inevitably affect and may well reduce BLS's client base.

(3)   Legal services are to be exposed to CCT. The Government presently intends to expose 33% of legal services to competition. Further information on this is awaited (including for instance how "legal services" are to be defined). Nonetheless the practice account initiative is in part a response to this challenge to control costs whilst maintaining quality.

4.   OBJECTIVES

The objectives of the business for 1993/1994 are set out in the four following sections: -

4.1 Operational Objectives

(1)   To review the organisational structure having regard to changing client demands and legislative requirements.

(2)   To ensure that each profit centre of the practice maximises efficiency.

(3)   To ensure that the cost of support services supplied by other Council departments represents value for money.

(4)   To provide sufficient training to ensure staff efficiency and the ability to respond to new demands.

(5)   To manage all resources within prescribed targets.

(6)   To ensure administrative and financial procedures are firmly established to facilitate the smooth transition to a practice account.

4.2 Financial Objectives

(1)   To achieve the profit target.

(2)   To ensure each profit centre of the Department achieves its income target.

(3)   To reduce costs.

4.3 Qualitative

(1)   To maintain the recognised expertise of BLS in all areas of work.

(2)   To be responsive to clients' needs

(3)   To meet service specifications which may be developed

4.4 Marketing Objectives

(1)   To identify new work opportunities within the Council.

(2)   Subject to legal constraints to identify work opportunities and to undertake work outside of the Council.

3

(3)   To respond to demand for new skills.

5.   ACTION PLAN

Introduction

The establishment of the practice account for the first
time means that in the first year the primary concern of
BLS as a business unit is to ensure that the necessary
mechanisms are put in place to ensure a smooth transition
to a practice account and to ensure quality and cost
control. Also to ensure that the respective position of
the Chief Solicitor and BLS in the form of the corporate
and contractor links and their relationship with Council
departments are established. To this end a number of
discrete projects are proposed, some internal to BLS's
operation as a business unit and others geared to the
Council's overall requirements for legal services.

A. Internal BLS Projects

(1) Business Objective Proposals

To translate the operational objectives into effect
proposals will be brought forward to implement and
progress the following objectives:-

- review of support services
- training
- cost reduction
- responsiveness to clients
- new work opportunities

(2) Service Delivery

The Action Plan sets out many of the standards expected
of the Service in terms of the service delivered and forms
an important part of the department's management and
accounting to Committee. These will continue and the
anticipated volumes and target performance for the
identified activities are set out at Appendix 3.

(3) Computerisation of legal services
Identify the scope for increased computerisation within
BLS.

(4) Provision of recharge specification

Analyse the usage of support services to ensure BLS is
receiving value for money.

4

B. Projects related to the overall development of the Council's legal services

(1) Service

To make proposals to the Chief Solicitor for the more effective delivery of legal services.

(2) Provision of Service Specification

To produce at the direction of the Chief Solicitor and in consultation with Client Departments detailed service specifications for selected areas of work to enable cost and performance to be evaluated.

(3) Basis for charging Client Departments

In conjunction with Client Departments to review and refine the methods used to charge clients for their use of legal services.

6. RESOURCE PLANNING

6.1 Manpower Plan

BLS establishment is currently set at   staff. The number actually in post at the 1st April, 1993 will total   during the year an additional Solicitor will be appointed, following the service development bid approved by the Policy and Resources committee at its last meeting. Table 1 below sets out the manpower plan.

TABLE 1 – MANPOWER PLAN

Profit Centres	Numbers in position at 1.4.93	Additions	Deletions	Numbers in position at 31.3.93
Property Planning and Development		–	–	
Family and Common Law			–	
Education, Employment and Competition		–	–	
Management and Administration		–	–	
	———	———	———	———
Total			–	
	———	———	———	———

During the course of the year the computerisation of key
work areas will be systematically introduced. In the early
days no savings are anticipated as it has already been
learned that the implementation of computer programmes
consumes large quantities of man hours. It is anticipated
however that savings will eventually be released. With the
experience gained from the early applications two things
will be possible. The release of manpower to develop
further applications which should lead to efficiency
savings in the long term. These are matters which will be
picked up and dealt with in the 1994/95 Business Plan.

6.2   Financial Plan

The gross cost of the practice for 1993/94 is
After allowing for 5% profit margin, calculated on the
gross cost of the services provided, a profit target of
has been set for 1993/94. Income for the year of
is therefore required from clients. As already
explained, the practice is divided into three profit
centres and an administrative unit. Table 2 below sets
out the financial plan for the practice on this structure.

Services will be charged to client departments on the basis
of an agreed tariff. The tariff includes a mixture of
hourly rate charges, unit charges and annual retainers,
details of which are set out in Appendix 4. Approximately
40% of the income for 1993/94 will derive from unit charges
and annual retainers. When required clients will also be
provided with forward estimates of likely cost or
individual fee budgets agreed. A forecast of the income
which is expected from each charge type for the three
profit centres has been included as Appendix 5.

TABLE 2

BEXLEY LEGAL SERVICES FINANCIAL PLAN (£'000)

	Property Planning & Development	Family & Common Law	Education, Employment & Competition	Total
INCOME				
less Direct Costs – Staffing – Transport – Office Expenses				
Sub-Total				
OPERATING PROFIT				
less Overheads – Support Costs – Management & Admin				
Sub-Total				
NET PROFIT				
Net Profit as a percentage of gross expenditure	5	5	5	5

7

The plan is based on assumptions for pay and price inflation consistent with the Council's overall financial policy, i.e. 3.5% price inflation, 4% pay inflation for Hay staff and 1.5% for non-Hay staff. The cost of overheads, which include management, administration and support services have been allocated to each profit centre pro rata to staffing costs.

6.3   Capital Investment

The only item of a capital nature within the BLS is the computer. This was acquired in 1990 and became operational in 1991. This year, work applications will be gradually put onto the system. No new investment is foreseen for 1993/94, but it is essential for the computer system to be kept under review to ensure that capacity is adequate, that new applications and updates are programmed, together with the essential planned replacement. This major piece of work will commence in 1993/94 with a view to the inclusion of what will become a rolling programme of proposals for the 1994/95 Workplan on

7.   PERFORMANCE MONITORING

Performance monitoring is carried out through a series of indicators which were previously included in the Action Plan. These have now been incorporated into this Business Plan and are now included in Appendix 3. Performance - financial and non-financial - will be monitored regularly and reported monthly to the Trading Services Steering Group chaired by the Chief Executive and quarterly to the General Purposes Sub-Committee.

8.   OUTLOOK FOR THE FUTURE

The purpose of business planning must be to enable the service to be run on a cost efficient basis whilst at the same time endeavouring to maintain a quality service and meet the Council's overall financial target. The objective must be to ensure that quality standards are established and that the Council is in a position to determine, in detail, the service levels that it requires. Then BLS must demonstrate that it deserves to be the service provider. Events will also be dictated by the steps taken by other departments in pursuit of the enabler/provider split. The position with regard to these issues will have clarified when the time comes to prepare the 1994/95 plan and careful regard will then be had to such issues and their likely effect.

APPENDIX 2

WORK UNDERTAKEN

DIRECTORATE OF HOUSING AND PERSONAL SERVICES

Social Services Department

Child Protection,
Mental Health and the Elderly

Housing Department

Possession Proceedings,
Homelessness,
Former Tenancy Arrears.

Environmental Services

Prosecution in respect of the environment,
Public Health consumer protection,
Weights and Measures,
Health and Safety,
Trade Description

DIRECTORATE OF EDUCATION

Schools and Further Education Department

Advice on education matters arising from Schools, further
education, Youth Service, phased development plans.

Involvement in specific projects

DIRECTORATE OF ENGINEERING AND SURVEYING

Engineers Department

Civil engineering projects
Highways
Compulsory purchase
Traffic regulation

Works Services Department

Compulsory competitive tendering

10

DIRECTORATE OF DEVELOPMENT

Valuers Department

Sales/Purchases
Leases/Licences
Property Transactions
Economic Development

Planning Department

Planning Inquiries
Planning Agreements
Planning Enforcement
Development Control/Forward Planning
Building Control

DIRECTORATE OF FINANCE

Finance Department

Debt Collection
Advice

Data Processing Department

Contract advice

DIRECTORATE OF ADMINISTRATION

Assistance to Chief Solicitor
Monitoring Officer
Corporate Tasks
Contract advice to Client units

Personnel Department

Personnel issues

ACTION PLAN – PERFORMANCE INDICATORS

Key Indicators to be Reported Quarterly

1. Achievement of chargeable hours   2384 per month

2. Percentage of Accounts passed   80%
   for payment without query

Operational Indicators to be reported annually

1.	Litigation Referrals County Court Possession Actions	350 to institute proceedings in 90% of cases within 1 month, and in 100% of cases within 2 months.
2.	Magistrates Court Statutory	500 To institute proceedings in 90% of cases within 1 month, and in 100% of cases within 2 months.
3.	Parking and Highways	250 To institute proceedings in 90% of cases within 1 month
4.	Sundry Debt Actions	400 100% of cases to be processed within 10 working days of receipt of relevant papers
5.	Land Transactions Sale of Council houses	250 Contract documents to be despatched in 95% of cases within 10 working days of receipt of instructions
6.	Other Transactions	250 Contract documents to be despatched in 95% of cases within 10 working days of receipt of instructions
7.	Contracts	250 To process 95% within 10 working days of receiving completed instructions

8. Section 330 Notices	30	85% to be served within 7 working days of receipt of all necessary information from the Chief Planning Officer.

Reminder letter with a second copy of Notice to be sent where the required response is not received within 21 days. |
9. Enforcement Notices	25	85% to be served within 14 days of the receipt of all necessary information
10 Public Inquiries		
(a) Rule 6 Statement of DoE and Appellant		Send at least 4 weeks before date of Inquiry
(b) Circular letter to Interested Parties		Send at least 4 weeks before date of Inquiry

TARIFF OF CHARGES

Hourly Rate Charges

£   per hour

> Section 38/104 A' Type Agreements
> Mortgages of Council Houses

£   per hour

> Redemption of Mortgages
> Home Loss payment/claims

£   per hour

> Parking Prosecutions
> Leases of Council houses
> Deeds of Variation (of leases)
> Possession Action
> Mortgage repossession
> Liquor licensing

£   per hour

> Other Prosecutions
> Economic Development Loans
> Release/variation of Restrictive Covenants

£   per hour

> Boundary enquiries
> Democratic process
> Service of notices
> Enforcement action
> Lease of shops
> Section 38/104 B' Type Agreements

£   per hour

> 'A' Type litigation
> Leases of land/property
> Sales/purchases of land/property
> Refund of Discounts
> Site appraisals
> Transfer of equity on Council mortgages
> Sales of lane
> Appropriations
> Audit of Deeds

14

Byelaws
Compensation Claims
Contract Law I
Surrender of Leases
Consents to Dealing
tendering procedures
Traffic Orders

£   per hour

Parks and Open Spaces
Compulsory Purchase Orders

£   per hour

'B' Type Litigation
Legislation
'A' Type Planning matters
'A' Type Public Inquiries/Tribunals
Rent reviews
Land development matters
Committee Meetings
Court liaison
Highway matters
Financial dealings
Member inquiry

£   per hour

Contract Law II
'B' Type Public Inquiry/Tribunals
Employment Law
Vetting/monitoring Committee reports
Reviewing delegation

£   per hour

Monitoring
Schools Admission Appeals
Community Care
Committee Business Review
Constitution
Quarterly Operations Reports

£   per hour

Externalisation/major corporate initiatives
Directorate Team

Retainer Charges

Total Income

1. Debt Collection

2. Housing General Advice

3. Legal Advice Directorates

4. Child Care

5. Advice on Legislation

6. 'B' Type Planning Matters

7. 'A' Type litigation for Chief Housing Officer (gf)

8. 'B' type litigation for Chief Housing Officer (gf)

Unit Charges

Unit Cost

1. 'A' type conveyancing licence (according to type)

2. Sale of Council Houses

3. Grant of Easement

4. 'B' type conveyances licence (according to type)

5. Housing Association mortgage

6. Preparation Agreement and Bond

7. Licence to Assign

16

APPENDIX 5

FORECAST OF INCOME (£'000) – 1993/94

Profit Centres	Total	Dev	Educ	H&PS	Admin	C.Sol	Fin	DES	Other
Property Planning & Development									
Hourly Charges									
Unit Charges									
Retainers									
Family & Common Law									
Hourly Charges									
Unit Charges									
Retainers									
Education, Employment & Competition									
Hourly Charges									
Unit Charges									
Retainers									
Total Target Income									
Less Contingency Provision									
Total Disaggregated to Clients									
PRACTICE/BUSINESS.1									

17

CIPFA

BUSINESS PLANS

A Compendium

LOCAL AUTHORITIES

Cheshire County Council

Finance and Management Group
Business Plan 1993

*FINANCE AND MANAGEMENT
GROUP*

Business Plan

1993-94

*COUNTY
FINANCE OFFICE*
Alan Cope

April 1993

Cheshire County Council

1 PURPOSE

Core purpose

- To ensure that Council business is underwritten with sound and timely financial advice.

- To ensure policy and expenditure planning, budget preparation and control, financial reporting and borrowing and investment are underpinned by robust financial procedures.

- To co-ordinate the whole of the Council's financial activities and fulfil the 'Head of Profession' role.

Clients

A key role of the County Finance Office is to support the whole Council in satisfying the wide range of statutory obligations and regulations. These include Section 151 of the Local Government Act 1972 and Section 114 of the Local Government Finance Act 1988.

In addition, it helps the Council to develop a clear financial strategy, manage its cash flow and assists in the allocation and management of its resources. A key element in this process is the construction of good management information systems.

The primary client is the corporate management of the Authority in the shape of the Policy Committee, the Finance and Management Sub-Committee and the Management Board. The corporate role includes working closely with service managers.

Structure

There are three operating units.

Policy Planning

Managing the Medium Term Strategy (MTS) process and supporting the Policy Committee and Management Board in evaluating policy options and determining priorities.

Management Accounting (including Education Finance)

Overseeing the Council's budget preparation, accounting and budgetary control activities and providing corporate financial advice.

Business Finance

Managing the Superannuation Fund and the Council's borrowing and lending and overseeing the strategy for the Council's approach to Compulsory Competitive Tendering and its capital assets.

COUNTY *finance*   1

Main Activities

Policy Planning and Performance Management

To enable the Council to plan and manage its activities with a full awareness of resource implications and the changing external financial environment.

To support the Policy Committee in ensuring a clear and consistent evaluation of policy options and in developing the medium term strategy.

To support the Management Board and Council in the effective management of resources and service performance through the development of the Resource Centre Management Process. This involves the preparation of business plans and the development and monitoring of performance criteria.

Financial Advice and Support

To provide corporate financial advice on strategic policy initiatives. To ensure that policy formulation follows best practice and takes full account of resource implications.

To oversee from an independent County-wide view, on behalf of the Policy Committee, the accounting and management of all service finances and provide advice to services and Members.

To co-ordinate the client requirements on the Exchequer Services function. To ensure that specifications and performance meet the requirements and give managers the information they need.

To provide, through the internal market, advice and accounting support to the Education Services Group.

Corporate Financial Management and 'Head of Profession'

To prepare the annual budget, accounts and annual report to ensure public accountability and stewardship.

To manage borrowing, lending and cash flow and provide advice in managing assets and resources.

To set a strategy for the Superannuation Fund and its investments.

To set and monitor corporate standards for cash and money management.

To manage the recruitment, training and career development of professional accounting staff throughout the Council.

2   THE OPERATING ENVIRONMENT

External Influences

The Finance Office plays a key role in managing externally and internally driven change. Current major challenges include Local Government Review and the financing of local government and reduced funding. At the same time the Council is seeking to improve the quality and performance of its service.

Although there are increased demands on the service it is required to make reductions of £x as part of the MTS. Furthermore, the size and shape of the Finance Office will need to be adjusted to reflect the changing demands and the finance available.

Internal Influences

The County Council has a strong reputation as an employer and training authority for finance staff. The effort put into recruiting, training and retaining professional staff has resulted in a more stabilised skills base. However, the age and experience profile has suffered. There is a continuing demand for finance skills in the wider public sector and the planned review of local government could well affect Cheshire's ability to maintain this position.

It is important to sustain the current level of training and personal development. This is with a view to ensuring that the needs of all service groups are covered.

The Finance Office now supplies financial services to the Education Services Group on an internal contract with the Group Director, Education Services. The arrangements are currently being reviewed but are felt to be successful and could well prove the basis for wider application.

3   CORPORATE INITIATIVES

CONTRIBUTION TO 1992-93 INITIATIVES

At the front of this document is a section giving details of common contributions across the Group's services. Any measures taken specifically by this service are set out below.

Closer to the Customer

The Finance Office has an important role in terms of public confidence and accountability. The Annual Report, financial reporting generally and the budget leaflet make important contributions to the public understanding of the Council's affairs.

Support is also provided to individual councillors and to all service groups. A survey is being undertaken of Council Members and officers, seeking views on performance.

The Budget Information Telephone Line is heavily used. A new system of local government finance - the Council Tax, has increased the emphasis on good relationships with the public.

Improved Communications

The Finance Office operates a network of regular meetings with staff and service groups. Staff appraisal operates at all levels.

A series of open-house training workshops has been held throughout the year on a wide variety of financial topics. These sessions have been very popular with large attendances.

Development of Performance Measures

The Finance Office has been instrumental in developing the Resource Centre Management Scheme and the internal market. It will continue to develop systems which sharpen management focus, improve accountability and help local managers to achieve their objectives and demonstrate performance.

NEW INITIATIVE FOR 1993-94

Quality of Service

The County Finance Office has held extensive briefing and training sessions for all staff. These have provided a factual briefing on the County Council's quality initiatives and the reasons behind them. In addition, staff have participated in discussions about their own jobs and working style so as to develop quality standards tailored for County Finance Office activities.

4   MEDIUM TERM OBJECTIVES

Sustaining and Improving Standards of Financial Management

To maintain high standards in all aspects of managing the Council's financial affairs in the face of change.

To develop the County-wide organisation of finance functions. They should have a proper focus on strategic and corporate activities, and also the ability to provide financial and accounting advice in a way which uses available skills to best effect.

To develop further the Resource Centre Management Scheme and the Internal Market, aimed at improving performance and the ability to monitor performance.

To lead the development of the revised arrangements for capital accounting.

To continue to develop the Council's monitoring of investment performance and financing strategy in the light of government requirements.

Helping the Council to Manage Change

To assist in the continuing development of Medium Term Planning, ensuring policy and decisions are based on sound information and advice.

To promote the understanding of the changing local government financing structure and financing and costing aspects of Local Government Review.

To support the Council in managing changes in its organisational shape and in meeting its accountability obligations.

5   PERFORMANCE IN 1992-93 AND ACTION PLAN FOR 1993-94

SUSTAINING AND IMPROVING STANDARDS OF FINANCIAL MANAGEMENT

Organisation and Staffing

1992-93

Measures were taken to combat the shortage of finance skills. These included market supplements, an expansion in training and extensive recruitment. They have helped stabilise the staffing position but at a significant financial cost and in terms of pressures on managers and staff. Stability is now required to enable the experience profile of the office to mature.

In 1992-93 the Finance Office became responsible for providing unified financial services to the Education Group involving some ... staff. A post implementation review is being carried out and all the signs are that the organisational change has been successful.

1993-94

There is the need to review skills and experience and match these to work priorities. Professional training will continue, though this will be constrained by the budgetary position.

The deployment of professional finance staff throughout the Council, and the potential for job rotation, will be reviewed both as a means of personal development and to respond to changing needs.

Effort will be put into finding improved methods of working and efficiency savings across the financial administration of the County Council.

To establish a clear client/contractor relationship with Exchequer Services.

Resource Centre Management

1992-93

The County-wide Resource Centre Management Scheme is a major Finance Office project. In 1992-93 it was reviewed and structural changes were made, including the extension to the Police Service. The emphasis is now on developing measurable performance criteria and testing their effectiveness.

1993-94

Ways will be examined of making the Resource Centre Plans process more effective on the political network, by allowing Members to concentrate on the key issues and changes.

Support will be provided to the Chief Constable in developing his Resource Centre Management Scheme. A priority is to devolve budget responsibility to front-line managers.

The Resource Centre Management Scheme will need to reflect the new capital asset requirements, trading accounts and charging for insurance cover.

Capital Investment and Financing

1992-93

The traditional allocation of capital financing costs to services has been discontinued. Cheshire is at an advanced stage in establishing an approach under which services will be charged for the use of capital assets.

The Treasury Management Code of Practice has been implemented.

1993-94

The 'asset register' will be completed. A pilot scheme will be introduced in Business Generation Centres and Smallholdings to test the new asset charging approach. A programme of implementation for all services will be developed by April 1994.

With advice from the Actuary, it is intended to review the operation of the Superannuation Fund's external investment managers.

HELPING THE COUNCIL TO MANAGE CHANGE

Policy, Expenditure and Resource Planning

1992-93

The MTS process was further developed in 1992-93. Despite reductions in external funding and fundamental changes in financing, the debate was kept on course to arrive at a 1993-94 budget.

The Finance Office promoted an understanding of the new Council Tax to be introduced in 1993, including seminars for Members and Managers.

1993-94

In the light of the deteriorating external financial scene, the MTS will be fundamentally reshaped leading up to the 1994-95 budget.

Assistance will be given to the induction of new members.

The unfavourable position of Cheshire's SSA, which has emerged over a number of years, will require fundamental review and rigorous presentation of arguments. The aim is to argue for a national review and debate for change.

The introduction of the Council Tax means there will be the need to improve the understanding of its operation and the cash flow relationships with collection authorities.

The Finance Office will lead the financial evaluation of structural options in preparation for the arrival of the Local Government Commission in 1994. This will be a major task using internal sources of information and liaison with other local authorities.

A 'Businesslike' Approach to Cheshire Services

1992-93

The 'internal market' is proving to be a far sighted initiative as legislation is now being drafted to require the production of statutory trading accounts in preparation for competitive tendering.

In 1992-93, client and supplier responsibilities were reviewed by a series of Consumer Panels. A better understanding of the concept of the 'enabling' authority emerged.

1993-94

The internal market will be operated on the basis of the Consumer Panel specifications, without ringfenced budgets.

During the year the internal market will be extended to all services and procedures will be developed for introduction in the 1994-95 financial year.

Some units will be involved in developing different approaches to service provision and management options.

The Changing Shape of Cheshire Services

1992-93

Services have received significant support in managing fundamental change, including the Education local management schemes, the transfer of FE, the restructuring of the Waste Disposal Service and Community Care.

1993-94

The Council and its Services continue to face significant change, and support will be needed.

The Finance Office will need to provide financial advice on strategic direction.

6 RESOURCES AND INCOME

	Budget £000	Actual £000	Variance £000

1991-92 Final
1992-93 Projected

1993-94	Internal Market £000	Charges to Clients		Total £000
		Strategic/ Regulatory £000	Corporate Functions £000	

SERVICES TO BE PROVIDED

Corporate Financial Management
Corporate Advice
Policy Planning
Budget & Performance Management
Support to Committees and Members
Accountancy Support

Gross Cost
Income from outside CCC
Internal Market charges to clients

COST TO THE
CORPORATE CLIENT

RESOURCES USED

Staff (XX full time equivalents)
Accommodation
Other Running Costs
Support Services

Gross Cost
Income from outside CCC (incl. Superannuation Fund)
Internal Market charges to clients

COST TO THE
CORPORATE CLIENT

Other Items:
External Audit Fee
Reimbursements
Total Budget Book Cost

The 1993-94 Capital Programme for the Group is £....

COUNTY *finance*   9

7 SERVICE PERFORMANCE

Key Indicators for 1993-94 (see schedule opposite)

Performance measurement has always been difficult. The Finance Office's products are mostly intangible, and the corporate client is not easily identified.

However, the setting of key indicators for performance is important. The schedule overleaf represents a hard attempt to do this.

Where products or timetables can be quantified they have been. Where possible, the schedule also seeks to specify quality standards.

Quality

Members and Senior Managers will make subjective judgements of the quality of the Finance Office services. They will make these judgements on the standard of products such as financial reports and on the speed and quality of responses to requests. A survey of Members, the Management Board and Heads of Service is underway on the quality of Finance Office products which begins a process of regular feedback. Particular emphasis has been placed on gaining staff commitment to the quality of service philosophy and Finance Office standards are shown in the schedule.

Independent Inspection

The External Auditor's report is an important measure of the quality and quantity of Finance Office achievements and is a true independent inspection. His 1991-92 report provides an unqualified opinion on the statement of accounts.

Monitoring and Review

Finance and Management Group has well established planning and performance review processes. The Service plans are supported by more detailed unit plans. The objectives and actions in the plans will form key tasks under the staff appraisal process.

More formal performance reports will be made to Finance and Management Services Sub-Committee as part of the County-wide framework.

Comparative Statistics

The CIPFA Support Statistics are not considered a good measure but they generally indicate that Cheshire's costs are broadly in line with the average for the family group.

KEY INDICATORS FOR 1993-94

SUSTAINING AND IMPROVING STANDARDS OF FINANCIAL MANAGEMENT

Organisation and Staffing	Deadline

• Achieve Quality of Service Standards adopted, including:
    Telephone - Answer calls within six rings
    Correspondence - Respond within five working days
	Continuously

• Review organisation/shape of the Finance Office and the County-wide finance function	July

Resource Centre Management

• Review Member involvement in the Resource Centre Plans process	September
• Assist Chief Constable to extend the Resource Centre Scheme into Police	October
• Integrate capital charging and insurance	March

Capital Investment and Financing

• Introduce pilot scheme of asset charging	April
• Review Superannuation Fund external investment management	October

General Financial Management

• Publish: S42 School Budget Statements
    1994-95 Budget Leaflet
    1994-95 Budget Book
	31 March
	3 March
	April

• Budget Information Line:
    answer queries from the public
    produce summary for members
	
	Promptly
	Regularly

• Prepare final accounts to the satisfaction of the External Auditor	July
• Publish Annual Report and Superannuation Fund Accounts	September
• Publish S42 School Expenditure Statements	31 October
• Make regular reports on borrowing and lending	Agreed timetable
• Submit all grant claims and statutory returns by the due dates	
• Analyse all service comparative statistics	Within 7 days

HELPING THE COUNCIL TO MANAGE CHANGE

Deadline

Policy, Expenditure and Resource Planning

* Assist the Management Board to fundamentally review the MTS

* Prepare 1994-98 MTS advice/draft capital programmes for Policy Panel — October

* Publish the Buff/Yellow/Green Books — Nov/Jan/Feb

* Provide induction training to new members — September

* Assist the Council to lobby government for a fairer SSA settlement — July

* Review cash flow relationship with districts — October

* Produce initial costings for Local Government Review — May

A 'Businesslike' Approach to Cheshire Services

* Implement internal market with 'unringfenced' budgets — April

* Extend internal market to all services — April

The Changing Shape of Cheshire Services

* Clear all committee reports with financial content and provide quality to committees — Committee Timetables

* Provide quality financial advice to members and services on service issues generally

CIPFA

BUSINESS PLANS

A Compendium

LOCAL AUTHORITIES

Delyn Borough Council

Financial Services Division Business Plan

Delyn BC is currently undertaking a widespread survey of 'customer' attitudes and has now published the newsletter referred to in part 2 section 2.9.

FINANCIAL SERVICES DIVISION

BUSINESS PLAN

CONTENTS

FINANCIAL SERVICES DIVISION

BUSINESS PLAN

Part One - Reviewing the Present

CONTENTS

1. INTRODUCTION

1.1. The Need for a Business Plan

We are a recently formed division within the Financial Services Directorate, being an amalgam of three previously separate sections - Management Accountancy, Customer Services and Paymaster Services.

It was because of the need to integrate a new "team", coupled with many uncertainties over our collective future that we decided to undertake the task of formally putting together a Business Plan for the Division.

It was felt that only by going through this process would we be able to plan ahead to meet the many changes which will undoubtedly be coming our way over the next couple of years. We also agreed that the putting together of the plan would involve **all** staff.

1.2. This Document

This document looks at the role of the Financial Services Division and what we should do to establish ourselves, following our recent reorganisation. It describes work planned for the period up to March 1995, against a background of change affecting the Authority, and objectives which the Council has set for itself.

This document serves as a basis for setting work plans of the teams which form the Division and the objectives of individual staff members. It also identifies the training requirements of all staff in order that they may meet their individual objectives.

This document was put together over a four month period, during which time many changes have occurred, particularly when "our way forward" was being agreed. Rather than re-write what had gone before, the document has been split into two halves, leaving the original review intact and changes highlighted in the introduction to Part Two where they had some impact on decisions required for the future.

2. OUR PRESENT POSITION

2.1. The Division Structure

On completion of the departmental reorganisation, the following management structure was approved for the Division :

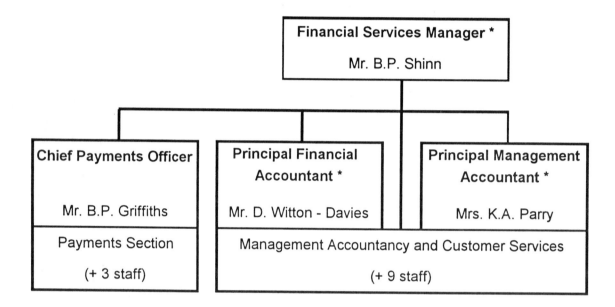

* Posts specifically identified as Client Officers, responsible directly to the Director of Financial Services for a range of services.

2.2. S.W.O.T. Analysis

Appendix 1 summarises our S.W.O.T. Analysis, which is looked at in more detail below. The purpose of the analysis was for us to analyse our present position critically through identifying the strengths and weaknesses of the team, and the opportunities and threats that face us.

Once identified, we have to ensure that strengths and opportunities are maximised, and weaknesses and threats are minimised. Some, however, are beyond our control.

2.2.1. Strengths

The following strengths of the team were identified :

a **Team Spirit**. Each section, individually, already has its own good team spirit, with genuine willingness to help colleagues. The Customer Accounts Section is fully integrated, physically, with the Accountancy Section, and partial integration of workloads has already taken place. The Paymaster Section is not physically located with the rest of the Division. We are confident, however, that team spirit will not suffer as a result of this.

b **The Team Itself.** We are a relatively young yet experienced team - many staff have had previous experience in other local authorities, financial services sector and industry. We are skilled, dedicated, enthusiastic, intelligent and adaptable. Indeed, it is these strengths that have seen us through some very changeable times over the last few years.

c **Low Staff Turnover.** Staff turnover has been very low over the last few years - only one member leaving in the last three years. This has given us continuity and saved some "on the job" training that might otherwise have been expected. This is also symptomatic of the other strengths of the team.

d **Training Opportunities.** Undoubtedly a strength which reflects on the authority generally. Training opportunities are excellent for accounting technician and professional qualifications and managerial development. In addition, attendance at one day seminars is available for training in new subject areas - either generally or specifically for individuals.

e **Working Environment.** Generally, the working environment is good. If required, private office facilities are available to all staff whether or not they have their own office. Working space is adequate.

f **New Technology.** Technology within the office is fairly modern, both in terms of hardware and software. Training on new developments is good. Improvements are continuous, particularly in personal computing. Expertise in new technology is widespread throughout the Division.

g **Systems.** Systems, both manual and computerised, are very good and adaptable. The diversity of systems is also considerable.

h **External Bodies.** The Division has a really first class reputation with external bodies, particularly with the District Audit Service, the Welsh Office, neighbouring authorities and financial institutions. Many of our internal training papers and documents are used as best practice guides for other organisations.

i **Captive Customers.** One of our main strengths is that we effectively have captive customers - insofar as it is not council policy to allow our customers, other departments etc., to seek provision of their financial services elsewhere. We also recognise that this might not always be the case.

j **Customers.** Our customers believe that we provide a good quality service. (Fuller analysis of customer opinion is given in Chapter 3.)

2.2.2. Weaknesses

The following weaknesses of the team were identified :

a **Low Staff Turnover.** Already identified as a strength, we also feel that low staff turnover is a weakness. It does not allow for much diversity of work for existing staff. It prevents promotion to better paid jobs as they do not become vacant. It also restricts the infusion of "new blood" to the Division.

b **Division Not Integrated.** Whilst not a major weakness, we feel that in the interests of team spirit and proper working integration it would be better if the Division were all in the same office.

c **Over-Staffing.** With many of our corporate systems now installed (for example, resource management and capital database), no requirement for new systems of similar input and the imminent reduction of "lost days" through completion of training courses, the Division finds itself forecasting, in the near future, an excess of workable hours available over those needed.

d **Back Up / Cover.** There are a few areas that lack sufficient cover or back up in the absence of certain staff for certain functions. Cover <u>is</u> available in all areas - but not always by the appropriate member of staff. This is particularly true in some specialised areas.

e **Reward Package.** The lack of flexibility in the reward package is considered to be a weakness. There is no scope to reward exceptional performance, except for contract staff. This does not mean, however, that all staff expect larger salaries, cars and bonuses etc..

f **Poor Use of Secretariat.** We generally feel that we do not make sufficient use of the secretarial services available to us - and for which we pay. The problem is two-fold. Firstly, we have not always been happy with the service we receive and, secondly, we do too much of our own typing (particularly on P.C.s) and photocopying. The latter is recognised as an inefficient use of our time.

g **Systems Documentation.** Whilst our systems themselves are identified as a strength, we accept that, generally, documentation was poor and, in some cases, non-existent. This could have serious implications if those "au fait" with the systems were unavailable and others were expected to use them without adequate documentation explaining how.

h **Planning.** It would not be fair to say that there is no planning at all. It would be fair, however, to say that it is spasmodic and usually for specific tasks/projects only. We, as a Division, lack any overall plan covering any meaningful time span.

2.2.3. Opportunities

There were few opportunities identified :

a **Business Planning.** Many services of the Council are actively considering the use of Business Planning. Income could be earned for the Division as Consultants for the implementation of Business Planning - particularly as the Division will have undertaken the exercise itself and can draw on its own experiences.

b **Market Ourselves.** Additional income could be generated if the Division were to actively market itself - even within the authority (its existing customers). This could be from business planning, internal trading accounts, financial evaluations, secondments or other projects that service managers may wish to undertake.

c **Quality Assurance.** The Council has a positive policy on BS5750 accreditation. The Division embraces the concept of Total Quality Management, and the opportunity to seek accreditation may be made available to it. The time and cost, however, would need to be evaluated against other work pressures before the Division embarked on this. It could, however, give the Division a substantial advantage in a compulsory competitive tendering situation.

d **Competitive Tendering.** Competition in other disciplines and services of local government will, undoubtedly, present income earning opportunities for the Division - in preparatory work and tender evaluations. Currently, however, the extension of tendering has been put back until restructuring (below) has taken place. (See Threats, also.)

e **Local Government Restructuring.** The proposals to restructure local government in Wales will require considerable input from the Division in the establishment of any new authority and in the "winding up" of Delyn. (See Threats, also.)

2.2.4. Threats

Whilst very few threats were identified, they were significant :

a **Competitive Tendering.** The continued expansion of services being subjected to compulsory tendering will, inevitably, result in a shrinking client base, for the Division, as external contractors take over the running of many services.

In addition, of course, our own services will be subjected to compulsory tender themselves, to some degree in the near future. There is a realistic possibility that some of us may lose our jobs as a result.

b **Local Government Restructuring.** Whilst this plan covers the period up to the proposed restructure of local government in Wales, there is, nonetheless, a threat to the Division beforehand. There is, and will increasingly be, some concern that we may not find employment within any new authority. This concern will vary with each individual within the Division and we may see an exodus of staff as the new authority approaches. This would be compounded by the inability to attract new (replacement) staff.

c **Client / Contractor Split.** Under the new Divisional structure, the three most senior posts are specifically identified as "clients". A complete client/contractor split before it is necessary (for competition purposes) will, without doubt, be divisive and could seriously damage the excellent team spirit that currently exists.

3. OUR CUSTOMERS

3.1. Who are our customers ?

Our costs are recharged to over 100 separate budget heads, but we have only 18 service level agreements (3 of which are to the separate arms of Delyn Leisure Management). Of these customers, 4 (Members, Chief Executive, Director of Financial Services and Head of Housing Services) provide approximately 60% of our income.

3.2. Customer Attitude Survey

A brief customer attitude survey was undertaken by the Financial Services Manager with all Heads of Service, Chief Officers and Directors of the authority. The summary of this survey is shown in Appendix 2, with commentary below :

3.2.1. Current Use of Services

As stated in the last chapter, we have 'captive customers' as it is against council policy to allow service managers to seek financial services from other agencies. That having been said, we are not adverse to service managers taking on some aspects of financial management themselves - provided that they accept the accompanying responsibility, it is cost effective to do so and, above all, quality is maintained.

The use of our services, however, varies with each customer. The summary (Appendix 2) reflects whether or not they are used, and not the degree of their use.

3.2.2. Future Requirements

The majority of customers surveyed gave business planning as a relatively high priority future requirement. This was closely followed by an identified need for assistance to help face the challenges of compulsory competitive tendering. The establishment of Internal Business Units / Service Level Agreements also featured prominently.

Two other requirements were specifically identified by the Chief Executive. Work in both these areas (local government reorganisation and financial arbitration) has already been undertaken by the Division.

3.2.3. Quality of Service Provided

On being questioned about the quality of services provided, the response was generally very favourable. A couple of the 'good' responses wavered between 'good' and 'very good'.

Most customers commented on the speed as well as quality of service - they got what they wanted when they wanted it and, very often, at very short notice.

There were no complaints, whatsoever, about the quality of any of the services provided.

3.2.4. Service Level Agreements

When asked whether or not Service Level Agreements had made them more aware of *what* they were paying for, the customers responses reflected the degree of pressure, or control, that their budgets were under. Many of those who replied positively agreed that they did not know fully what their costs were or what, precisely, they were getting for their money. All felt that as Business Units were established, they would need to take a greater interest in financial management.

3.2.5. The Future

When asked how they would like to see payment for financial services developed in the future, there was no consensus of opinion amongst our customers.

Two gave a preference for the Division to be subjected to competitive tender, although in both cases this was on the basis of 'we are (or will be), so why shouldn't you be ?'.

3.3. <u>Future Surveys</u>

A far more detailed and widespread survey needs to be carried amongst all our internal customers to ascertain exactly what the majority (not just the most senior officers of the Authority) think of the services we provide.

Consideration will also be given to whether or not we survey our external customers - although with the services concerned it is very unlikely that complaints would not arise if errors did occur.

Careful consideration will need to be given to the wording of questions in any future survey. Previous attempts at finding out what changes our customers want have achieved a NIL response.

4. BUDGET AND RESOURCES

4.1. <u>Resources</u>

a **Staff.** The largest and best resource of the Division is, undoubtedly, its staff. Our establishment is 16 full-time permanent staff. Currently we employ 15 permanent and 1 temporary staff. The temporary post is in lieu of a recent vacancy and maternity leave cover and, subject to future review (this business plan), will terminate in July 1993, when the permanent post will either be filled or given up

b **New Technology.** Hardware, within the Division, consists of 9 mainframe terminals and 6 personal computers (one of which also acts as a mainframe terminal) and numerous local printers. The PCs vary in age, power and software - ideally, they should all be capable of operating Lotus 1-2-3, Amipro and Freelance Graphics (preferably in Windows). The Division also pays for mainframe systems that it uses as well as systems development work. To this extent, the Division is tied to the Computer Section as only in exceptional circumstances will we be allowed to obtain bespoke software packages from external agencies.

c **Departmental Overheads.** The Division has to bear recharges from other parts of the department. Some costs of the Director of Financial Services are borne by the Division, and we pay for our use of the typing and secretarial services. The use would be more efficient if their word-processing software was compatible with the software we use on our PCs.

d **Charges from other Departments.** The three largest recharges are for personnel, training and legal services. Again, under existing Council policy, there is little we can do to reduce these costs. We are unable to seek the provision of these services elsewhere and are required to have personnel staff involved in job recruitment, interviewing etc.

11

e **Accommodation.** Accommodation costs include maintenance, heating and lighting etc. Costs of the building are recharged on an occupancy (square footage) basis. Once the new capital accounting proposals are introduced we may find ourselves being charged market rents which will be higher and, therefore, adversely impact our profitability.

f **Other Running Costs.** These include telephones (recharged on the basis of number of extensions rather than calls made), insurances, printing, stationery, postages etc. Costs within our control are kept to a minimum wherever possible - but "output" (reports etc.) is increasing in volume and is also being presented to increasingly high standards, both of which have higher costs associated with them.

4.2. <u>1993/94 Budget</u>

The Budget, for the Division, in 1993/94 is estimated to be :

	£
<u>Remuneration Costs</u> : including salaries, leased cars, bonuses and employer oncosts.	
<u>Recharges from</u> : Director of Financial Services, Typing and Secretarial Support. Computer Services - Hardware and Systems etc. Personnel, Training and Legal Services.	
Accommodation.	
Other Running Costs : telephones, insurances, printing, stationery, postages etc.	
<u>Total Expenditure</u>	
<u>Income</u> (through Service Level Agreements)	
FORECAST PROFIT FOR YEAR :	

In addition, capacity exists to undertake Business Planning consultancy work (525 hours) generating a further £18,375 income - to be charged to the appropriate "customer" cost centre.

5. OBJECTIVES AND PRIORITIES

5.1. Objectives

The following objectives of the team have been identified :

a To contribute towards the development and implementation of the strategic and corporate plans of the Council, so that it may achieve its social and economic priorities as outlined in "Delyn through the 90's".

b To represent the Council so that its policies and interests are pursued to optimum effect.

c To provide a range of efficient and effective financial services in a way which is responsive to the needs of all our customers.

d To provide financial information and advice to service managers and Members so that they are able to monitor and control their activities and understand the financial implications of proposed courses of action.

e To assist with the efficient and effective discharge of a range of financial duties associated with the post of Chief Financial Officer in accordance with statutory requirements.

f To safeguard the jobs and conditions of all those employed within the Division.

5.2. Mission Statement

The following mission statement, encompassing all of our objectives, was agreed :

To provide an efficient, effective and economic service for the benefit of all our customers in a way which maximises the career enhancement and future prospects of all staff within the Division.

5.3. Priorities

In order that the objectives can be met, the following priorities have been agreed :

a To distribute duties, ensuring adequate back up / cover, within the Division in order that these priorities may be met.

b To identify training requirements, whether technical or managerial, and implement a training plan for individuals in order that they may perform duties efficiently and effectively.

c To introduce and monitor performance targets and measures for each member within the Division.

d To implement a formal staff appraisal system.

e To draw up service specifications for each function within the Division.

f To draw up working manuals for each function within the Division.

g To identify appropriate performance indicators for each function within the Division.

h To market and actively seek consultancy work within the Council and neighbouring authorities.

6. OUR OPTIONS

6.1. Client Function

The threat of competitive tendering highlights the need for a client role within the Division. With the three senior officers of the Division having been denoted as "Client Officers", and with each having client role accountabilities built into their performance targets, there was no option other than to identify client functions as separate duties.

Client functions include :

a Liaison with customers to ascertain current and future requirements of the services provided by the Division.

b The drawing up of service specifications, with performance measures, to be undertaken by the "contractor" - which represents all the requirements of all customers.

c Monitor and report on the performance on the delivery, by contractors, of the service specifications.

6.2. The Options

The options, so far as the Division was concerned, related to what degree the client / contractor roles should be separated if it was to minimise threats and weaknesses and maximise opportunities and strengths. Three options were considered :

a Voluntary Competitive Tender

b Facilities Management

c Remain In-house

6.3. Voluntary Competitive Tender

This would entail the formal separation of the Division into Client and Contractor sections. Decisions would need to be made on which services should be subjected to tender - whether or not some core services would be placed within the client or contracting arm of the Division.

In a formal tender situation there is no doubt that an "in-house" bid would NOT win as many firms would relish the opportunity to have a working contract in readiness for compulsory competitive tendering, and tender accordingly. Many of us would then be made redundant (although some may be taken on by the contract winner) which is contrary to the objectives of the Division (paragraph 5.1.f, page 13).

6.4. Facilities Management

The decisions required here are virtually identical to those for voluntary competitive tendering. The significant difference to the contract details would be the specific inclusion of safeguards for employees - they would have to be employed, on no less terms and conditions than they currently enjoy, by the contract winners. Usually such safeguards are only for 12 months - they could be for longer, but this becomes less attractive financially for prospective tenderers.

There could be advantages, to staff, in working for a well-known private firm - but there would be no guarantee of employment beyond that specified in the contract.

6.5. Remain In-house

It was agreed that jobs and conditions of those employed within the Division were best safeguarded by remaining in-house, although as local government reorganisation draws nearer, the Facilities Management option might become more attractive and warrant further consideration.

6.6. Client / Contractor Split

Having concluded that our best option is to keep services in-house, the only other choice we had to make was whether or not we adopted a formal client / contractor split within the Division - effectively making ourselves two separate units.

With compulsory competitive tendering being very unlikely to be introduced before local government restructuring, there was very little to commend the adoption of a formal split. The following observations were made :

a The duties of the "client" officers should already be performed by the Division's managers.

b Not all the duties of the client officers were appropriate for senior staff.

c There would be insufficient client work for three posts, as identified. Other functions, such as "core" activities would need to performed by them too.

d There would be a management "gap" in any contracting unit which excluded the three most senior members of the Division. This would incur additional expense to fill and would, therefore, be self-defeating.

e To formally identify and separate core and contractor functions would be needlessly contentious and divisive.

f Client and contractual management roles could be undertaken by the same person. Whilst no formal contract exists, this is not seen as a conflict of interest.

It is appreciated that asking individuals to carry out a mixture of Client and Contractor duties may lead to some difficulties. It is, however, considered to be the best alternative. The mechanisms to ensure that this arrangement succeeds are available through job accountabilities, targets and performance measures for the three "client" officers.

S.W.O.T. ANALYSIS	
STRENGTHS	**WEAKNESSES**
Team Spirit.	Low staff turnover.
The Team Itself.	Division not integrated.
Low staff turnover.	Over staffing.
Training Opportunities.	Insufficient back up / cover.
Working Environment.	Lack of flexibility in reward package.
New Technology.	Poor use of Secretariat.
Systems.	Many systems not documented.
Reputation with external bodies.	No business plan.
Captive customers.	
Responsive to customers' needs.	
OPPORTUNITIES	**THREATS**
Business Planning.	Competitive Tendering.
Market Ourselves.	Local Government Restructuring.
Quality Assurance.	Client / Contractor Split.
Competitive Tendering.	
Local Government Restructuring.	

APPENDIX 2

Services - Used Currently	1	2	3	4	5	6	7	8	9	10	11	12	13	14	15	16	17	18
Budget Preparation and Monitoring	♦	♦	♦	♦	♦	♦	♦	♦	♦	♦	♦	♦	♦	♦	♦	♦	♦	♦
Final Accounts and associated statements	♦	♦	♦	♦	♦	♦	♦	♦	♦	♦	♦	♦	♦	♦	♦	♦	♦	♦
Payment of Salaries	♦	♦	♦	♦	♦	♦	♦	♦	♦	♦	♦	♦	♦	♦	♦	♦	♦	
Payment of Wages	♦		♦		♦	♦		♦	♦	♦		♦	♦	♦	♦		♦	
Payment of Creditors	♦	♦	♦	♦	♦	♦	♦	♦	♦	♦	♦	♦	♦	♦	♦	♦	♦	♦
Provision / Administration of Car Loans	♦	♦	♦	♦	♦	♦	♦	♦	♦	♦	♦	♦	♦	♦	♦	♦	♦	
Sundry Debtor Invoicing		♦	♦	♦	♦	♦	♦	♦	♦	♦	♦	♦			♦		♦	♦
Insurance - Provision and Administration	♦	♦	♦	♦	♦	♦	♦	♦	♦	♦	♦	♦	♦	♦	♦	♦	♦	♦
Financial Input to Publications	♦			♦	♦		♦		♦	♦				♦	♦		♦	♦
Financial Advice - Working Parties	♦			♦	♦			♦							♦			♦
Resource Management	♦	♦	♦	♦	♦	♦	♦	♦	♦	♦	♦	♦					♦	
Service Level Agreements	♦	♦	♦	♦											♦			
Target Savings	♦	♦	♦	♦	♦	♦	♦	♦	♦	♦		♦			♦		♦	
Financial Procedures	♦	♦	♦	♦	♦	♦	♦	♦	♦	♦		♦		♦	♦		♦	♦
New Legislation	♦				♦			♦	♦	♦				♦	♦		♦	♦
Value Added Tax	♦	♦	♦	♦	♦	♦	♦	♦	♦	♦	♦	♦	♦	♦	♦	♦	♦	♦
Report Implications	♦	♦	♦	♦	♦	♦	♦	♦	♦	♦	♦	♦		♦	♦	♦	♦	♦
Competitive Tendering	♦								♦	♦	♦						♦	♦
Other General Advice	♦	♦	♦	♦	♦	♦	♦	♦	♦	♦	♦	♦	♦	♦	♦	♦	♦	♦
Future Requirements																		
Local Government Reorganisation	♦																♦	♦
Financial Arbitration	♦																	
Business Planning	♦	♦	♦	?	♦	♦	♦	♦	♦	♦					?	♦	♦	
Service Level Agreements					♦	♦	?			?					♦		♦	
Competitive Tendering					♦	♦	♦	♦		♦					♦	♦	♦	♦
Quality of Service Provided																		
Very Good	♦	♦	♦	♦	♦	♦		♦		♦	♦				♦		♦	♦
Good							♦		♦			♦	♦	♦				
Adequate																♦		
Poor																		
Very Poor																		
Have SLAs made you more aware of what you are paying for ?	N	Y	Y	Y	N	N	Y	Y	Y	Y	N	Y	Y	Y	Y	N	Y	Y
Future Service Payments																		
Provide own services									♦			♦	♦					
Competitive Tender										♦				♦				
SLAs with specified outputs & penalties						♦												
SLAs with specified outputs	♦				♦		♦				♦						♦	♦
No change		♦	♦	♦								♦			♦			

Key :

1. Chief Executive

2. Chief Legal Services Officer

3. Chief Personnel Services Officer

4. Assistant Chief Executive

5. Director of Development & Environmental Services

6. Head of Technical Services

7. Head of Planning Services

8. Head of Environmental Health Services

9. Director of Housing & Client Services

10. Head of Housing Services

11. Head of Client Services

12. Head of Leisure Services

13. Delyn Leisure Management

14. Delyn Commercial Contractors

15. Revenues Manager

16. Information Technology Manager

17. Director of Financial Services

18. Chairman of P.R.F. Committee

Delyn Borough Council - Financial Services Division - Business Plan

FINANCIAL SERVICES DIVISION

BUSINESS PLAN

Part Two - The Way Forward

CONTENTS

1. INTRODUCTION

1.1. Changes since "Reviewing the Present"

Since conducting the review of our present position, some changes have occurred which have significant bearing on our way forward :

a Two more staff (a Finance Assistant and Management Accountant) have resigned having obtained promotion in other local authorities. Action was taken to replace the Finance Assistant immediately as the existing vacant post (Part I, paragraph 4.1.a, page 11) is also a Finance Assistant and it was clear that we could not give up both posts. The need for the Management Accountant post will be reviewed as part of the Business Plan process.

b

c The White Paper on Local Government Restructuring in Wales has been published, confirming the introduction of unitary authorities from April 1995 and that central services CCT will not take place before these new authorities are formed.

2. OUR PLAN OF ACTION

2.1. Purpose

A plan is required to :

a Maximise our strengths and opportunities;

b Minimise, so far as possible, our weaknesses and threats; and

c Achieve our agreed objectives and priorities.

Once agreed, the resources required for the successful implementation of the plan need to be determined and any surplus/shortfall in existing budgets and resources identified.

2.2. Duties

A weakness specifically identified was the lack of back up / cover in specific areas within the Division, which has been compounded by the recent departure (due to promotions elsewhere) of two finance assistants who provided cover for each other. This will be addressed by identifying "Deputies" responsible for providing cover in each area of work.

2.3. Service Specifications

The Client Officer will be responsible for drawing up the service specifications for functions identified, by the deadlines shown.

The service specification is to detail :

a A brief description of the relevant function;

b Any statutes, Codes of Practice etc. to be complied with;

c All outputs required (what is to be achieved); and

d Deadlines and performance indicators by which service provision will be measured.

2.4. Working manuals

The responsible officers are to draw up working manuals for their respective functions. The working manuals detail the "inputs" required to meet the "outputs" demanded by the service specifications.

Working manuals are to include :

a Details of each persons responsibility, and who should deputise in their absence;

b Details of documentation and procedures to be followed; and

c Details of systems to be employed and how they work (system manuals).

Appendix 1 identifies the Client Officer, Responsible Officer and "Deputy" for each function within the Division.

2.5. Training Requirements

No specific professional or managerial training needs were identified.

Many of the deputies will require training in the functions they are to cover. This will be provided in-house by the responsible officer and/or client officer.

A widespread training need was identified in the use of Lotus 1-2-3, Amipro and Freelance Graphics, which is currently used (and extensively so) on three PCs only. (See paragraph 2.8, also.)

2.6. Staff Appraisal / Performance

The Council is currently introducing a standard staff appraisal system, which is welcomed. Performance targets and measures are nothing new to some of our staff , and we may have to change our existing practices to complement (and avoid duplication with) the standard appraisal system.

2.7. Work Plans

Work plans for 1993/94 have been agreed with all staff and these are detailed in Appendix 5.

2.8. Resources

a New Technology

In order to make more efficient use of new technology, all the PCs and software need to be standardised throughout the Division. Lotus 1-2-3, Amipro and Freelance Graphics are the "standard" packages used by many local authorities and other businesses. These have recently been installed in the Secretariat and this would allow better use of their services as data and reports could be easily transferred from one PC to another.

To standardise the new technology within the Division would entail the upgrading of three PCs, and purchase of software for each. A laptop PC is also required for training and work at home. With the network being installed, we could release 3 other PCs, 1 mainframe terminal and 3 printers for use elsewhere within the authority. The net cost of this is estimated at £9,500. Our maintenance charges will reduce by £1,560 a year.

b Staff

With the improved use of technology and secretarial services (above), the Division can meet all of its objectives and priorities with 15 (14 full-time and 1 part-time) rather than 16 full-time staff. Most of the duties of the Management Accountant will be absorbed by other staff - the one exception being that the Division will not be able to offer consultancy services for the introduction of Business Planning

In recognition of additional duties and responsibilities being undertaken by the Finance Officer (Post No. FS0502), it is recommended that the post be regraded to Scale 4/6 (rather than Scale 4/5).

It was agreed that the two vacant permanent posts be relinquished, the temporary post would continue whilst maternity leave cover was needed (July 1993) and thereafter reduce to 15 hours a week (except for 10 weeks from November, when 35 hours a week will be required to undertake work on F.A.S).

Some staff also have titles that no longer reflect their grade and/or jobs. It was felt that these should be addressed now, particularly as job titles may have greater significance in the establishment of the new unitary authorities. Appendix 2 details proposed titles, grades and jobholders.

It was also agreed that a bid for the new technology requirements (above) be submitted to the Management Team, with this Business Plan, on the basis that the Division would save £27,100 in 1993/94 (and £32,100 a year thereafter) through the revised staffing structure.

c Accommodation

With staff having a more integrated role within what were once different sections, a couple actually work in more than one office due to the Division not being physically integrated. Whilst this is far from ideal, it is accepted that it is unrealistic, due to cost alone, to expect the situation to change in the lifetime of Delyn.

d Use of Secretariat

Having identified poor use of the Secretariat as a weakness, a "charter" was drawn up spelling out exactly what service was required of the Secretariat by the Division. This coupled with the introduction of Ami-pro in the Secretariat should improve the situation in the near future.

d Budget Implications

The full budgetary implications (at current prices) of the above are detailed in Appendix 3, with a full analysis of income (service level agreements) given in Appendix 4.

2.9. Market ourselves

By the end of June 1993, the Division will produce a newsletter ("Finance Matters") which will include :

a What the Division does;

b Who does what within the Division;

c Identification of Client Officers, and what their responsibilities are;

d Latest News / information which may be interesting or useful; and

e A sales pitch for our corporate services (business planning etc.)

This will be circulated to members, officers, neighbouring authorities and any other interested parties.

2.10. Future Reviews

Working in a dynamic environment means that the Business Plan needs to be reviewed regularly, in order that it is up to date with all changes that have occurred in the meantime and, more importantly, that it's objectives and priorities are being achieved.

This plan will be reviewed, by all staff within the Division, by the end of October 1993 or when the next vacancy occurs within the Division - whichever is the sooner.

3. CONCLUSION

3.1. The Process

The process of putting this plan together has taken just over four months. It has been time well spent, with a few lively debates, particularly when conducting the S.W.O.T. Analysis - which was the first time strengths, weaknesses, opportunities and threats had been addressed collectively.

3.2. What have we achieved ?

We have achieved what we set out to do, although the final product is not what many imagined it would be at the outset :

a The Division has established itself as a team.

b Weaknesses identified are being positively tackled.

c Workplans, training and computer requirements have all been agreed. All staff have a greater awareness of what everybody else has to do.

3.3. The Plan Itself

This plan is intended as an internal document for the Division - an integral part of the management of the Division. It will, however, have a wider audience with it being "reported" to :

a Management Team. Authority for the plan was given by Management Team with a view to us, acting on a consultancy basis, introducing plans throughout the authority. Whilst the consultancy service may no longer be relevant, this plan may serve as a useful guide.

b Members' Review Panel and Personnel Sub Committee. Authority will be needed to introduce the proposed staffing and grading changes.

FUNCTION	CLIENT	RESPONSIBLE OFFICER	DEPUTY (IES)
Treasury Services : Policy Management Leases Bank Reconciliation			
Paymaster Services : Wages Salaries Creditors Car Loans Car Claims Members' Allowances			
Budgetary Services : General Fund Revenue Housing Revenue Account Salaries Wages Capital Expenditure Capital Financing D.C.C. D.L.M. Rechargeable Works			
Corporate Services : Internal Business Units Target Savings			
Other Services : F.A.S. Concessionary Fares Insurances - Policy Insurances - Claims Sundry Debtors - Industry Sundry Debtors - Other Housing Act Advances RTB Mortgages Morgan Grenfell Mortgages Members' Services			

FINANCIAL SERVICES DIVISION - PROPOSED STAFFING

Post   **Holder**   **Grade**

APPENDIX 3

Revised Budget 1993/94 and 1994/95

	1993/94	1994/95
	£	£
Remuneration Costs : including salaries, leased cars, bonuses and employer oncosts.		
Recharges from :		
Director of Financial Services, Typing and Secretarial Support.		
Computer Services - Hardware and Systems etc.		
Computer Hardware / Software Bid		
Personnel, Training and Legal Services.		
Accommodation.		
Other Running Costs : telephones, insurances, printing, stationery, postages etc.		
Total Expenditure		
Income (through Service Level Agreements)		
FORECAST PROFIT FOR YEAR :		
LESS Original Profit Forecast (Part One, page 12)		
Savings to Delyn Borough Council		

The savings to the Council may be available (subject to Management Team's approval) to "buy-in" Business Planning consultancy services, if required.

APPENDIX 4

FINANCIAL SERVICES DIVISION - 1993/94 INCOME SUMMARY

	SLA/01 Members £	SLA/02 C Exec £	SLA/03 DFS £	SLA/04 ITM £	SLA/05 Rev M £	SLA/06 DDES £	SLA/07 Health £	SLA/08 Planning £	SLA/09 Housing £	SLA/10 DCC £	SLA/11 Leisure £	SLA/12 DLM £	SLA/15 Legal £	SLA/16 Personnel £	SLA/17 Admin £	SLA/18 Client S £	TOTAL £
FIXED INCOME																	
Revenue Monitoring																	
Capital Monitoring																	
Treasury Management																	
Financial Assistance																	
Concessionary Bus Pass																	
Insurances																	
Housing Advances																	
Sundry Debtors																	
Wages																	
Salaries																	
Creditors																	
Car Loans / Claims																	
Members Allowances																	
VARIABLE INCOME																	
Committee (Meetings)																	
Committees (Reports)																	
Members - Advice																	
Working Parties																	
Corporate Assignments																	
Publications																	
Forward Planning																	
New Legislation																	
Competitive Tendering																	
Rechargeable Works																	
TOTAL																	

FINANCIAL SERVICES DIVISION - WORKPLAN FOR 1993/94

Income earning activities

	Apr	May	Jun	Jul	Aug	Sep	Oct	Nov	Dec	Jan	Feb	Mar
Budget Preparation												
Budget Monitoring			Peak			Peak						
Final Accounts												
Treasury Management												
Committee Meetings / Reports												
Working Parties												
Target Savings												
Business Planning					Deferred for the time being.							
Internal Business Units / SLAs				As agreed with customers and Director of Financial Services								
Annual Report												
Budget "Action Pack"												
Economic Development Strategy												
Statement of Accounts												
Treasury Policy Statement & Associated Reports												
Forward Planning												
New Legislation					As and when required							
Rechargeable Works												
Financial Assistance Scheme	Peak								Peak			
Concessionary Bus Passes							Peak					
Insurances												
Housing Advances	Peak											
Sundry Debtors												
Salaries and Wages	Peak					Back Pay ?						Peak
Creditors												
Members Allowances			Peak									
Car Loans / Claims												

FINANCIAL SERVICES DIVISION - WORKPLAN FOR 1993/94

Non - Income earning activities

Activity	Apr	May	Jun	Jul	Aug	Sep	Oct	Nov	Dec	Jan	Feb	Mar
Financial Services Newsletter												
Performance Review / Appraisal												
Workplan Review												
Service Level Agreements												
Resource Management System Review												
Business Plan Review												
Service Specifications and Work Manuals for :												
Budgetary Services				Specification					Manual			
Rechargeable Works		Specification			Manual							
Financial Assistance Scheme			Specification		Manual							
Concessionary Fares Scheme			Specification					Manual				
Insurances - Policy Renewal					Specification			Manual				
Insurances - Claims Procedures					Specification			Manual				
Sundry Debtors - Industry							Specification				Manual	
Sundry Debtors - Other							Specification				Manual	
Salaries			Spec					Manual				
Wages			Spec					Manual				
Creditors		Spec						Manual				
Members' Allowances		Spec	Manual									
Car Loans	Spec				Manual							
Car Claims (travelling)	Spec				Manual							
Housing Act Advances					Specification						Manual	
RTB Mortgages					Specification						Manual	
Morgan Grenfell Mortgages					Specification						Manual	

The workplans for all 15 individual staff members, within the Division, have been agreed. In order to save paper (and costs), they have only been reproduced in a few plans, where their circulation is deemed particularly relevant.

Anyone who wishes to see these workplans should contact the Financial Services Manager.

CIPFA

BUSINESS PLANS

A Compendium

LOCAL AUTHORITIES

Ross & Cromarty District Council

Leisure Services Activity Plan 1993/94

Ross & Cromarty District Council

Leisure Services Activity Plan 1993/94

This activity plan is one of a range presented to the District Council. Plans are produced in the same format for:

- development services

- environmental services

- housing services

- central services
    - chief executive's
    - legal services
    - architectural services
    - financial services
    - administrative services.

Each activity plan is subject to review throughout the year and detailed financial information is presented separately.

ROSS & CROMARTY
DISTRICT COUNCIL

COMHAIRLE
Rois is Chrombaidh

ACTIVITY PLANS

Activity Plans: Leisure Service Interests

(i)   Arts Development
(ii)   Heritage Management
(iii) Landscape Maintenance and Development
(iv) Leisure Centres
(v)   Leisure Development
(vi) Play Equipment

ACTIVITY: ARTS DEVELOPMENT

ACTIVITY MANAGER: ARTS DEVELOPMENT OFFICER

1. OBJECTIVES

(a) To provide the people of Ross and Cromarty with good access to a wide range of opportunities for involvement in arts activities.

(b) To support and develop arts initiatives for, and with, local arts organisations, groups and individuals.

(c) To create training and employment opportunities for local individuals and arts workers.

(d) To raise the awareness of, and involvement in, arts activities by the people of Ross and Cromarty.

2.	KEY RESULT AREAS	COMMENTARY
(a)	To provide opportunities for people to participate in and be audience to, a wide range of arts activities.	In the first 5 months of the year approximately 16,000 people have been involved in workshops, residencies, projects, exhibitions and performances.
(b)	To maximise the value of arts provision.	Approximately 24% earned and grant-related income from individual art form and promotion budgets.
(c)	To provide information on Arts activities and events.	Achieved high standard of publicity for summer activities. Plans to launch new "What's On" in December in association with Ross-Shire Journal. Circulation 30,000.
(d)	To provide geographical access to arts provision.	Arts activities have taken place in 31 towns and villages throughout the District.

3.	KEY TASKS	COMMENTARY
(a)	To consoldiate the work of the 6 Artists in Residence.	Major combined arts project planned Winter 93/94 involving all Artists in Residence.
(b)	To develop collaborative links with other sections in Leisure Services.	Successful collaborations with Museums Section: Vikings Project, Scotland's Music Projects and Cromarty Courthouse Exhibition.
(c)	To establish a Drama Training Scheme.	Y.T. Placement Scheme in operation.

4. RESOURCES	1993/94 BUDGET	ADJUSTED ACTUAL TO 31 JULY 1993	PROJECTED OUT-TURN 1993/94	VARIANCE
REVENUE EXPENDITURE				
STAFF COSTS	135,872	44,290	134,886	(986)
PROPERTY COSTS	11,294	2,913	11,729	435
SUPPLIES AND SERVICES	4,400	3,368	7,297	2,897
ADMINISTRATION/OTHER COSTS	79,445	55,490	84,683	5,238
TOTAL OPERATING COSTS	231,011	106,061	238,595	7,584
LOAN CHARGES	1,949	650	1,949	
CENTRAL ADMIN. ALLOCATION	29,544	9,848	29,544	
TOTAL GROSS COST	262,504	116,559	270,088	7,584
INCOME	35,160	11,187	35,532	372
TOTAL NET EXPENDITURE	227,344	105,372	234,556	7,212

COMMENTARY:

(1) Supplies and Services - Increased activity in Visual Arts. Costs of materials and equipment used in new commission should be offset by elements in Scottish Arts Council annual grant.

(2) Other costs:

- Reduction in Scottish Council Grants (Drama and Dance) approximately £4,000.

- Overspend in Grants budget due to £2,450 granted to Cromarty Arts Trust by Chief Executives Office. Expenditure lodged in Arts budget until contingency funds are arranged.

5. COST EFFECTIVENESS MEASURES

STANDARD	COMMENTARY
(a) 24% earned income for each art form budget reading	Average 24%
(b) Subsidy per head for Summer Activities Programme - £3	Average £2.50

6. ACCOUNTS COMMISSION INDICATORS

INDICATOR	COMMENTARY

ACTIVITY:- HERITAGE MANAGEMENT

ACTIVITY MANAGER:- MUSEUMS DEVELOPMENT OFFICER

1 OBJECTIVES

a) To enable the people of Ross and Cromarty to preserve and interpret their heritage through well managed facilities which support the economic and social infrastructure of their community.

b) To deliver a quality outreach programme which makes the natural and human heritage of the District accessible and enjoyable to locals and visitors.

c) To preserve and document the history and heritage of the District and make it accessible to the public.

2.	KEY RESULTS	COMMENTARY
a)	To enable museums to provide a quality service to the public.	The museums are succeeding in being re-registered. The Highland Museum of Childhood has been Registered by the Museums and Galleries Commission. Target review meetings are being held and no major problems are being reported. The Museums have attracted approximately 60,000 visitors to date.
b)	To provide opportunities for people to participate in heritage events and activities.	These have attached 9,000 participants to date.
c)	To collect, collate and make available, information on the history and heritage of Ross and Cromarty.	Although the Council's collections are being maintained above Registration standards, there is little opportunity to actively progress information gathering. This will be addressed in the 1994/95 Activity Plan.

3.	KEY TASKS	TARGET
a)	To set up and open a pilgrimage heritage centre in Tain.	On target for June 1994 opening.
b)	To run a Viking Festival.	Cancelled due to lack of sponsorship. Local events attracted 1085 visitors including 470 children to Dingwall Museum.
c)	To run an outreach programme which effectively covers the whole District.	On target.
d)	To input into the production of visitor orientated heritage trails.	A west coast churches trail is being developed. A "Kings Route" trail from Fortrose to Tain is under discussion.
e)	Advise and support independent museums in the District.	This continues and has involved 47% of the Museum Development Officers time.

4. RESOURCES	1993/94 BUDGET	ADJUSTED ACTUAL TO 31 JULY 1993	PROJECTED OUT-TURN 1993/94	VARIANCE	
REVENUE EXPENDITURE					
STAFF COSTS	46,271	18,805	50,735	4,464	1
PROPERTY COSTS	3,652	2,046	5,137	1,485	2
SUPPLIES AND SERVICES	26,000	14,233	27,000	1,000	3
ADMINISTRATION/OTHER COSTS	78,663	66,076	78,962	299	4
TOTAL OPERATING COSTS	154,586	101,160	161,834	7,248	
LOAN CHARGES	24,952	8,317	24,952	–	
CENTRAL ADMIN ALLOCATION	29,544	9,848	29,544	–	
TOTAL GROSS COST	209,082	119,325	216,330	7,284	
INCOME	4,000	1,027	5,050	1,050	
TOTAL NET EXPENDITURE	205,082	118,298	211,280	6,198	

COMMENTARY:

1.   Increase salary costs and mileage.

2.   Unexpected building maintenance costs.

3.   Matched by increased income from grants.

4.   Increased telephone costs.

5. COST EFFECTIVENESS MEASURES	
STANDARD	COMMENTARY
Subsidy per head for Museum visitors of £1.80.	On target.
Subsidy per head for Museum activities of £2.80.	On target.

ACTIVITY: Landscape Maintenance and Development

ACTIVITY MANAGER: Landscape Development and Client Officer

1 OBJECTIVES

(a)   The provision and maintenance of quality landscape including
       formal amenity areas and informal rereational areas, sportsfields,
       woodlands, road verges, picnic area, special habitats and
       landscape features.

(b)   To contribute to the quality of life of the residents and the
       visitors to the District through the provision of physical and
       visual amenity.

(c)   To conserve, enhance and protect the natural environment of the
       District.

2 KEY RESULT AREA	STANDARDS
(a) The effective undertaking of the client role for all landscape issues affecting the District Council.	85 contract instructions issued to date. Expenditure targets in specific client areas monitored. P.I. = average cost of landscape maintenance £3,227.00 per hecture.
(b) The addition of new and the re-appraisal of existing landscape areas.	Proposed development of management plans and re-appraisal of existing landscape schemes delayed by failure of technical assistant bid and budget restrictions.
(c) To reflect the Council's Environmental Strategy in all Landscape matters.	Proposals to diversify Council's landscape holdings in line with environmental strategy to be debated in forthcoming Policy Space. Woodland Development strategy in preparation.

4. RESOURCES:	1993/94 BUDGET	ADJUSTED ACTUAL TO 31 JULY 93	PROJECTED OUT-TURN 1993/94	VARIANCE
REVENUE EXPENDITURE				
STAFF COSTS	32,919	11,851	33,544	625
PROPERTY COSTS	47,914	21,730	47,567	(347)
SUPPLIES AND SERVICES	2,474	892	3,126	652
CONTRACT COSTS	385,718	140,303	397,225	11,507
ADMINISTRATION/OTHER COSTS				
TOTAL OPERATING COSTS	469,025	174,776	481,462	12,437
LOAN CHARGES	177,254	59,084	177,254	
CENTRAL ADMIN. ALLOCATION				
TOTAL GROSS COST	646,279	233,860	658,716	12,437
INCOME	26,776	11,722	24,000	(2,776)
TOTAL NET EXPENDITURE	619,503	222,138	634,716	15,213

COMMENTARY:

(1)   £20K of Contractor cost budget lodged in C.F.C.R. Projected outurn takes account of only £10K being allocated to this source because of difficulties in attributing actual works which meet C.F.C.R guidelines.

(2)   Contract Costs - overspend of £4,000 due to Leisure Contract budget figure being set prior to final costs being determined.

(3)   Income - no grant from Countryside 1967 Act £3,000.

5.	COST EFFECTIVENESS MEASURES	STANDARDS
Contract Instruction		85 issued to date.
Monitoring of Contract		Ongoing. Default Notices - two to date and two Renewal Works Notices.

6.	ACCOUNTS COMMISSION INDICATORS	
INDICATOR		**COMMENTARY**
Average cost of landscape maintenance per hectare.		£3,227.00

ACTIVITY: LEISURE CENTRES

ACTIVITY MANAGER: LEISURE MANAGERS

1. OBJECTIVES

(a) To provide and maintain high quality facilities.

(b) To enable all sections of the community to fulfil their leisure aspirations.

(c) To seek out and respond to changing customer needs.

(d) To operate facilities and activities cost effectively.

2.	KEY RESULT AREAS	COMMENTARY
(a)	Standard of facility provision.	Meeting leisure management contract specifications and standards for quality of maintenance and provision of facilities.
(b)	Level of Participation.	Participation figures are generally on target for this time of year.
(c)	Provision of opportunities and activities.	Autumn programme of activities now operating with increased opportunities available.
(d)	Safety.	Staff training programme operating to ensure safe procedures and standards are maintained by qualified staff.
(e)	To provide "safety net" funding for community run facilities - Poolewe Swimming Pool and Averon Leisure Centre.	Ongoing.

3.	KEY TASKS	COMMENTARY
(a)	Improve energy efficiency through duct insulation and fuel regulation at Dingwall.	Funding agreed by Leisure Services Committee from contract profits to progress in November 1993.
(b)	Upgrade and relocate fitness facilities at Invergordon.	Fitness room now relocated. Funding for improvements agreed by Leisure Services Committee profits. To progress in November 1993.
(c)	Complete swimming pool and set up necessary staffing and administrative procedures at Ullapool.	Staff training in progress to ensure necessary qualified personnel for opening.
(d)	Effect a six month review of operation of community run facilities.	Meetings with Managers of Poolewe Swimming Pool and Averon Leisure Centre planned during October 1993.

4. RESOURCES	1993/94 BUDGET	ADJUSTED ACTUAL TO 31 JULY 1993	PROJECTED OUT-TURN 1993/94	VARIANCE
REVENUE EXPENDITURE				
STAFF COSTS	137,145	42,209	136,127	(1,018)
PROPERTY COSTS	225,836	75,695	220,501	(5,335)
SUPPLIES AND SERVICES	48,867	13,157	49,583	716
CONTRACT COSTS	233,432	71,739	220,472	(12,960)
ADMINISTRATION/OTHER COSTS	241,945	129,539	242,551	606
TOTAL OPERATING COSTS	887,225	332,339	869,234	(17,991)
LOAN CHARGES	288,833	96,278	288,833	
CENTRAL ADMIN. ALLOCATION	46,547	15,514	46,547	
TOTAL GROSS COST	1,222,605	444,131	1,204,614	(17,991)
INCOME	358,130	112,450	351,334	(6,796)
TOTAL NET EXPENDITURE	864,475	331,681	853,280	(11,195)

COMMENTARY:

(1)   Contract Costs – £13,000 underspend in Invergordon due to budget being set prior to final costs being established.

(2)   Property Costs – an underspend of approximately £4,000 is projected for the Alness Swimming Pool rent and insurance charges.

(3)   Income – a £7,000 shortfall is projected based on admissions for the first four months.

5. COST EFFECTIVENESS MEASURES	
STANDARD	COMMENTARY
Income as percentage of operating costs.	Currently approximately 34% and in line with Centre targets.
Contract income to exceed expenditure	5% profit target being achieved.

	INDICATOR	COMMENTARY
	6. ACCOUNTS COMMISSION INDICATORS	
(a)	Average attendance per opening hour for swimming and leisure pools.	Attendance and financial statistics are routinely collected. Measurement statistics required for the indicators are currently being drawn up with Contract Compliance Unit.
(b)	Average attendance per square metre for other indoor sport and leisure facilities excluding pools in a combined complex.	
(c)	Percentage of total operating expenditure for year met from customer income for pools and other indoor facilities.	

ACTIVITY: LEISURE SERVICES - LEISURE DEVELOPMENT

ACTIVITY MANAGER: DEPUTE DIRECTOR
                             CENTRAL SUPPORT OFFICER
                             LEISURE DEVELOPMENT OFFICER

---

1. OBJECTIVES

Central Support

(a) Provide efficient administrative systems and support for all sections of Leisure Services.

(b) Co-ordinate administrative systems between Leisure Centres and Central Services.

(c) Provide a central source of information on Leisure Services activities and developments.

Grants

(a) To help stimulate the development and growth of quality facilities and opportunities.

(b) To act as enabler for local voluntary organisations to lead their own development projects.

(c) To act as a catalyst in the attraction of outside funding for local projects.

Leisure Development

(a) To encourage and promote participation and enjoyment in sporting/leisure/activities/events by all sections of the community by creating opportunities to take part in a wide range of activities at all levels.

(b) To promote activities throughout Ross and Cromarty.

(c) Raise standards and skills levels and promote and develop health and fitness programmes.

2. KEY RESULT AREAS	COMMENTARY
<u>Central Support</u>	
(a) Provide administration service to all sections including process of invoices, accounts, income, booking of classes, events, venues, etc.	Ongoing
(b) Offer advice service to Local Voluntary Organisations.	Ongoing
(c) Ensure a high quality of marketing, publicity and media coverage for Leisure Services activities.	Ongoing
<u>Grants</u>	
(a) To provide support and advice to groups considering one off projects, purchases or events.	Ongoing
(b) To stimulate use of swimming facilities by those in remote West areas by assisting travel costs.	Ongoing
<u>Leisure Development</u>	
(a) To provide a varied programme of leisure activities throughout Ross and Cromarty.	53 sessions operating weekly during term time on East Coast, 21 on West Coast. Summer programme of events attracted 2,060 attendances.
(b) To provide opportunities for people to participate in leisure activities and events.	Opportunities increased by 22%.
(c) To co-operate and work with agencies involved with sport and sport development at a local, regional and national level.	Development work ongoing with Team Sport Scotland - Hockey and Football. Projects planned with Scottish Rugby Union and Scottish Sports Council - consultation continues with other agencies interested in developing sport in Ross and Cromarty.

3. KEY TASKS	COMMENTARY
Central Support	
(a) Review the work of Leisure Services Central Administration Section.	Implementation of revised income, receipt and recording procedures. Complete. Monitoring - ongoing.
(b) Develop Leisure Services Database for all classes, events and Summer Activities Programme.	Complete and in use.
(c) Actively seek sponsorship for a variety of activities and special events.	Assisting Activity Managers in preparing sponsorship bids - ongoing. Sponsorship achieved for the Summer Activities Brochure.
(d) Manage a range of equipment, including mini bus which may be borrowed by groups and individuals.	Review of administration of bookings system complete. Storage agreed by Leisure Services Committee - September 1993.
Grants	
(a) In consultation with other Services offering grants, devise a policy for their provision and promotion.	Discussions scheduled for October/November 1993.
(b) Ensure District Council involvement in projects receives full recognition.	Ongoing.
Leisure Development	
(a) On-going development of coaches.	6 courses have been organised. Another 8 to run before March 94.
(b) To have coaches trained in target sports.	3 coaches trained for pre-school, 6 for aerobics, 3 for canoe instruction, 14 badminton coaches.
(c) Improve public awareness of importance of health and fitness programme.	This initiative has not progressed, date put back to Feb/March 94.
(d) Increase level of opportunities to participate in sport and leisure activities.	5 new activities introduced to programme.
(e) Organise competition for District wide participation.	Date set for March 94.

RESOURCES	1993/94 BUDGET	ADJUSTED ACTUAL TO 31 JULY 1993	PROJECTED OUT-TURN 1993/94	VARIANCE
REVENUE EXPENDITURE				
STAFF COSTS	232,047	88,550	246,297	14,250
PROPERTY COSTS	14,269	4,159	14,074	(195)
SUPPLIES AND SERVICES	37,805	14,744	39,731	1,926
ADMINISTRATION/OTHER COSTS	81,087	38,678	82,859	1,772
TOTAL OPERATING COSTS	365,208	146,131	382,961	17,753
LOAN CHARGES	40,159	13,386	40,159	
CENTRAL ADMIN. ALLOCATION	343,617	114,539	343,617	
TOTAL GROSS COST	748,984	274,056	766,737	17,753
INCOME	144,291	52,874	142,511	(1,780)
TOTAL NET EXPENDITURE	604,693	221,182	624,226	19,533

COMMENTARY:

(1)   Staff costs - £14,000 overspend in Admin. due to:

- -2% vacancy prov. unutilised £5,000

- -£3,500 extra cost for temporary employees assisting with administration workload.

- -£3,500 for changes to administrative support following transfer of Assistant to the Director post to Chief Executives Service - omitted from continuation budget

- -£2,000 increase travel costs

(2)   Supplies and Services - £2,000 overspend due to increased costs arising from new mini bus

(3)   Income - £2,000 under on budget figure in fees and charges for Leisure Officers

5.   COST EFFECTIVENESS MEASURES

STANDARD	COMMENTARY
Leisure Development - Ratio Income to Expenditure - 16.4%	Achieved for period.

6.   ACCOUNTS COMMISSION INDICATORS

INDICATOR	COMMENTARY
None.	

ACTIVITY:	PLAY EQUIPMENT
ACTIVITY MANAGER:	DEPUTE DIRECTOR OF LEISURE SERVICES

1. OBJECTIVES

(a) To provide opportunities for challenge, physical and mental stimulus in a safe environment, close to home.

(b) To ensure an equitable spread of opportunities throughout the District, for a variety of age groups.

2.	KEY RESULT AREAS	COMMENTARY
(a)	Maintenance - Monitor work of contractor - litter clearance, structural inspections.	Ongoing
(b)	Installation programme - ensure annual is updated and completed.	Ongoing

3.	KEY TASKS	COMMENTARY
(a)	Inititate two spot checks per month to ensure compliance with contract specification.	Ongoing
(b)	Prepare site investigations and begin community consultation for the design of new areas.	Begun by end June 1993. 1993/94 installation programme began September 1993.
(c)	Prepare annual review of works programme	For March 1994

RESOURCES	1993/94 BUDGET	ADJUSTED ACTUAL 31 JULY 1993	PROJECTED OUT-TURN 1993/94	VARIANCE
REVENUE EXPENDITURE				
STAFF COSTS				
PROPERTY COSTS				
SUPPLIES AND SERVICES				
CONTRACT COSTS	61,050	17,806	60,870	(180)
ADMINISTRATION/OTHER COSTS				
TOTAL OPERATING COSTS	61,050	17,806	60,870	(180)
LOAN CHARGES				
CENTRAL ADMIN. ALLOCATION				
TOTAL GROSS COST	61,050	17,806	60,870	(180)
INCOME	9,205		4,900	(4,305)
TOTAL NET EXPENDITURE	51,845	17,806	55,970	4,125

COMMENTARY:

1) Income - £4,000 under projected figure. £5,000 now forecast for 1993/94.

5. COST EFFECTIVENESS MEASURES

STANDARD	COMMENTARY

CIPFA

BUSINESS PLANS

A Compendium

LOCAL AUTHORITIES

South Somerset District Council

Development Services Department
Service Plans 1994 - 1997

South Somerset District Council

Development Services Department
Service Plans 1994-1997

South Somerset District Council produce service plans in the same format for:

◆ chief executive's department

◆ community services department

◆ development services department

◆ resources department

◆ South Somerset Contractors.

In addition to the development services department service plan an outline of the overall process and a summary of the annual service planning and performance review cycle are reproduced.

The district council also produces for each of the activities listed above:

◆ details of 'Past Achievements' – an annual review

◆ details of 'Present Activities' – action plans for the year indicating objectives, key actions, performance indicators, and lead officers.

Please note that the service plan which follows is in draft form prior to agreement by members.

SOUTH SOMERSET DISTRICT COUNCIL

SERVICE PLANNING AND PERFORMANCE REVIEW

A system of strategic management based on the Annual Service Planning and Performance Review Cycle opposite is being established throughout the authority. This process is designed to make sure the authority identifies, in a structured way, what needs to be done, ensures appropriate targets are set and measures performance against them. In addition to the setting of corporate goals and constant monitoring, there are five key stages in the annual cycle.

- <u>Service Plans</u> provide a vision of the development of each service over a three year period. They are prepared following an analysis of the implications of the past, consideration of ongoing action and attempts at assessing the future. Emphasis is placed on year one of each service plan which allows the next stages of the cycle to be implemented more easily.

- <u>Priorities</u> which are established through the budget setting process. The early exposure of members to all service plans allows wide debate in the identification of priorities before the Chancellor's Autumn Statement. Once the authority's total budget is known, estimates for the next financial year can be allocated to each unit/service.

- <u>Action Plans</u> which managers produce by drawing on the service plans and taking into account unit/service budgets when they are announced. Action Plans follow a common format:

  - the long term aim of the unit/service;
  - the medium term objectives which will fulfil that aim;
  - the short term actions by which the unit/service will seek to achieve those objectives;
  - performance indicators which establish targets and may be used to evaluate achievement.

- <u>Performance Appraisal</u> which has operated for individual staff since 1986. Unit action plans form the basis for setting staff's team and personal objectives. At the same time, individual performance during the previous year is evaluated. The gradual introduction of the system of strategic management is ensuring that the objectives against which individual performance is reviewed match up with corporate goals.

- <u>Annual Reviews</u> which make a comparison between what was proposed for the services with what was actually achieved. As well as looking back over the previous 12 months, the reviews consider issues which have emerged and which may have an impact on the future of services. They also highlight areas in which improvements might be made. In due course, these are likely to become proposals for action in the subsequent three year rolling service plan.

The incremental implementation of the cycle which commenced in the autumn of 1991, enables efforts to be devoted to developing and refining each stage at the appropriate point of the year. This flexible approach is proving effective in the establishment of a system which is contributing to the authority's aim of maintaining South Somerset as an attractive place in which to live and work, with a healthy environment and a Council which provides accessible, high quality public services at a reasonable cost.

RDP1-93SERVICE

Annual Service Planning and Performance Review Cycle

What are we setting out to do?
COUNCIL STRATEGY
- Prepared by Councillors
- Sets Corporate Values/Goals
- Review in light of external changes

(Life of Council)

What would we like to do?
SERVICE PLANS
- Prepared by Directors
- Needs and resources identified
- 3 year rolling programme

(August - September)

What can we do?
PRIORITIES
- Decided by Councillors
- External considerations
- Budgets agreed

(October - January)

How do we manage performance?
MONITORING
- By all continuously
- Progress reports
- Revise if necessary

(Ongoing)

What will we do?
ACTION PLANS
- Prepared by Unit Managers
- Key Actions and Performance Measures
- 1 Year life span

(February - March)

What about our staff?
PERFORMANCE APPRAISAL
- Based on individuals
- Set next year's objectives
- Review last year's performance

(April - May)

How have we done?
ANNUAL REVIEW
- Prepared by Directors
- Reviews Unit achievements
- Identifies key service issues

(June - July)

SERVICE PLANS 1994-97

General Introduction

Service Plans are a key element of the authority's service planning and performance review process which is displayed opposite. The draft service plans contained in this document set out officers' aspirations. They will be presented to committees during October and November 1993, when members will be given the opportunity to agree priorities and determine clearly what they would like the Council to achieve over the next three years.

In drafting their proposals during August and September 1993, Unit Managers and Directors considered changes and improvements to services. They took into account external factors and other changes which are likely to influence those services. For the first time, managers explicitly show how they intend to consult the people of South Somerset in ensuring their needs are met during the next three years.

Officers have concentrated in detail on the action for 1994-95, the first year of these service plans. Earlier in 1993, they were invited to look for ways of making savings so that anticipated difficulties in balancing the budget in 1994-95 could be avoided. This exercise was successfully completed and, where appropriate, changes have been incorporated in these service plans.

A few words should be mentioned about the position of South Somerset Contractors (S.S.C.) No separate service plans for the Direct Services Organisation (D.S.O.) have been included in this document and the five year Business Plan adopted in March 1990 is still relevant. There are, however, serious concerns about the ability of S.S.C. to remain competitive in the light of increasing outside interest in district council work. Many other D.S.O.'s are in difficulty and it is with the interests of both the Council and the D.S.O. in mind that a feasibility study has been commissioned to look at ways forward.

Other equally daunting challenges lie ahead. Indeed, it might be said that the authority has reached a watershed.

Even before these service plans are implemented, the Department of the Environment's decision on Local Government Reorganisation in this region should be known. Whatever the outcome, an issue which could turn out to be a more severe test is the compulsory competition faced by our professional services. In addition, local authorities are being urged to review their internal management arrangements in order to strengthen the role of members.

At the same time as trying to accommodate these challenges, the Council wishes to extend the involvement of local communities in decision making and sharing power.

Considerable progress has been made in getting closer to communities and improving service quality over the last two years. This is due to a combination of factors; reorganisation in November 1991, the flexibility of our staff and training and development support through a period of rapid change. This was acknowledged by an independent management consultant who evaluated the authority against the national "Investors in People" standard in July 1993.

At the beginning of the year, the Council made a formal commitment to Somerset TEC to pursue the Investors in People Standard. This is a national standard for training and development and, once achieved, would confirm that the Council is working in line with good practice with regard to people development. Pursuance of the standard during 1994 will be integrated into other activities already planned and the resource implications are minimal.

Becoming recognised as an Investor in People will underpin the authority's belief that the people who work for the Council are our most valuable resource. It is they who will see us through the uncertainties ahead and bring about the achievements intended in these service plans.

Mel Usher,
Chief Executive

SERVICE PLANS 1994-97

Introduction - Development Services Department

In introducing the Department's Service plan for 1994-97, it would be unrealistic not to set this in the context of Local Government Review. At the future pattern unfolds, we will need positive plans which encourage managers and staff to feel enthusiastic about the prospect of playing a part in creating a new organisation, or at least ensuring that our good services and practices are carried forward.

Reflecting upon the Department's services in the context of the coming changes, here are some brief thoughts about the way forward. The future is clearer for some than for others.

- Regulatory services such as Building Control and Development Control will be carried forward into a new authority, although the organisational framework may vary - there is every reason to maintain and improve our present high standards and keep abreast of good practice.

- The South Somerset Local Plan must be completed at least to "deposit" stage before a new authority commences. The Policy team see this as a clear aim and will remain motivated by it. After that, a reappraisal of priorities would have been needed anyway.

- Environmental considerations are acquiring increased emphasis in planning and appropriate specialist support will continue to be needed for development control and policy preparation, unless standards are to slip and for the maintenance of the District's historic heritage.

- Activities such as highway agency functions and maintenance of public buildings and car parks must be carried on effectively up to "handover" stage. Neglect of assets would be irresponsible, but there may be a temptation not to make longer term investments.

For other service areas the picture is less clear.

- The future of contracts with the Water Companies is in doubt - Wessex have made it clear that they will take a fresh view according to what kind of authority emerges but cost effectiveness will be their primary consideration. We are working on the assumption that a new authority will want an agency of some kind, and must keep in close touch with Wessex to see if their thinking can be influenced.

- Areas of discretionary spending are already under scrutiny due to financial restrictions. The Council will, no doubt, wish to continue to re-appraise its priorities for spending on projects and grants depending on emerging circumstances. This would affect the work of Architectural Services, Technical Services and Environment Units.

- Compulsory Competitive Tendering for the construction-related services (Architecture, Engineering and Property Management) will not be introduced here until after LGR, but we must do what preparation we can now. The current approach is to defer firm conclusions about structural change in the short term, until the form of new authority is known, but move ahead in pursuing the "good business practices" needed (which are justifiable anyway on efficiency grounds) - clear objectives, customer liaison, good accounting practice, time recording and analysis, formal commissioning of work, quality controls, reducing direct and indirect costs etc.

The implications of CCT for the Architectural Services and Technical Services Units are arguably more fundamental to their future than Local Government Review and it is not surprising that preparing for it features prominently in both Units' Key Actions for 1994/95. A study of the best way to approach competition for the construction-related services will be completed later this year and its findings will need to be implemented next year, alongside the preparations for introducing new authorities.

Next year's Key Actions should also be seen in the context of:
- a slow rise in the level of development activity
- the need to pursue greater efficiency due to expenditure restrictions
- increased public expectations and scrutiny of performance, for example, through the Citizen's Charter.

Recent reductions in staffing, coupled with the Council's likely difficulty in meeting Service Plan bids for items such as IT equipment may make it difficult to sustain current standards for some services. Nevertheless, it will be evident from the Unit Service Plans which follow that there is a commitment by the Department's Managers to the further development of its services, despite the difficulties which lie ahead.

John Clotworthy
Director of Development Services

ARCHITECTURAL SERVICES UNIT

AIM: **To provide professional architectural and building surveying services for the Council.**

ANALYSIS OF CURRENT POSITION

Service	1993/94 Budget Provision Net £
* Architectural Services	146,040
* Public Offices	555,440
* Commercial property	-267,840

The Unit provides a non-statutory support service. The extent of the architectural work is governed by the Council's capital programme. Projects are also undertaken on a fee basis for Housing Associations, Town and Parish Councils and for other organisations as permitted by the "Goods and Services" Act. The maintenance of the Council's Public Buildings is carried out within budgets agreed by the relevant Committee within overall constraints.

ANTICIPATED CHANGES IN SERVICE 1994/97

Compulsory Competitive Tendering

* The Government's proposals to extend CCT to architectural services and property management have fundamental implications for the Unit.

Client Base

* The role of the Authority as a primary supplier of rented housing is changing from supplier to enabler. Although feasibility work is carried out for the Authority and some schemes of a hostel nature, the majority of new build commissions are from Housing Associations. The Unit also acts as architect for the other non-housing building work of the Authority which varies as aspirations and funds allow.

Council House Modernisation

* There still remains across the District a substantial number of housing units requiring modernisation to bring them to current standards. We will respond to the programme agreed.

Structural Repairs to Local Authority Housing

* Progress with a rolling programme of structural repairs will depend upon resources.

Computer Aided Drafting

* The change from a drawing board based process for production of drawings to the use of the Computer Aided Design system will continue.

Public Conveniences

* The Unit became responsible for the maintenance and repair of public conveniences in 1993/94.

Property Maintenance

* A proper level of funding needs to be maintained for the care of the Authority's non-housing building stock. Under-funding of this function will lead to deterioration and increased costs in the future. If this Authority is successful in its bid for unitary status there will be profound changes in the property portfolio. The implications will have to be addressed.

Energy Management

* It is estimated that up to a fifth of the nation's fuel bill could be saved through increasing energy efficiency. Next to transport, energy use in building is the single largest producer of carbon dioxide emissions within the UK contributing to the global warming effect. This Council's total energy bill per annum is some half a million pounds. It may well be that all the Authority's buildings are running at optimum efficiency; the suspicion remains that there are savings to be made - unless resources are made available for investigation we will not know. Alternative sources of energy for use in Council offices will need to be investigated.

COMMUNITY CONSULTATION AND USER SURVEYS 1994/97

* The Unit remains committed to a "user friendly" service and will endeavour to maintain this approach with its clients within the Authority and to outside

1

commissioners. Feedback will be sought about the quality of architectural design work. The nature of our work includes little contact with the general public. Consultation is carried out with local residents affected by projects.

The Building Maintenance Section monitors its relationship with its main customers, but a comprehensive survey will be carried out when time permits.

KEY ACTIONS 1994/95

Compulsory Competitive Tendering

* By far the most important matter that will require attention is the proposed introduction of CCT for architectural and property management functions. Service Review and Service Days must address the issues and options, including possible changes in departmental structure.

Client Base

* Maintain the agreement whereby Housing Associations commission the Unit for schemes built on the Authority's land. Carefully monitor the fees paid against the time spent so there is no cross-subsidisation by the District Council. Agree fees with internal clients and monitor.

The workload to be assessed and programmed in order that there is always sufficient capacity to carry out the Authority's work. The South Somerset District Council remains our most important client.

Council House Modernisations

* To promote a "community architecture" approach to the modernisation programme with full tenant involvement and consultation.

Computer Aided Drafting

* Disseminate within the unit the knowledge which already exists to maximise the capabilities of the existing system, explore its potential and provide a further work station if justified.

Property Maintenance

* A Planned Maintenance system has been introduced which identifies future need priorities and budgetary requirements. The system requires an annual update. Responsive maintenance budgeting will still be based on historical data.

* In the short term new boilers are required at the Octagon Theatre and the offices at 91 Preston Road. Extensive repairs are required at Crewkerne, Church

Street offices. In the longer term all the air handling plant and ductwork at Brympton Way will need to be cleaned.

* The extension to Petters Way in Yeovil and the refurbishment of Churchfields, Wincanton and its return to the Public Offices budget, will have been completed in 1993/94 which completes the programme for buildings for Area Offices.

* The windows at the Somerton Area Office are in a poor state of repair. The building is Grade II* and the rolling programme of repairs should continue.

* In 1993/94 security systems were fitted to offices which will need maintenance and repair.

* Monitor disabled access to public buildings in accordance with the Citizens' Charter and carry out modifications when practicable.

* No checks are made to confirm that the terms of repairing property are being honoured by tenants and this should be addressed.

Energy Management

* The Audit Commission has published performance indicators for building types which give an indication of the recommended level of energy use. A system for the monitoring and analysis of energy use and the identification of cost effective savings should be investigated.

* Alternative sources of energy for use in Council offices will be investigated.

FINANCIAL IMPLICATIONS

Work by the Architectural Unit for outside bodies is carried out on a fee basis, thus reducing the cost of the Unit to the Authority.

To provide a proper maintenance programme will require further resources. Its advantages financially are closer budgetary control and the improvement in value of an expensive asset.

Energy management could be self-financing in cost terms.

SERVICE PLANS 1994-97

Resource implications - Excluding Inflation

	1994/95 £	1995/96 £	1996/97 £
1993/94 Base Budget as at 30.6.93	1,016,710	1,016,710	1,016,710
Committed/Unavoidable Growth:			
Running costs and maintenance of security systems	5,000	5,000	5,000
Cleaning air handling system, Brympton Way	-	-	15,000
Wincanton, Churchfields	1,000	1,000	1,000
	6,000	6,000	21,000
Other Growth:			
Planned property maintenance:			
- administration	5,000	5,000	5,000
Somerton Area Office Windows	3,000	3,000	-
Energy management	5,000	2,500	2,500
Computer Aided Drafting - upgrade	2,000	2,000	2,000
	15,000	12,500	9,500
Service Review Savings:			
Delete one Senior Arch. Assistant post (net of lost income)	-2,000	-2,000	-2,000
Reduce R & M budgets by 10%	-15,000	-15,000	-15,000
	-17,000	-17,000	-17,000
Net Resource Implications of Service Plan	4,000	1,500	13,500
Forecast Net Expenditure	1,020,710	1,018,210	1,030,210

CAPITAL	1994/95	1995/96	1996/97
New boilers to 91 Preston Road Offices	25,000		
Repairs to Crewkerne Offices, Church Street.	100,000		

SERVPLN.93\ARCHIT.GB

BUILDING CONTROL UNIT

AIM: **To provide an effective Building Control Service, committed to ensuring that Building Work satisfies the Building Regulations and that other statutory and non-statutory functions for which the Unit is responsible are discharged.**

ANALYSIS OF CURRENT POSITION

Service	1993/94 Budget Provision
Building Control	£200,760 (net)

In the main, the services provided by the unit are statutory, involving the checking of deposited plans and the inspection of building work on site for compliance with the Building Regulations, dealing with dangerous structures and monitoring demolition work.

Other services provided by the unit are of a support nature and these include the inspection of buildings and sites for Public Entertainment Licences and the provision of specialist advice for other units.

The Department of the Environment increased Building Control fees in October 1992 and this has assisted in raising the unit's fee income. For most areas of work the increase was approximately 9.4%, but fees in connection with domestic extensions and certain alterations were raised by 50%.

ANTICIPATED CHANGES IN SERVICE 1994/97

Service Planning

*   The Unit continues to absorb the effects of the significant amendments to the Building Regulations introduced last year. The effects of these have increased both the administrative and technical operations of processing Building Regulation applications.

    In addition to the workload implications, there is the need for further technical training which due to the complexity and cost will need to continue over an extended period to ensure that all the appropriate technical staff in the Unit are adequately trained.

*   Further amendments to the Building Regulations

have been circulated in draft form for comment by the Department of the Environment. These relate to thermal insulation and ventilation requirements - Parts L and F respectively. The proposal involves increasing the standards of both parts and it is anticipated they will be introduced in the next 12 months.

*   Despite some indications earlier in the year, any increase in application numbers has been very slow and inconsistent. It is difficult to anticipate whether the situation will change in the immediate future. However, if the workload does increase then the Unit's present staffing level, which is already finely balanced, will be unable to continue to provide the current standard of service. Furthermore, there is also the risk of being unable to fulfil aspects of the Council's Building Control policy. Therefore consideration would need to be given to financing one of the frozen Building Control Surveyor posts on the establishment and this has been indicated in the table at the end of this report.

Local Licences (Public Entertainment)

*   The number of premises and sites continue to increase, along with the complexity of many of the applications, particularly those for large outside events.

Self-Financing

*   The principal fee regulations are currently being reconsidered by the Department of the Environment after circulating extensive revisions in draft form for comment. It is still the Government's intention to move towards self-financing for building control; as yet there is no publicised timetable.

Competition

*   The Department of the Environment continue to refine the criteria and procedure for authorising Approved Inspectors in order to encourage further

1

private sector competition to the Local Authority building control service. At present there is still one competitor operating primarily in the new domestic market.

COMMUNITY CONSULTATION AND USER SURVEYS 1994/97

* During the next 12-18 months, it is intended to undertake some form of customer research in order to obtain a user's eye view of the service provided by the Unit. This will probably take the form of a questionnaire similar to that sent out to builders, architects and DIY householders early in 1992.

KEY ACTIONS FOR 1994/95

Service Planning

* Continue monitoring staffing and workload levels in connection with both the Building Regulation and Local Licensing functions. Having completed a successful trial (which was well received by our customers) with two mobile 'phones, extend the facility to two other areas by purchasing two further mobile 'phones.

Self-financing

* Undertake further research and monitoring of the unit's operating costs to be in a position to set our own fees.

Competition

* Promote, at the appropriate opportunities, the Council's Building Control service to primarily consolidate the existing customer base and wherever possible attract new customers from our competitor(s).

Information Technology

* For technical and administrative purposes, and for managerial information, the unit relies heavily on computer and word processor systems. To avoid delays to customers due to down time, a programme of replacing the hardware is needed to ensure prompt and regular service delivery on a daily basis.
Purchase two PCs.

FINANCIAL IMPLICATIONS

The cost implications of the above actions and other financial details of the Unit's operation are shown in the table below.

In the event of the need to fill one of the Building Control Surveyor posts currently frozen, there is the possibility that the total cost may not be totally offset by a corresponding increase in fee income.

SERVICE PLANS 1994-97

Resource implications - Excluding Inflation

	1994/95 £	1995/96 £	1996/97 £
1993/94 Base Budget as at 30.6.93	152,160	152,160	152,160
Committed/Unavoidable Growth:			
Increase in Consultants' Fees	3,500	5,000	6,500
Other Growth:			
Additional Building Control Surveyor post	26,000	26,000	26,000
Replacement IT	2,500	2,500	2,500
Training Building Regulations Changes	1,000	1,000	1,000
2 additional mobile 'phones	1,300	1,300	1,300
	30,800	30,800	30,800
Service Review Savings:			
Other Sources of Finance:			
Increase Building Control Fee income	-10,000	-15,000	-20,000
Net Resource Implications of Service Plan	24,300	20,800	17,300
Forecast Net Expenditure	176,460	172,960	169,460

SERVPLN.93\BLDCON.SF

DEVELOPMENT CONTROL UNIT

AIM: **To control land use and development efficiently and effectively for the benefit of the community of South Somerset.**

ANALYSIS OF CURRENT POSITION

1993/94 budget provision - £141,700 (net).

Making decisions on planning applications and responding to planning appeals are a statutory duty. Investigating unauthorised developments, tree preservation, responding to pre-and post-application discussion and liaison with the public (including Parish Councils) are not a statutory duty but have long been considered to be good development control practice.

ANTICIPATED CHANGES IN SERVICE 1994/97

General

* Consider further improvements in the quality of the service as set out in the Audit Commission's study 'Building in Quality', the model charter guide for development control and consider the suggestions set out in the District Planning Officers' Quality Aspirations Index.

* Strike proper balance between workload and staffing level.

* Consider how the service can best be delivered pre and post LGR, including investigation of devolvement to Area Offices.

* Future legislative requirements and Central Government advice anticipated, eg PPG 15 Historic Buildings and Conservation Areas.

Applications

* Examine ways of assessing the quality of design of recently built development.

* Examine the appropriateness of open space for subsequent adoption by the Council.

Costs

* Prepare for the service having to meet the full recovery of application processing costs.

COMMUNITY CONSULTATION AND USER SURVEY 1994/97

* Full consultation on applications, appeals and enforcement always takes place with the public, parish councils, other interested parties, Members.

* Extensive customer satisfaction survey May 1993 with 5 groups of customers (professional applicants, occasional applicants, those who had made representations, those regularly consulted and Parish Councils). Outcome mainly complimentary but implement appropriate improvements.

* Sample customer satisfaction survey.

KEY ACTIONS FOR 1994/95

* Implement appropriate improvements to the service:-

  - as set out in the model charter guide and District Planning Officer Society's Quality Aspirations Index;

  - as highlighted in response to customer satisfaction survey;

  - by extending the duty officer system.

* Assist Assistant Chief Executive in considering feasibility of providing extended development control services in Area Offices.

* Progress consideration of ways to measure the quality of newly built development and apply in selected cases.

* Monitor workload/income and ensure staffing level is appropriate for it.

1

*   Establish the costs of providing the component parts of the service.

FINANCIAL IMPLICATIONS

Application levels remain the same as last year; fee level has reduced slightly. The start of an economic recovery proclaimed in some quarters is not being reflected in development activity at the present time.

SERVICE PLANS 1994-97

Resource implications - Excluding Inflation

	1994/95 £	1995/96 £	1996/97 £
1993/94 Base Budget as at 30.6.93	284,050	284,050	284,050
Service Review Savings: Delete one technical post Charge applicants for preparing Section 106 Agreements	-15,000 -19,000	-15,000 -19,000	-15,000 -19,000
	-34,000	-34,000	-34,000
Forecast Net Expenditure	250,050	250,050	250,050

SERVPLN.93\DEVCON.PJB

PLANNING ENVIRONMENT UNIT

AIM: **To conserve and enhance the quality and diversity of the built and natural environment through the effective application of specialist professional expertise.**

ANALYSIS OF CURRENT POSITION

Service	1993/94 Budget Provision
Conservation & Environment	£193,140

There is a statutory obligation on local authorities to ensure the preservation or enhancement of conservation areas and a particular duty to prepare proposals to that end. Extra care is to be taken considering planning applications for development affecting listed buildings. Authorities are also under a special duty to consider the preservation and planting of trees.

ANTICIPATED CHANGES IN SERVICE 1994/97

Conservation Area Management

* New planning policy guidance, plus the refocussing of English Heritage resources and possible increases in planning controls in conservation areas, will make a positive approach to preserving and enhancing conservation areas necessary. Area appraisals, policy statements, design briefs and general advice leaflets will need to be prepared on a regular basis.

Historic Buildings Conservation

* Withdrawal of English Heritage funding for Town Schemes and other grant aid will impose greater burdens on local authorities to promote and assist the proper maintenance, repair and alteration of historic buildings.

Environmental Design Advice

* Key sites identified for development should be subject to appraisal and preparation of a design brief at an early stage so as to identify environmental impact and design constraints.

Environmental Improvement Schemes

* New ways should be investigated of encouraging community involvement in maintaining and improving the local environment.

Countryside Planning

* A targeted approach to the preparation of management plans for landscape and nature conservation will be developed.

Historic Parks and Gardens

* Recognition of the District's heritage of designed landscapes needs to be extended so that restoration and better maintenance can be promoted.

COMMUNITY CONSULTATION AND USER SURVEYS 1994/97

* Ongoing communication with listed building owners through data base mail shots.

* All environmental improvement schemes involve community participation.

* Countryside planning and historic landscapes rely on co-operation with landowners.

* Conservation area management requires better communication with residents and property owners.

* The environmental concern and enthusiasm of young people should be enlisted wherever possible.

KEY ACTIONS FOR 1994/5

* Continue programme of conservation area appraisals and commence preparation of publicity material.

1

* Maintain historic building activity at current level.

* Seek involvement in appraisal of key sites, and preparation of briefs for them.

* Canvass Parish/Town Councils and local schools to invite new initiatives for environmental improvements.

* Complete landscape strategy.

* Consider designation of Registered Parks and Gardens as conservation areas.

FINANCIAL IMPLICATIONS

To maintain level of service in countryside planning and make new agréements, annual payments will increase. Publication of design guides (nearing completion) in appropriate illustrated form requires increase in publication budget. Triennial Design Award Scheme due in 1995.

SERVICE PLANS 1994-97

Resource implications - Excluding Inflation

	1994/95 £	1995/96 £	1996/97 £
1993/94 Base Budget as at 30.6.93	202,150	202,150	202,150
Other Growth:			
Countryside Planning Management Agreements	1,500	3,000	4,500
Publication of design guides and conservation area appraisals	1,500	1,500	1,500
Design Award Scheme 1995	-	3,000	-
	3,000	7,500	6,000
Service Review Savings:			
Delete vacant part-time post	-4,000	-4,000	-4,000
Stop support for SCC schemes	-15,790	-15,790	-15,790
	-19,790	-19,790	-19,790
Net Resource Implications of Service Plan	-16,790	-12,290	-13,790
Forecast Net Expenditure	185,360	189,860	188,360

SERVPLN.93\ENVIRON.TJ

PLANNING POLICY UNIT

AIM: To maintain up-to-date planning policies and guidelines for the whole District in order to ensure the pattern and character of land use and development in South Somerset is related as closely as possible to the physical, economic and social needs of all sections of the community.

ANALYSIS OF CURRENT POSITION

Service	1993/94 Budget Provision
Planning Policy	£304,700 (net)

With the introduction of the Planning and Compensation Act 1991, each local planning authority is required to prepare a Local Plan for its area; the Government expects "to see substantially complete coverage" by such plans by February 1997. The Town and Country Planning Act 1990 requires local planning authorities to keep under review matters which may be expected to affect the development of their area. Government advice is that plans should be reviewed regularly.

ANTICIPATED CHANGES IN SERVICE 1994/97

Local Plans

* Completion of work on Local Plans covering only part of the District, with the adoption of the Chard & Ilminster Local Plan.

* Continuing preparation of District-wide South Somerset Local Plan in accordance with approved timetable, leading to Public Local Inquiry probably in latter part of 1995/96.

* Improve communication with members of the public and other participants in the Local Plan process.

* Improve the quality of appearance and ease of use of Local Plan documents, particularly maps and plans but also text.

Other Activities

* Respond to and anticipate emerging development pressures.

* Continue to improve service of providing/analysing statistical data.

* Input into emerging strategic planning guidance, particularly Structure Plan Alteration No. 3.

COMMUNITY CONSULTATION AND USER SURVEYS 1994/97

* Publicity and consultation on approved South Somerset Local Plan:-

  - formal deposit;
  - recommended changes;
  - proposed modifications;
  - supplementary planning guidance.

* Follow-up customer surveys to establish effectiveness of publicity and consultation procedures.

KEY ACTIONS FOR 1994/95

Local Plans

* Possible re-opening of Yeovil Area Local Plan Public Local Inquiry in respect of Northover, Ilchester.

* Chard and Ilminster Local Plan: Proceed to adopt Local Plan.

* South Somerset Local Plan: revise text and graphics for printing (ready for formal public consultation on deposit plan in 1994/95).

1

Resources

* Retain additional staff to cope satisfactorily with expected workload, ie planning officer (Sc. 5/6/SO1) to provide policy input and to specialise in statistical analysis.

* Enter into Service Contract to ensure continued availability of process camera.

FINANCIAL IMPLICATIONS

The key actions listed will have significant financial implications. These arise particularly from the requirement to prepare a single District-wide Local Plan, which has the effect of concentrating expenditure rather than, as hitherto, allowing a rolling programme of preparing individual Local Plans over a period of years. Substantial costs will have to be borne, particularly in achieving widespread publicity and public participation and in holding a Public Inquiry into formal objections.

The timing of the Local Plan preparation costs shown in the table below is based on the assumption that formal deposit of the Local Plan will take place in Spring 1995 and that a Public Local Inquiry will be held in Winter 1995/96.

	1994/95 £	1995/96 £	1996/97 £
1993/94 Base Budget as at 30.6.93	187,180	187,180	187,180
Committed/Unavoidable Growth: Public Local Inquiries (including Inspector & Programme Officer)	5,000	23,000	277,000
Other Growth: Retention of additional Planning Officer Service Contract for Process Camera	- 1,250	- 1,250	- 1,250
	1,250	1,250	1,250
Net Resource Implications of Service Plan	6,250	24,250	278,250
Forecast Net Expenditure	193,430	211,430	465,430

SERVPLN.93\POLICY.GH

SEWERAGE SERVICES UNIT

AIM: **The satisfactory provision of the sewerage function under contract to the Water Companies in accordance with District Council policy.**

ANALYSIS OF CURRENT POSITION

Service	1993/94 Budget Provision
* Sewerage Services	£306,440
* Projected income from Water Companies	£399,192
* Sewerage guarantees	£677,000

Sewerage services are carried out under an agency contract with the Wessex Water and South West Water Companies. With the exception of the requirement on this Council to display a copy of the statutory sewer record, these are not mandatory functions.

The Unit manages an operational revenue budget of approximately £270,000 and a capital budget of £1.8 M on behalf of the Water Companies.

Sewerage Guarantees arise as a result of deficit payments due on rural sewerage requisition schemes and are not a mandatory function.

ANTICIPATED CHANGES IN SERVICE 1994/97

* Introduction of infrastructure charge to rural sewerage requisition schemes where relaxation of charge not granted.

* Greater emphasis on alternative methods of overcoming pollution problems in rural areas not benefitting from requisition schemes.

* Greater emphasis on fee bid tenders for Water Company design work on project specific basis - possibly in competition with Water Company in-house staff.

* In order to remain competitive there will be a continuing move towards an IT based environment with increased dependency on computer based storage and design/analysis systems.

* Introduction of statutory sewer records in computer based, digitised format; initially in tandem with hard copy records.

COMMUNITY CONSULTATION AND USER SURVEY 1994/97

* Continuation of consultation and post contract satisfaction surveys with Parish Councils and householders in villages subject to sewerage requisitions.

* Continuation of bi-annual meeting with senior Water Company staff to assess our compliance with performance standards.

* Consultation with Parish Councils, householders and other interested parties in villages with known domestic pollution problems but low priority for sewerage requisition.

KEY ACTIONS FOR 1993/94

* Ensure public awareness of origin and basis of sewerage infrastructure charge.

* Investigate and report on options for improving domestic sewerage arrangements in villages not benefitting from sewerage requisitions. Consider technical, legal and financial implications with emphasis on enabler rather than provider role where possible.

* Fee bid against detailed design brief. Regular comparison of actual costs against appropriate design stage for project management purposes. Access to design salaries information via computer network system to be arranged.

* Notwithstanding outcome of LGR, consider options available for cross boundary co-operation (joint

1

arrangements) in sewerage contract areas.

*   Maintain and develop Unit's computational facilities and expertise. Explore areas where AutoCad facility may be enhanced and exploited.

*   Ensure training for key personnel in computerised sewer records area.

*   Negotiate reduction of accountancy information required by Water Company, thereby reducing support service costs.

*   Review costs associated with private drain clearance to ensure that budget available is sufficient to cover bad debts.

*   Consider introduction of quality assurance procedures to design work.

FINANCIAL IMPLICATIONS

SERVICE PLANS 1994-97

Resource implications - Excluding Inflation

	1994/95 £	1995/96 £	1996/97 £
D639 - Sewerage Services 1993/94 Base Budget as at 30.6.93	306,440	306,440	306,440
Forecast Net Expenditure	306,440	306,440	306,440
D310 Sewerage Guarantees (GRF) **Base Budget**	620,900	620,900	620,900
Committed/Unavoidable Growth:	119,000	229,000	266,000
Other Growth:	-	-	74,000
Forecast Net Expenditure	739,900	849,900	960,900

NOTES:

Committed Growth on sewerage requisition schemes as committed at Council, 1st July 1993 (Minute No. 17).

96/97 Other Growth refers to Ashill and Charlton Musgrove which have yet to be formally committed by Council. Note that Lovington/Alford, South Cadbury and North Barrow not included as subject to review.

SERVPLN.93\SEWERAGE.LS

SUPPORT SERVICES UNIT

AIM: To provide a high quality, responsive administration service to the Development Services Department.

ANALYSIS OF CURRENT POSITION

Service	1993/94 Budget Provision
* Support Services	£515,690 (net)

The Unit provides support to other Units and the level of support is determined by the needs of those Units.

ANTICIPATED CHANGES IN SERVICE 1994/97

Records Services

* The new service level agreement with Ordnance Survey provides map data in digital format. This will necessitate the purchase of IT equipment to manage and distribute this data. Digitised OS data will facilitate the introduction of electronic data storage to replace the ageing map overlays, which are themselves nearing the end of their serviceable life and urgently need redrafting.

Development Control Administration

* The devolution of services to area offices would require procedural changes to ensure data required by area staff is up to date, available and of consistent quality.

General Administration

* Various performance indicators are being put in place, enabling closer monitoring of workload and performance.

* The microfiche printing service for officers and the public is well below standard, hampered by poor quality and inadequate reader and printing facilities. This service must be improved.

Reception

* Customer Care and Citizen's Charter initiatives have emphasised the importance of providing quality in 'front line' services. Customers are now demanding a higher level of service.

* The image quality on the microfiche reader used by the public has deteriorated to the point where it is in urgent need of replacement.

Integrated Information Systems

* As increasing reliance is being placed on the Department's IT systems, the significance of downtime experienced due to hardware failures has become more apparent. Elderly equipment is still in front line service; in addition the two file servers will require replacement in the next year or two.

* The network cabling within the Preston Road Offices has been altered many times to allow for relocation of equipment, office moves, etc. The number of cable joints and the routing of the cable (eg, adjacent to heating pipes) is leading to failures.

* In the event of further devolution, Area Office IT equipment will need upgrading since staff will need instant access to comprehensive data across the networks.

COMMUNITY CONSULTATION AND USER SURVEYS 1994/97

* Improve present arrangements for monitoring customer and user satisfaction through the use of surveys and statistical data.

KEY ACTIONS FOR 1994/95

Records Services

* Introduce electronic data storage of records.

1

General Administration

*   Further improve monitoring of output and performance.

*   Purchase a replacement microfiche reader/printer.

Development Control Administration

*   Set up a document image processing system whereby planning file and other data can be centrally managed and stored but instantly available to area office staff.

Reception

*   Purchase replacement microfiche reader.

Integrated Information Systems

*   Continue the rolling programme of computer hardware replacement to ensure that obsolete, inefficient and unreliable hardware is removed from front line service.

*   Replace one of the Preston Road file servers.

*   Upgrade Area Office IT equipment if further devolution of services occurs.

FINANCIAL IMPLICATIONS

The key actions which have cost implications are shown in the table below.

SERVICE PLANS 1994-97

Resource implications - Excluding Inflation

	1994/95 £	1995/96 £	1996/97 £
1993/94 Base Budget as at 30.6.93	503,530	503,530	503,530
Committed/Unavoidable Growth:			
Digital Ordnance Survey/Records Data Storage	20,000	10,000	10,000
IT equipment - planned replacement	15,000	15,000	15,000
Replace File Servers	19,000	-	19,000
	54,000	25,000	44,000
Other Growth:			
Microfiche reader/printer	10,000	-	-
Microfiche reader	-	500	-
IT Leasing Replacement (Note 1)	-	15,000	20,000
Document Image Processing System	18,000	8,000	8,000
A3 Colour Laser Printer	-	15,000	-
Upgrade Area Office IT equipment (Note 2)	5,000	-	-
	33,000	38,500	28,000
Service Review Savings:			
Reduced IT expenditure	-5,500	-5,500	-5,500
Reduce Records post to part-time	-7,000	-7,000	-7,000
Abandonment of Contaminated Land Register	-31,000	-31,000	-31,000
	-43,500	-43,500	-43,500
Other Sources of Finance:			
IT Leasing (Note 1)	-	-28,500	-39,500
Net Resource Implications of Service Plan	43,500	-8,500	-11,000
Forecast Net Expenditure	547,030	495,030	492,530

Notes:

1. Leases will not be renewed, some replacement IT equipment will need to be purchased.
2. If Development Control is devolved to Area Offices.

SERVPLN.93\SUPPORT.AT

3

TECHNICAL SERVICES UNIT

AIM: **To meet efficiently and effectively the Council's requirements for engineering and other technical expertise.**

ANALYSIS OF CURRENT POSITION

The Unit provides services through three sections:-

* Operations
* Engineering design
* Technical liaison

The cost of running the unit in 1993/94 is £376,010.

The main direct services for which the unit is responsible are:-

1993/94 Budget Provision

Service	Net £
* Public Transport	13,370
* Car Parks	-96,510
* Land Drainage	84,760
* Waste Collection	956,950
* Public Conveniences	314,720
* Street Cleaning	436,370
* Highways (incl.Agency)	-44,310
* Street Naming & Numbering	12,790

The waste collection and street cleaning services are statutory functions, the contracts for which will be re-tendered in 1998 and 1994 respectively, although this may be affected by LGR. Whilst not statutory, aspects of some other services provided are essential, such as public convenience maintenance and cleaning, car park maintenance and operation, and maintenance of sewage treatment plants. Most of the highway service is carried out under an agency agreement and the majority of the service is a statutory function.

Engineering design is a support service, the extent of which depends upon the capital programme of this Council and the County Council.

Technical liaison supports a range of statutory functions such as development control, adoption of roads and sewers, footpath diversions, street naming and numbering, land charge searches and Street Works notices.

ANTICIPATED CHANGES IN SERVICE 1994/97

Compulsory Competitive Tendering

* The Government's proposals to extend CCT to engineering services have fundamental implications for the Unit.

Car Parking

* A planned maintenance approach is being adopted to the repair of the fabric of the car parks in order to preserve the value of the asset. Environmental improvements are incorporated in the planned maintenance process and high environmental standards are aimed for in new designs.

* In the Yeovil area there is an imbalance of use of car parks due to changed retail patterns which it is hoped will be corrected if development proceeds at the eastern end of the town.

* Car parking administration has recently been transferred to the Unit and arrangements for the car park inspections are changing to rely more on casual staff rather than permanent staff.

* Demand for new car parks in the small towns and large villages continues and the challenge of funding convenient sites and meeting environmental standards requires considerable design and evaluation time.

Waste Collection

* Possible changes in the sites for waste disposal have not yet materialised but are expected in the lifetime of this plan. Increasing demands on some elements of the service are being dealt with effectively.

1

Street Cleansing

*   Although LGR may delay the preparation of a new contract, work will commence shortly on consultation for the new specification prior to re-tender.

Highways

*   Several new systems are in place in the light of changes in legislation and contractual arrangements.

*   The County Council has recently changed its policy on traffic calming and the Unit will now only be responsible for schemes in the Excepted Area. The demand is increasing and additional funds will be needed if this is to be met. A new joint funding policy has yet to be considered.

*   Some duties have been devolved to Yeovil Town Council and these will need to be carefully monitored in the early stages.

Land Drainage

*   A reduction in staff will result in a poorer service to the general public, although the Council's direct responsibility for maintenance, etc will be dealt with.

Engineering Design

*   The Capital Programme continues to be difficult to forecast and there is little sign that improvement can be expected in the foreseeable future.

*   The imminent introduction of CCT to professional services will impact particularly on the design services, although the majority of the work of the Unit will be affected to some extent.

*   Private sector style quotations for design work are now available and will increase.

Technical Liaison

*   It appears that the construction industry is beginning to come out of recession and this is reflected in the increasing work load. As demand increases there will be less opportunity to work on extraneous activities and to help other sections.

*   Further computerisation of the Water Authority liaison work is expected over the coming years.

*   Street naming and numbering continues to receive a high public profile and the current budget is barely sufficient to meet the demand. This is made

worse by increasing levels of vandalism.

Housing Site Sewage Treatment

*   The National Rivers Authority's policy will be monitored to identify programme of work of repair and replacement of plants and possible need to increase financial provision if NRA policy changes.

Capital Programme

*   Capital Projects will continue to be promoted in line with Council policy and within financial restraints. The Capital Programme will inevitably identify more than can be afforded and it is important to ensure that a balanced programme is agreed each year. Identify projects where special financing might be appropriate, eg Supplementary Credit Approvals will be identified.

COMMUNITY CONSULTATION AND USER SURVEYS 1994/97

Feedback will be sought from individual clients about their satisfaction with the quality of engineering design work. Consultation is carried out with local residents affected by projects such as traffic calming schemes.

The Technical Liaison Section monitors its relationship with its main customers, but a comprehensive survey will be carried out when workload permits.

KEY ACTIONS FOR 1994/95

General

By far the most important matter that will require attention is the proposed introduction of CCT for many of the Technical Services Unit functions. Service Review and Unit Service Days must address the issues and options, including possible changes in departmental structure.

Car Parking

Monitor use of car parks using newly introduced management programmes to identify shortfall or corrections in imbalance that might be possible.

Street Cleansing

Obtain comments of Area Committees and Parish Councils and report to Planning & Development Committee on proposals for new Contract unless timing of LGR delays the implementation date.

Highways

Make financial provision for traffic calming in the Excepted Area as a result of the change in County Council funding policy.

Engineering Design

*   Continue to develop commercial approach to obtaining design work and monitor costs and performance to assist transition to CCT.

*   Consider the various options to achieve success in the CCT exercise.

FINANCIAL IMPLICATIONS

Staff reductions which have resulted in savings are being incorporated in the budget. Nil growth is assumed with the exception of the provision for traffic calming as a result of a change in County Council policy.

SERVICE PLANS 1994-97

Resource Implications - Excluding Inflation

	1994/95 £	1995/96 £	1996/97 £
1993/94 Base Budget as at 30.6.93	1,789,590	1,789,590	1,789,590
Other Growth:			
Land Drainage - increase maintenance	-	10,000	10,000
Traffic Calming	50,000	50,000	50,000
	50,000	60,000	60,000
Service Review Savings:			
Land Drainage - reduce maintenance	-10,000	-10,000	-10,000
Land Drainage Post	-15,000	-15,000	-15,000
2 Car Park Inspector Posts	-20,000	-20,000	-20,000
	-45,000	-45,000	-45,000
Net Resource Implications of Service Plan	5,000	15,000	15,000
Forecast Net Expenditure	1,794,590	1,804,590	1,804,590

SERVPLN.93\TECHNICA.JGW